REFLECTIONS ON THE PHILOSOPHY OF THE HISTORY OF MANKIND

CLASSIC EUROPEAN HISTORIANS

A SERIES EDITED BY LEONARD KRIEGER

Johann Gottfried von Herder

REFLECTIONS ON THE PHILOSOPHY OF THE HISTORY OF MANKIND

Abridged and with an Introduction
by Frank E. Manuel

THE UNIVERSITY OF CHICAGO PRESS
CHICAGO & LONDON

THE UNIVERSITY OF CHICAGO PRESS, CHICAGO 60637
The University of Chicago Press, Ltd., London W.C. 1

Published 1968

Library of Congress Catalog Card Number: 68–24012

Printed in the United States of America

Series Editor's Preface

THE ideas and the methods that make up the contemporary western approach to history are essentially those that have been worked out in the study of European history. For the "Classic European Historians" whose works are reprinted in this series, the general attributes of history were those appropriate to the developing quality of the European past, and this past, conversely, could be known only on the assumption of these attributes. Since general historiography and European history have thus been mutually dependent in the career of the historical discipline, a series devoted to its innovators affords materials for both fields.

In the case of Herder, the connection between the two fields is evident in the parallel nature of his legacy to both, for he illuminated both historiography and European history by showing them in their external relations with a broader context—historiography with the philosophy of history and European history with world history. With Professor Manuel's perceptive introduction to guide us, we may see in Herder's comprehensive view of the historical plane and its European dimension the exoteric origins of what would later become the covert assumptions behind each.

Following a tradition that went back to St. Augustine and that would go on through Marx and Engels, Herder wrote philosophy of history that was virtually indistinguishable from the universal history in which it was embodied. Then as now, the philosophy of history dealt with the connections between the principles that underlie our knowledge of historical reality and the principles that underlie our knowledge of reality in general, but whereas our emphasis now is on the connection between the principles of historical and general knowledge, the emphasis then, in the long tradition represented by Herder, was on the connection between the principles of historical and general reality. For us, consequently, philosophy of history has become a distinct field, focused on the epistemological and moral assumptions of the historian and separated from the actual history for which it only provides the frame. For Herder and his ilk, on the contrary, philosophy of history elaborated the schemes of the fundamental life-forces that were at work in the actual process of human history. Since the only coherent order in the record of historical events thus derived from cosmic or human principles that lay outside history, and since the concrete evidence for the reality of those principles lay in the specific forms they took within history, philosophy of history was intimately commingled with history itself.

But if Herder belongs to an older tradition, his place in that tradition is at a point of its juncture with the new autonomous approach to history and sheds light on how the principles of the old approach could feed into the assumptions of the new. Professor Manuel shows the delicate balance of Herder's commitment to and departure from the typical tenets of the Enlightenment, and in terms of this balance Herder's adaptation of the secularized blend of history and philosophy of history to the requirements of the emerging specialized disciplines becomes clear. Through its principles of the popular locus and the many-faceted expressions of nature's life-force, Herder's philosophy of history provided general historiography, soon to arise as the self-conscious methodology of an independent historical profession, with a basis for including all kinds of cultural activity within the purview of history. Again, through its exaltation of language as the main vehicle of cultures, his philosophy of history stimulated the philological studies and techniques that were to bulk so large in the particular methods of the new historiography associated with Leopold von Ranke and Theodor Mommsen.

Similarly, in the realm of history proper Herder's approach to universal history, under Professor Manuel's analysis, makes explicit some of the presuppositions that historians of Europe have subsequently carried along with them, usually unrecognized even by themselves. The convergence of world history with the history of Europe and its tributaries; the concomitant conversion of the equal valuation of all peoples and eras on the stage of world history into the rising hierarchy of eras along the linear line of progress when attention is narrowed to the European scene; and the preference for depicting the history of Europe as the history of its several nations: all these familiar habits we can trace back to Herder.

Finally, Herder not only influenced the historians who followed him, but he has something to say to us directly. For we are at the other end of the historical sequence whose origins he witnessed. For us too the search for the lines that will associate the history that we know, as well as the way we know it, with fundamental patterns of human behavior has become an urgent challenge. And for us too the relationship between the European history which has supplied us with our canons of historical judgment and the world history which our age calls upon us to understand is a live problem. On both counts, we can sympathize with the dilemmas which Herder faced when he tried to unify the effects of God, nature, and culture in history and when he tried to reconcile the claims of humanity as a whole with the claims of its several nations in the depiction of man's earthly destiny. And we can learn, from the magnificent achievement in the *Reflections,* that when his conception is broad enough and his execution honest enough an historian's inconsistencies can extend his grasp of the past and equip him to cope with the rich variety of the life that falls within it.

LEONARD KRIEGER

Editor's Introduction

Almost everything that Herder composed—and the musical analogy is deliberate—became a part of his philosophical history. Some works address themselves directly to this subject: the brilliant, youthful sketch, full of ironies and ambiguities, entitled *Auch eine Philosophie der Geschichte zur Bildung der Menschheit* (*"Another Philosophy of History Concerning the Development of Mankind,"* 1774); the provocative, prize-winning essay, *Ursachen des gesunknen Geschmacks bei den verschiedenen Völkern, da er geblühet* (*"Causes of the Decline of Taste among Peoples Where It Once Flourished,"* 1775); the masterpiece of his mature years, presented in this volume, *Ideen zur Philosophie der Geschichte der Menscheit* (*"Reflections on the Philosophy of the History of Mankind,"* 1784–91); and the rather inchoate *Briefe zu Beförderung der Humanität* (*"Letters for the Advancement of Humanity,"* 1793–97), by a garrulous scholar whose ideas are so diffuse that they often revert to an original chaos. But other writings, those on primitive poetry, mythology, the spirit of Christianity, the literary achievements of all nations, the origin of language, aesthetics, and even the abortive attempt at a philosophical critique of his former professor Immanuel Kant, can be assimilated as mammoth footnotes to the major themes of his philosophy of history.

To submit Herder's variant formulations in the thirty-three volumes assembled in the classical Suphan edition of his works to the canons of consistency and Aristotelian logic is a vain and futile effort. Rudolf Haym, his most eminent biographer, in a work published in 1880 which shows no signs of aging, compared the *Ideen* to a bush whose branches and twigs sprouting in wild profusion end up by breaking each other. If Herder could not hold to a set position even within a single work, stability should certainly not be expected in a body of writings that spans more than three decades.

Most twentieth-century scholarly argumentation about the essence of Herder's thought—and the debates seem interminable—is analogous to a dispute about which brilliant flower in a luxuriant tropical garden is its most characteristic expression. Did his work advocate cultural nationalism for all peoples or was it merely a nativist reaction against contemporary frenchifiers of the German spirit? Was he a primitivist worshiper of folk culture or the ideological bearer of the values of the German bourgeoisie in its formative stage? Was he an exponent of the Enlightenment concepts of Humanity and Reason, one of the educators of German liberalism, or was he still at heart an enthusiastic German Pietist and the propagator of irrationalism? Was he the father of a virulent form of aggressive nationalism in central and eastern Europe? A militant exponent of Germandom who can be attached to that long line culminating in the Nazis? Was he the crucial figure in the modern historicist revolution? A philosophical eighteenth-century precursor of Darwin? A racist? With the exception of the last epithet, which unfortunately found its way into Collingwood's *Idea of History* and was thus spread in the English-speaking world, Herder was all of these things—and more.

He was not without bombast. The Pietist "enthusiasm" of his background transferred itself to all manner of secular artistic enthusiasms, which shifted with his life history. But for all their changeability, his passions and antagonisms were psychologically of a piece, even if the critic who approaches Herder as he might a tightly reasoned text of Immanuel Kant will be driven to distraction. He was one of those who spoke with tongues, like Meister Eckhardt and Luther before him, Hamann his contemporary, and Nietzsche and Spengler after him. Such men are ordinarily the despair of analytical Anglo-Saxon and French historians.

Herder's capacity for *Einfühlung*, empathy, makes him sound at his worst dilettantish and at his best a great interpreter of states of feeling in other historical epochs. It is no accident that when Michelet was communicating Vico to France, his colleague Edgar Quinet was performing the same service for Herder. In the romantic tradition Herder sought to express individuality, but he was not blind to universals. He and Vico stand together as ideal masters for one kind of historian—the man who sees the particular as impregnated with the universal, but still seeks to recreate the particular in all its uniqueness. Herder could evoke the genius of both the living and the dead—of Goethe and of ancient Hebrew poetry—no mean achievement.

Herder became a German cultural idol not only among liberals and reactionaries, who each saw only one side of his face, but among all those who believed in cultural riches for their own sake, who reveled in a full larder of historical experiences, in the sheer joy of variety and the plenitude of things. If this makes him an ideological representative of advanced bourgeois culture, well and good. But Herder's pretension to living through all states of being in all times and places, the expansive ideal for which he stands, is, one must now admit, less ecumenical and all-inclusive than would have been imagined a generation ago. It is rather bookish, literary, restricted to the corpus of Western aesthetic and philosophical expression, ornamented with a smattering of orientalia and reflections about primitives culled from the voluminous travel literature that he devoured. He was a proper pastor, after all, and a supervisor of educational institutions in Weimar. Goethe's "affairs" shocked him and so did European drunkenness, "immorality," and excess. One does not have to look hard for Herder's German, middle-class prejudices and nostalgic longings. But, for all its limitations, his attempt to open wide the floodgates of historical experience among all peoples, great and small, who ever inhabited the globe, is one of heroic proportions, and his steadfast refusal to identify history with the history of states is still a fighting doctrine, not the mere whipping of a dead horse.

Herder's interpretation of God's overall design in the governance of the world is as epoch-making as his discovery of a new historical consciousness. Most eighteenth-century thinkers who contemplated world history philosophically felt a reasonable pride in the achievements of the European civilization to which they belonged. They were not as alienated from their society as some recent commentators have fancied. They could contrast their own world of law with the barbarism of the Middle Ages. The *Encyclopédie* had revealed to them—both the writers and the readers—what a wealth of knowledge had been accumulated in all fields of human activity since the restoration of the arts and sciences, and if there were areas on the continent where superstition and prejudice still darkened existence, the philosophes seemed to be steadily gaining ground, pouring illumination into the most dismal crannies of priestly dominion. Despite the persistence of religious and political persecution, the philosophes, even the skeptical among them, saw themselves winning more battles than they were losing. If this was so, why should they not go on from triumph to triumph developing the arts and sciences forever?

Here sober historical reflection gave some French and German thinkers pause. In France the political and aesthetic ideal with which the intellectuals identified themselves was the age of Augustus and the Antonines, in Germany, the age of Pericles. But these comparisons which inflated their pride also worried them as historians. The Roman Empire began to collapse precisely at the moment of its greatest triumph. Was this to be the destiny of their own glorious civilization? Would their institutions of order and civility give way before a new barbarian invasion, or would some inner disease sap the strength of their robust and thriving world? All the historical examples they could muster pointed to the pessimist conclusion that in fact the most magnificent creations of human genius had fallen into ruins. No empire, however powerful, that had not declined; no age of flowering genius that had not been followed by a long period of aridity. How could enlightened Europe escape the destiny that had overwhelmed all other societies?

And indeed, many eighteenth-century philosophical historians foresaw the demise of their own civilization. Death was natural and inevitable. Decadence was the inescapable aftermath of growth and maturity. Studying past empires might still serve a salutary end: the course of the diseases that afflicted previous states could be observed in order to prolong the lifespan of existing civilization. Though death could not be avoided, the doctor of societies might at least stave off the doom as long as possible. A man did not disdain the advice of a wise physician merely because he knew he could not live forever.

Widespread as was this attitude, another body of thought was being shaped in France which dared to defy those who brooded on the transient character of human institutions. The Enlightenment was the great divide. The spell had been broken and new forces set in motion that would allow mankind to enjoy an eternally blooming state of civilization without interludes of barbarism. Men of the future would be born into a civilization, mature and creative, that would last forever. For those possessed with this optimist spirit, analysis of the past would yield an answer to an ominous question: What was there in present-day society of so essentially different a character that it could achieve immortality? What corrosive evils of the past had been and would be eradicated? The burden of proof was upon the newcomers who made bold to imagine an unprecedented, unnatural fate, infinite progress for contemporary society. The usual response in France pointed to the development of the arts and sciences, which it was believed had attained so great a momentum that they could never decelerate. A rather sophisticated theory of inevitable and infinite perfectibility embracing ever wider areas of the globe reached its epitome in the writings of Turgot and Condorcet.

Although there were supporters of this French thesis on the eastern side of the Rhine, there were other writers in Germany who, because of their deeply religious roots in a pessimist Protestant view of human destiny, could not accept the facile French idea of the cosmopolitan, unitary, progression of the human mind, the elimination of decay and death as if by fiat.

Herder, the outstanding representative of a new German philosophical history that ran counter to the French current of linear, rationalist progression, altered the traditional historical perspective and the universe of historical discourse in a revolutionary manner. The history of mankind was conceived as a development not only of the human mind, the parochial French view, but also of the multicolored expressions of human nature beyond the rational. Shifting his emphasis from the history of individual polities, however great, to the whole world history of mankind, Herder maintained that while the life cycles of particular states had to end in death, culture itself knew no decline, as hegemony passed from one world center to another.

To carry conviction, this new viewpoint had to demonstrate that there was in fact a single humanity with a history, despite the more immediate and arresting observation that the world was an agglomerate of widely dispersed and divergent races, peoples, and cultures, with a bewildering variety of languages, beliefs, and customs. Here the musical analogy came to Herder's rescue. There were an infinite number of variations on the theme of man; each one had a finite existence; but as each came into being and was fulfilled in time, total humanity grew ever richer. In the course of history all possible combinations of human sensibility, the form-giving elements in the varieties of experience, would make their appearance. There was no historical death, because every culture that had ever been or would be fashioned, from the worm-eating Californians through the Greeks, became a part of one world symphony with an ever grander orchestration. Hegel later made this conception more rationalist and restrictive by envisaging a limited number of embodiments of World-Spirit, defined primarily in terms of subject-object relationships, and by tracing them in simple sequence chronologically and geographically from East to West, from ancient despotic China to nineteenth-century Germany. Herder allowed for no such formal chronological arrangement. Despite the semblance of historical sequence in which his cultures are introduced in parts of the *Ideen,* their filiations are tenuous. The possible cultural manifestations of the human are infinite, unpredictable, disorderly.

The superficial style of living in the German principalities where Herder spent his years was an imitation of the French court, and in a sense his whole creative intellectual vision may be looked upon as a rejection of this artificially imposed way of life, with its emphasis upon the progress of arts, sciences, and civility, defined in French terms. Of course the French way—like the American way in our own time—was viewed by foreign eyes too simplistically, as a monolith to be accepted or refused in its entirety. The "rationalism" and generalizing quality of French thought which Herder denounced was a straw man of his own making. In his treatment the French love of mathematical abstraction, which became the butt of his caustic irony, was primarily a foil for a new way of looking at the world. His organismic sense, his romantic holism, his demand that the perception of experience be unmathematical, more concrete, adjectival, colorful, more varied and emotive, less rigid and uniform, his refusal to accept the simple traditional body-soul, reason-emotion dichotomy, was a counterattack from the East of great magnitude. Feeling was knowledge of a superior order to French reason, he argued.

Any philosophic document of the past that even remotely lent itself to this outlook was assimilated by Herder (whatever the original intentions of the author may have been). Spinoza's pantheism, for example, his apparent abolition of the matter-spirit division, and the emotional quality of his conception of God served to make Herder a Spinozist. From Leibniz he derived the feeling for continuous process, the sense of individuation, and the glorification of the particular in a world harmony that are so vital for modern historical consciousness.

Herder broke the bounds of what would be included in history with an impetuosity that makes previous enlargements of the historical vision puny extensions. Reading the French philosophical histories from Turgot through Comte, one is still impressed with their fundamental Europeocentrism and the finiteness, even narrowness, of their historical appreciation of "otherness." Herder believed in the individuality of each *Volk,* or agglomeration of people, wherever and whenever it had appeared and its equivalent (or almost equivalent) status in the history of mankind. Any body of men who achieved a form of life, a cultural configuration, was a noble manifestation of mankind, of God's creation, of power, of energy, of nature—the particular rhetorical choice varies from passage to passage. In broad acceptance of the infinite variety of human cultures, Herder broke through both traditional religious and political molds that had confined Christian Europeans for centuries. He has no antecedents of comparable vigor and few descendants. In fact his vision was so large that it failed to sustain itself in German thought. Kant bluntly rejected it from the outset, and Hegel, too, with one sweep denied history to the primitive, waiting for the emergence of an organized state before he would deign to consider a cultural form as an admissible embodiment of Spirit. Marx in this respect did not follow Hegel, and there are idealizations of patriarchal society in his writings to which Hegel would never have subscribed, though Marx paused at this early stage only as a way station to a utopian vision of man, not as something of worth in itself.

Herder not only gave status to the culture of primitives, winning the appreciation of explorers like Johann Forster for his capacity to look at these peoples from within instead of regarding them as mere objects to be converted or "civilized"; he also placed a new valuation on the earliest form of expression of all peoples, the mythic. Admittedly such an outlook bears with it "reactionary" dangers, and Herder's work has merged with streams of thought that have been blatantly anti-progressist in a political sense, racist, and existentialist to the point of entirely rejecting the rational. But the notion that a thinker should be held morally responsible before some self-appointed historical Grand Judge for the subsequent fortune of his thought is a patent absurdity. The history of Herder's thought is, after all, the history of other men's thoughts about him.

In bestowing significance upon the history of all peoples Herder rather consistently refused to engage in comparisons among them. Each *Volk* contained the principle of its individuality within itself; it was a self-respecting monad. The Christian Pietist conception of souls equal in the eyes of God was extended to peoples throughout world history. Herder's use of the term *Volk* is characteristically loose. It embraces the chosen people of Israel, the Greeks, the Egyptians, the Romans, the Germans, as well as tiny tribes of American Indians and Negroes in the African bush. A *Volk* is virtually any group that has a name and a culture. If there is a mythology, a folk poetry, a separate religion, a cuisine, a recognizably different pattern of sense perceptions, the *Volk* is identifiable. But Herder's canopy also includes peoples that have no artifacts, or hardly any, and little mythology. There is, however, no folk without a religion, he affirms in conscious disavowal of the Baylian and Humian discoveries in the travel reports that there were nations of atheists.

The history of the world for Herder is the history of these *Völker*, their formation as a consequence of the interpenetration of their physical environment and their being, their creation of a mythic cosmology, a music, and a poetry, above all, a language. The union of their original nature, their genius, and the environment reaches a climax in a form-giving moment—it is not quite clear whether this is the discovery of religious or of linguistic identity. But nothing static results. The process of change is continuous as long as the people is alive. It may become subject to disruption during the course of its wanderings to a new environment; it may suffer the evils of invasion; and it will inevitably die. Some cultures outlive themselves, dragging out their monotonous existences, stinking corpses (Hegel will adapt this concept without acknowledgment). But except for the cultures that outlast their creativity, Herder makes all moments of time in all cultures worthy of respect. His was a Christianization of the historic process as well as a democratization to a degree that had never been achieved before. As intellectuals in Central Europe read Herder, they found in his work a justification for the existence of the embryonic nations to which they belonged, and he became the chosen philosopher of the new cultural nationalism that destroyed the Hapsburg empire.

There is an ideal, natural way to self-fulfillment for each *Volk* analogous to an individual's development from birth to the grave. Unfortunately, peoples have broken the bounds of their natural habitat, have destroyed and been destroyed, have contaminated other cultures and been contaminated. The tragic, unnatural episodes of world history are the subjection of cultures to the vicissitudes of such experience. Herder is a moral historical judge: the monad of *Volk* individuality can be lost and has been. That which is mixed is rarely good, that which imitates is a defilement, and that which is forced lacks authenticity. Somehow a culture can never survive imperial extension. Rome, both Romes, are evil symbols.

"Even the best should not mature too soon." This is the final reflection of the fourth volume of the *Ideen.* Herder conceived of an optimum time sequence for the development of *Volk* potentialities, natural, biological time. Condorcet had a vision of improvement accelerated at an increasing rate of speed like a mechanical instrument subject to an ever greater impetus. Herder had an infinite variety of ideal growth times, each appropriate to a different *Volk.* Not all plants and all creatures have the same life cycle and the same rate of growth. What is perfect for one is deadly for another. The environment helps determine what is the fitting rate of growth and so does the original genius. There is no overall rule of development except the natural one, which is idiosyncratic. What is natural is what occurs in a given environment where alien elements have not intruded either to stimulate growth artificially or to stunt it.

Herder made a great point of distinguishing his universal history from the canonical French study of the eighteenth century, Montesquieu's *Spirit of the Laws,* even though he had derived from Montesquieu the insight that climate affected the spirit of nations. He quickly set himself in opposition to the use to which the Frenchman had put his generalization. He saw Montesquieu as making false abstractions from existential reality and the complexity of history when he set up the traditional categorization of three types of states, the monarchical, the aristocratic, and the democratic. No state form could really be repeated in a different part of the globe even though it might bear the same name. Montesquieu had described states in terms of their avowed constitutional principles, what they said they were; Herder knew that "verbal principles" of governments had little relationship with the reality of practice, performance, or existence. Montesquieu had taken his constitutional examples out of context; they were made timeless, spaceless, and characterless. For Herder peoples had existed and grown only in these three dimensions. True philosophical history would have to be based upon an acceptance of the peculiarities of time, place, and national character as essential elements. Philosophical generality would follow these three forces through the details of *Volk* history. The result would be the authentic living, colorful pageant of the interplay of the three variables. The cyclical principle of the unfolding of history would always be the same, the separate *Volk* experience always different.

There are in Herder subtle attempts to relate the individual, the *Volk*, and Humanity as three organic beings which grow in accordance with an inner genetic principle. Their interaction is one of the most difficult for him to establish, and he often evades problems by effusive language. The analogy between the individual and the *Volk* is most satisfactory since both have life cycles, individual characters and spirits, and both are subject to accident, premature death, or the corruption of their souls by alien influence. The individual cannot express himself in cosmopolitan terms, for however extraordinary his genius he is limited by the realities of space, the original spirit of the *Volk* into which he was born, and the character of the time in its life cycle. Towering as his individual genius may be, it is impossible for a man to transcend these restrictions, for he cannot define himself except in terms of a particular religion, a specific language, a communal pattern of feeling, using images which have been inculcated into his being through the inherited traditions of education, transmitted and kept alive in folk songs, religious ritual, and speech. These are not limitations in any mechanical sense, they are vehicles of differentiated character which exclude from being all other things but themselves. When Herder analyzed the creation of a genius he considered it as an expression of the *Volk* spirit: a man could not think freely in all possible forms and languages—he was born to one only. If a man tried to assimilate what was not his natural *Volk* spirit, he would never be able to give utterance to a harmonious song, for its bastard quality would obtrude.

The connection between the *Volk* and Humanity is a far thornier problem. At times the analogy is merely extended: Humanity is to the *Volk* as the *Volk* is to the individual. Humanity, too, has a growth, though it is everlasting, and if you look upon the whole world you will see Humanity timelessly evolving. In the course of this development numerous individual elements, *Völker,* are born, create, and die, while Humanity lives eternal. But there is no necessary transmission of the creations of one *Volk* to another, and even when there is contact through war and commerce there is rarely a spiritual relationship, because the inner core of a *Volk* spirit is hard, virtually impenetrable. Thus there is no progress of the human mind in the sense in which the concept was used in France. The parallel between Humanity-*Volk* and *Volk*-individual applies in a limited way. The *Volk* expresses itself in certain modes that are common to all Humanity. All peoples have religion, art, a form of reason, and morals: this is the sense in which Humanity is one. In their natural state *Völker* are not bestial but uniquely human in what they have to express. All peoples partake of humanity in different forms, however; they are variant renderings of the common Humanity, as distinguished from bestiality or a higher angelic form of creation in the great chain of being. This was the import of Herder's vigorous attack on Kant's theory of distinct, original races, four or five types with different degrees of humanity—Kant thought the blacks were inferior. For Herder Humanity is one, and a *Volk*—unless corrupted (this is the implicit caveat)—can express only fully human values and ideas. Progress is the gradual expression of all possible *Volk* configurations. These forms are not created simultaneously, for it is the divine purpose that they be revealed through the passage of time.

All mankind is naturally inclined to humanness, *Humanität,* but it must be fostered and developed. *Humanität* has manifested itself quintessentially not in the state and the organization of power but in music, literature, art, and science, in that order of importance. The state as an expression of energy plays a dubious role in history. Herder is violently hostile to the new, aggressive, Prussian kingdom of Frederick II, and he is no admirer of Louis XIV or his successors. The state is usually described as a destructive force that crushes cultural flowers, amalgamates forms, extinguishes spirit. The Europeans as conquerers and colonizers of the world are depicted as ravishers of primitive peoples; the ancient Romans, praised for their virtues at home, are enemies of humanity when they become imperial masters.

There are times when Herder is so absorbed with describing the individual *Völker* that he seems to rest content with the mere presentation of a world cultural historical geography—a history of the birth, rise, and decline of cultures in different places at different times, with some moral lessons about the evils of cultural miscegenation and cultural conquest, some preference for the early growth stages of culture, the creative moments, over the repetitive ones which betoken senility. But not always is he satisfied with this description of the history of cultures in a neutral, biological rhythm. The French conception of progress is an eternal challenge to him. Has there been progress in human happiness and virtue, or no? With this problem he wrestled all his life, and it would be false to impute to him a simple, definitive answer. The tenor of Book XIV of his *Reflections on the Philosophy of the History of Mankind* is markedly more favorable to a general theory of gradual perfectibility, albeit not a linear one, than the *Letters for the Advancement of Humanity,* which sometimes wanders off into a gloomy prospect. At moments Herder cavalierly dismissed those who extolled the arts and sciences as evidence of progress, particularly the technological triumphs of modern civilization that had increased human power and multiplied pleasure-creating gadgets. He drew upon a vast body of illustration equating luxury with effeminacy and moral degeneration, so that it was easy to reject an augmentation of pleasure as proof of superiority of any kind. Herder, like most of his compatriots, was still close to Rousseau's paradox and he was an upright Pietist. The worth of the expansion of human technological power through invention was at best doubtful; in a telling passage he asked whether the end to which power was employed was not the more central concern.

But there were long sections in the *Ideen* where in common sense terms Herder viewed Western European civilization—the chain from Greece and Rome to the present—as a progressive unity, and there he approached a simple middle-class optimism in which the growing acceptance of the bourgeois virtues of orderliness, peace, diligence, workmanship, and gentleness was witnessed and praised. He celebrated the extension of the reign of reasonableness, justice, and law in Europe, and the mitigation of cruelty. The last books of the *Ideen* are a kind of bourgeois history of Western civilization in progress, despite occasional relapses, to which Condorcet himself might have assented. Herder seems to be bestowing approbation upon the development of the arts and sciences which the author of the more ironic *Auch eine Philosophie der Geschichte* mocked. If the manuscript papers on the French Revolution, which were not published during his lifetime, are attached to this bourgeois history, the difference between Herder and Condorcet is small indeed. Both are antidespotic and libertarian, in favor of commerce and the mercantile ideal, antimilitary and antiaristocratic, if not completely egalitarian.

No one outdid Herder in the zeal of his Protestant animosity against the Roman Catholic hierarchy; and yet even he could concede in the last sections of the *Ideen* that perhaps this oppressive institution had served a purpose in binding together the barbarous peoples of the Middle Ages, who otherwise might have engaged in endless fratricidal warfare and left Europe a

Mongolian desert. While the hostile forces of the Church and the Empire were subjecting the body of Europe to pressures and counterpressures, a third force arose, a good middle class that believed in knowledge, utilitarian activity, and industriousness, a force that ultimately prevailed and made it possible to dispense with both bellicose knights and the obscurantist papacy. The true Europe emerged as a culture of business, science, and art. Its genius revealed itself above all in its capacity for work. If Europe had been as rich as India it would not have felt the stimulus of need, if it had not been traversed by great rivers it would have been another Tartary, if it had been as isolated from the past as America its real genius would not have come to fruition. But the confluence was perfect: there were rivers and needs, and it had a good cultural heritage from Greece and Rome—an optimal set of conditions for the flowering of its unique splendor. For all Herder's preaching of the equality of nations, he cannot in the end restrain a measure of enthusiasm for Europe. He does not quite shout its superiority over all other previous and contemporaneous expressions of Humanity, but he surely implies that Europe is its jewel. The bulk of the *Ideen* is, after all, devoted to Europe despite his reverence for exotic peoples throughout the globe.

Herder thus leaves the historian with a number of models that are sometimes contradictory. It is best to look at these variegated designs in his own spirit of the moment, as the ways in which he experienced history at different times in his long literary life. He has many descendants who refuse to recognize one another because he cast his seed in strange wombs and sired his progeny at different times of life. But there are some elements in his world history that are remarkably constant.

Of all the philosophers of history, Herder was perhaps the most richly intuitive. Eschewing a traditional Western European and Graeco-Roman fixation, which has persisted well into the twentieth century among historians, he pushed the geographic dimensions of the historical in all directions. Even the bounds of the planet earth were broken as he toyed with evolutionary conceptions of the universe. The historical included the primitive as well as the civilized, and the aboriginal was not a mere prelude to the more advanced. Every moment of historical experience had worth. Moreover, Herder's history was not restricted to rational intent and to action expressed primarily in the state. He invented the concept of the national soul defined and described in feeling tones, not in terms of power relations. The cultural emanations of peoples rather than their political acts were the stuff of history. Masterpieces of religion, music, poetry, and art became history's major events and central meaning. Science and technology, too, played a role, but of lesser importance. Emotion took its place alongside reason—perhaps it even assumed a position of primacy as a creative force. In Herder cultural history is no longer on sufferance, boxed and isolated in a few sections at the end of a chronicle of royal exploits, after the manner of Voltaire. Herder turned conventional history writing upside down, relegating the political and the military to the lower end of the table, to be devalued and demeaned as lesser manifestations of the human spirit.

The original text of the *Ideen* was composed of twenty books, eleven of which may be considered theoretical, and nine, descriptive of specific societies. Since the scope of the present edition does not permit the reproduction of the whole, a selection has been made without breaking up any single book. Of the books of historico-philosophical generality, the first six, which abound in cosmological and biological reflections that are today rather outlandish, have been omitted. Our text begins with Books VII and VIII, the heart of Herder's doctrine of national genius and climate, and then moves on to Book XV, his definition of Humanity. Instead of giving a sampling of Herder on the Eskimos, the Africans, and the American Indians (Book VI) and a rather sketchy treatment of the Far East (Book XI), the Germanic and Slavic nations (Book XVI), and the early barbarian kingdoms in Europe (Book XVIII), it seemed wisest to concentrate upon his presentation of the Near Eastern and European cultures that he knew so profoundly and to make a unit of the books that cover their history: Book XII on the Babylonians, the Persians, the Hebrews, the Phoenicians, and the Egyptians; Book XIII on Greece; Book XIV on the Etruscans and the Romans; Book XVII on early Christianity; Books XIX and XX on medieval Christian Europe, the Arab world, and the birth of modern times.

The translation was made by T. O. Churchill and was originally published in London in 1800. Although many turns of phrase, the capitalization of some substantives, the spelling, and the punctuation are outmoded, into this version the spirit of Herder's writing has been successfully transfused.

FRANK E. MANUEL

Contents

REFLECTIONS ON THE PHILOSOPHY OF THE HISTORY OF MANKIND

I

National Genius and the Environment

BOOK VII

THE picture of nations hitherto sketched must be considered only as the foreground, serving as a basis to farther observations: while its groups answer the purpose of the *templa* of the augurs in the skies, forming definite spaces for our contemplation, and aids to our memory. Let us see what they afford towards a philosophy of our species.

CHAPTER 1

Notwithstanding the Varieties of the human Form, there is but one and the same Species of Man throughout the Whole of our Earth

No two leaves of any one tree in nature are to be found perfectly alike; and still less do two human faces, or human frames, resemble each other. Of what endless variety is our artful structure susceptible! Our solids are decomposable into such minute and multifariously interwoven fibres, as no eye can trace; and these are connected by a gluten of such a delicate composition, as the utmost skill is insufficient to analyse. Yet these constitute the least part of us: they are nothing more than the containing vessels and conduits of the variously compounded, highly animated fluid, existing in much greater quantity, by means of which we live and enjoy life. "No man," says Haller, "is exactly similar to another in his internal structure: the courses of the nerves and blood vessels differ in millions and millions of cases, so that amid the variations of these delicate parts, we are scarcely able to discover in what they agree."[1] But if the eye of the anatomist can perceive this infinite variety, how much greater must that be, which dwells in the invisible powers of such an artful organization! So that every man is ultimately a world, in external appearance indeed similar to others, but internally an individual being, with whom no other coincides.

And since man is no independent substance, but is connected with all the elements of nature; living by inspiration of the air, and deriving nutriment from the most opposite productions of the Earth, in his meats and drinks; consuming fire, while he absorbs light, and contaminates the air he breathes; awake or asleep, in motion or at rest, contributing to the change of the universe; shall not he also be changed by it? It is far too little, to compare him to the absorbing sponge, the sparkling tinder: he is a multitudinous harmony, a living self, on whom the harmony of all the powers that surround him operates.

The whole course of a man's life is change: the different periods of his life are tales of transformation, and the whole species is one continued metamorphosis. Flowers drop and wither; others sprout out and bud: the vast tree bears at once all the seasons on its head. If, from a calculation of the insensible perspiration alone, a man of eighty have renovated his whole body at least four and twenty times;[2] who can trace the variations of matter and its forms through all the race of mankind upon the Earth, amid all the causes of change; when not one point on our complicated Globe, not one wave in the current of time, resembles another? A few centuries only have elapsed since the inhabitants of Germany were Patagonians: but they are so no longer, and the inhabitants of its future climates will not equal us. If now we go back to those times, when every thing upon Earth was apparently so different; the times for instance, when elephants lived in Siberia and North America, and those large animals existed, the bones of which are to be found on the Ohio; if men then lived in those regions,

---

[1] Preface to Buffon's *Nat. Hist.*, Vol. III.

[2] According to Bernoulli: see Haller's *Physiolog.*, Vol. VIII, l. 30, where will be found a multitude of observations on the changes of human life.

how different must they have been from those, who now inhabit them! Thus the history of man is ultimately a theatre of transformations, which He alone can review, who animates all these figures, and feels and enjoys in them all. He builds up and destroys, improves and alters forms, while he changes the World around them. The wanderer upon Earth, the transient ephemeron, can only admire the wonders of this great spirit in a narrow circle, enjoy the form that belongs to him in the general choir, adore, and disappear with this form. "I too was in Arcadia": is the monumental inscription of all living beings in the ever-changing, ever-renewing creation.

As the human intellect, however, seeks unity in every kind of variety, and the divine mind, its prototype, has stamped the most innumerable multiplicity upon the Earth with unity, we may venture from the vast realm of change to revert to the simplest position: *all mankind are only one and the same species.*

How many ancient fables of human monsters and prodigies have already disappeared before the light of history! and where tradition still repeats remnants of these, I am fully convinced, more accurate inquiry will explain them into more beautiful truths. We are now acquainted with the ourang-outang, and know, that he has no claim to speech, or to be considered as man: and when we have a more exact account of the ourang-kubub, and ourang-guhu, the tailed savages of the woods in Borneo, Sumatra, and the Nicobar islands will vanish.[3] The men with reverted feet in Malacca,[4] the probably rickety nation of dwarfs in Madagascar, the men habited like women in Florida,

[3] Even Marsden mentions these in his history of Sumatra, but only from hearsay. Monboddo, in his work on the *Origin and Progress of Language,* Vol. I, p. 219 and following, has collected all the traditions respecting men with tails he could find. Professor Blumenbach, *De generis humani varietate* (On the varieties of the human species), has shown from what sources the delineations of tailed men of the woods have been derived.

[4] Sonnerat also, in his *Voyage aux Indes* (Voyage to India), Vol. II, p. 103, speaks of these, but from report merely. Commerson has revived the story of dwarfs in Madagascar after Flaucourt; but later travellers have rejected it. On the hermaphrodites of Florida see Heyne's critical essay in the *Comment. Societ. Reg. Götting.* (Memoirs of the Royal Society of Göttingen), for the year 1778, p. 993.

and some others, deserve such an investigation as has already been bestowed on the albinoes, the dondoes, the Patagonians, and the aprons of the Hottentot females.[5] Men, who succeed in removing wants from the creation, falsehoods from our memory, and disgraces from our nature, are to the realms of truth, what the heroes of mythology were to the primitive world; they lessen the number of monsters on the Earth.

I could wish, too, that the affinity of man to the ape had never been urged so far, as to overlook, while seeking a scale of Being, the actual steps and intervals, without which no scale can exist. What for example can the rickety ourang-outang explain in the figure of the Kamtschadale, the little pigmy in the size of the Greenlander, or the pongo in the Patagonian? for all these forms would have arisen from the nature of man, had there been no such thing as an ape upon the Earth. And if men proceed still farther, and deduce certain deformities of our species from an intermixuture with apes, the conjecture, in my opinion, is not less improbable than degrading. Most of these apparent resemblances of the ape exist in countries where no apes are to be found; as the reclining skulls of the Calmucs and Mallicollese, the prominent ears of the Pevas and Amicuans, the small hands of some savages in Carolina, and other instances, testify. Even these appearances, as soon as we have surmounted the illusion of the first view, have so little of the ape, that the Calmuc and the Negro remain completely men, even in the form of the head, and the Mallicollese displays capacities, that many other nations do not possess. In fact, apes and men never were one and the same genus, and I wished to rectify the slight remains of the old fable, that in some place or other upon the Earth they lived in community, and enjoyed no barren intercourse.[6] For each genus Nature has done enough, and to each has given its proper progeny. The ape she has divided into as many species and varieties as possible, and extended these as

[5] See Sparmann's *Voyage*, p. 177.

[6] In the *Auszügen aus dem Tagebuch eines neuen Reisenden nach Asien* (Extracts from the journal of a late traveller in Asia), Leipsic, 1784, p. 256, this is asserted anew, still only from report.

far as she could: but thou, O man, honour thyself: neither the pongo nor the gibbon is thy brother: the American and the Negro are: these therefore thou shouldst not oppress, or murder, or steal; for they are men, like thee: with the ape thou canst not enter into fraternity.

Lastly, I could wish the distinctions between the human species, that have been made from a laudable zeal for discriminating science, not carried beyond due bounds. Some for instance have thought fit, to employ the term of *races* for four or five divisions, originally made in consequence of country or complexion: but I see no reason for this appellation. Race refers to a difference of origin, which in this case either does not exist, or in each of these countries, and under each of these complexions, comprises the most different races. For every nation is one people, having its own national form, as well as its own language: the climate, it is true, stamps on each its mark, or spreads over it a slight veil, but not sufficient to destroy the original national character. This originality of character extends even to families, and its transitions are as variable as imperceptible. In short, there are neither four or five races, nor exclusive varieties, on this Earth. Complexions run into each other: forms follow the genetic character: and upon the whole, all are at last but shades of the same great picture, extending through all ages, and over all parts of the Earth. They belong not, therefore, so properly to systematic natural history, as to the physico-geographical history of man.

CHAPTER 2

The one Species of Man has naturalized itself in every Climate upon Earth

OBSERVE yon locusts of the Earth, the Kalmuc and Mungal: they are fitted for no region but their own hills and mountains.[7] The light rider flies on his little horse over immense tracts of the

[7] For particular regions see Pallas and others already quoted. The account given by G. Opitz of his life and imprisonment among a Kalmuc horde at Yaik would be a very descriptive picture of their mode of living, if it were not embellished with so many of the editor's remarks, which give it an air of romance.

desert; he knows how to invigorate his fainting courser, and by opening a vein in his neck, to restore his own powers, when he sinks with fatigue. No rain falls on many parts of these regions, which are refreshed solely by the dew, while inexhaustible fertility clothes the earth with continually renovated verdure. Throughout many extensive tracts no tree is to be seen, no spring of fresh water to be discovered. Here these wild tribes, yet preserving good order among themselves, wander about among the luxuriant grass, and pasture their herds: the horses, their associates, know their voices, and live like them in peace. With thoughtless indifference sits the indolent Kalmuc, contemplating the undisturbed serenity of his sky, while his ear catches every sound, that pervades the desert his eye is unable to scan. In every other region of the Earth the Mungal has either degenerated or improved: in his own country he is what he was thousands of years ago, and such will he continue, as long as it remains unaltered by Nature or by art.

The Arab of the desert belongs to it, as much as his noble horse, and his patient, indefatigable camel.[8] As the Mungal wanders over his heights, and among his hills, so wanders the better-formed Bedouin over his extensive Asiatic-African deserts; also a nomad, but a nomad of *his own* region. With this his simple clothing, his maxims of life, his manners, and his character, are in unison; and, after the lapse of thousands of years, his tent still preserves the wisdom of his forefathers. A lover of liberty, he despises wealth and pleasure, is fleet in the course, a dextrous manager of his horse, of whom he is as careful as of himself, and equally dextrous in handling the javelin. His figure is lean and muscular; his complexion brown; his bones strong. He is indefatigable in supporting labour, bold and enterprising, faithful to his word, hospitable and magnanimous, and, connected with his fellows by the desert, he makes one common cause with all. From the dangers of his mode of life he has imbibed wariness and shy mistrust; from his solitary abode, the feelings of revenge, friendship, enthusiasm, and pride.

[8] Beside the many ancient travels in Arabia see those of Pagès, Vol. II, p. 62–87.

Wherever an Arab is found, on the Nile or the Euphrates, on Libanus or in Senegal, nay even in Zanguebar or the islands of the Indian Ocean, if a foreign climate have not by length of time changed him into a colonist, he will display his original Arabian character.

The Californian, on the verge of the earth, in his barren country, exposed as he is to want, and amid the vicissitudes of his climate, complains not of heat or cold, eludes the force of hunger, though with the utmost difficulty, and enjoys happiness in his native land. "God alone can tell," says a missionary,

> how many thousand miles a Californian, that has attained the age of eighty, must have wandered over before he finds a grave. Many of them change their quarters perhaps a hundred times in a year, sleeping scarcely three nights together on the same spot, or in the same region. They lie down wherever night overtakes them, without paying the least regard to the filthiness of the soil, or endeavouring to secure themselves from noxious vermin. Their dark brown skin serves them instead of coat and cloak. Their furniture consists of a bow and arrows, a stone for a knife, a bone or sharp stake to dig up roots, the shell of a tortoise for a cradle, a gut or a bladder to carry water, and, if they be peculiarly fortunate, a pouch made of the fibres of the aloe, somewhat in the fashion of a net, to contain their utensils and provision. They feed on roots, and all sorts of small seeds, even those of grass, which they collect with great labour; nay, when pressed by want, they pick them out of their own dung. Every thing that can be called flesh, or barely resembles it, even to bats, grubs, and worms, is to be reckoned among the dainties, on which they feast; and the leaves of certain shrubs, with their young shoots, leather, and spungy bones, are not excluded from their list of provision, when urged by hunger. Yet these poor creatures are healthy: they live to a great age, and are strong; so that it is uncommon to see a man grayheaded, and never but at a late period. They are always cheerful; forever jesting and laughing; well made, straight, and active; they can lift stones and other things from the ground with their two foremost toes; they walk as erect as a dart to the extreme of old age; and the children go alone before they are a year old. When weary of talking, they lie down and sleep, till awakened by hunger, or the desire of eating: and as soon as they are awake, the laugh, the talk, and the jest, recommence. Thus they go on, till worn out by old age, when they meet death with calm indifference.

"The inhabitant of Europe," continues the missionary, "may envy the happiness of the Californian: but for this the native of California is indebted solely to his perfect indifference whether he possess much or little in this world, and his absolute resignation to the will of God in all the occurrences of life." [9]

In this manner I might go on, and exhibit climatic pictures of several nations, inhabiting the most different regions, from Kamtschatka to Tierra del Fuego: but why should I give these brief sketches, since every traveller, who sees with accuracy, or feels as a man, gives the shade of the climate to every little stroke of his delineations? In India, the grand resort of commercial nations, the Arab and the Chinese, the Turk and the Persian, the Christian and the Jew, the Negro and the Malay, the Japanese and the Gentoo, are clearly distinguishable: [10] thus every one bears the characters of his country and way of life on the most distant shores. The ancient allegorical tradition says, that Adam was formed out of the dust of all the four quarters of the Globe, and animated by the powers and spirits of the whole Earth. Wherever his children have bent their course, and fixed their abode, in the lapse of ages, there they have taken root as trees, and produced leaves and fruit adapted to the climate. Hence let us deduce a few consequences, which seem to explain to us many things, that might otherwise be deemed striking singularities in the history of man.

In the first place it is obvious why all sensual people, fashioned to their country, are so much attached to the soil, and so inseparable from it. The constitution of their body, their way of life, the pleasures and occupations to which they have been accustomed from their infancy, and the whole circle of their ideas, are climatic. Deprive them of their country, you deprive them of every thing.

"It has been remarked," says Cranz,

> of the six Greenlanders, who were brought over to Denmark, that, notwithstanding all the friendly treatment they received,

[9] *Nachrichten von Kalifornien* (Account of California), Mannheim, 1773.

[10] See Mackintosh's *Travels*, Vol. II, p. 27.

and the abundance of stockfish and train-oil, with which they were supplied, their eyes were often turned toward the north and their native country, with melancholy looks and piteous sighs; and at length they attempted to make their escape in their canoe. A strong gale having driven them on the coast of Scania, they were brought back to Copenhagen, when two of them died of grief. Two of the others again ran away, and only one of them was retaken, who wept bitterly whenever he saw a child in its mother's arms; whence it was inferred, that he had a wife and children, for no one was able to converse with him, or prepare him for baptism. The last two lived ten or twelve years in Denmark, and were employed in the pearl-fishery at Coldingen, but were so hard-worked in winter, that one of them died. The other, again attempting to escape, was retaken thirty or forty leagues from land, when he too died of grief.[11]

No words can express the sorrow and despair of a bought or stolen negro slave, when he leaves his native shore, never more to behold it while he has breath. "Great care must be taken," says Römer,

that the slaves do not get hold of a knife, either in the fort, or aboard the ship. To keep them in good humour on their passage to the West Indies requires the utmost exertion. For this purpose violins are provided, with fifes and drums; they are permitted to dance; and they are assured, that they are going to a pleasant country, where they may have as many wives as they please, and plenty of good food. Yet many deplorable instances have been known of their falling upon the crew, murdering them, and letting the ship drive ashore.[12]

But how many more deplorable instances have been known of these poor stolen wretches destroying themselves in despair! Sparmann informs us, from the mouth of a slavedealer, that at night they are seized with a kind of frenzy, which prompts them to commit murder, either on themselves or others; "for the painful recollection of the irreparable loss of their country and their freedom commonly awakes by night, when the bustle of

[11] *Gesch. von Grönland* (History of Greenland), p. 355.
[12] Römer's *Nachrichten von der Küste Guinea* (Account of the Coast of Guinea), p. 279.

the day ceases to engage their attention." [13] And what right have you, monsters! even to approach the country of these unfortunates, much less to tear them from it by stealth, fraud, and cruelty? For ages this quarter of the Globe has been theirs, and they belong to it: their forefathers purchased it at a dear rate, at the price of the Negro form and complexion. In fashioning them the African sun has adopted them as its children, and impressed on them its own seal: wherever you convey them, this brands you as robbers, as stealers of men.

Secondly. Thus the wars of savages for their country, or on account of its children, their brethren, torn from it, or degraded and oppressed, are extremely cruel. Hence, for instance, the lasting hatred of the natives of America toward Europeans, even when these behave to them with tenderness: they cannot suppress the feeling: "This land is ours; you have no business here." Hence the treachery of all savages, as they are called, even when they appear altogether satisfied with the courtesy of European visitors. The moment their hereditary national feelings awake, the flame they have long with difficulty smothered breaks out, rages with violence, and frequently is not appeased, till the flesh of the stranger has been torn by the teeth of the native. To us this seems horrible; and it is so, no doubt: yet the Europeans first urged them to this misdeed: for why did they visit their country? why did they enter it as despots, arbitrarily practising violence and extortion? [14] For ages it had been to its inhabitants the universe: they had inherited it from their fathers, and from them too they had inherited the barbarous practice of destroying in the most savage manner all, who would deprive them of their territory, tear them from it, or encroach upon their rights. Thus to them an enemy and a stranger are the same: they resemble the *muscipula*, which,

---

[13] Sparmann's *Voyages*, p. 73. This humane traveller has interspersed through his work many melancholy accounts of the capture and treatment of slaves, p. 195, 612, etc.

[14] See the editor's remarks on the unfortunate Marion's *Voyage à la Mer du Sud* (Voyage to the South Sea): also R. Forster's preface to the *Journal of Cook's last Voyage*, Berlin, 1781, and the accounts of the conduct of the Europeans.

rooted to its soil, attacks every insect that approaches it: the right of devouring an unbidden or unfriendly guest is the tribute they exact; as *Cyclopical* a tribute as any in Europe.

Lastly, I cannot pass over those joyful scenes, when a stolen son of nature revisits his paternal shores, and is restored to the bosom of his country. When the worthy Fuli priest, Job Ben Solomon, returned to Africa, every Fuli embraced him with brotherly affection, "he being the second of their countrymen, that had ever returned from slavery." [15] How ardently had he longed for this! How little was his heart satisfied with all the tokens of friendship and respect he received in England, which, as an enlightened, good-hearted man, he gratefully acknowledged! He was never at ease, till he was certain of the ship, that was to carry him home. This longing depends not on the state or advantages of a man's native land. The Hottentot Coree threw away all his European accoutrements, useful as they might be, to share again the hardships of his countrymen.[16] Instances might be cited from almost every climate, and the most inhospitable countries have the strongest attractions for their natives. Even the difficulties surmounted, to which body and mind are formed from infancy, impart to the natives that love of country and climate, which the inhabitants of fertile and populous plains feel much less, and to which the citizen of an European metropolis is almost a stranger. It is time, however, to investigate the term climate more narrowly; and while some build so much upon it, in the philosophy of the history of man, and others almost deny its influence altogether, I shall venture on nothing more than problems.

CHAPTER 3

What is Climate? and what Effect has it in forming the Body and Mind of Man?

THE two most fixed points of our Globe are the poles: without these it could not revolve, nay probably could not be a globe. If

[15] *Allg. Reisen,* Vol. III, p. 127 and following.

[16] *Ibid.,* Vol. V, p. 145. For other examples see Rousseau, in the notes to his *Discourse on the Inequality of Men.*

we knew the genesis of the poles, and the laws and effects of the magnetism of our Earth on the various bodies it contains, should we not have found the warp, which Nature, in the formation of beings, afterwards variously interwove with other superiour powers? But, notwithstanding the many and fine experiments that have been made, as yet we know little of it on the whole: we are still in the dark with respect to the basis of all climates from the polar regions.[17] At some period, perhaps, the magnet will render us the same service in the sphere of physical powers, as it has already full as unexpectedly on sea and land.

The revolution of our Globe about its own axis, and round the Sun, affords us a nearer indication of climates; but here too the application of even generally admitted laws is difficult and deceptive. The zones of the ancients have not been confirmed by our later knowledge of foreign parts, as, physically considered, they were founded on ignorance of them. It is the same with our calculations of heat and cold from the quantity and angle of the solar beams. As a mathematical problem, the effect of these has been industriously calculated with the greatest accuracy; but the mathematician himself would deem it an abuse of his rule, if the philosopher, in writing the history of climates, should build conclusions on it, without admitting exceptions.[18] In one place the proximity of the sea, in another the wind, here the height of the land, there its depth, in a fifth place the vicinity of mountains, in a sixth rain or mist, gives such a particular local qualification to the general law, that we frequently find the most opposite climates in places bordering upon each other. Beside this, it is evident from modern experiments, that every living being has its own mode of receiving and evolving heat; nay, that the more elaborate the organization of a creature, and the more active the vital power it exerts, the greater capacity it possesses of generating relative heat and

[17] See Brugmann, *Über den Magnetismus* (On magnetism), propositions 24–31.

[18] See Kästner's elucidation of Halley's Method of calculating heat, in the *Hamburg Magazine,* p. 429 and following.

cold.[19] The old position, that man can live only in a climate, the heat of which does not exceed that of the blood, has been confuted by experience: on the other hand, the modern systems of the origin and effect of animal heat are far from having attained sufficient perfection, for us in any wise to think of a climatology of the human frame merely, not to mention the faculties of the mind, and their arbitrary application. Every one indeed knows, that heat extends and relaxes the fibres, attenuates the fluids, and promotes perspiration; and that thus it is capable in time of rendering the solids light and spongy, etc. This law remains incontestable on the whole; [20] and in consequence, from it and its antagonist, cold, many physical phenomena have been already explained: [21] but general inferences from this principle, or from a part of it, as relaxation or perspiration for instance, to whole nations and countries, nay to the most delicate functions of the human mind, and the most accidental ordinances of society, are all in some measure hypothetical; and this the more, in proportion as the head that considers and arranges them is acute and systematic. They are contradicted almost step by step, by examples from history, or even by physiological principles; because too many powers, partly opposite to each other, act in conjunction. It has even been objected to the great Montesquieu, that he has erected his climatic spirit of laws on the fallacious experiment of a sheep's tongue. It is true, we are ductile clay in the hand of Climate; but her fingers mould so variously, and the laws, that counteract them, are so numerous, that perhaps the genius of mankind alone is capable of combining the relations of all these powers in one whole.

---

[19] Crell's *Versuche über das Vermögen der Pflanzen und Thiere Wärme zu erzeugen und zu vernichten* (Experiments on the capacities of plants and animals to generate and destroy heat), Helmstadt, 1778; Crawford's "Experiments on the Power of Animals to Produce Cold," *Philosophical Transactions,* Vol. LXXI, Part II, Art. 31.

[20] See the *Pathology of Gaubius,* Chap. V, X, etc.

[21] See Montesquieu, Castillon, Falconer, not to mention a number of less important tracts.

Heat and cold are not the sole principles of the atmosphere, that act upon us; for it appears from late observations, to be a magazine of other powers, which combine with us to our detriment or advantage. In it operates the stream of electric fire; a powerful substance, of the influence of which on the animal machine we yet know little: and we are fully as ignorant how it is received into the human body, and what changes it undergoes in it. We live by the inspiration of air: yet its balsam, our vital aliment, is a mystery to us. If now we add the various and almost innumerable local modifications of its component parts, from the effluvia of different substances; if we recollect the frequent instances of extraordinary, often terrible, and for ages inextinguishable, diseases, that have arisen from an invisible malignant seed, to which the physician is unable to give any other name than that of miasma; if we reflect on the secret poison, that has brought us the smallpox, the plague, syphilis, and many other disorders, which in the course of time have disappeared; and consider how little we know, not of the *harmattan* and *simoom,* the *sirocco* and north-east wind of Tatary, but of the constitution and effects of our own winds: how many introductory labours shall we perceive to be wanting, ere we arrive at a physiologico-pathology, to say nothing of a climatology, of all the sensitive and cogitative faculties of man! in the mean time, every judicious attempt deserves its laurels, and posterity will have many honourable ones, to bestow on the present times.[22]

Lastly, the elevation or depression of a region, its nature and products, the food and drink men enjoy in it, the mode of life they pursue, the labours in which they are employed, their clothing, even their ordinary attitudes, their arts and pleasures, with a multitude of other circumstances, which considerably influence their lives, all belong to the picture of changeable climate. What human hand can reduce this chaos of causes and effects to a world of order, in which every individual thing, and every individual region, shall enjoy its rights, and no one re-

[22] See Gmelin, *Über die neueren Entdeckungen in der Lehre von der Luft* (On the modern discoveries in aerology), Berlin, 1784.

ceive too much or too little? The best and only thing we can do is, to examine particular regions climatically, after the manner of Hippocrates, with his sagacious simplicity, and then slowly, slowly deduce general inferences.[23] The natural historian and physician are here the pupils of Nature, and the teachers of the philosopher. To them we and posterity also are already indebted for several materials, collected in different regions, toward a general doctrine of climates and their effects upon man. But here we must content ourselves with general remarks, as we cannot descend to particular observations.

1. *As our Earth is a globe, and the firm land a mountain raised above the sea, a climatic community, affecting the life of every thing living, is promoted on it by various causes.* Not only is the climate of every region periodically changed by the alteration of day and night, and the revolution of the seasons; but the jarring of the elements, the mutual action of sea and land upon each other, the situation of mountains and plains, the periodical winds, that arise from the motion of the Globe, the changes of the season, the appearance and disappearance of the Sun, and many less important causes, maintain this salutiferous union of the elements, without which every thing would stagnate in drowsiness and corruption. We are surrounded by an atmosphere; we live in an electric ocean: but both, and probably the magnetic fluid with them, are in continual motion. The sea emits vapours; the mountains attract them, and send them down in rain and streams on every side. Thus winds relieve each other: thus years, or periods of years, fulfill their climatic days. Thus different regions and ages follow one another; and every thing on our Globe combines in one general connexion. Had the Earth been flat, or angular, as the Chinese have dreamed, its corners might have produced climatic monsters, incompatible with its present regular structure, and diffusive movement. The Hours dance in a circle round the throne of Jove, and what is formed under their feet is only an imperfect perfection, because all originates from the union of things

[23] See Hippocrates, *De aere, locis, et aquis*, particularly the second part of the treatise. He is my principal author on the subject of climate.

various in kind: but from an internal love and conjunction with one another, the children of Nature, sensible Regularity and Beauty, are every where produced.

2. *The habitable land of our Earth is accumulated in regions, where most living beings act in the mode best adapted to them; and this situation of the quarters of the Globe influences all its climates.* Why does the cold in the southern hemisphere commence so near the line? The natural philosopher answers, "because there is so little land, so that the cold winds and ice of the south pole extend themselves to a great distance." Thus we perceive what would have been our fate, had the whole of our firm land been scattered about in islands. Now three quarters of the Globe, lying in contact, warm each other: the fourth, being remote from them, is on this account colder; and in the South Sea, a very little beyond the line, degeneracy and deformity begin with the deficiency of the land. Fewer species of the more perfect animals also dwell there. The southern hemisphere was made the grand reservoir of water for our Globe, that the northern might enjoy a better climate. Thus, whether we consider the World geographically, or climatically, we find Nature intended mankind to be neighbourly beings, dwelling together, and imparting to each other climatic warmth, and other benefits, as well as the plague, diseases, and climatic vices.

3. *By the formation of the land on the frame of the mountains, not only were its climates infinitely diversified for the great variety of living beings, but the degeneration of the human species was provided against as much as possible.* Mountains were necessary to the Earth; but we find Mungals and Tibetians only on one ridge of them; the lofty Cordilleras, and many others their fellows, are uninhabitable. Barren deserts, also, are rare, from the mountainous structure of the Earth: for the mountains rise as conductors of the clouds, and pour out from their horns of plenty fertilizing streams. The barren shore, the bleak or marshy border of the sea, is every where more recently formed land; and consequently men have taken possession of it later, and when their powers were already improved. The vale of Quito was inhabited unquestionably

before Tierra del Fuego; Cashmire, sooner than New Holland or Nova Zembla. The middle and broadest part of the earth, the land of the finest climate between sea and mountains, was the nursery of our species, and is even now the most fully peopled part of the Globe.

There is no question, but, as climate is a compound of powers and influences, to which both plants and animals contribute, and which every thing that has breath promotes in its reciprocating mutations, so man is placed in it as a sovereign of the Earth, to alter it by art. Since he stole fire from Heaven, and rendered steel obedient to his hand; since he has made not only beasts, but his fellow man also, subservient to his will, and trained both them and plants to his purposes; he has contributed to the alteration of climate in various ways. Once Europe was a dank forest; and other regions, at present well cultivated, were the same. They are now exposed to the rays of the Sun; and the inhabitants themselves have changed with the climate. The face of Egypt would have been nothing more than the slime of the Nile, but for the art and policy of man. He has gained it from the flood; and both there, and in farther Asia, the living creation has adapted itself to the artificial climate. We may consider mankind, therefore, as a band of bold though diminutive giants, gradually descending from the mountains, to subjugate the earth, and change climates with their feeble arms. How far they are capable of going in this respect futurity will show.

4. Finally, if it be allowable to speak in general terms on a subject, which rests so completely on particular cases, local or historical, I will insert, with a little variation, some cautions, that Bacon gives with respect to the history of revolutions.[24] The action of climate extends itself indeed to bodies of all kinds, but chiefly to the more delicate, to fluids, the air, and the ether. It operates rather on the mass, than on the individual: Yet on this, through that. It is not confined to points of time, but prevails through long periods: though it is often late before it

[24] *Baco de Augm. Scient.* l. 3.

becomes obvious, and then perhaps is rendered so by slight circumstances. Lastly, climate does not force, but incline: it gives the imperceptible disposition, which strikes us indeed in the general view of the life and manners of indigenous nations, but is very difficult to be delineated distinctly. Sometime possibly a traveller may be found, who will pursue without prejudice or exaggeration the *spirit of climate.* At present our duty is rather to note the living powers, for which each climate is formed; and which, by their existence, induce in it various changes and modifications.

CHAPTER 4

The genetic Power is the Mother of all the Forms upon Earth, Climate acting merely as an Auxiliary or Antagonist

How must the man have been astonished, who first saw the wonders of the creation of a living being![25] Globules, with fluids shooting between them, become a living point; and from this point an animal forms itself. The heart soon becomes visible, and, weak and imperfect as it is, begins to beat: the blood, which existed before the heart, begins to redden: soon the head appears: soon eyes, a mouth, the senses, and limbs, display themselves. Still there is no breast, yet there is motion in the internal parts: there are no bowels, yet the animal opens its mouth. The little brain is not yet inclosed in the head; or the heart, in the breast: the ribs and bones are like a spider's web: but quickly the wings, feet, toes, hips, appear, and the living creature receives more nourishment. What was naked becomes covered: the breast and head close: the stomach and bowels are still pendulous. These also at length assume their proper form, as more matter is furnished: The integuments contract and ascend: the belly closes: the animal is formed. It now swims no longer, but assumes a recumbent posture: it wakes and sleeps by turns: it moves, it rests, it cries, it seeks an exit, and comes complete in all its parts into the light of day. What would he who saw this wonder for the first time call it? There, he would say, is a *living organic power:* I know not whence it came, or

[25] See Harvey, *De generat. animal.*, Wolf's *Theor. Generat.*, etc.

what it intrinsically is: but that it is there, that it lives, that it has acquired itself organic parts out of the chaos of homogeneal matter, I see: this is incontestable.

If he observed farther, and saw, that each of these organic parts was fashioned as it were *in actu,* in its own operation: the heart formed itself no otherwise than by a confluence of the channels, that existed before it; as soon as the stomach was perceptible, matter to be digested was in it. It was the same with the arteries and all the vessels: the contents existed before what was to contain them, the fluids before the solids, the spirit before the body, in which it is merely clothed. If he observed this, would he not say, that the invisible power did not fashion arbitrarily, but only *reveal* itself as it were according to its internal nature? [26] It becomes visible in a mass appertaining to it, and must have *the prototype of its appearance in itself,* whence or wherever it may be. The new creature is nothing but the realization of an idea of creative Nature, who never thinks inactively.

If he go farther and observe, that this creation is promoted by maternal or solar warmth; but that the egg will produce no living fruit, notwithstanding the preference of the necessary warmth and materials, unless quickened by the father: what would he suppose, but that the principle of heat may indeed have some affinity to the principle of life, which it promotes, yet that the cause, which sets this organic power in action, to give the dead chaos of matter a living form, must actually lie in the union of two living beings? Thus we, thus all living creatures, are formed; each after the kind of its organization; but all according to the evident laws of an analogy, that prevails universally with every thing, that lives upon this Earth.

Lastly, when it appears, that this vital power does not quit the finished creature, but *continues to display itself actively* in him; no longer creating indeed, for he is created, but supporting, vivifying, nourishing: from the moment he enters the World, he performs all the vital functions for which, nay in some measure in which, he was made; the mouth opens, as

[26] Wolf's *Theor. Generat.*, p. 169, b. 180–216.

opening was its first action, and the lungs respire; the vocal organs emit sound, the lips suck, the stomach digests; he lives, he grows, all the external and internal parts assist each other; they attract, reject, and assimilate, with associated action and sympathy, and assist one another in pain and disease in a thousand wonderful and incomprehensible ways: what would he, what would any one, who saw this for the first time, say, but that the innate genetic vital power still *resides* in the creature, that was formed by it, in all its parts, and in each after its proper manner, that is organically? It is present in him every where in the most multifarious manner; for only by its means is he a living whole, self-supporting, growing, and acting.

This vital power we all have in us: it assists us in sickness and in health, assimilates homogeneal subtances, separates heterogeneal matters, and expels such as are injurious; at length it grows feeble with age, and lives in some parts even after death. It is not the faculty of reason: for this assuredly did not fashion the body, which it does not know, and which it employs merely as an imperfect adventitious instrument, to execute its thoughts. Yet this faculty is connected with the vital power, as all the powers of nature are connected: for even incorporeal thought depends on the health and organization of the body, and all the desires and propensities of our hearts are inseparable from animal warmth. All these are natural *facts,* which no hypothesis can shake, no logic of the schools overturn: the enunciation of them is the most ancient philosophy of the Earth, as probably it will be the last.[27] Certainly as I know that I think, yet know not my thinking faculty; as certainly do I see and feel that I live, though I know not what the vital principle is. This principle is innate, organical, genetic: it is the basis of my natural powers, the internal genius of my being. Man is the most perfect of earthly creatures, only because in him the finest organic powers

[27] Hippocrates, Aristotle, Galen, Harvey, Boyle, Stahl, Glisson, Gaubius, Albinus, and many others of the greatest observers or philosophers of the human species, compelled by experiment, have admitted this vital principle, only bestowing on it various appellations, or sometimes not sufficiently discriminating it from collateral powers.

we know act with the most elaborately organized instruments. He is the most perfect animal plant, a native genius in human form.

If the principles hitherto advanced be just, and they are founded on indisputable experience, our species cannot in any way degenerate, but by the operation of these organic powers. Whatever climate may effect, every man, every animal, every plant, has his own climate; for every one receives all external impressions in his own manner, and modifies them according to his organs. Even in the minutest fibre man is not affected as a stone, as a hydatid. Let us consider some steps, or shades, of this degeneration.

The first step in the degeneration of the human species exhibits itself in the external parts: not as if these suffered or acted of themselves, but because the power dwelling in us acts from within to without. By the most wonderful mechanism it strives to expel from the body what is incongruous or detrimental to it: the first alterations of its organic structure, therefore, must be perceptible on the confines of its domain; and accordingly the most striking varieties of the species affect only the skin and hair. Nature protects the internal essential form, and drives out as far as possible the aggrieving matter.

If the altered external power proceed farther, its effects show themselves in the same way as the vital principle itself acts, *in the way of nutrition and propagation.* The Negro is born fair: the parts that first grow black in him are evident signs, that the miasma of his change, which the external air merely developes, acts genetically. The age of puberty, as well as a multitude of facts observed in diseases, shows us the extensive sway, that the powers of nutrition and propagation possess in the human body. By these the remotest parts of the body are connected; and in the degeneration of the species these parts suffer in conjunction. Hence, the skin and sexual parts excepted, the ears, the neck and voice, the nose, the lips, the head, &c., are precisely the parts, in which most changes appear.

Finally, as the vital principle connects all the parts together, and the organization is a complicated knot, which has properly neither beginning nor end, it is easy to comprehend, that the most internal change of any consequence must ultimately become visible even in the parts possessing the greatest solidity, the relations of which are altered, by means of the internal power that is affected, from the crown of the head to the sole of the foot. Nature does not easily yield to this change: even in monstrous births, when she has been forcibly disturbed in her operations, she has astonishing ways of reparation, as a defeated general displays most skill in a retreat. The various national forms of people however testify, that even this, the most difficult change of the human species, is possible: and it is rendered so by the multifarious complication and delicate mobility of our frame, with the innumerable powers that act upon it. But this difficult change is effected only from within. For ages particular nations have moulded their heads, bored their noses, confined their feet, or extended their ears: Nature remains true to herself; and if for a time she be compelled to take a course she would not, and send fluids to the distorted parts; she proceeds on her own way, as soon as she can recover her liberty, and produces her own more perfect image. If the deformity be genetic, and effected in the natural way, the case is totally different: it is then hereditary, even in particular parts. Let it not be said, that art or the Sun has flattened the Negro's nose. As the figure of this part is connected with conformation of the whole skull, the chin, the neck, the spine; and the branching spinal marrow is as it were the trunk of the tree, on which the thorax and all the limbs are formed; comparative anatomy satisfactorily shows, that the degeneration has affected the whole figure, and none of these solid parts could be changed without an alteration of the whole.[28] Thus the Negro form is transmitted in hereditary succession, and is capable of being rechanged no otherwise than genetically. See the Negro in Europe: he remains as he was. Let him marry a white woman, and a single generation will effect a change, which the

[28] See Sömmering, *Über die körperliche Verschiedenheit des Mohrer vom Europäer* (On the bodily difference between the Negro and the European), Mentz, 1784.

fair-complexioned climate could not produce in ages. So it is with the figures of all nations: regions alter them very slowly; but by intermixture with foreigners, in a few generations every Mungal, Chinese, or American feature vanishes.

If it be agreeable to the reader to pursue this path, let us go on a few steps farther.

1. It must be obvious to every observer, that, *amid the innumerable varieties of the human figure, certain forms and proportions not only reoccur, but pertain exclusively to each other.* With artists this is an acknowledged fact: and we see in the statues of the ancients, that they placed this proportion, or symmetry as they termed it, not merely in the length and breadth of the limbs, but also in their harmonic adjustment to the spirit of the whole. The characters of their gods and goddesses, their youths and heroes, were so determinate in their whole conformation, that they are in some degree to be known from single limbs, and no one figure will admit of an arm, a breast, a shoulder, that belonged to another. The genius of a particular living being exists in each of these forms, which serves it merely as a shell, and characterizes itself in the least attitude or motion as distinctly as in the whole. Among the moderns, the Polyclete of our country,[29] Albert Durer, has industriously examined the measure of various proportions of the human body; and thus rendered it obvious to every eye, that the figures of all the parts differ with their proportions.[30] What would it be, if a man united Durer's accuracy with the spirit and taste of the ancients, and studied the differences of the genetic forms and characters of men, in their concordant figures! Thus, I think, Physiognomy would return to her old natural way, to which her name points; and in which she would be neither Ethognomy, nor Technognomy, but the expositor of the living *nature* of a man, the interpreter as it were of his

[29] This epithet can allude only to the canon of proportions, which Polyclete is said to have established in one of his figures: Plin. L. XXXIV, c. 8: for surely neither the materials nor the style of the Sicyonian genius were those of Albert of Nuremberg.

[30] Albert Durer's four books on human proportion, Nuremberg, 1528.

genius rendered visible. As within these bounds she remains true to the analogy of the whole, which is most conspicuous in the face, Pathognomy must be her sister, Physiology and Semeiotics her friends and assistants: for the external figure of man is but the case of his internal mechanism, a consistent whole, in which every letter forms a part of the word indeed, but only the whole word has a determinate signification. It is thus we practise and apply physiognomy in common life: the experienced physician sees from a man's make and countenance to what diseases he is subject, and the physiognomic eye even of a child observes the natural disposition of a man in his person, that is, the form in which his genius discloses itself.

Farther. *Are not these forms, these concords of harmonizing parts, capable of being noted, and reduced like letters as it were to an alphabet?* Not that we must expect this system of letters ever to be complete, as there is no such thing as a perfect alphabet in any language; but a careful study of these living orders of human columns unquestionably opens a wide field for the science of character. If in this pursuit we were not to confine ourselves to Europe, and still less to our common idea of the summit of health and beauty, but followed living Nature throughout the Globe, in whatever harmony of congruous parts she displays herself, variously diversified, yet ever one: numerous discoveries respecting the concent and melody of living powers in the human structure would undoubtedly reward our exertions. Nay it is probable, this study of the natural consent of forms in the human body would carry us farther, than the doctrine of complexions and temperaments, often attempted, though commonly to little purpose. The most acute observers have made little progress here, because they have wanted a determinate alphabet, to note the differences, that were to be expressed.[31]

As the physiology of life must every where carry the torch before such a *figural history of the formation and diversification*

[31] I find this doctrine reduced to great simplicity in Metzger's miscellaneous Works, Vol. I. Platner too, and some others, have their acknowledged merits on this head.

of the human species, the wisdom of Nature, who fashions and alters forms only according to one law of multifariously compensating goodness, would be visible at every step. Why, for example, did the creative mother separate species from each other? For no other reason, but to make and preserve the image of their conformation more perfect. We know not how many of the present species of animals may have approached nearer to each other in an earlier age of our Earth; but we see, that *their boundaries are now genetically separated.* In the wild state, no beast couples with one of a different kind: and if the despotic art of man, or the wanton indolence, to which pampered animals yield, cause a deviation from their real propensities, Nature permits not her unchangeable laws to be surmounted by art or debauchery. Either the union is unproductive, or the forced illegitimate offspring is propagated only among the nearest species. Nay, among these bastard species themselves, we perceive the deviation nowhere but in the extreme parts of the figure, as in the degeneration of the human species already described: if the internal essential form had been susceptible of alteration, no living creature could have preserved its identity. Thus in consequence of the fundamental laws of creative nature, and the genetic essential type of each genus, neither a centaur, nor a satyr, neither a Scylla, nor a Medusa, is within the sphere of procreation.

3. Lastly, *the most exquisite means employed by Nature, to unite variety and stability of form in her genera, were the creation and union of the two sexes.* With what wonderful delicacy and spirit do the features of the two parents unite in the countenances and make of their children! as if their souls had been transfused into them in different proportions, and the multifarious natural powers of organization had been divided between them. That diseases and features, nay that tempers and dispositions, are hereditary, is known to all the world: even the forms of ancestors long departed frequently return in the course of generations in a wonderful manner. Equally undeniable, though not easy to be explained; is the influence of the bodily and mental affections of the mother on the foetus; many

lamentable examples of the effects of which have been borne till death. Thus Nature has turned into each other two currents of life, to endow the future creature with one complete natural power, which will live in it according to the features of both the parents. Many a declining race is again restored by a cheerful healthy mother: many a debilitated youth must first be awakened to a living natural creature in the arms of his wife. In the genial formation of man Love is the most powerful of all deities: he ennobles races, and revives the declining: a ray of the divinity, the sparks of which kindle the flame of human life, and make it burn here more vividly, there more obscurely. Nothing, on the contrary, counteracts the plastic genius of Nature more than cold antipathy; or disgusting convenience, which is even worse. This brings persons together, who were never designed for each other, and perpetuates miserable beings, never in harmony with themselves. No brute has yet sunk so low, as man has fallen from this cause of degeneracy.

CHAPTER 5

Concluding Remarks on the Opposition between Genesis and Climate

If I mistake not, the hints, that have been given, may be considered as the commencement of the line, that marks this opposition. No man will expect, for instance, that the rose should become a lily, the dog a wolf, in a foreign climate: for Nature has drawn determinate lines round her species, and permits a creature rather to disappear, than essentially deface or falsify its figure. But, that the rose can admit of variation, that the dog can acquire something wolfish, is conformable to experience: yet here the variation is producible only by flow or speedy violence done to the resisting organic powers. Thus both the contending principles act with great force, yet each in its own way. Climate is a chaos of causes, very dissimilar to each other, and in consequence acting slowly and in various ways, till at length they penetrate to the internal parts, and change them by habit, and by the genetic power itself: this resists long, forcibly, uniformly, and like itself; but as it is not independent of external affections, it also must accommodate itself to them in length of time.

To an extensive view of the opposition in general, I would prefer an instructive examination of particular cases, of which history and geography afford us an ample store. We know, for example, what effect the adoption of the mode of life of the natives, or the retaining of their own European customs, has had on the Portuguese colonies in Africa, or the Spanish, Dutch, English, and German settlers, in America and the East Indies. When all these were accurately investigated, we might proceed to more ancient transitions; as for instance of the Malays to the islands, the Arabs to Africa and the East Indies, and the Turks to the countries conquered by them; and thus go on to the Mungals, the Tatars, and lastly the swarm of nations, that covered Europe in the course of the great migration. We should never overlook the climate from which a people came, the mode of life it brought with it, the country that lay before it, the nations with which it intermingled, and the revolutions it has undergone in its new seat. If this inquiry were carried through those ages of which we have authentic accounts, we might probably arrive at conclusions respecting those more early migrations, of which we know nothing but from the traditional tales of ancient writers, or the coincidences of language and mythology; for in fact all, or most of the nations upon Earth at least, have sooner or later migrated. Thus, with the assistance of a few maps for the convenience of inspection, we should obtain a *physico-geographical history of the descent and diversification of our species* according to periods and climates, which at every step must afford us important results.

Without anticipating the labours of the inquiring mind, that shall undertake this task, I will introduce a few facts from modern history, as brief examples of my preceding examination.

1. *Too sudden, too precipitate transitions to an opposite hemisphere and climate are seldom salutary to a nation;* for Nature has not established her boundaries between remote lands in vain. The history of conquests, as well as of commercial companies, and especially that of missions, afford a melancholy, and

in some respects a laughable picture, if we delineate this subject and its consequences with impartiality, even from the narrations of the parties themselves. We shudder with abhorrence when we read the accounts of many European nations, who, sunk in the most dissolute voluptuousness and insensible pride, have degenerated both in body and mind, and no longer possess any capacity for enjoyment and compassion. They are fullblown bladders in human shape, lost to every noble and active pleasure, and in whose veins lurks avenging death. If to these we add the wretches, to whom both the Indies have proved insatiate graves; if we read the histories of the diseases of foreign climates, given by English, French, and Dutch physicians; and if we then turn our eyes to the pious missionaries, who have not been so ready to quit the garb of their order, and their European mode of life; what instructive inferences press upon us, which alas! belong to the history of man!

2. *Even the European industry of less debauched colonies in other quarters of the Globe is not always able to avert the effect of climate.* It is observed by Kalm, that the Europeans in North America arrive earlier at the age of puberty, but at the same time sooner grow old and die, than in their native country. "It is nothing uncommon," says he,

> to find little children answer questions put to them with astonishing readiness and vivacity, and yet not attain the age of Europeans. Eighty or ninety years are seldom reached by one born in America of European parents, though the aborigines frequently live much longer: and the natives of Europe commonly live much longer in America, than such of their children as are born in that country. The women sooner cease childbearing, some as early as the age of thirty: and it is generally observed, that the offspring of the European colonists lose their teeth soon and prematurely, while the Americans retain their teeth white and sound to the end of their lives.[32]

This passage has been improperly quoted as a proof of the unhealthiness of America with respect to her own children: but it is to foreigners only that she is a stepmother, who, as Kalm

[32] *Göttingen Collection of Travels,* Vols. X and XI *passim.*

observes, dwell in her bosom with different constitutions and manners.

3. *Let it not be imagined, that human art can with despotic power convert at once a foreign region into another Europe,* by cutting down its forests, and cultivating its soil: for its whole living creation is conformable to it, and this is not to be changed at discretion. Even Kalm informs us, from the mouths of American Swedes, that the speedy destruction of the woods, and cultivation of the land, not only lessened the number of edible birds, which were found in innumerable multitudes in the forests and on the waters, and of fishes with which the brooks and rivers swarmed, and diminished the lakes, streams, rivulets, springs, rains, thick long grass of the woods, etc.; but seemed to affect the health and longevity of the inhabitants, and influence the seasons. "The Americans," says he,

> who frequently lived a hundred years and upwards before the arrival of the Europeans, now often attain scarcely half the age of their forefathers: and this, it is probable, we must not ascribe solely to the destructive use of spirits, and an alteration in their way of life, but likewise to the loss of so many odoriferous herbs, and salutary plants, which every morning and evening perfumed the air, as if the country had been a flower-garden. The winter was then more seasonable, cold, healthy, and constant: now the spring commences later, and, like the other seasons, is more variable and irregular.

This is the account given by Kalm; and however local we may consider it, still it shows, that Nature loves not too speedy, too violent a change, even in the best work, that man can perform, the cultivation of a country. May we not also attribute the debility of the civilized Americans, as they are called, in Mexico, Peru, Paraguay, and Brazil, to this among other things, that we have changed their country and manner of living, without the power or the will of giving them an European nature? All the nations, that live in the woods, and after the manner of their forefathers, are strong and bold, live long, and renovate their vigour like their own trees: those on the cultivated land, deprived of shade and moisture, decline miserably; their souls are left behind in the woods. Read, as an example, the affecting history of a simple flourishing family, drawn from its wilds by Dobritzhofer.[33] Both the mother and daughter soon died; and both in dreams continued to call on their son and brother left behind, till death closed his eyes without the aid of disease. This alone renders it comprehensible, how nations, that once were valiant, active, and resolute, should in a short time sink into such a state of weakness, as the Jesuits of Paraguay and travellers in Peru describe: a weakness of which we cannot read without sorrow. In the course of ages this subjugation of Nature may have its good effects in particular places; though I doubt this, if it were generally practicable: but for the first races, both of the civilizers and civilized, it appears to have none; for Nature is every where a living whole, and will be gently followed and improved, not mastered by force.[34] Nothing has been made of any of the savages, who have been suddenly brought into the throng of an European city: from the splendid height, on which they were placed, they longed for their native plains, and for the most part returned inexpert and corrupted to their ancient way of life, which also they were now rendered incapable of enjoying. It is the fame with the forcible alteration of savage climates by European hands.

O sons of Dedalus, emissaries of Fate, how many instruments are in your hands for conferring happiness on nations by humane and compassionate means! and how has a proud insolent love of gain led you almost every where into a different path! All newcomers from a foreign land, who have submitted to naturalize themselves with the inhabitants, have not only enjoyed their love and friendship, but have ultimately found, that their mode of life was not altogether unsuitable to the climate: but how few such are there! how seldom does an European hear from the native of any country the praise, "he is a rational man like us!" And does not Nature revenge every insult offered her? Where are the conquests, the factories, the invasions, of former times, when distant foreign lands were visited by a

[33] Dobritzhofer's *Geschichte der Abiponer* (History of the Abiponians), Vol. I, p. 114.

[34] See Williamson's attempt to explain the causes of change of climate, in the Berlin Collection, Vol. VII.

different race, for the sake of devastation or plunder! The still breath of climate has dissipated or consumed them, and it was not difficult for the natives to give the finishing stroke to the rootless tree. The quiet plant, on the other hand, that has accommodated itself to the laws of Naure, has not only preserved its own existence, but has beneficially diffused the seeds of cultivation through a new land. Future ages may decide, what benefit, or injury, our genius has conferred on other climates, and other climates on our genius.

BOOK VIII

As it would be with one, who, from navigating the sea, should attempt a voyage through the air, so it is with me, now that, having gone over the figure and natural powers of man, I come to his mind, and attempt to investigate its variable faculties, as they exist throughout the wide World, from indirect, defective, and partly questionable accounts. The metaphysician has here a much easier task. He sets out with establishing a certain idea of the mind, and from this deduces every thing, that can be deduced, wherever, or under whatever circumstances, it may be found. The philosopher of history can proceed on no abstract notion, but on history alone; and he is in danger of forming erroneous conclusions, if he do not generalize at least in some degree the numerous facts before him. I shall attempt to explore the way, however: yet, instead of launching out into the ocean, I shall rather coast along the shore; or, to speak in plain terms, confine myself to undoubted facts, or such as are generally considered so, distinguishing them from my own conjectures, and leaving it to those who are more fortunate, to arrange and employ them in a better manner.

CHAPTER 1

The Appetites of the human Species vary with their Form and Climate; but a less brutal Use of the Senses universally leads to Humanity

All nations, the diseased albinoes perhaps excepted, enjoy the five or six senses of man: the men without feeling of Diodorus, and the nations of deaf and dumb, are proved fabulous in modern history. Yet he, who attends only to the difference of the external senses among us, and then considers the innumerable multitudes living in all the climates of the Earth, will find himself contemplating an ocean, where wave loses itself in wave. Every man has a particular proportion, a particular harmony as it were, between all his sensitive feelings; so that, in extraordinary cases, the most wonderful appearances frequently occur, to show the state of an individual on this or that occasion. Hence physicians and philosophers have already formed whole collections of singular and peculiar feelings, that is of idiosyncrasies, which are in many instances equally rare and inexplicable. For the most part these are observed only in disease, or unusual incidents, not in the common occurrences of life. Language too has no terms for them; as every man speaks and understands according to his own perceptions alone, and different organizations of course want a common standard for their different feelings. Even in the clearest sense, that of seeing, these differences display themselves, not only with respect to distance, but also to the figure and colour of things: hence so many painters have their peculiarities of outline, and almost every one his particular style of colouring. It is not the part of the philosophy of the history of man to exhaust this ocean, but by some striking differences to call our attention to the more delicate, that lie around us.

The most general and necessary sense is that of feeling: it is the basis of the rest, and one of the greatest organic preeminences of man.[35] It has conferred on us dexterity, invention, and art; and contributes more perhaps to the formation of our ideas, than we imagine. But how different is this sense, according as it is modified by the way of life, climate, application, exercise, and native irritability of the body! To some American nations, for example, an insensibility of the skin is ascribed, conspicuous even in women, and under the most painful operations.[36] If the

---

[35] See Metzger on the bodily excellences of man over brutes, in his *Vermischten Medicinischen Schriften* (Miscellaneous Medical Tracts), Vol. III.

[36] Robertson's *History of America,* Vol. I, p. 562.

fact be true, I conceive it easily explicable both from corporal and mental circumstances. For ages many nations in this quarter of the Globe have exposed their naked bodies to the piercing winds, and the stings of insects; and, to protect them in some measure from these, have besmeared them with acrid unguents. They also pluck out the hair, which promotes the tenderness of the skin. Alkaline roots and plants, and the meal of acrimonious vegetables, are used by them as food; and the close sympathy between the organs of digestion, and the seat of feeling, the skin, is well-known, this sense completely failing in consequence of it in many diseases. Even their immoderate indulgence in eating, after which they will endure hunger to a degree equally uncommon, seems to confirm this insensibility, which is also a symptom of many of their diseases, and consequently must be reckoned among the advantages and disadvantages of their climate.[37] With it Nature has gradually armed them against evils, which greater sensibility would have rendered insupportable; and with them Art has followed the steps of Nature. The North Americans suffer pain and torment with heroic insensibility, from principles of honour. They are formed to it from infancy; and in this the women yield not to the men. Thus stoic apathy under bodily pain is to them a natural habitude: and their feebler appetite for pleasure, notwithstanding the vivacity of their natural powers in other respects, and even that lethargic insensibility, in consequence of which many subjugated nations appear as if in a waking dream, seem deducible from this cause. Brutes therefore must they have been, who, from a still greater want of human feeling, have abused, or put to painful trials, a want, which Nature bestowed on her children for their solace and convenience.

Experience has shown, that an immoderate degree of heat or cold scorches up or benumbs the external feeling. Nations that walk barefoot on the sands acquire a sole as hard as iron; and instances have been known of such persons standing on burning coals for twenty minutes. Corrosive poisons can so change

---

[37] Ulloa, Vol. I, p. 188.

the skin, that a man may plunge his hand into melted lead; and rigorous cold, as well as anger and other passions of the mind, also contributes to deaden the feeling.[38] This sense on the other hand appears most exquisite in regions, and under a mode of life, that are most favourable to the gentle contraction of the skin, and an harmonious extension as it were of the nerves of touch. The East Indian enjoys perhaps in the highest perfection the organs of sense. His palate, which has never been blunted by strong drink or stimulating food, tastes the slightest accidental flavour in pure water; and his fingers imitate the most delicate works in such a manner, that the copy is not to be distinguished from the original. His mind is calm and serene, an echo of the gentle feelings, that every thing around him excites. So play the waves about the swan: so whisper the winds through the thin foliage of spring.

Next to the warmth and serenity of the climate, nothing contributes so much to this exquisiteness of feeling, as cleanliness, temperance, and motion: three physical virtues, in which many nations, that we term uncivilized, exceed us, and which the inhabitants of the most delightful countries appear particularly to claim as their own. Keeping the mouth clean, frequent bathing, love of exercise in the open air, and even the healthy and voluptuous rubbing and extension of the body, which was as well known to the Romans, as it is now common among the Indians, Persians, and many Tatar nations through a considerable tract of country, promotes the circulation of the fluids, and maintains the elastic tone of the muscular fibres. The inhabitants of the most fertile country live temperately: they have no conception, that an unnatural stimulation of the nerves, and a daily overloading of the vessels, can be pleasures, for which man was created: the caste of Bramins have tasted neither flesh nor wine from the beginning of the World. Now since the effects of these on the whole system of sensation in brutes are apparent, must they not operate much more powerfully on the flower of all organizations, man? Moderation in sensual enjoy-

[38] Haller's *Physiology*, Vol. V, p. 16.

ment without doubt contributes more effectually to the philosophy of humanity, than a thousand learned and artificial abstract considerations.

All people of coarse feelings, in a savage state, or rigorous climate, are gluttonous; as they are frequently obliged to suffer hunger afterwards: for the most part, too, they eat whatever comes in their way. Nations possessing finer senses love more delicate pleasures. Their meals are simple, and they eat daily the same food: but then they are fond of luxurious unguents, fine perfumes, pomp, and convenience; and their highest pleasure is sensual love. If we were talking merely of the fineness of organs, there can be no doubt, which way the preference would incline: for no polished European would hesitate, to choose between the fat and train-oil of the Greenlander, and the aromatics of the Hindoo. But it is a question, in spite of our verbal polish, to which of the two we approach nearest upon the whole. The Hindoo places his happiness in tranquillity undisturbed by passion, in an uninterrupted enjoyment of serenity and pleasure. He breathes voluptuousness: he floats on a sea of pleasing dreams, and exhilarating fragrance. On the other hand, what are the objects of our luxury? for what does it disturb the whole World, and plunder every quarter of the Globe? New and pungent spices for a blunted palate; foreign fruits and food, which are often jumbled together in such a medley, that we cannot taste their proper flavour; intoxicating liquors, that bereave us both of our senses and our peace; whatever can be invented to exhaust nature by exciting it, are daily the grand aim of our lives. By these, conditions are distinguished: by these, nations are made happy. Happy! Why do the poor suffer hunger, and with benumbed senses drag on a wretched life of toil and labour? That the rich and great may deaden their senses in a more delicate manner, without taste, and probably to the eternal nourishment of their brutality. "The Europeans eat every thing," says the Hindoo, whose more exquisite smell revolts at the mere effluvia of what they swallow. According to his ideas, he can rank them only in the caste of the pariahs, who, as a mark of supreme contempt, are allowed to eat what they please. In many countries, too, the Mohammedans call the Europeans unclean beasts; and this not merely from religious antipathy.

It can hardly be possible, that Nature should have given us a tongue, in order that the gratification of a few papillae on it should be the aim of a laborious life, or the cause of wretchedness to others. She endowed it with the sense of taste, partly to sweeten the duty of satisfying the calls of hunger, and enticing us to labour by more pleasing motives: and partly also to be the scrupulous guard of our health; but this it has long ceased to be in all nations addicted to luxury. The cow knows what is salutary for herself, and selects her food with apprehensive caution: noxious and poisonous plants she avoids, and is seldom mistaken. Men, who live among beasts, can discriminate their food like them; but lose this faculty, when they come to associate with mankind, as the Indians, who relinquish the simplicity of their diet, lose the purity of their smell. Nations, that enjoy healthful freedom, still possess much of this guiding sense. They seldom or never err with respect to the products of their own country: nay, the North American can trace his enemy by the smell, and by this the Carib distinguishes the footsteps of different nations. Thus man may heighten his most sensual, his animal powers, by cultivating and exercising them: but the highest perfection of them consists in a due proportion of them all, adapted to a truly human life, so that no one be lost, and no one predominate. This proportion varies with country and climate. The inhabitant of hot countries eats with eager appetite food to us highly disgusting: for his nature requires it, as a medicine, as an antidote.[39]

Lastly, the sight and hearing are the noblest senses, for which man is particularly formed by his organization; for in him the organs of these senses are more artfully constructed, than in any other animal. How acute have the sight and hearing been rendered by many nations! The Calmuc sees smoke, where nothing can be perceived by an European eye: the shy Arab

---

[39] Wilson's *Observations on the Influence of Climate,* p. 93, etc.

hears far around in his silent desert. If these acute and fine senses be exercised with unremitting attention, the consequence is obvious: for we see in many nations how far practice can carry a man beyond the unpractised, even in the most trifling things. People who live by hunting know every tree and bush in their country: the North Americans never lose their way in their forests: they travel in quest of their enemies hundreds of miles, and return again to their huts. Dobritzhofer informs us, that the civilized Guaranies imitate with astonishing exactness any piece of delicate workmanship, that is set before them, but verbal descriptions convey scarcely any ideas to their minds: this is the natural consequence of their education, in which the understanding is formed by present visible objects, not by words; while on the other hand men taught by words have often heard so much, that they are incapable of seeing what is before their eyes. The understanding of the free son of Nature is divided as it were between the eye and the ear: he knows with accuracy the objects he has seen, he relates with precision the tales he has heard. His tongue stammers not, as his arrow deviates not from its mark: for how should his mind err, or hesitate, with respect to what it has seen and heard with precision?

Nature has disposed things well for a creature, the first buds of whose understanding and well-being arise only from the perceptions of the senses. If our bodies be sound, if our senses be well-ordered and exercised; the foundations of a serenity and internal satisfaction are laid, the loss of which speculative reason cannot easily repair. The ground of man's physical happiness every where consists in his living where it is his lot to live, enjoying what is set before him, and perplexing himself as little as possible with provident or retrospective care. If he confine himself to this point, he is vigorous and tranquil: but if, while he should enjoy and think only on the present, he suffer his thoughts to wander, how does he distract and enfeeble himself, often leading a more painful life than the brute, happily restricted to a narrow sphere! The free child of Nature contemplates his parent, and is enlivened, without knowing it, by the sight of her garb; or he follows his occupations, and, while he enjoys the revolving seasons, scarcely grows old with any increase of days. His ear, undisturbed by imperfect thoughts, and unperplexed by written symbols, hears perfectly what it hears: it eagerly takes in words, which, indicating determinate objects, are more satisfactory to the mind than volumes of barren abstract terms. Thus lives, thus dies the savage; satisfied, but not glutted, with the simple pleasures, that his senses enable him to enjoy.

But Nature has conferred another beneficent gift on our species, in leaving to such of its members as are least stored with ideas the first germ of superiour sense, exhilarating music. Before the child can speak, he is capable of song, or at least of being affected by musical tones; and among the most uncultivated nations music is the first of the fine arts, by which the mind is moved. The pictures, which Nature exhibits to the eye, are so various, changeable, and extensive, that imitative taste must long grope about, and seek the striking in wild and monstrous productions, ere it learns justness of proportion. But music, however rude and simple, speaks to every human heart; and this, with the dance, constitutes Nature's general festival throughout the Earth. Pity it is, that most travellers, from too refined a taste, conceal from us these infantile tones of foreign nations. Useless as they may be to the musician, they are instructive to the investigator of man: for the music of a nation, in its most imperfect form, and favourite tunes, displays the internal character of the people, that is to say, the proper tone of their sensations, much more truly and profoundly, than the most copious description of external contingencies.

The more in general I trace the whole sensibility of man, in his various regions and ways of life, the more do I find Nature every where a kind parent. Where an organ is less capable of being gratified, she excites it less, and leaves it for ages in a gentle slumber: where she has refined and expanded an organ, she has disposed means to gratify it fully: so that the whole Earth, with this checked or heightened organization of man, sounds to her ear as a well-tuned instrument, from which every possible note is, or will be, produced.

CHAPTER 2

The human Fancy is every where organic and climatic, but it is every where led by Tradition

Of a thing that lies without the sphere of our perception we know nothing: the story of a king of Siam, who considered ice and snow as nonentities, is in a thousand instances applicable to every man. The ideas of every indigenous nation are thus confined to its own region: if it profess to understand words expressing things utterly foreign to it, we have reason to remain long in doubt of the reality of this understanding.

"The Greenlanders," says the worthy Cranz,

> are fond of hearing tales of Europe; but they can comprehend nothing unless illustrated by some comparison. "The town, or the country," for instance, "has so many inhabitants, that several whales would hardly suffice to feed them a day: they do not eat whales, however, but bread, which grows out of the ground like grass, and the flesh of animals that have horns; and they are carried about on the backs of large strong beasts, or drawn along by them upon a wooden stage." On hearing this, they call bread, grass; oxen, reindeer; and horses, great dogs; are struck with admiration, and express a wish to live in such a fine fruitful country, till they are informed, that it frequently thunders, and no seals are to be procured there. They willingly hear of God and divine things, also, as long as you do not contradict their superstitious fables.[40]

From the same author I will compose a catechism of their theologico-natural philosophy, showing, that they can neither answer nor comprehend European questions, otherwise than according to the circle of their own conceptions.[41]

> *Question.* Who created Heaven and Earth, and every thing that you see?
>
> *Answer.* That we cannot tell. We do not know the man. He

[40] *Gesch. von Grönland* (History of Greenland), p. 225.
[41] Sect. V, VI.

must have been a very mighty man. Or else these things always were, and will always remain so.

Q. Have you a soul?

A. O yes. It can increase and decrease: our angekoks can mend and repair it: when a man has lost his soul, they can bring it back again: and they change a sick soul for a fresh sound one from a hare, a reindeer, a bird, or a young child. When we go a long journey, our soul often stays at home. At night, when we are asleep, it wanders out of the body: it goes a hunting, dancing, or visiting, while the body lies still.

Q. What becomes of it after death?

A. Then it goes to the happy place at the bottom of the sea. Torngarsuck and his mother live there. There it is always summer, bright sunshine, and no night: and there, too, is good water, with plenty of birds, fishes, seals, and reindeer, all of which may be caught without any trouble, or taken out of a great kettle ready boiled.

Q. And do all men go thither?

A. No: only good people, who were useful workmen, have done great actions, caught many whales and seals, endured much, or been drowned at sea, died in the birth, etc.

Q. How do these get thither?

A. Not easily. They must spend five days or more in scrambling down a bare rock, which is already covered with blood.

Q. But do you not see those beautiful heavenly bodies? Are not they more probably the place of our future abode?

A. It is there, too, in the highest Heaven, far above the rainbow; and the journey thither is so quick and easy, that the soul can repose the same evening in his house in the moon, which was once a Greenlander, and dance and play at bowls with the other souls. Those northern lights are the souls playing at bowls and dancing.

Q. And what do they there besides?

A. They live in tents, by a vast lake, in which are multitudes of fishes and birds. When this lake overflows, it rains upon Earth; if the banks were to break down, it would cause an universal deluge. But in general only the vile and worthless go to Heaven; the diligent go to the bottom of the sea. Those souls must often suffer hunger, are lean and feeble, and can have no rest for the quick turning round of the sky. Bad people and sorcerers go thither: they are tormented by ravens, which they cannot keep out of their hair, etc.

Q. What do you believe was the origin of mankind?

A. The first man, Kallak, came out of the earth, and his wife soon after came out of his thumb. She bore a Greenland woman, and the woman bore *Kablunæt,* that is, foreigners and dogs: hence both dogs and foreigners are incontinent and prolific.

Q. And will the world endure for ever?

A. Once already it has been overwhelmed, and every body drowned, except one man. He struck the earth with his staff, a woman came out, and they repeopled the World. It now rests on its supporters, but they are so rotten with age, that they often crack; so that it would long ago have fallen down, if our angekoks were not continually repairing them.

Q. But what think you of those beautiful stars!

A. They were all formerly Greenlanders, or beasts, who have travelled up thither on particular occasions, and appear pale or red according to the difference of their food. They that you see there meeting are two women visiting each other: that shooting star is a soul gone on a visit: that great star (the Bear) is a reindeer: those seven stars are dogs hunting a bear: those (Orion's belt) are men who lost themselves hunting seals, could not find the way home, and so got among the stars. The Sun and Moon are a brother and sister. Malina, the sister, was assaulted by her brother in the dark: she endeavoured to escape by flight, ascended into the sky, and became the Sun: Anninga pursued her, and became the Moon. The Moon is continually running round the virgin Sun, in hopes to catch her, but in vain. When he is weary and exhausted (in the last quarter) he goes seal hunting, at which he continues some days, and then he returns again as fat as we see him in the full Moon. He is glad when women die, and the Sun is pleased at the death of men.

I should be little thanked for my trouble, were I to go on thus exhibiting the fancies of various nations. If any one should be found desirous of travelling through these realms of imagination, the true Limbo of vanity, which extend to every part of the World, I wish he may be endued with the spirit of calm observation, which, free from all hypotheses of the descent and similitude of nations, shall be in all places as it were at home, and know how to render every folly of our fellow-creatures instructive. For my part, I have only to extract some general observations from this kingdom of living shadows formed by musing nations.

1. *Climates and Nations are universally marked in it.* Compare the Greenland mythology with the Indian, the Laplandic with the Japanese, the Peruvian with that of Negroland; a

complete geography of the inventing mind. If the Voluspa of the Icelander were read and expounded to a Bramin, he would scarcely be able to form a single idea from it; and to the Icelander the Vedam would be equally unintelligible. Their own mode of representing things is the more deeply imprinted on every nation, because it is adapted to themselves, is suitable to their own earth and sky, springs from their mode of living, and has been handed down to them from father to son. What is most astonishing to a foreigner they believe they most clearly comprehend; he laughs at things, on which they are most serious. The Indians say, that the destiny of a man is written on his brain, the fine lines of which represent the illegible letters of the book of Fate: the most arbitrary national ideas and opinions are frequently such brain-drawn pictures, lines of the fancy most firmly interwoven with both body and mind.

2. Whence is this? Have all these tribes of men invented their own mythology, and thus become attached to it as their own property! By no means. They have not invented, but *inherited it.* Had they produced it themselves, their own reflection might have carried them from the bad to better, which has not been the case. When Dobritzhofer represented to a whole tribe of brave and intelligent Abiponians, how ridiculous it was in them, to be terrified at the menaces of a conjuror, who threatened to turn himself into a tiger, and whose claws they fancied they already felt: "you daily kill real tigers in the field," said he to them, "without being afraid; why are you alarmed in such a dastardly manner at an imaginary one, that does not exist?" "You, father," answered a valiant Abiponian, "have no accurate ideas of our affairs. The tigers in the field we fear not, because we see them: there we kill them without difficulty. The artificial tigers we dread, because we cannot see them, and consequently are unable to kill them." [42]

This, I conceive, is the key of the mystery. Were all notions as clear to us, as those we acquire by the sight; had we no other ideas, than those which we derive from visual objects, or can

---

[42] *History of the Abiponians,* Vol. I.

compare with them; the source of errour and deception would be stopped, or at least soon discoverable. But at present most national fictions spring from verbal communications, and are instilled into the ear. The ignorant child listens with curiosity to the tales, which flow into his mind like his mother's milk, like choice wine of his father, and form its nutriment. They seem to him to explain what he has seen: to the youth they account for the way of life of his tribe, and stamp the renown of his ancestors: the man they introduce to the employment suited to his nation and climate, and thus they become inseparable from his whole life. The Greenlander and Tungoose see in reality all their lives only what they heard of in their infancy, and thus they believe it to be evidently true. Hence the timid practices of so many nations, even far remote from each other, in eclipses of the Sun or Moon: hence their trembling belief in spirits of the air, sea, and other elements. Wherever there is motion in nature; wherever any cause seems to exist and produce change, without the eye being able to discover the laws, by which the change is effected; the ear hears words, which explain to it the mystery of what is seen, by something unseen. The ear is in general the most timorous, the most apprehensive, of all the senses: it perceives quickly but obscurely: it cannot retain and compare things, so as to render them clear, for its objects hasten to the gulf of oblivion. Appointed to awaken the mind, it can seldom acquire clear and satisfactory information, without the aid of the other senses, particularly the eye.

3. Thus it appears *among what people the imagination is most highly strained:* among those namely, who love solitude, and inhabit the wild regions of nature, deserts, rocks, the stormy shores of the sea, the feet of volcanoes, or other moving and astonishing scenes. From the remotest times the deserts of Arabia have fostered sublime conceptions, and they who have cherished them have been for the most part solitary, romantic men. In solitude Mohammed began his Koran: his heated imagination rapt him to Heaven, and showed him all the angels, saints, and worlds: his mind was never more inflamed, than when it depicted the thunders of the day of resurrection, the

last judgment, and other immense objects. To what extent has the superstition of the Shamans spread itself! From Greenland and the three Laplands, over the whole benighted coast of the Frozen Ocean, far into Tatary, and almost throughout the whole of America. Magicians every where appear, and fearful images of nature every where form the world in which they dwell. Thus more than three fourths of the Globe receive this faith: for even in Europe most nations of Finnish or Slavian origin are still addicted to the sorceries of the worship of Nature, and the superstition of the Negroes is nothing but Shamanism moulded to their genius and climate. In the polished countries of Asia, indeed, this is suppressed by positive, factitious religion, and political institutions: yet it is discernible, wherever it can peep out, in solitude, and among the populace; till on some of the islands in the South Sea it again rules with powerful sway. Thus the worship of Nature has gone round the Globe, and its reveries have seized on those local objects of power and alarm, on which human wants confine. In ancient times it was the worship of almost all the nations upon Earth.

4. *That the way of life and genius of each nation have powerfully cooperated in this,* scarcely requires to be mentioned. The shepherd beholds nature with different eyes from those of the fisherman or hunter: and again, in every region these occupations differ as much as the character of the people, by whom they are exercised. I was astonished, for instance, to observe in the mythology of the Kamtschadales, dwelling so far to the north, a lasciviousness, that might have been more naturally expected from a southern nation: but their climate and genetic character afford us some explanation of this anomaly.[43] Their cold land is not without burning mountains and hot springs: benumbing cold and melting heat there contend against each other; and their dissolute manners, as well as their gross mythological tales, are the natural offspring of the two. The same may be said of the fables of the passionate, talkative

[43] See Steller, *Kraschenninikow,* etc.

Negro, which have neither beginning nor end:[44] the same of the fixed concise mythology of the North American:[45] the same of the flowery reveries of the Hindoo, which breathe, like himself, the voluptuous ease of Paradise.[46] The gods of the last bathe in seas of milk and honey: his goddesses repose on cooling lakes, in the cups of fragrant flowers. In short, the mythology of every people is an expression of the particular mode, in which they viewed nature; particularly whether from their climate and genius they found good or evil to prevail, and how perhaps they endeavoured to account for the one by means of the other. Thus even in the wildest lines, and worst-conceived features, it is a philosophical attempt of the human mind, which dreams ere it awakes, and willingly retains its infant state.

5. Men generally consider the angekoks, conjurers, magicians, shamans, and priests, as the inventors of these tales, to blind the people; and think they have explained the whole, when they call them deceivers. That they are so in most places is very true: but let it be remembered, that they also are people, and the dupes of tales older than themselves. They were born and brought up amid the imaginations of their tribe: their consecration was attended with fasting, solitude, intention of the fancy, and exhaustion of body and mind; so that no one became a conjurer, till his familiar had appeared to him, and the business was first accomplished in his own imagination, which he afterwards carried on during his whole life for others, with repetition of similar exaltations of the mind, and debilitations of the body. The coolest travellers have been astonished by many juggling tricks of this kind, seeing such effects of the power of imagination, as they could scarcely have believed possible, and often knew not how to explain. Of all the powers of the human mind the imagination has been least explored, and is probably the most inexplicable: for, being connected

---

[44] See Römer, Bossmann, Mueller, Oldendorp, etc.

[45] See Lafiteau, le Beau, Carver, etc.

[46] Baldeus, Dow, Sonnerat, Holwell, etc.

with the general structure of the body, and with that of the brain and nerves in particular, as many wonderful diseases show, it seems to be not only the band and basis of all the finer mental powers, but the knot, that ties body and mind together; the bud, as it were, of the whole sensual organization, expanding to the higher use of the thinking faculties. Thus it is necessarily the first, that descends from parents to children; as many instances of deviation from the course of nature, and the undeniable similitude of the external and internal organization, even in the most accidental circumstances, sufficiently prove.

It has long been questioned, whether there be innate ideas: and in the common acceptations of the words the answer must certainly be in the negative. But if we understand them to signify a predisposition to receive, connect, and expand certain ideas and images, nothing appears to make against the affirmative, and every thing for it. If a child can inherit six fingers, if the family of the *porcupine-man* in England could derive from their parent his unnatural excrescences, if the external form of the head and face be often transmitted, as it evidently is, from father to son; would it not be strange, that the form of the brain, perhaps even in its finest organic divisions, should not be hereditary likewise? Diseases of the imagination, of which we have no idea, prevail in many nations: and all the countrymen of those, who are so affected, compassionate them, because they feel in themselves the genetic disposition to the same disease. Among the valiant Abiponians, for instance, a periodical madness prevails, of which the madman has no consciousness in the intervals: he is in health, as he was before, only his soul, they say, is gone out of him. In many nations, in order to give vent to this evil, dream-feasts have been established, in which the visionaries are permitted to do whatever comes into their minds. Dreams, indeed, are of astonishing force among all people of warm imaginations: nay probably they were the first muses, the parents of poetry and fiction. They introduced men to forms and things, which no eye had seen, but the desire of which lay in the human mind: for what could be more natural, than that the beloved dead should appear in dreams to those they left behind, and that they, who had lived so long with us awake, might now wish to live with us at least as shades in a dream? The history of nations will show how Providence has employed the instrument of imagination, by which man might be acted upon so powerfully, simply, and naturally: but it is horrible, when deceit or despotism abuses it, and renders subservient to its purposes that ocean of human fancies and dreams, which no one has yet been able to subdue.

Great Spirit of the World, with what eyes dost thou contemplate all the shadowy forms and visions, that course each other on this our globe! for we are shadows, and dreams of shadows are all that our fancies imagine.[47] As little as we are capable of respiring pure air, as little can pure reason impart itself wholly at present to our compound clay-formed shell. Yet, amid all the errours of the imagination, the human species is moulding to it: men are attached to figures, because they express things and thus through the thickest clouds they seek and perceive rays of truth. Happy the chosen few, who proceed, as far as is possible in our limited sphere, from fancies to essences, that is from infancy to manhood, and whose clear understandings go through the history of their brethren with this end in view. The mind nobly expands, when it is able to emerge from the narrow circle, which climate and education have drawn round it, and learns from other nations at least what may be dispensed with by man. How much, that we have been accustomed to consider as absolutely necessary, do we find others live without, and consequently perceive to be by no means indispensable! Numberless ideas, which we have often admitted as the most general principles of the human understanding, disappear, in this place and that, with the climate, as the land vanishes like a mist from the eye of the navigator. What one nation holds indispensable to the circle of its thoughts, has never entered into the mind of a second, and by a third has been deemed injurious. Thus we wander over the Earth in a labyrinth of human fancies: but the question is; where is the central point of the labyrinth, to which all our wanderings may be traced, as refracted rays to the Sun?

---

[47] Pindar.

CHAPTER 3

The practical Understanding of the human Species has every where grown up under the Wants of Life; but every where it is a Blossom of the Genius of the People, a Son of Tradition and Custom

It has been customary, to divide the nations of the Earth into hunters, fishermen, shepherds, and husbandmen; and not only to determine their rank in civilization from this division, but even to consider civilization itself as a necessary consequence of this or that way of life. This would be very excellent, if these modes of life were determined themselves in the first place: but they vary with almost every region, and for the most part run into each other in such a manner, that this mode of classification is very difficult to apply with accuracy. The Greenlander, who strikes the whale, pursues the reindeer, and kills the seal, is occupied both in hunting and fishing; yet in a very different manner from that, in which the Negro fishes, or the Araucoan hunts on the deserts of the Andes. The Bedouin and the Mungal, the Laplander and the Peruvian, are shepherds: but how greatly do they differ from each other, while one pastures his camels, another his horses, the third his reindeer, and the last his pacoes and llamas. The merchants of England differ not more from those of China, than the husbandmen of Whidah from the husbandmen of Japan.

Want alone, even when there is no deficiency of powers in a nation to obey its demands, seems equally incapable of producing civilization: for as soon as the Indolence of man has rendered him contented under his Necessities, and both together have begotten the child he names Convenience, he persists in his condition, and cannot be impelled to improve it without difficulty. Other causes cooperate to determine the mode of life of a people: but let us at present consider it as fixed, and inquire what active powers of the mind are displayed in its various forms.

Men who live on roots, herbs, and fruits, will remain inactive, and their faculties will continue limited, if some particular motives do not impel them to civilization. Born in a fine climate, and descended from a gentle race, they are gentle in their lives: for why should contention take place among men, on whom bountiful Nature bestows every thing without toil? Their arts and inventions, too, extend only to their daily wants. The islanders, whom Nature feeds with vegetable productions, particularly the salubrious breadfruit, and clothes in a delightful climate with the rind of trees, lead a tranquil happy life. Birds, we are told, sat on the shoulders of the natives of the Ladrone Islands, and sang undisturbed: with the use of the bow they were unacquainted, for no beast of prey obliged them, to have recourse to weapons of defence. They were strangers to fire, also; for the mildness of their climate rendered it unnecessary. The same might be said of the people of the Caroline and other happy islands in the southern ocean; only in some of them society had arrived at a higher degree of civilization, and more arts and manufactures had arisen from various causes. Where the climate was less temperate, men were necessitated to live more hardly, and with less simplicity. The New Hollander pursues his opossum and kanguroo, shoots birds, catches fish, and eats yams: he has united as many ways of life as his rude convenience required, till he had rounded them as it were into a circle, in which he could live happily after his fashion. It is the same with the New Caledonian and New Zealander; nor must we except even the miserable inhabitants of Tierra del Fuego. They had their canoes of bark, bows and arrows, baskets and pitchers, huts and fire, clothes and hatchets; and consequently the commencement of all the arts, by means of which the most enlightened nations upon Earth have attained their present civilization; only with them, under the pressure of benumbing cold, and amid their dreary rocks, every thing has remained in the rudest state. The Californian displays as much understanding, as his country and way of life afford or require. So does the native of Labradore, and of every country on the most barren verge of the earth. Every where men have reconciled themselves to necessity, and from hereditary habit live happy in the labours, to which they are compelled. What makes not a part of their wants they despise: actively as the Eskimaux plies his oar, he has not yet learned to swim.

On the great continents of our globe men and beasts crowd more together; and in consequence brutes have contributed in various ways, to exercise the human intellect. The inhabitants of many morasses in America, indeed, have been obliged to have recourse to snakes and lizards, to the iguana, the armadillo, and the alligator: but most nations have been hunters in a nobler mode. What does a North or South American require, to fit him for the way of life, to which he is destined? He knows the beasts of his chase, their abodes, manners, and artifices, and arms himself against them with strength, address, and exercise. The boy is educated, to aspire to the fame of a hunter; as the son of a Greenlander, to seek renown by catching seals: this forms the subject of the discourse, the songs, the tales of famous deeds, that meet his ears; this is represented to his eyes in expressive actions, and animating dances. From his infancy he learns, to fabricate and employ the implements of the chase: weapons are his toys, and women the objects of his contempt; for the narrower the sphere of life, and the more determinate the object, in which perfection is sought, the sooner will this be attained. Nothing interrupts the course of the aspiring youth, but every thing tends rather to stimulate and encourage him, as he lives exposed to the eyes of his countrymen, in the state and occupation of his father. If a man were to compose a book of the arts of various nations, he would find them scattered over the whole Earth, and each flourishing in its proper place. Here the Negro leaps into the surf of a sea, into which no European would venture: there he climbs a tree, on which our eye can scarcely follow him. This fisherman pursues his trade with such art, as if he fascinated his prey: that Samoiede encounters the white bear, and opposes him singly: for yonder Negro, uniting strength with address, two lions are not more than a match. The Hottentot attacks the rhinoceros and hippopotamus: the inhabitant of the Canary Isles traverses the steepest rocks, leaping like a chamois from crag to crag: the strong manly wife of the Tibetian carries the stranger over the loftiest mountains of the Earth. The children of Prometheus, composed of the parts and instincts of all animals, have excelled every one of these in arts and capacities, in one place or another, after having learned from them, whatever they have acquired.

That men have learned most of their arts from nature and animals, cannot be doubted. Why does the inhabitant of the Ladrone Islands clothe himself with the bark of trees? or the American and Papoo adorn themselves with feathers? Because the former lives amid trees, and obtains from them his food; and the elegant plumage of their birds is the most beautiful object, that occurs to the sight of the latter. The hunter clothes himself like the game he pursues, and takes lessons in architecture from the beaver of his lakes: others build their huts like nests on the ground, or, with the birds, fix them upon trees. The beak of a bird was the model, from which men formed their arrows, and spears; as the figure of the canoe was taken from that of a fish. From the snake they learned the pernicious art of poisoning their weapons; and the singularly extensive custom of painting the body was equally an imitation of birds and beasts. What! thought man, shall these be so beautifully adorned, so distinguishingly coloured, while I bear a pale uniform skin, because my indolence refuses, to prepare the covering my climate does not require? Hence he began to paint and embroider himself with symmetry. Even nations, that were not strangers to the use of clothes, envied the ox his horns, the bird his crest, the bear his tail, and made them objects of imitation. The North Americans relate with gratitude, that maize was brought to them by a bird: and the use of most indigenous medicines was unquestionably learned from animals. But all these things required the sensual minds of free children of Nature, who, living with these animals, think themselves not infinitely exalted above them. It is difficult for an European in other parts of the world even to discover, what the natives daily use: after many endeavours, they are obliged to obtain the secret from these either by force or entreaty.

But man went incomparably farther, when he attracted animals about him, and finally brought them under his yoke. The immense difference between neighbouring nations, living with or without these auxiliaries to their powers, is evident. Whence came it, that America, on its first discovery, was so far behind the old world, and the Europeans could treat its inhabitants like a flock of defenceless sheep? It depended not on corporal powers alone, as the examples of all the numerous savage nations show: in growth, in swiftness, in prompt address, they exceed, man for man, most of the nations, that play at dice for their land. Neither was understanding, as far as it relates to the individual, the cause: the American knew how to provide for himself, and lived happily with his wife and children. It arose, therefore, from art, weapons, close connexion, and principally from domesticated animals. Had the American possessed the horse, the warlike majesty of which he tremblingly acknowledged; had the fierce dog, which the Spaniard sent against him as a fellow-soldier in the pay of his Catholic majesty, been his; the conquest would have been more dearly purchased, and at least a retreat to their mountains, deserts, and plains, would have remained open to a nation of horsemen. Even now, all travellers say, the horse makes the greatest difference between the American nations. The horsemen in the northern part of America, and still more in the southern division of that continent, are so superiour to the poor slaves of Mexico and Peru, that a man would scarcely suppose them to be neighbouring sons of the same climate. The former have not only maintained their freedom, but are become more manly both in body and mind, than they were probably at the discovery of their country. The horse, which the oppressors of their brethren employed as an unconscious instrument of fate, may at some future period perhaps be the deliverer of the whole land; as the other domestic animals, that have been introduced into it, have already been in some measure conducive to a more comfortable life, and may hereafter possibly become auxiliary means of a degree of civilization peculiar to the west. But as all this is in the hand of Fate, to the same Fate must be ascribed, what was in the nature of this quarter of the Globe, that it was so long unacquainted with either horse, ass, ox, dog, sheep, goat, hog, cat, or camel. It had fewer kinds of quadrupeds, because the land was less extensive, separated from the old world, and in great part probably later emerged from the bosom of the ocean than the other continents; so that it had fewer to tame. The paco and llama, the camel-sheep of Mexico, Peru, and Chili, were the only tameable and domesticated beasts: for even the Europeans, with all their understanding, have been unable to add any to these, or render either the quiqui or puma, the sloth or tapir, an animal of domestic utility.

In the old world, on the contrary, how many animals are domesticated! and how much have they assisted the active mind of man! But for the horse and camel, the deserts of Arabia and Africa would be inaccessible: the sheep and the goat have been aids to domestic economy; the ox and the ass, to agriculture and trade. The human animal, in a state of simplicity, lives in friendship and society with these beasts; he treats them with kindness, and acknowledges his obligations to them. It is thus the Arab, thus the Mungal, lives with his horse, the shepherd with his flock, the hunter with his dogs, the Peruvian with his llama.[48] It is also generally known, that all animals subservient to the purposes of man are more useful, in proportion to the humanity of the treatment they receive: they learn to understand and have an affection for man: capacities and inclinations are developed in them, which are to be found neither in the wild animal, nor in such as are abused by man, which lose even the powers and instincts of their species in stupid fatness, or degraded forms. Thus man and beast have improved themselves together in a certain sphere: the practical understanding of man has been strengthened and extended by the beast; the capacity of the beast, by man. When we read of the dogs of the Kamtschadales, we are almost in doubt, which is the more rational creature, the Kamtschadale or his dog.

In this sphere the first active exertion of the human mind

[48] Read in Ulloa, for instance, of the childish joy, with which the Peruvian dedicates a llama to his service. The manner, in which other nations live with their beasts, is sufficiently known from the accounts of various travellers.

stands still: nay it is difficult, for any nation accustomed to it, to quit; and every one particularly dreads submission to the yoke of agriculture. Notwithstanding the fine arable lands to be found in North America; much as every nation values and defends its property; however highly some have been taught by Europeans, to prize gold, brandy, and certain of the conveniences of life: still the tilling of the ground, with the cultivation of maize, and a few garden vegetables, is left to the women, as well as the whole care of the huts; the warlike hunter could never bend his mind, to become a gardener, shepherd, or husbandman. The savage, as he is called, prefers the active free life of Nature to every consideration: surrounded with perils, it awakens his powers, his courage, his resolution, and rewards him with health in the field, with independent ease in his hut, with respect and honour among his tribe. He wants, he desires, nothing more: and what addition to his happiness could he derive from another state, with the advantages of which he is unacquainted, and to the inconveniences of which he cannot submit? Read the various unadorned speeches of those, whom we call savages, and say, whether sound sense and natural justice be not conspicuous in them. The frame of man, too, in this state, is as much improved, though with a rude hand, and to few purposes, as it is capable of being improved in it: he is formed to a contented equanimity, and to welcome death with calmness, after the enjoyment of a life of permanent health. The Bedouin and Abiponian are both happy in their condition: but the former shudders at the thought of inhabiting a town, as the latter does at the idea of being interred in a church when he dies; according to their feelings, it would be the same as if they were buried alive.

Even where agriculture has been introduced, it has cost some pains, to limit men to separate fields, and establish the distinction of mine and thine: many small Negro nations, who have cultivated their lands, have yet no idea of it; for, say they, the earth is common property. They annually parcel out the ground among them, till it with little labour, and as soon as the harvest is gathered in, the land reverts to its former common state.

Generally speaking, no mode of life has effected so much alteration in the minds of men, as agriculture, combined with the enclosure of land. While it produced arts and trades, villages and towns, and, in consequence, government and laws; it necessarily paved the way for that frightful despotism, which, from confining every man to his field, gradually proceeded to prescribe to him, what alone he should do on it, what alone he should be. The ground now ceased to belong to man, but man became the appertenance of the ground. Soon even the consciousness of powers, that had been used, was lost by their disuse: the oppressed, sunk in cowardice and slavery, were led from wretchedness and want into effeminate debauchery. Hence it is, that, throughout the whole World, the dweller in a tent considers the inhabitant of a hut as a shackled beast of burden, as a degenerate and sequestrated variety of the species. The former feels pleasure in the severest want, while seasoned and rewarded by freedom in act and will: on the other hand, the greatest dainties are poisons, when they benumb the mind, and deprive the frail mortal of worth and independence, the sole enjoyments of his precarious life.

Imagine not, that I seek to derogate from the value of a mode of living, which Providence has employed as a principal instrument for leading man to civil society: for I myself eat the bread it has produced. But let justice be done to other ways of life, which, from the constitution of our Earth, have been destined, equally with agriculture, to contribute to the education of mankind. Land is cultivated in our manner by the smallest portion of the inhabitants of the Earth, and Nature, herself, has pointed out to the rest their different modes of living. The numerous nations, that live on roots, rice, fruits, fishing, fowling, and hunting, the innumerable nomades, although perhaps they now purchase bread from their neighbours, or sow a little corn themselves, and all the nations, that cultivate land without having a fixed property in it, or by means of their women and slaves, are not, properly speaking, husbandmen: what a small part of the World remains, therefore, for this artificial way of life! If Nature have any where attained her end, she has attained it everywhere. The practical understanding of man was intended, to blossom and bear fruit in all its varieties: and hence such a diversified Earth was ordained for so diversified a species.

CHAPTER 4

The Feelings and Inclinations of Men are every where conformable to their Organization, and the Circumstances in which they live; but they are every where swayed by Custom and Opinion

SELF-PRESERVATION is the first object of every existing being: from the grain of sand to the solar orb, every thing strives, to remain what it is: for this purpose instinct is impressed on the brute; for this, reason, the substitute of instinct, is given to man. In obedience to this law, he every where seeks food at the impulse of inexorable hunger: from his infancy, without knowing why or wherefore, he strives to exercise his powers, to be in motion. The weary does not call for sleep; but sleep comes, and renovates his existence: the vital powers relieve the sick, when they can, or at least strive to remove the disease. Man defends his life against every thing, that attacks it; and even without being sensible, that Nature has taken measures, both within and around him, for his support.

There have been philosophers, who, on account of this instinct of self-preservation, have classed man with the beasts of prey, and deemed his natural state a state of warfare. It is evident, there is much impropriety in this. Man, it is true, is a robber, in tearing the fruit from the tree; a murderer, in killing an animal; and the most cruel oppressor on the face of the Earth, while with his foot, and with his breath perhaps, he deprives of life innumerable multitudes of invisible creatures. Every man knows the attempts of the gentle Hindoo and extravagant Egyptian philosophy, to render man a perfectly harmless creature: but to the eye of the speculatist they appear to have been in vain. We cannot look into the chaos of the elements; and if we refrain from devouring any visible animal, we cannot avoid swallowing a number of minute living creatures, in water, air, milk, and vegetables.

But away with these subtilties, and, considering man among his brethren, let us ask: is he by nature a beast of prey toward his fellows, is he an unsocial being? By his make he is not the former; and by his birth the latter still less. Conceived in the bosom of Love, and nourished at the breast of Affection, he is educated by men, and receives from them a thousand unearned benefits. Thus he is actually formed in and for society, without which he could neither have received his being, nor have become a man. Insociability commences with him, when violence is done to his nature, by his coming into collision with other men: but this is no exception, as here he acts conformably to the great universal law of self-preservation. Let us inquire what means Nature has invented, to satisfy and restrain him as much as possible even here, and prevent a state of general warfare among mankind.

1. As man is the most artfully complicated of all creatures, so great a variety of genetic character occurs in no other. Blind imperious instinct is wanting to his delicate frame; but in him the varying currents of thoughts and desires flow into each other, in a manner peculiar to himself. Thus man, from his very nature, will clash but little in his pursuits with man; his dispositions, sensations, and propensities, being so infinitely diversified, and as it were individualized. What is a matter of indifference to one man, to another is an object of desire: and then each has a world of enjoyment in himself, each a creation of his own.

2. Nature has bestowed on this diverging species an ample space, the extensive fertile Earth, over which the most different climates and modes of life have room to spread. Here she has raised mountains, there she has placed deserts or rivers, which keep men separate: on the hunter she has bestowed the extensive forest, on the fisherman the ample sea, on the shepherd the spacious plain. It is not her fault, that birds, deceived by the fowler's art, fly into his net, where they fight over their food,

peck out each other's eyes, and contaminate the air they breathe: for she has placed the bird in the air, and not in the net of the fowler. See those wild species, how tamely they live together! no one envies another; each procures and enjoys what he wants in peace. It is repugnant to the truth of history, to set up the malicious discordant disposition of men crowded together, of rival artists, opposing politicians, envious authors, for the general character of the species: the rankling wounds of these malignant thorns are unknown to the greater part of mankind; to those who breathe the free air, not the pestilential atmosphere of towns. He who maintains laws are necessary, because otherwise men would live lawlessly, takes for granted, what it is incumbent on him to prove. If man were not thronged together in close prisons, they would need no ventilators to purify the air: were not their minds inflamed by artificial madness, they would not require the restraining hand of correlative art.

3. Nature, too, has shortened, as far as she could, the time, that men must remain together. Man requires a long time to educate; but then he is still weak: he is a child, quickly provoked, and as easily forgetting his anger; often displeased, but incapable of bearing malice. As soon as he arrives at years of maturity, a new instinct awakes in him, and he quits the house of his father. Nature acts in this instinct: she drives him out, to construct his own nest.

And with whom does he construct it? With a creature as dissimilarly similar to himself, and whose passions are as unlikely to come into collision with his, as is consistent with the end of their forming an union together. The nature of the woman is different from that of the man: she differs in her feelings, she differs in her actions. Miserable he, who is rivalled by his wife, or excelled by her in manly virtues! She was destined to rule him by kindness and condescension alone, which render the apple of discord the apple of love.

I will not pursue the history of the dispersion of mankind any farther: with their division into different houses and families, the foundations of new societies, laws, manners, and even languages, were laid. What do we learn from these different, these unavoidable dialects, which occur upon our Earth in such infinite numbers, and frequently at such little distance from each other? We learn, that the object of our diffusive parent was not to crowd her children together, but to let them spread freely. As far as it may be, no tree is permitted to deprive another of air, so as to render it a stunted dwarf, or force it to become a crooked cripple, that it may breathe with more freedom. Each has its place allotted it, that it may ascend from its root by its own impulse, and raise its flourishing head.

Peace, therefore, not war, is the natural state of mankind when at liberty: war is the offspring of necessity, not the legitimate child of enjoyment. In the hand of Nature it is never an end, cannibalism itself even included, but here and there a severe and melancholy mean, with which even the mother of all things could not entirely dispense, but which, as a compensation, she has employed for various, higher, and more valuable purposes.

Before we proceed to the afflicting consideration of enmity, let us therefore examine delightful love: love, which extends its sway over all the Earth, though every where appearing in different forms.

As soon as the plant has attained its full growth, it blossoms: thus the time of blossoming is regulated by the period of growth, and this by the impulse of the solar heat. The early or late arrival of man at maturity equally depends on climate, and the various circumstances connected with it. The age of puberty differs astonishingly in different regions, and under different modes of life. The Persian maiden marries at eight, and becomes a mother in her ninth year: our ancient German heroines attained the age of thirty, before they thought of love.

It is obvious to every one, how much this difference must alter the relation of the sexes to each other. The Eastern virgin is a child, when she is married: she blooms early, and quickly fades: the maturer husband treats her as a child, or as a flower. Since in those warmer regions the stimulus of physical desire not only awakes earlier in both sexes, but operates more intensely, what step could be more natural for the man, than to abuse the superiority of his sex, and endeavour to form a garden of these perishable flowers? The consequences of this step to the human species were far from trifling. It was not merely, that the jealousy of the husband confined his numerous wives in a haram, where their improvement could not possibly keep pace with that of the men: but as the females were educated from their infancy for the haram, and the society of women, nay the child was frequently sold or betrothed at two years of age; how could it be otherwise, than that the general behaviour of the man, domestic economy, education of children, and lastly even the fecundity of the women, must in time be affected by this abuse? It is sufficiently proved, for instance, that too early marriage on the part of the wife, and too powerful a stimulus on the part of the husband, contribute neither to the fertility of the sex, nor excellence of form. Indeed the accounts of various travellers render it probable, that in several of these countries more females are actually born than males; and if this be true, it may be both an effect of polygamy, and a cause promoting its continuance. It is certain, this is not the only case, in which art, and the licentiousness of man, have turned Nature out of her course: for elsewhere Nature maintains a pretty exact proportion between the births of both sexes. But as woman is the most delicate production of our Earth, and love the most powerful engine, that acts throughout the whole creation, the manner, in which women are treated, must be the first critical point of distinction in the history of our species. Every where woman has been the first object of contentious desire, and from her nature not less the first failing stone in the human edifice.

For examples let us accompany Cook on his last voyage. While in the Society and other islands the female sex appeared to be wholly dedicated to the rites of Cytherea, so as not only to refuse nothing for a nail, an ornament, a feather, but even the husband was ready to barter his wife for any trifle he wished to possess; the scene completely changed with the climate and character of other islanders. Where the men appeared armed with the hatchet of war, the women were more confined to their houses; and the ruder manners of the husband rendered the wife more strict, so that neither her charms nor deformities were exposed to the eyes of the world. There is no circumstance, I believe, which so decisively shows the character of a man, or a nation, as the treatment of women. Most nations, that acquire subsistence with difficulty, degrade the female sex to domestic animals, and impose on them all the labours of the hut: the husband imagines bold, dangerous, manly enterprise sufficiently excuses him from submitting to more trifling occupations, and leaves these to his wife. Hence the extreme subjection of the women in most savage nations throughout the World: and hence the little respect paid the mother by her sons, as soon as they arrive at years of maturity. They are early initiated in perilous undertakings, so that the superiority of the man is frequently occurring to their minds, and a rude disposition to toil or danger soon takes place of a more tender affection. From Greenland to Caffraria this contempt of the women prevails in all uncultivated nations; though it appears among every people, and in every particular region, in a different form. The wife of the Negro is far beneath her husband in slavery, and at home the wretched Carib imagines himself a king.

But the feebleness of the woman seems not to have been the only circumstance, that has rendered her subordinate to the man; in most places her greater sensibility, her artfulness, and in general the more delicate mobility of her mind, appear to have contributed to it still more. The Asiatics, for instance, cannot conceive, how the unbounded liberty of the women, as in Europe, the seat of female empire, can subsist without exposing the men to extreme peril: with them, they are persuaded, every thing would be in a perpetual state of commotion, if these artful creatures, easily moved, and ready to attempt any thing, were not under restraint. The only reasons assigned for many tyrannical customs are, that the women formerly brought on themselves such rigid laws by such or such an action, and the men were compelled to have recourse to them for their own peace and security. It is thus they account for the inhuman custom of burning wives with their husbands in Hindustan: the life of the husband, they say, would never have been safe, but for this dreadful remedy, which impels the wife, to sacrifice herself with him: and when we read of the ardent passions of the women in those countries, the fascinating charms of the Indian dancing girls, and the cabals of the haram among the Turks and Persians, we are led to think something of the kind not incredible. The men were incapable of securing from sparks the inflammable tinder, which their voluptuousness had composed; and too weak and indolent, to unravel the immense web of female capacities and contrivances, and turn them to better purposes: accordingly, as weak and voluptuous barbarians, they fought their own quiet in a barbarous manner; and subjected by force those, whose artfulness their understanding was unable to sway. Read what the Greeks and Asiatics have said of women, and you will find materials for explaining their singular fate in most warm climates. The whole, it must be confessed, is ultimately ascribable to the men, whose stupid brutality did not eradicate the evil, they have so lamely attempted to restrain; as appears, not only from the history of civilization, which, by a rational education, has placed woman on a level with man, but from the example of some uncivilized yet intelligent nations. The ancient German, in his wild forests, understood the worth of the female sex, and enjoyed in them the noblest qualities of man, fidelity, prudence, courage, and chastity: but to this his climate, his genetic character, and every part of his way of life, contributed. He and his wife grew, like their oaks, slowly, unexhausted, and strong: the stimulus of seduction his country did not supply; and both the general condition and necessity inclined each sex to virtue. Daughters of Germany, be not insensible of the fame of those, from whom ye are descended, and aspire to emulate them: there are few nations, on whose females history has conferred equal renown; and there are few nations, in which the husband has so honoured the virtues of the wife, as in ancient Germany. The women of most nations in a similar state were slaves: your mothers were the friends and counsellors of their husbands, and every worthy woman among you is so now.

Let us proceed to the virtues of women, as they display themselves in the history of mankind. Even among the most savage people the woman is distinguished from the man by more delicate civility, and love of ornament and decoration: and these qualities are discernible, even where the nation has to contend against an unfriendly climate, and the most distressing want. Every where the woman adorns herself, however scanty the materials she is able to procure. So in the early spring the Earth, rich in life, sends forth at least a few inodorous blossoms, to show what she is capable of effecting in other seasons.

Cleanliness is another female virtue, to which woman is impelled by nature, and excited by her desire to please. The regulations, nay often supererogatory laws and customs, by which all unvitiated nations keep women when labouring under disease in a state of separation, that no injury may accrue from them, reflect disgrace on many civilized people. They are in consequence unacquainted with a great part of the weaknesses, which among us are both the effects, and again new causes, of that deep degeneracy, which licentious, diseased effeminacy transmits to a wretched offspring.

The gentle endurance, the indefatigable activity, for which the softer sex, when not corrupted by the abuses of civilization, are distinguished, deserve still greater commendation. They bear with resignation the yoke, that the rude superiority of strength in man, his love of idleness and inaction, and lastly the faults of their ancestors, have entailed on them as an hereditary custom; and the most perfect examples of this are often found among the most wretched people. It is not from dissimulation, that in many regions the marriageable females must be compelled by force to submit to the drudgery of the wedded state: they run from their hut, they flee into the desert: with tears they put on the bridal garland, the last flower of their freer, playful youth. Most of the epithalamiums of such nations are meant to encourage and console the bride, and are composed in a melancholy strain, at which we are apt to laugh, because we are insensible of their innocence and truth.[49] The bride takes a tender leave of all, that was dear to her youth, quits the house of her parents, as one dead to them for ever, loses her former name, and becomes the property of a stranger, who in all likelihood will treat her as a slave. She must sacrifice to him every thing, that is most dear to a human being, her person, her liberty, her will, nay probably her life and health; and all for the gratification of a passion, to which the modest virgin is yet a stranger, and which will soon be drowned in a sea of inconveniences. Happy is it, that Nature has endowed and adorned the female heart with an unspeakably affectionate and powerful sense of the personal worth of man. This enables her to bear also his severities: her mind willingly turns from them to the contemplation of whatever she considers as noble, great, valiant, and uncommon in him: with exalted feelings she participates in the manly deeds, the evening recital of which softens the fatigue of her toilsome day, and is proud, since she is destined to obedience, that she has such a husband to obey. Thus the love of the romantic in the female character is a benevolent gift of Nature; a balsam for the woman, and an animating reward for the man: for the most valuable prize of the youth was ever the love of a maiden.

Lastly must be mentioned that sweet maternal affection bestowed on woman by Nature; almost independent of cool reason, and far remote from the selfish desire of reward. The mother loves her child, not because he is amiable, but as a living part of herself, the child of her heart, the copy of her nature. Hence her bowels yearn with compassion for his sufferings; her heart beats higher at his happiness; her blood flows more placidly, while he receives the stream from her breast. These maternal feelings pervade every uncorrupted nation upon Earth: no climate, by which all other things are changed, could alter this: the most depraved customs of society alone can in time perhaps render enervating vices more pleasing than

[49] See some of them in the *Volkslieder* (Popular songs), Vol. I, p. 33, Vol. II, p. 96–98, 104.

the tender pains of maternal love. The Greenlander suckles her son three or four years, because her climate affords no food proper for infants: she submits to all the perversities arising from the latent insolence of the future man with indulgent forbearance. The Negress displays more than manly strength, when a monster attacks her child: we read with astonishment instances of maternal magnanimity contemning life. Lastly, when the tender mother, whom we call a savage, is deprived of her chief consolation, the object of her care, and that for which she values life, her feelings surpass description:[50] How then can these nations be deficient in sentiments of true female humanity, unless perhaps want and mournful necessity, or a false point of honour and some barbarous hereditary custom, occasionally lead them astray? The germes of every great and noble feeling not only exist in all places, but are universally unfolded, as much as the way of life, climate, tradition, or peculiarity of the nation will permit.

If these things be so, the husband would not remain inferior to the wife: and what manly virtue can we conceive, that has not found some place of the Earth or other, in which to flourish? Aspiring courage, to be a sovereign on Earth, and to enjoy life with freedom, but not with inactivity, is the first virtue of the man. This has formed itself most extensively and diversely; as it has been almost every where fostered by necessity, and every region, every variation of manners, has given it a different turn. Thus man soon sought fame in perils; and to surmount them was the most precious jewel of his life. This disposition descended from father to son: the rudiments of education promoted it, and in a few generations the tendency became hereditary. No other man is affected by the sound of the horn, and the voice of the hound, like him who is born a hunter: to this the impressions he received in his childhood contribute. Nay frequently the countenance of the hunter, and the structure of his brain, are transmitted to his posterity. It is the same with all the other ways of life of free, active nations.

[50] See Carver's *Travels*, p. 338, etc., the lamentations of the Naudowessee woman, who had lost her husband, and her son of four years old.

The songs of a people are the best testimonies of their peculiar feelings, propensities, and modes of viewing things; they form a faithful commentary on their way of thinking and feeling, expressed with openness of heart.[51] Even their customs, proverbs, and maxims, express not so much as these: but still more should we learn from the characteristic dreams of a nation, if we had examples of them, or rather if travellers would note them. In dreaming, and at play, man exhibits himself just as he really is, but in the former most.

Paternal love is the second virtue, which is best displayed by a manly education. The father early inures his son to his own mode of life: teaches him his art, awakens in him the sense of fame, and in him loves himself, when he shall grow old, or be no more. This feeling is the basis of all hereditary honour and virtue: it renders education a public, an external work: it has been the instrument of transmitting to posterity all the excellencies and prejudices of the human species. Hence in almost all nations and tribes the mutual joy, when the son arrives at manhood, and equips himself with the implements or weapons of his father: hence the deep sorrow of the father, when he loses this his proudest hope. Read the lamentations of the Greenlander for the loss of his son,[52] listen to the complaints of Ossian on the death of his Oscar, and in them you will perceive the bleeding wounds of the paternal heart, the noblest of the manly breast.

The grateful love of the son to his father is certainly but a slight return for the affection, with which the father has loved his son: but this too is the design of Nature. When the son becomes a father, his heart acts in the line of descent upon his children: the full stream is ordained to flow downward, not upward; for thus only the ever growing chain of new races can be upheld. It is not therefore to be reprobated as unnatural, if some nations, oppressed by want, prefer the child to the de-

[51] See the *Volkslieder* (Popular songs), partly in general, partly the northern songs in particular, Vol. I, p. 166, 175, 177, 242, 247, Vol. II, p. 210, 245.

[52] *Volkslieder,* Vol. II, p. 128.

cayed parent; or, as some accounts say, even accelerate the death of those, who are worn out by age. It is not hatred, but melancholy necessity, or rather cool benevolence, from which this springs: as they cannot feed the aged, as they cannot take them with them, they choose rather with friendly hand, to bestow on them an easy death, than leave them to perish by the fangs of wild beasts. Cannot a friend, when impelled by necessity, deprive his friend of life, however painful the task may be; and thus confer on him, whom he is unable to save, the only benefit in his power? But, that the fame of the father lives and acts immortally in the minds of his descendants, appears in most nations, from their songs and wars, their history and traditions, and still more especially from their rooted esteem for that way of life, which they have received as an inheritance.

Finally, common perils excite common courage: thus they knit the third and noblest tie of man, *friendship*. In countries and modes of life, that render union in enterprise necessary, heroic minds are found wearing the bonds of friendship through life and death. Such were those friends of the heroic ages of Greece, whose fame will live immortally: such were those renowned Scythians; and such are still to be found among nations addicted to hunting, war, or adventures of any kind, amid woods and deserts. The husbandman knows only a neighbour, the mechanic a workfellow, whom he aids or envies: the merchant, the man of letters, the courtier—how remote are they from that chosen, active, tried friendship, with which the wanderer, the prisoner, the slave who groans with another in one chain, are much better acquainted! In times of need, on occasions of exigence, minds unite: the dying man calls on his friend, to avenge his blood, and rejoices in the hope of meeting him beyond the grave. The friend thirsts with an unquenchable desire to take vengeance for the death of him, to whom he is attached, to deliver him from prison, to assist him in the combat, and to share with him the meed of glory. An united tribe, among little nations, is nothing but a band of sworn friends, segregated from all the rest, whether in love or hatred. Such are the Arabian tribes; such are many of the Tatar hordes; and such are most of the nations of America. The bloodiest wars between them, which seem to disgrace humanity, originally sprung from the noble sentiment of an injury done to the honour of the tribe, or an offence committed against its friendship.

I shall not at present pursue this subject through the different forms of government of the male or female sovereigns of the Earth. For, since in all, that has hitherto been said, we find no grounds to explain, why one man should rule over thousands of his fellows by right of birth; why he should exact from them obedience to his will without conditions and without control, send thousands of them to be killed without contradiction, dissipate the wealth of the state without rendering any account of it, and beside this lay the most oppressive taxes precisely on the poor: since we are still less capable of deducing from the original dispositions of Nature, why a bold and valiant people, that is to say thousands of worthy men and women, frequently kiss the feet of a weak creature, or worship the sceptre, with which a madman tears their flesh from their bones; still less what god or demon it is, that inspires them, to submit their understanding, their abilities, nay frequently their lives, and all the rights of man, to the will of one, and deem it their greatest joy and happiness, that the despot should beget a future despot like himself; since all these things appear at first view the most inexplicable enigma of human nature, and happily, or unhappily, to the greater part of the Earth this form of government is unknown; we cannot reckon them among the primitive, necessary, universal laws, that Nature has imposed upon mankind. Husband and wife, father and son, friend and enemy, are determinate relations and names: but the ideas of leader and king, an hereditary legislature and judge, an arbitrary sovereign and ruler of the state, in his own person and in those of all his posterity yet unborn, require a different explanation, from what we can here bestow on them. Let it suffice, that we have hitherto considered the Earth as a seminary of natural senses and endowments, arts and capacities, mental faculties and virtues, in considerable variety: but how far man is qualified, or enabled, to procure himself happiness thereby, or where the standard of happiness is to be found, let us now proceed to inquire.

CHAPTER 5

The Happiness of Man is in all Places an individual Good; consequently it is every where climatic and organic, the Offspring of Practice, Tradition, and Custom

THE very name of happiness [53] implies, that man is neither susceptible of pure bliss, nor capable of creating felicity for himself. He is the child of Accident, who has placed him on this spot, or on that, and determined his capacity of enjoyment, and the kind and measure of his joys and sorrows, according to the country, time, organization, and circumstances, in which he lives. It would be the most stupid vanity to imagine, that all the inhabitants of the World must be Europeans to live happily. Should we ourselves have become what we are out of Europe? He who placed us here, and others there, undoubtedly gave them an equal right to the enjoyment of life. Happiness is an internal state; and therefore its standard is not seated without us, but in the breast of every individual, where alone it can be determined: another has as little right to constrain me to adopt his feelings, as he has power to impart to me his mode of perception, and convert his identity into mine. Let us not place, therefore, from indolent pride, or too common presumption, the form and standard of human happiness higher or lower, than it has been fixed by the creator; for he alone knows, what a mortal can attain upon Earth.

1. Our complexly organized bodies, with all their senses and limbs, have been bestowed on us for use, for exercise. Without

[53] Being derived from *hap*, chance. The terms here contrasted in the original are *seligkeit* and *glueckseligkeit:* the former, which I have rendered bliss, implies the permanent felicity of the other world; to this *glueck*, signifying chance, or fortune, is prefixed to express the casual felicity of this. Our language has not two words expressing precisely the same ideas, and contrasted in a similar manner; so that I am obliged to content myself with the term happiness, pointing out the contingency implied in its derivation.

this our fluids stagnate; our organs become languid; and the body, a living corpse, dies long before its decease; it perishes by a slow, miserable, unnatural death. If Nature, therefore, would secure us the first indispensable foundation of happiness, health, she must bestow on us exercise, toil, and labour, and rather compel man thereby to a state of wellbeing, than leave him to dispense with it. Hence, as the Greeks say, the gods sold every thing to mortals at the price of labour; not out of envy, but from kindness; for the greatest enjoyment of existence, the sensation of active striving powers, lies in this very struggle, in this striving after the comforts of ease. Human nature languishes only in those climates, or conditions, in which enervating idleness, in which voluptuous indolence entombs the body alive, and renders it a pallid carcase, or a burden to itself; in other countries, in other modes of life, even in the most severe, the most energetic growth, the healthiest and most beautiful symmetry of the limbs, prevail. Turn over the history of nations, and read what Pages says, for example, of the make of the Chactaws and Tegaws, of the characters of the Bissagoans, Hindoos, and Arabs: even the most unfavourable climates make little difference in the duration of life, and want itself strengthens the cheerful son of need for the performance of health-giving labour.[54] Even the mal-conformations of the body, that occur here and there upon the Earth as genetic characters or hereditary modes, are less detrimental to health, than our artificial embellishments, our many forced unnatural ways of life: for what is a larger lobe of the ear of an Arracanese, the eradicated beard of an East or West Indian, or perhaps a perforated nose, to the straightened, tortured breast, bent knee, misshapen foot, distorted or rickety form, and compressed bowels, of so many delicate male and female Europeans? Let us therefore thank Providence, that, as health is the foundation of all physical happiness, it is so diffused over the Earth. Nations, to whom we are inclined to think Nature has played the stepmother, are perhaps her most favoured chil-

[54] *Voyages de Pagès* (Pagès's travels), p. 17, 18, 26, 52, 54, 140, 141, 156, 167, 188, etc.

dren: for, if she have prepared them no idle feast of pleasing poisons, she has presented to them from the hard hand of labour the cup of health, and an internal invigorating vital warmth. Children of the rosy morn, they bloom to the last: a frequently careless serenity, an internal sensation of well-being, is to them happiness, is to them the end and enjoyment of life: could any other, could happiness more sweet and durable, be conferred upon them?

2. We boast of the refinement of our mental powers: but let melancholy experience teach us, that every refinement does not promote happiness; nay, many an instrument becomes unfit for use by its very delicacy. Contemplation, for instance, can form the pleasure only of a few idle men: and to them, like opium to the Asiatics, it is frequently an enervating, consuming, stupefying, visionary pleasure. The waking, healthy use of the senses, an understanding employed about the real concerns of life, vigilant attention, accompanied with active recollection, quick determination, and happy effect, alone constitute what we call presence of mind, real mental vigour, which repays itself with the consciousness of a present active power, with happiness and joy. Think not, sons of men, that a premature disproportionate refinement or cultivation is happiness; that the dead nomenclature of all the sciences, the holiday use of all the arts, can secure to a living being the science of life: the feeling of happiness is not acquired from words learned by rote, or a knowledge of the arts. A head stuffed with knowledge, even of golden knowledge, oppresses the body, straitens the breast, dims the eye, and is a morbid burden to the life of him who bears it. The more we divide our mental powers by refinement, the more the inactive powers decay: stretched on the scaffold of art, our limbs and faculties wither while displayed with ostentation. The blessing of health arises only from the use of the whole mind, and of its active powers in particular: let us thank Providence, therefore, for not rendering the human species in general too refined, and the Earth an auditory of the learned sciences. In most nations and conditions of men, the mental powers are kindly left bound together in a firm knot,

and developed only where need requires. Most nations of the Earth act and think, love and hate, hope and fear, laugh and cry, like children: at least, therefore, they enjoy the happiness of the childish dreams of infancy. Unhappy he, who first takes the pains, to dive beneath the surface for the happiness of life!

3. As our wellbeing is rather a quiet feeling, than a brilliant thought; so our lives are embellished with love and joy much more from the feelings of the heart, than from the effects of the most profound understanding. How good, therefore, has our common mother been, in rendering the source of goodwill toward ourselves and others, the true humanity of our species, for which it was created, almost independent of motives and artificial incentives. Every living being rejoices in his existence: he inquires not, he does not scrupulously examine, why he exists: his existence is to him an end, and his end is existence. No savage commits suicide, as no beast destroys himself: he propagates his species, without knowing to what purpose; and in the severest climate submits to every toil and labour, merely that he may live. The simple, rooted feeling of existence, for which there is no equivalent, is happiness, therefore: a drop from the infinite ocean of the Allblissful, who is in all, and feels and enjoys himself in all. Hence that imperturbable joy and tranquillity, which many Europeans admire in the countenances and lives of foreigners, because their restless anxiety prevents them from entertaining similar feelings: hence, too, that openhearted benevolence, that anticipating unconstrained courtesy, which we find in all happy nations, not compelled to defence or revenge. From impartial accounts, this is so generally diffused over the Earth, that it might be deemed the characteristic of man; were it not, alas, equally the character of his equivocal nature, to restrain this frank benevolence, this courteous tranquillity and joy in himself and others, at the call of reason or fancy, to guard against future want. Why should not a creature happy in himself see others happy about him, and endeavour what he can to promote their being so? But while we ourselves, surrounded with wants, increase our necessities still more by our own art and contrivance, our being is

contracted, and the clouds of distrust, anxiety, labour, and care, obscure a countenance formed for open participating joy. Yet even here Nature has taken the human heart in hand, and moulded the sensible clay in such various ways, that where she could not gratify with giving, she has sought at least to satisfy in refusing. The European has no idea of the boiling passions and imaginations, that glow in the Negro's breast; and the Hindoo has no conception of the restless desires, that chase the European from one end of the World to the other. The savage cannot gratify his passions in voluptuousness, and therefore they incline more to composure and tranquillity: on the other hand, where the flame of benevolence scatters light sparks all around, it quickly kindles, and perishes in these sparks. In short, the human feelings have received every form, that could find a place in the various climates, states, and organizations of our Globe: yet every where the happiness of life consists not in a tumultuous crowd of thoughts and feelings, but in their relation to the actual internal enjoyment of our existence, and what we reckon as part of our existence. No where upon Earth does the rose of happiness blossom without thorns: but what proceeds from these thorns is every where, and under all its forms, the lovely though perishable rose of vital joy.

If I err not, from these simple data, the truths of which every heart must feel, a few lines may be drawn, which determine at least many doubts and mistakes concerning the destination of the human species. How, for instance, can it be, that man, as we know him here, should have been formed for an infinite improvement of his mental faculties, a progressive extension of his perceptions and actions? nay, that he should have been made for the state, as the end of his species, and all preceding generations properly for the last alone, which is to be enthroned on the ruined scaffolding of the happiness of the rest? The sight of our fellow-creatures, nay even the experience of every individual life, contradicts this plan attributed to creative Providence. Neither our head nor our heart is formed for an infinitely increasing store of thoughts and feelings; our hand is not made, our life is not calculated for it. Do not our finest mental powers decay, as well as flourish? Do they not even fluctuate with years and circumstances, and relieve one another in friendly context, or rather in a circular dance? And who has not found, that an unlimited extension of his feelings enfeebles and annihilates them, while it gives to the air in loose flocks what should have formed the cord of love, or clouds the eyes of others with its ashes? As it is impossible, that we can love others more than ourselves, or in a different way; for we love them only as part of ourselves, or rather ourselves in them; that mind is happy, which, like a superiour spirit, embraces much within the sphere of its activity, and in restless activity deems it a part of itself: but miserable is that, the feelings of which, drowned in words, are useful neither to itself nor others. The savage, who loves himself, his wife, and child, with quiet joy, and glows with limited activity for his tribe, as for his own life, is, in my opinion, a more real being, than that cultivated shadow, who is enraptured with the love of the shades of his whole species, that is of a name. The savage has room in his poor hut for every stranger, whom he receives as his brother with calm benevolence, and asks not once whence he comes. The deluged heart of the idle cosmopolite is a hut for no one.

See we not, then, my brethren, that Nature has done all she could, not to diffuse, but to circumscribe us, and to accustom us to the sphere of our lives? Our senses and powers have their measure: the Hours of our days and lives take hands only in rotation, while those that come relieve those that depart. It is a trick of the fancy, when the old man still dreams, that he is a youth. Is that concupiscence of the mind, which, forerunning even desire, is momentarily changing to disgust, the pleasure of Paradise? Is it not rather the Hell of Tantalus, the bottomless buckets of the vainly labouring Danaids? Thy sole art below, O man, is moderation: Joy, the child of Heaven, for whom thou pantest, is around thee, is in thee, the daughter of Temperance and calm Enjoyment, the sister of Content and Satisfaction with thy being in life and death.

Still less comprehensible is it, how man should be made for the state, so that his first true happiness must necessarily spring from its constitution: for how many people upon Earth are entirely ignorant of all government, and yet are happier than many, who have sacrificed themselves for the good of the state? I will not enter upon the benefits or mischiefs, which this artificial form of society brings with it: but it may be observed, as every art is merely an instrument, and the most complicated instrument necessarily requires the most prudence and delicacy in managing it, this is an obvious consequence, that with the greatness of a state, and the intricate art of its constitution, the danger of rendering individuals miserable is infinitely augmented. In large states, hundreds must pine with hunger, that one may feast and carouse: thousands are oppressed, and hunted to death, that one crowned fool or philosopher may gratify his whims. Nay, as all politicians say, that every well constituted state must be a machine regulated only by the will of one, what increase of happiness can it bestow, to serve in this machine as a thoughtless member? or, probably indeed, contrary to our better knowledge and conscience, to be whirled round all our lives on an Ixion's wheel; that leaves the tormented wretch no hope of comfort, unless perhaps in strangling the activity of his free, self-governing mind, as a fond father would his darling babe born to misery; to seek happiness in the insensibility of a machine? O, if we be men, let us thank Providence, that this was not made the general destination of mankind. Millions on this Globe live without government: and must not every one of us, even under the most exquisite government, if he will be happy, begin where the savage begins, seeking to acquire and maintain health of body and soundness of mind, the happiness of his house and of his heart, not from the state, but from himself? Father and mother, husband and wife, son and brother, friend and man, are natural relations, in which we may be happy: the state gives us nothing but instruments of art, and these, alas! may rob us of something far more essential, may rob us of ourselves.

Kindly considerate was it therefore in Providence, to prefer the easier happiness of individuals to the artificial ends of great societies, and spare generations these costly machines of state as much as possible. It has wonderfully separated nations, not only by woods and mountains, seas and deserts, rivers and climates, but more particularly by languages, inclinations, and characters; that the work of subjugating despotism might be rendered more difficult, that all the four quarters of the Globe might not be crammed into the belly of a wooden horse. No Nimrod has yet been able to drive all the inhabitants of the World into one park for himself and his successors; and though it has been for centuries the object of united Europe, to erect herself into a despot, compelling all the nations of the Earth to be happy in her way, this happiness-dispensing deity is yet far from having obtained her end. Weak and childish must our creative mother have been, had she constructed the sole and genuine destination of her children, that of being happy, on the artificial wheels of some latterlings, and expected the end of the creation from their hands. Ye men of all the quarters of the Globe, who have perished in the lapse of ages, ye have not lived and enriched the Earth with your ashes, that at the end of time your posterity should be made happy by European civilization: is not a proud thought of this kind treason against the majesty of Nature?

If happiness be to be met with upon Earth, it is in every sentient being, it must be in every one by Nature, and assisting art must become nature in him to produce enjoyment. Every man has the standard of his happiness within himself: he bears about him the form, to which he is fashioned, and in the pure sphere of which alone he can be happy. For this purpose has Nature exhausted all the varieties of human form on Earth, that she might find for each in its time and place an enjoyment, to amuse mortals through life.

II

Humanity the End of Human Nature

BOOK XV

"Thus every thing in history is transient: the inscription on her temple is, evanescence and decay. We tread on the ashes of our forefathers, and stalk over the entombed ruins of human institutions and kingdoms. Egypt, Persia, Greece, Rome, flit before us like shadows: like ghosts they rise from their graves, and appear to us in the field of history.

"When any political body has outlived its maturity, who would not wish it a quiet dissolution? Who does not shudder, when, in the circle of living active powers, he stumbles over the graves of ancient institutions, which rob the living of light, and narrow their habitations? And when the present race has cleared away these catacombs, how soon will its institutions have a similar appearance to another, and be in like manner levelled with the earth!

"The cause of this transitoriness of all terrestrial things lies in their essence, in the place they inhabit, and in the general laws, to which our nature is subject. Man's body is a fragile, ever-renovating shell, which at length can renew itself no longer: but his mind operates upon Earth only in and with the body. We fancy ourselves independent; yet we depend on all nature: implicated in a chain of incessantly fluctuating things, we must follow the laws of its permutation, which are nothing more than to be born, exist, and die. A slender thread connects the human race, which is every moment breaking, to be tied anew. The sage, whom time has made wise, sinks into the grave; that his successor may likewise begin his course as a child, perhaps madly destroy the work of his father, and leave to his son the same vain toil, in which he too consumes his days. Thus year runs into year: thus generations and empires are linked together. The Sun sets, that night may succeed, and mankind rejoice at the beams of a new morn.

"Now were any advancement observable in all this, it would be something: but where is it to be found in history? In it we every where perceive destruction, without being able to discern, that what rises anew is better, than what was destroyed. Nations flourish and decay: but in a faded nation no new flower, not to say a more beautiful one, ever blooms. Cultivation proceeds; yet becomes not more perfect by progress: in new places new capacities are developed; the ancient of the ancient places irrevocably pass away. Were the Romans more wise, or more happy, than the Greeks? are we more so than either?

"The nature of man remains ever the same: in the ten thousandth year of the World he will be born with passions, as he was born with passions in the two thousandth, and ran through his course of follies to a late, imperfect, useless wisdom. We wander in a labyrinth, in which our lives occupy but a span; so that it is to us nearly a matter of indifference, whether there be any entrance or outlet to the intricate path.

"Melancholy fate of the human race! with all their exertions chained to an Ixion's wheel, to Sisyphus's stone, and condemned to the prospect of a Tantalus. We must will; and we must die, without having seen the fruit of our labours ripen, or learned a single result of human endeavours from the whole course of history. If a people stand alone, its characters wear away under the hand of Time: if it come into collision with others, it is thrown into the crucible, where its impression is equally effaced. Thus we hew out blocks of ice; thus we write on the waves of the sea: the wave glides by, the ice melts; our palaces, and our thoughts, are both no more.

"To what purpose then the unblessed labour, to which God has condemned man as a daily task during his short life? To what purpose the burden, under which every one toils on his way to the grave; while no one is asked, whether he will take it up or not, whether he will be born on this spot, at this period, and in this circle, or no? Nay, as most of the evils among mankind arise from themselves, from their defective constitutions and governments, from the arrogance of oppressors, and from the almost inevitable weakness both of the governors and the governed; what fate was it, that subjected man to the yoke of his fellows, to the mad or foolish will of his brother? Let a man sum up the periods of the happiness and unhappiness of nations, their good and bad rulers, nay the wisdom and folly, the predominance of reason and of passion, in the best: how vast will be the negative number! Look at the despots of Asia, of Africa, nay of almost the whole Earth: behold those monsters on the throne of Rome, under whom a World groaned for centuries: note the troubles and wars, the oppressions and tumults, that took place, and mark the event. A Brutus falls, and an Anthony triumphs: a Germanicus dies, and a Tiberius, a Caligula, a Nero, reign: Aristides is banished: Confucius is a wanderer upon the Earth: Socrates, Phocion, Seneca, are put to death. Every where, it must be confessed, is discoverable the proposition: 'what is, is; what can be, will be; what is susceptible of dissolution, dissolves:' a melancholy confession, however, which universally proclaims, that rude Violence, and his sister, malignant Cunning, are every where victorious upon Earth."

Thus man doubts, and redoubts, after much apparent historical experience: nay, this melancholy complaint has in a certain degree the superficies of all earthly occurrences in its favour: hence I have known many, who on the wide ocean of human history imagined they had lost that god, whom on the firm ground of natural knowledge they beheld with their mental eye in every stalk of grass, in every grain of dust, and adored with overflowing heart. In the temple of the earthly creation, every thing appeared to them full of omnipotence, and benevolent goodness: in the theatre of human actions, on the contrary, for which the periods of our life are calculated, they beheld nothing but a stage of conflicting sensual passions, brutal powers, destructive arts, or evanescent good purposes. To them history is a spider's web, in a corner of the mundane mansion, the intricate threads of which display abundant traces of destructive rapine, while its melancholy centre, the spider by which it was spun, nowhere appears.

Yet, if there be a god in nature, there is in history too: for man is also a part of the creation, and in his wildest extravagances and passions must obey laws, not less beautiful and excellent than those, by which all the celestial bodies move. Now as I am persuaded, that man is capable of knowing, and destined to attain the knowledge of every thing, that he ought to know; I step freely and confidently from the tumultuous scenes, through which we have been wandering, to inspect the beautiful and sublime laws of nature, by which they have been governed.

CHAPTER 1

Humanity is the End of human Nature; and, with this End, God has put their own Fate into the Hands of Mankind

THE end of whatever is not merely a dead instrument must be implicated in itself. Were we created, to strive with eternally vain endeavours after a point of perfection external to ourselves, and which we could never reach, as the magnet turns to the north; we might not only pity ourselves as blind machines, but the being likewise, that had condemned us to such a state of tantalism, in forming us for the purpose of such a malignant and diabolical spectacle. Should we say in his exculpation, that some good at least was promoted, and our nature preserved in perpetual activity, by these empty endeavours, incapable of ever attaining their object; it must be an imperfect, ferocious being, that could deserve such an exculpation: for in activity that never attains its end can lie no good; and he has weakly or maliciously deceived us, by placing before our eyes such a dream, from a purpose unworthy of him. But happily we are taught no such doctrine by the nature of things: if we consider mankind as we know them, and according to the laws that are intrinsic to them, we perceive nothing in man superiour to humanity; for even if we think of angels, or of gods, we conceive them as ideal, superiour men.

Humanity the End of Human Nature

We have seen, that our nature is evidently organized to this end: for it our finer senses and instincts, our reason and liberty, our delicate yet durable health, our language, art, and religion, were bestowed.[1] In all states, in all societies, man has had nothing in view, and could aim at nothing else, but humanity, whatever may have been the idea he formed of it. For it, the arrangements of sex, and the different periods of life, were made by nature; that our childhood might be of long continuance, and we might learn a kind of humanity by means of education. For it, all the different modes of life, throughout the wide World, have been established, all the forms of society introduced. Hunter, or fisherman, shepherd, husbandman, or citizen, in every state man has learned to discriminate food, and construct habitations for himself and his family; to clothe and adorn either sex, and regulate his domestic economy. He invented various laws, and forms of government, the object of all which was, that every one might exercise his faculties, and acquire a more pleasing and free enjoyment of life, undisturbed by others. For this purpose, property was secured, and labour, arts, trade, and an extensive intercourse between persons, facilitated: punishments were invented for culprits, rewards for the deserving; and numberless moral practices for people of different classes, in public and private life, and even in religion, were established. For this, wars were carried on, treaties were made; by degrees a sort of law of nations and of war, and various compacts of hospitality and commerce were framed, so that man might meet compassion and respect beyond the confines of his own country. Thus whatever good appears in history to have been accomplished, humanity was the gainer; whatever foolish, vicious, or execrable, was perpetrated, ran counter to humanity: so that in all his earthly institutions man can conceive no other end, than what lies in himself, that is, in the weak or strong, base or noble nature, that God gave him. Now if throughout the whole creation we know nothing, except by what it is, and what it effects, man's end upon Earth is shown us by his nature and history, as by the clearest demonstration.

---

[1] Book IV.

Let us take a retrospect of the regions, over which we have been wandering: in all the civil establishments from China to Rome, in all the varieties of their political constitutions, in every one of their inventions, whether of peace or war, and even in all the faults and barbarities that nations have committed, we discern the grand law of nature: let man be man; let him mould his condition according as to himself shall seem best. For this nations took possession of their land, and established themselves in it as they could. Of women and of the state, of slaves, clothing, and habitations, of recreation and food, of science and of art, every thing has been made, in the different parts of the Earth, that man thought was capable of being made for his own or for the general good. Thus we every where find mankind possessing and exercising the right of forming themselves to a kind of humanity, as soon as they have discerned it. If they have erred, or stopped at the half way of an hereditary tradition; they have suffered the consequences of their errour, and done penance for the fault they committed. The deity has in nowise bound their hands, farther than by what they were, by time, place, and their intrinsic powers. When they were guilty of faults, he extricated them not by miracles, but suffered these faults to produce their effects, that man might the better learn to know them.

This law of nature is not more simple, than it is worthy of God, consistent, and fertile in its consequences to mankind. Were man intended to be what he is, and to become what he was capable of becoming, he must preserve a spontaneity of nature, and be encompassed by a sphere of free actions, disturbed by no preternatural miracle. All inanimate substances, every species of living creature that instinct guides, have remained what they were from the time of the creation: God made man a deity upon Earth; he implanted in him the principle of self-activity, and set this principle in motion from the beginning, by means of the internal and external wants of his nature. Man could not live and support himself, without learning to make use of his reason: no sooner, indeed, did he begin to make use of this, than the door was opened to a thousand errours and mistaken attempts; but at the same time, and even through these very mistakes and errours, the way was cleared to a better use of his reason. The more speedily he discerned his faults, the greater the promptitude and energy with which he applied to correct them: the farther he advanced, the more his humanity was formed; and this must be formed, or he must groan for ages beneath the burden of his mistakes.

We see, too, that Nature has chosen as wide a field for the establishment of this law, as the abode of mankind would allow: she organized man as variously as the human species could be organized on this Earth. She placed the Negro close to the ape; and she offered for solution the grand problem of humanity, to all people, of all times, from the intellect of the Æthiop to the most refined understanding. Scarcely a nation upon Earth is without the necessaries of life, to which want and instinct guide: for the greater refinement of man's condition more genial climates produce a race of finer mould. But as all beauty and perfection of order lie in the midst of two extremes; the most beautiful form of reason and humanity must find its place in the temperate middle region. And this it has abundantly found, according to the natural law of this general fitness. For though scarcely any of the Asiatic nations can be absolved from that indolence, which rested satisfied too early with good institutions, and regarded hereditary forms as sacred and unalterable; yet they must be excused, when the vast extent of their continent is considered, together with the circumstances to which they were exposed, particularly beyond the mountains. Upon the whole, their first attempts at the promotion of humanity, early as they were, considered each in its place and time, deserve praise; and still less can we refrain from acknowledging the progress made by the more active nations on the coasts of the Mediterranean sea. These shook off the despotic yoke of ancient forms of government and traditions, and gave thereby an example of the great and good law of human destiny: that, whatever a nation, or a whole race of men, wills for its own good with firm conviction, and pursues with energy, Nature, who has set up for man's aim neither despots nor traditions, but the best form of humanity, will assuredly grant.

The fundamental principle of this divine law of nature reconciles us wonderfully not only with the appearance of our species all over the Globe, but likewise with its variations through the different periods of time. Every where man is what he was capable of rendering himself, what he had the will and the power to become. Were he contented with his condition, or were the means of his improvement not yet ripened in the ample field of time; he remained for ages what he was, and became nothing more. But if he employed the instruments God had given him for his use, his understanding, power, and all the opportunities that a favourable current conveyed to him; he raised himself higher with art, and improved himself with courage. If he did not this, his very indolence showed, that he was little sensible of his misfortune: for every lively feeling of injustice, accompanied by intelligence and strength, must become an emancipating power. The long submission to despotism, for instance, arose by no means from the overbearing might of the despots: the easy, confiding weakness of their subjects, and latterly their patient indolence, were its great and only supports. For, it must be confessed, it is easier to bear with patience, than to redress ourselves with vigour; and hence so many nations have forborn to assert the right, that God has conferred on them in the divine gift of reason.

Still there is no doubt, generally speaking, that what has not yet appeared upon Earth will at some future period appear: for no prescription is a bar to the rights of man, and the powers, that God has implanted in him, are ineradicable. We are astonished, to see how far the Greeks and Romans advanced in a few centuries, in their sphere of objects: for, though the aim of their exertions was not always the most pure, they proved, that they were capable of reaching it. Their image shines in history, and animates every one, who resembles them, to similar and better exertions, under the same and greater assistance of fate. In this view the whole history of nations is to us a school, for instructing us in the course, by which we are to reach the lovely goal of humanity and worth. So many celebrated nations of old attained an inferiour aim: why should not we succeed in the pursuit of a purer and more noble object? They were men like us: their call to the best form of humanity was ours, according to the circumstances of the times, to our knowledge, and to our duties. What they could perform without a miracle, we can and ought to perform: the deity assists us only by means of our own industry, our own understanding, our own powers. When he had created the Earth, and all its irrational inhabitants, he formed man, and said to him: "be my image; a god upon Earth; rule and dispose. Whatever of noble and excellent thy nature will permit thee to produce, bring forth: I will assist thee by no miracle; for I have placed thy own fate in thy own hand: but all my sacred, eternal laws of nature will be thy aids."

Let us consider some of these natural laws, which, according to the testimony of history, have promoted the progress of humanity in our species; and, as truly as they are the natural laws of God, will continue, to promote it.

CHAPTER 2

All the destructive Powers in Nature must not only yield in the Course of Time to the maintaining Powers, but must ultimately be subservient to the Consummation of the Whole

EXAMPLE *the first.* As the substance of future worlds lay floating in infinite space, the creator of these worlds was pleased, to leave matter to form itself by means of the internal energies imparted to it. Toward the centre of the whole, the Sun, whatever could find no course of its own, or was attracted by the superiour power of this orb, bent its way. Whatever found another centre of attraction revolved in like manner around it, and either tended to its great focus in an elliptical orbit, or flew off in a parabola or hyperbola, and returned no more. Thus the ether purified itself: thus from a confused fluctuating chaos arose an harmonious system of worlds, according to which earths and comets have revolved for ages in regular orbits round their sun: an eternal proof, that *order arose out of confusion by means of divine implanted powers.* As long as this grand and simple law of all powers numbered and balanced against each other endures, the structure of the universe stands firm; for it is founded on a divine rule and quality.

Second example. In like manner as our Earth formed itself from a shapeless mass into a planet, its elements struggled and contended upon it, till each found its place; so that, after much wild confusion, all are now become subservient to the harmoniously regulated orb. Land and water, air and fire, seasons and climates, winds and currents, and all its atmospherical phenomena, obey one great law of its form and density, its motion and distance from the Sun, and are regulated in harmony with these. Those innumerable volcanoes, that once flamed on the surface of our Earth, flame on it no longer: the ocean no longer boils with those vitriolic effusions, and other matters, that once covered the surface of our land. Millions of creatures have perished, that were fated to perish: whatever could preserve itself abides, and still, after the lapse of thousands of years, remains in great harmonious order. Wild animals and tame, carnivorous and graminivorous insects, birds, fishes, and man, are adapted to each other; and among all these, male and female, birth and death, the term and stages of life, wants and enjoyments, necessities and gratifications. Not, however, at the will of a daily changing, inexplicable order; but according to evident laws of nature, inherent in the structure of the creatures themselves, that is, *in the relation of all the organic powers, which have animated and maintained themselves on our planet.* As long as the natural law of this structure and relation endures, its consequences will likewise endure; namely harmonious order between the animate and inanimate parts of our creation, which, as the interiour of our Earth evinces, was producible only by the destruction of millions.

What? and shall not this law, conformable to the internal powers of nature, educing order out of chaos, and converting into regularity the confusion of human affairs, prevail in the life of man? Undoubtedly it does: we bear its principle within us, and it must and will act suitably to its nature. All the errours of man are mists of truth: all the passions of his breast are wild impulses of a power, which yet knows not itself, but, according to its nature, acts only for the best. Even the tempests of the ocean, those frequent engines of ravage and destruction, are the offspring of an harmonious order of things, to which they are not less subservient than the gentle zephyr. It is hoped a few observations may be placed in such a light, as to confirm this pleasing truth.

1. As the storms of the sea occur less frequently than moderate gales, so in the human species nature has benevolently ordered, *that fewer destroyers than preservers should be born.* It is a divine law in the animal kingdom, that not so many lions and tigers are capable of existence, and actually exist, as sheep and doves: in history we find the same beneficent disposition of things; so that we have a much smaller number of Nebuchadnezzars, Cambyses, Alexanders, Syllas, Attilas, and Genghis-Khans, than of less ferocious generals, or quiet peaceful monarchs. To the production of the former either very inordinate passions, and faulty natural dispositions, are requisite, whence they appear to the Earth as fiery meteors instead of associate planets; or singular circumstances of education, rare occurrences of early habit, or the imperious demands of hostile, political necessity, stir up these scourges of divine wrath, as they are called, against mankind, and keep up their relentless swing. If it be true, therefore, that Nature deviates not from her course on our account, when, among the innumerable varieties of form and temperament she produces, she occasionally exhibits to the World men of unruly passions, spirits of destruction, not of perservation; still it remains in men's own power, not to entrust their flocks to these wolves and tigers, and even to tame them by the laws of humanity. The wild ox no longer appears in Europe, which formerly enjoyed its forest domains in every part of it; and Rome at length found it difficult, to procure the number of African monsters, she required for her amphitheatres. In proportion as lands are cultivated, deserts are diminished, and their wild inhabitants become more rare. In the human species the increasing civilization of man has had a similar effect; his disposition to unruly

Progressivism by contingent evil.

passions giving way with his decrease of strength, a more delicate creature was formed. With all this, irregularities are possible; and these frequently rage more perniciously, from being founded on infantile weakness, as the examples of many Roman and Eastern despots show: however, as a spoiled child is always more easy to restrain than a bloodthirsty tiger, Nature, with her corrective regulations, has taught us the way to rule the lawless, and tame the insatiable savage, by increasing diligence. If there be no longer regions of dragons, to employ the arms of the giants of antiquity, we require no Herculean destructive powers against men themselves. Heroes of this stamp may pursue their bloody game on Caucasus, or in Africa, and there seek new minotaurs to encounter: the society in which they live possesses the undoubted right itself to destroy all the flame-breathing oxen of a Geryon. It suffers by its own fault, if it tamely yield itself up to them as a prey; as it was the fault of the nations themselves, that they did not unite against desolating Rome with all the force of a common league, to maintain the freedom of the World.

2. *The progress of history shows, that, as true humanity has increased, the destructive demons of the human race have diminished in number; and this from the inherent natural laws of a self-enlightening reason and policy.*

In proportion as reason increases among mankind, men must learn from their infancy to perceive, that there is a nobler greatness, than the inhuman greatness of tyrants; and that it is more laudable, as well as more difficult, to form, than to ravage a nation, to establish cities, than to destroy them. The industrious Egyptians, the ingenious Greeks, the mercantile Phenicians, not only make a more pleasing figure in history, but enjoyed, during the period of their existence, a more useful and agreeable life, than the destroying Persians, the conquering Romans, the avaricious Carthaginians. The remembrance of the former still lives with fame, and their influence upon Earth will continue eternally with increasing power; while the ravagers, with their demoniacal might, reaped no farther benefit, than that of becoming a wretched, luxurious people, amid the ruins of their plunder, and at last quaffing off the poisoned draught of severe retaliation. Such was the fate of the Assyrians, Babylonians, Persians, Romans: even the Greeks received more injury from their internal dissensions, and from their luxury in many cities and provinces, than from the sword of the enemy. Now as these are fundamental principles of a natural order, which not only shows itself in particular cases of history, or in fortuitous instances; but is founded on its own intrinsic properties, that is, on the nature of oppression and an overstretched power, or on the consequences of victory, luxury and arrogance, as on the laws of a disturbed equiponderance, and holds on coeternally with the course of things: why must we be compelled to doubt, that this law of Nature is not as generally acknowledged as any other, and does not operate, from the forcibleness with which it is perceived, with the infallible efficacy of a natural truth? What may be brought to mathematical certainty, and political demonstration, must be acknowledged as truth, soon or late; for no one has yet questioned the accuracy of the multiplication table or the propositions of Euclid.

Even our brief history already demonstrates beyond all doubt, that the increased diffusion of true knowledge among people has happily diminished their inhuman, mad destroyers. Since the downfall of Rome there has arisen no other cultivated nation in Europe, which has founded the whole of its constitution on war and conquest; for the military nations of the Middle Ages were rude and savage. In proportion as they advanced in civilization, and learned to have a regard for their property, the more amiable and peaceful spirit of industry, of agriculture, of trade, and of science, forced itself upon them unnoticed, or indeed often against their wills. Men learned to use without destroying, as what was destroyed was no longer capable of being used; and thus in time, from the nature of the case itself, a peaceful balance between nations took place; for, after centuries of wild warring, all began to perceive, that the object of every one's wish was not to be attained, unless they contributed to promote it in common. Even that, which of all things appeared most to require exclusive possession, commerce, could take no other way; as it is a law of nature, against which passions and prejudice are ultimately of no avail. Every commercial nation of Europe now laments, and will hereafter lament still more, what envy or superstition once prompted it foolishly to destroy. As reason increases, the object of navigation willl proportionably turn from conquest to trade; which is founded on reciprocal justice and courtesy, on a progressive emulation to excel in arts and industry, in short, on humanity and its eternal laws.

Our minds feel inward satisfaction, when they not only perceive the balm, which flows from the laws of human nature, but see it spread, and make its way among mankind, even against their wills, from its natural force. God himself could not divest man of the capability of errour; but he implanted this in the nature of human mistakes, that soon or late they should show themselves to be such, and become evident to the calculating creature. No prudent sovereign of Europe now governs his provinces, as did the kings of Persia, or even the Romans themselves; if not from philanthropic motives, yet from a clearer insight into the business, as with the course of time political calculation has become more certain, easy, and perspicuous. A madman only would build Egyptian pyramids in our days; and any one, that should attempt such useless enterprises, would be deemed insane by all the rational part of the World, if not from his want of love for the people, yet from considerations of economy. The bloody combats of gladiators, and barbarous fights with animals, are no longer suffered among us: the human species has run through these wild tricks of youth, and learned at length to see, that its mad frolics cost more than they are worth. In like manner, we no longer require the poor oppressed slaves of the Romans, or helots of Sparta; because in our constitutions we know how to obtain more easily from free beings, what they accomplished with more danger, and even expense, by means of human animals: nay the time must come, when we shall look back with as much compassion on our inhuman traffic in Negroes, as on the ancient Roman Slaves, or Spartan helots; if not from humanity, yet from calculation. In short, we have to thank God, for having given us, with our weak fallible nature, reason, that immortal beam from his sun, the essence of which it is to dispel night, and show things in their real forms.

3. *The progress of arts and inventions puts into the hands of man increasing means of restraining or rendering innocuous, what Nature herself cannot eradicate.*

The surface of the sea must be ruffled by storms, and the mother of all things could not dispense with them for man's advantage. But what did she bestow on him, to compensate these? The art of navigation. These very storms excited man, to invent the elaborate structure of his complicated ship, which enables him not merely to escape the storm, but to profit by its rage, and sail on its wings.

The wandering mariner, tossed on the ocean, could not call the sons of Tyndarus to appear and direct him on his course; accordingly he himself invented his guide the compass, and fought in the skies his Dioscuri, the Sun, the Moon, and the stars. Thus equipped with art he launched out on the boundless ocean, and braved it from the equator to the Arctic Circle.

Nature could not take from man the destructive element of fire, without depriving him of manhood itself: but then, what did she bestow on him by means of fire? Multifarious art: art not only to set bounds to the devouring poison, and render it innocent, but even to employ it for a thousand beneficial purposes.

It is the same with the raging passions of man, as with these storms on the ocean, with this raging element of fire. By and in these the human species has sharpened its reason, and invented a thousand means, regulations, and arts, not only to restrain them, but even to turn them to advantage, as all history shows. A race of men without passions would never have cultivated their understanding; they would have still lain as troglodytes in some cave.

Man-devouring war, for example, was during ages the trade of robbery rudely exercised. It was long the practice of men swayed by turbulent passions; for while personal strength, cunning, and address, were its requisites, it could cherish only the dangerous virtues of robbers and murderers, even in those who possessed the most laudable qualities; as the wars of ancient times, of the Middle Ages, and even some of modern date, abundantly testify. But in the midst of this depraving trade the art of war was invented, perhaps involuntarily; for the inventors of this art perceived not, that it would sap the foundations of war itself. In proportion as the art of fighting became a profound study, and various mechanical inventions were introduced into it, the passions and brute strength of individuals became useless. Soldiers were converted into mere machines, moved by the mind of a single general, and at the order of a few commanders; till at length sovereigns alone were permitted to play this dangerous and costly game, while in ancient times almost all warlike nations were continually in arms. We have seen proofs of this in several Asiatic nations, and not less in the Greeks and Romans. The latter were for centuries almost constantly in the field: the Volscian war continued 106 years; the Samnite, 71: the city of Veii was besieged ten years, like a second Troy: and the destructive Peloponnesian war of 28 years among the Greeks is sufficiently known. But as in all wars, to fall in battle is the least of evils, while the diseases and devastation, that attend the motions of an army, or the siege of a town, with the lawless spirit of plunder, that then pervades all ranks and conditions, are much greater evils, which passion-stirring war calls forth in a thousand frightful forms; we may thank the Greeks and Romans, and still more the inventors of gunpowder and firearms, for having reduced the most savage trade to an art, and latterly indeed the most honourable art of crowned heads. Since kings have personally engaged in this game of honour, with armies as devoid of passion as numerous, we are secured from sieges of ten years duration, or wars of seventy, carried on merely for the honour of the commander; for the very magnitude of an army is sufficient to prevent the continuance of war. Thus, conformably to an unalterable law of nature, the evil itself has produced some good; the art of war having suppressed in a certain degree the practice of warfare. This art has likewise diminished plunder and devastation, if not from philanthropy, yet for the honour of the general. The laws of war, and the treatment of prisoners, are become incomparably milder, than they were even among the Greeks; not to mention the public security, which first existed merely in warlike states. The whole Roman empire, for instance, enjoyed security in its highways, as they were covered by the wings of its eagles; while travelling was dangerous to a foreigner in Asia and Africa, and even in Greece, because in these countries a general spirit of security was wanting. Thus the poison was converted into a medicine, as soon as it came into the hands of art: generations indeed were swept away, but the immortal whole outlived the sufferings of the parts that disappeared, and learned good even from evil.

If this be true of the art of war, it must still more of the science of politics; the study of which, however, is more intricate, as in it centres the welfare of a whole nation. Even the savages of America have their politics; yet in how confined a state! being of advantage indeed to a few particular families, but by no means securing the whole people from ruin. Several little nations have exterminated one another; others are so thinned, that a similar fate probably awaits many of them, from their unequal contest with the smallpox, spirituous liquors, and the avarice of Europeans. The more the political system of a state became an art, both in Asia and Europe, the more stable it was in itself, and the more closely it was connected with others, so that one could not fall without the rest. Thus stands China, thus Japan; ancient edifices, the foundations of which lie deep beneath their walls. The constitution of Greece, the principal republics of which contended centuries for the balance of power, was still more elaborate. Common dangers united them: and had the union been perfect, these active people would have withstood Philip and the Romans with no less glory, than they once gained against Xerxes and Darius. The defective politics of the neighbouring nations alone gave

Rome her advantage: separately they were attacked; separately they were conquered. Rome experienced a similar fate, when she declined in the arts of war and politics: so did Judea; and so did Egypt. No people, whose state is well regulated, can perish, even supposing them to be conquered, as China shows even with all its faults.

The utility of an art profoundly understood is more evident, when we speak of the internal economy of a country, its trade, its administration of justice, its sciences, and its manufactures. In all these it is obvious, the greater the art, the more the advantage. A true merchant employs no deception, because deceit never leads to wealth: as the man of real learning never makes a parade of false science; as the judge, who deserves the name, is never knowingly unjust; for this would be to confess themselves tyroes, not masters of their arts. As certainly must the time come, when the irrational politician will be ashamed of his ignorance; and when it will be as absurd and ridiculous, to be a tyrannical despot, as it has ever been detestable. It will then be clear as day, that every irrational politician reckons with an erroneous multiplication table, and that, however great the sums he calculates, no real advantage is obtained from them. For this history is written; and in the course of it the proofs of this proposition will become evident. All the faults of government must precede, and exhaust themselves as it were; that, after all their disorders, man may at length perceive the happiness of his species to depend not on anything arbitrary, but on an essential law of nature, on reason and equity. To the developement of this law we now proceed; and may the internal force of truth stamp light and conviction on the proposition.

CHAPTER 3

The human Race is destined to proceed through various Degrees of Civilization, in various Mutations; but the Permanency of its Welfare is founded solely and essentially on Reason and Justice

First *natural law.* It is demonstrated in physical mathematics, that *to the permanent condition of a thing a sort of perfection is requisite, a maximum or minimum, arising out of the mode of action of the powers of that thing.* Thus, for example, our Earth could not possess durability, if its centre of gravity did not lie deep within it, and all its powers act to and from this, in equiponderating harmony. Every stable being, therefore, bears in itself, according to this beautiful law of nature, its physical truth, goodness, and necessity, as the grounds of its stability.

Second natural law. It is in like manner demonstrated, *that all perfection and beauty of compound, limited things, or systems of them, rest on such a maximum.* Thus similitude and difference, simplicity in means and diversity in effects, the slightest application of power to attain the most certain or profitable end, form a kind of symmetry and harmonious proportion, universally observed by Nature, in her laws of motion, in the form of her creatures, in the greatest things and in the least; and imitated by the art of man, as far as his powers extend. In this, many rules limit each other, so that what would be greater according to one is diminished by another, till the compound whole attains the most beautiful form, with the greatest economy, and at the same time internal consistency, goodness, and truth. An excellent law, which banishes from Nature every thing arbitrary, and all disorder; and displays to us, even in every variable and limited part of the creation, a rule of the highest beauty.

Third natural law. It is equally proved, that, *if a being, or system of beings, be forced out of this permanent condition of its truth, goodness, and beauty, it will again approach it by its internal powers, either in vibrations, or in an asymptote; as out of this state it finds no stability.* The more active and multifarious the powers, the less is the imperceptible straight course of the asymptote possible, and the more violent the vibrations and oscillations, till the disturbed subject attain an equilibrium of its powers, or harmony in their movements, and therewith the permanent condition essential to it.

Now as mankind, both taken as a whole, and in its particular individuals, societies, and nations, is a permanent natural system of the most multifarious living powers; let us examine, wherein its stability consists; in what point its highest beauty, truth, and goodness, unite; and what course it takes, in order to reapproach its permanent condition, on every aberration from it, of which many are exhibited to us by history and experience.

1. The human species is such a copious scheme of energies and capacities, that, as every thing in nature rests on the most determinate individuality, its great and numerous capacities could not appear on our planet otherwise than *divided among millions.* Every thing has been born, that could be born upon it; and every thing has maintained itself, that could acquire a state of permanence according to the laws of Nature. Thus every individual bears within himself that symmetry, for which he is made, and to which he must mould himself, both in his bodily figure, and mental capacities. Human existence appears in every shape and kind, from the most sickly deformity, that can scarcely support life, to the superhuman form of a Grecian demigod; from the passionate ardour of the Negro brain, to the capacity for consummate wisdom. Through faults and errours, through education, necessity, and exercise, every mortal seeks the symmetry of his powers; as in this alone the most complete enjoyment of his existence lies: yet few are sufficiently fortunate, to attain it in the purest, happiest manner.

2. As an individual man can subsist of himself but very imperfectly, *a superiour maximum of cooperating powers* is formed with every society. These powers contend together in wild confusion, till, agreeably to the unfailing laws of nature, opposing regulations limit each other, and a kind of equilibrium and harmony of movement takes place. Thus nations modify themselves, according to time, place, and their internal character: each bears in itself the standard of its perfection, totally independent of all comparison with that of others. Now the more pure and fine the maximum on which a people hit, the more useful the objects to which it applied the exertions of its nobler powers, and, lastly, the more firm and exact the bond of union, which most intimately connected all the members of the state, and guided them to this good end; the more stable was the nation itself, and the more brilliant the figure it made in

history. The course that we have hitherto taken through certain nations shows how different, according to place, time, and circumstances, was the object for which they strove. With the Chinese it was refined political morality; with the Hindoos, a kind of retired purity, quiet assiduity in labour, and endurance; with the Phenicians, the spirit of navigation, and commercial industry. The culture of the Greeks, particularly at Athens, proceeded on the maximum of sensible beauty, both in arts and manners, in science and in political institutions. In Sparta, and in Rome, men emulated the virtues of the patriot and hero; in each, however, in a very different mode. Now as in all these most depended on time and place, the ancients will scarcely admit of being compared with each other in the most distinguished features of national fame.

3. In all, however, we see the operation of *one principle,* namely *human reason,* which endeavours to produce unity out of multiplicity, order out of disorder, and out of variety of powers and designs one symmetrical and durably beautiful whole. From the shapeless artificial rocks, with which the Chinese ornaments his garden, to the Egyptian pyramid, or the ideal beauty of Greece, the plan and design of a reflecting understanding is every where observable, though in very different degrees. The more refined the reflections of this understanding were, and the nearer it came to the point, which is the highest in its kind, and admits no deviation to the right or to the left; the more were its performances to be considered as models, for they contain eternal rules for the human understanding in all ages. Thus nothing of the kind can be conceived superiour to an Egyptian pyramid, or to several Greek and Roman works of art. They are simple solutions of certain problems of the understanding, which admit no arbitrary supposition, that the problems are perhaps not yet solved, or might be solved in a better way; for in them the simple idea of what they ought to be is displayed in the easiest, fullest, and most beautiful manner. Every deviation from them would be a fault; and were they to be repeated and diversified in a thousand modes, we must still return to that single point, which is the highest of its kind.

4. Thus through all the polished nations, that we have hitherto considered, or shall hereafter consider, *a chain of cultivation may be drawn*, flying off in extremely divergent curves. In each it designates increasing and decreasing greatness, and has maximums of every kind. Many of these exclude or limit one another, till at length a certain symmetry takes place in the whole; so that were we to reason from one perfection of any nation concerning another, we should form very treacherous conclusions. Thus, because Athens had exquisite orators, it does not follow, that its form of government must likewise have been the best possible; or that, because the Chinese moralize so excellently, their state must be a pattern for all others. Forms of government refer to a very different maximum, from that of beautiful morals, or a pathetic oration; notwithstanding, at bottom, all things in any nation have a certain connexion, if it be only that of exclusion and limitation. No other maximum, but that of the most perfect bond of union, produces the most happy states; even supposing the people are in consequence obliged to dispense with many shining qualities.

5. But in one and the same nation every maximum of its commendable endeavours ought not and cannot endure for ever; since it is but one point in the progress of time. This incessantly moves on; and the more numerous the circumstances, on which the beautiful effect depends, the sooner is it liable to pass away. Happy if its master pieces remain as rules for future ages; since those that immediately succeed approach them too near, and will probably obliterate by attempting to excel them. Even the most active people frequently sink most speedily from the boiling to the freezing point.

The history of particular sciences and nations has to calculate these maxima, and I wish we had such a history only of the most celebrated nations during the periods best known. At present we speak only of human history in general, and of its state of permanence in every form and climate. This is nothing else than *humanity*, that is, *reason and equity in all conditions, and in all occupations of men.* And this indeed it is, not through the will of a sovereign, or the persuasive power of tradition, but through natural laws, on which the essence of man reposes. Even his most corrupt institutions cry aloud: "had not a glimmering of equity and reason been retained in us, we should long have ceased to be, nay we never should have existed." As the whole tissue of human history proceeds from this point, to it we must carefully bend our view.

First. What it is we esteem, and after which we inquire, in all human works? Reason, plan, and purpose. If these be wanting, nothing human is accomplished, a blind power is displayed. Wherever our understanding roams throughout the wide field of history, it seeks only itself, it finds only itself. The nearer it approaches pure truth, and the good of mankind, in all its undertakings; the more durable, useful, and beautiful are its works, and the more their rules meet the hearts and minds of all people, in all ages. Socrates and Confucius, Plato, Cicero, and Zoroaster, agree unanimously in what constitutes clear understanding, and just morals: in spite of their various differences, they have all laboured to one point, on which our whole species rests. As the wanderer enjoys no greater delight, than when he every where discovers, even unexpectedly, the traces of a thinking, feeling mind, like his own; so are we delighted when in the history of our species the echo of all ages and nations reverberates nothing from the noblest minds, but truth and benevolence towards man. As my reason seeks the connexion of things, and my heart rejoices when it perceives it; so has every honest man fought it: though, probably, from the point of view which his situation afforded, he saw it differently, and differently described it. Where he erred, he erred both for himself and me, as he warned me against similar errours. Where he guides me truly, instructs, solaces, animates me, he is my brother; a sharer in the same soul of the World, the one human reason, the one human truth.

Secondly. As there is not a more pleasing sight in all history, than that of a man of goodness and understanding, who, in spite of all the changes of fortune, remains the same in every period of his life, and in every thing he does; so our pity is excited in a thousand ways, when we perceive even in great and good men errours of the understanding, which, according to the laws of nature, cannot fail to bring upon them necessary pains. We too frequently meet with these fallen angels in history, and have to lament the weakness of the moulds, that human reason employs for her instruments. How little can a mortal bear, without bending underneath the load! how little that is extraordinary can come in his way, without turning him from it! A slight honour, a glimpse of good fortune, or an unexpected occurrence in life, is a sufficient ignis fatuus, to mislead one into quagmires, or over precipices: another is ignorant of his own powers, attempts what is above his strength, and faints under the enterprize. We are seized with sentiments of compassion, when we perceive such, unfortunately fortunate, on the point of deviating from the path of reason, justice, and happiness, which they feel the want of strength any longer to pursue. Behind them stands the grasping fury, and impels them against their will to overstep the line of moderation: they are now in her hand, and probably will suffer during the remainder of their lives the consequences of a slight folly, and dereliction of reason. Or if Fortune have raised them too high, and they feel themselves on her highest pinnacle, what presents itself to their foreboding minds, but the inconstancy of this fickle goddess, and misfortune bursting from the very seeds of their success? In vain, compassionate Cæsar, didst thou turn aside thy face, when the head of thy defeated enemy Pompey was brought to thee, and build a temple to Nemesis. Already thou hadst passed the confines of Fortune, as well as the banks of the Rubicon; the goddess was now behind thee, and thy bloody corse was doomed, to fall at the feet of the statue of that very Pompey. The constitutions of countries experience a similar fate, as they depend on the reason or folly of a few, who are their rulers, or by whom their rulers are swayed. The most beautiful institutions, which promised mankind the most profitable fruits for ages, have often been torn to pieces by the folly of an individual, who has felled the tree, instead of lopping a few of its branches. Success is most difficult to be born by whole realms, as well as by individuals; whether they be governed by monarchs and despots, or by senates and the people. The people and the despot are the least capable of perceiving the warning nod of the goddess of fate: dazzled by the splendour of vainglory, or made giddy by the sound of a name, they rush beyond the bounds of prudence and humanity, and perceive the consequences of their folly too late. This was the fate of Rome, of Athens, and of many nations; as well as of Alexander, and most of the conquerors, that have disturbed the peace of the World: for Injustice is the ruin of every country, as Folly of every human undertaking. These are the furies of Fate: Misfortune is no more than their younger sister, the third member of the fearful confederacy.

Great father of mankind, what an easy yet difficult lesson hast thou given thy family upon Earth for the whole of their task! They have nothing to learn, but reason and justice alone: if they practise these, light gradually enters their minds, goodness their hearts, perfection their states, happiness their lives. Endowed with these gifts, and making proper application of them, the Negro may form his society as well as the Greek, the troglodyte as well as the Chinese. Experience will lead each farther; and Reason, united with Equity, will give consistence, beauty, and symmetry, to his undertakings. But if he desert these, the essential guides of his life, what can give stability to his good-fortune, and save him from the furies of Inhumanity?

Thirdly. It follows likewise, that, whenever the equilibrium of reason and humanity is disturbed among men, a return to it seldom occurs, except by violent oscillations from one extreme to the other. One passion kicks up the scale of reason, another drives it down, and thus history goes on for years and ages, before the period of tranquillity returns. Thus Alexander destroyed the equilibrium of an extensive region of the World; and it was long after his death before the storm subsided. Thus Rome disturbed the peace of the Globe for more than a thousand years; and half a World of savage nations was requisite for the slow restoration of its quiet. The peaceable progress of an asymptote could by no means be expected, in these convulsions of countries and nations. The channel of cultivation on our Earth, with its abrupt corners, its salient and reentering angles, scarcely ever exhibits a gentle stream, but rather the rushing of a torrent from the mountains. Such are the effects of human passions. It is evident, too, that the general composition of our species is calculated and established on such alternating vibrations. As our walk is a continual falling to the right and to the left, and yet we advance at every step, so is the progress of cultivation in races of men, and in whole nations. Individually we often try both extremes, before we hit the point of rest, as the pendulum oscillates from side to side. Generations are renewed in continual change; and in spite of all the direct precepts of tradition, the son advances in his own way. Aristotle was assiduous to distinguish himself from Plato, Epicurus from Zeno, till more tranquil posterity could at last impartially profit by both extremes. Thus, as in the machine of our body, the work of time proceeds to the good of the human race by necessary opposition, and acquires from it permanent health. But through whatever turnings and angles the stream of human reason may wind and break, it arose from the eternal fountain of truth, and by virtue of its nature can never be lost in its course. Whoever draws from it, draws life and duration.

For the rest, both reason and justice hinge *on one and the same law of nature,* from which the stability of our being likewise flows. Reason weighs and compares the relations of things, that she may dispose them in durable symmetry. Justice is nothing else than a moral symmetry of reason, the formula of the equilibrium of contending powers, on the harmony of which the whole creation reposes. Thus one and the same law reaches from the Sun, and from all the suns in the universe, to the most insignificant human action: one law upholds all beings, and their systems; *the relation of their powers to periodical rest and order.*

CHAPTER 4

From the Laws of their internal Nature, Reason and Justice must gain more Footing among Men in the Course of Time, and promote a more durable Humanity

All the doubts and complaints of men, respecting the uncertainty and little observable progress of good in history, arise from this, that the melancholy wanderer sees too little on his way. If he extended his view, and impartially compared with each other the times, that we most accurately know from history; farther, if he dived into the nature of man, and weighed what truth and reason are; he would doubt as little of their progress, as of the most indisputable physical truth. For thousands of years our sun and all the fixed stars were supposed to be immovable: a fortunate telescope now permits us no longer to doubt of their movement. So in some future age, a more accurate comparison of the periods exhibited in the history of our species will not merely give us a superficial view of this exhilarating truth, but, in spite of all apparent disorder, will enable us to calculate the laws, according to which this progress is effected by the power of human nature. Standing on the verge of ancient history, as on a central point, I shall do no more than cursorily note a few general principles, which will serve as leading stars, to guide us on our future way.

First. *Times connect themselves together, in virtue of their nature; and with them the child of Time, the race of mankind, with all its operations and productions.*

No sophistical argument can lead us to deny, that our Earth has grown older in the course of some thousands of years; and that this wanderer round the Sun is greatly altered since its origin. In its bowels we perceive how it once was constituted; and we need but look around us, to see its present constitution. The ocean foams no longer; it is subsided peaceably into its bed: the wandering streams have found their shores; and plants and animals have run through a progressive series of years in their different races. As not a sunbeam has been lost upon our Earth since its creation; so no falling leaf, no wasted seed, no carcase of a decaying animal, and still less an action of any living being, has been without effect. Vegetation, for example, has increased, and extended itself as far as it could: every living race has spread within the limits nature assigned it, through the means of others: and even the senseless devastations of man, as well as his industry, have been active implements in the hand of Time. Fresh harvests have waved over the ruins of the cities he has destroyed: the elements have strewed the dust of oblivion upon them; and soon new generations have arisen, who have erected new buildings upon the old, and even with their ancient remains. Omnipotence itself cannot ordain, that effects shall not be effects: it cannot restore the Earth to what it was thousands of years ago, so that these thousands of years, with all their consequences, shall not have been.

Already therefore a certain progress of the human species is inseparable from the progress of Time, as far as man is included in the family of Time and Earth. Were the progenitor of mankind now to appear, and view his descendants, how would he be astonished! His body was formed for a youthful Earth; his frame, his ideas, and his way of life, must have been adapted to that constitution of the elements, which then prevailed; and considerable alteration in this must have taken place, in the course of six thousand years or upwards. In many parts America is no longer what it was when discovered: two thousand years hence, its ancient history will have the air of romance. Thus we read the history of the siege of Troy, and seek in vain the spot where it stood; in vain the grave of Achilles, or the godlike hero himself. Were a collection of all the accounts, that have been given of the size and figure of the ancients, of the kind and quantity of their food, of their daily occupations and amusements, and of their notions of love and marriage, the virtues and the passions, the purpose of life and a future existence, made with discriminating accuracy, and with regard to time and place, it would be of no small advantage toward a history of man. Even in this short period, an advancement of the species would be sufficiently conspicuous to evince both the consistency of ever-youthful Nature, and the progressive changes of our old mother Earth. Earth nurses not man alone: she presses all her children to one bosom, embraces all in the same maternal arms: and, when one changes, all must undergo change.

It is undeniable, too, that this progress of time has influenced the mode of thinking of the human species. Bid a man now invent, now sing an Iliad; bid him write like Æschylus, like

Sophocles, like Plato: it is impossible. The childish simplicity, the unprejudiced mode of seeing things, in short the youthful period of the Greeks, is gone by. It is the same with the Hebrews, and the Romans; while on the other hand we are acquainted with a number of things, of which both the Romans and the Hebrews were ignorant. One day teaches another, one century instructs another century: tradition is enriched: the muse of Time, History, herself sings with a hundred voices, speaks with a hundred tongues. Be there as much filth, as much confusion, as there will, in the vast snowball rolled up by Time; yet this very confusion is the offspring of ages, which could have arisen only from the unwearied rolling on of one and the same thing. Thus every return to the ancient times, even the celebrated year of Plato, is a fiction, is, from the ideas of the World and of Time, an impossibility. We float onward: but the stream that has once flowed, returns no more to its source.

Secondly. *The habitations of mankind render the progress of the human species still more evident.*

Where are the times when people dwelled as troglodytes, dispersed about in caves, behind their walls, and every stranger was an enemy? Merely from the course of time no cave, no wall, afforded security: men must learn to know one another; for collectively they are but one family, on one planet of no great extent. It is a melancholy reflection, that every where they first learned to know one another as enemies, and beheld each other with astonishment as so many wolves: but such was the order of nature. The weak feared the strong; the deceived, the deceiver; he who had been expelled, him who could again expel him; the unexperienced child, every stranger. This infantile fear, however, and all its abuses, could not alter the course of nature: the bond of union between nations was knit, though, from the rude state of man, in a rough manner. Growing reason may burst the knots, but cannot untwist the band, and still less undo the discoveries, that have once been made. What are the geologies of Moses and Orpheus, Homer and Herodotus, Strabo and Pliny, compared with ours? What was the commerce of the Phenicians, Greeks, and Romans, to the trade of Europe? Thus with what has hitherto been effected the clew to the labyrinth of what is to be done is given us. Man, while he continues man, will not cease from wandering over his planet, till it is completely known to him: from this neither storms nor shipwreck, nor those vast mountains of ice, nor all the perils of either pole, will deter him; no more than they have deterred him from the first most difficult attempts, even when navigation was very defective. The incentive to all these enterprizes lies in his own breast, lies in man's nature. Curiosity, and the insatiable desire of wealth, fame, discovery, and increase of strength, and even new wants and discontents, inseparable from the present course of things, will impel him; and they by whom dangers have been surmounted in former times, his celebrated and successful predecessors, will animate him. Thus the will of providence will be promoted both by good and bad incentives, till man knows and acts upon the whole of his species. To him the Earth is given; and he will not desist, till it is wholly his own, at least as far as regards knowledge and use. Are we not already ashamed, that one hemisphere of our planet remained for so long a time as unknown to us, as if had been the other side of the Moon?

Thirdly. *In consequence of the internal nature of the human mind, its activity has hitherto been employed solely on means of grounding more deeply the humanity and cultivation of our species, and extending them farther.*

How vast the progress from the first raft that floated on the water to an European ship! Neither the inventor of the former, nor the many inventors of the various arts and sciences that contribute to navigation, ever formed the least conception of what would arise from the combination of their discoveries: each obeyed his particular impulse of want or curiosity: but it is inherent in the nature of the human intellect, and of the general connexion of all things, that no attempt, no discovery, can be made in vain. Those islanders, who had never seen an European vessel, beheld the monster with astonishment, as some prodigy of another World; and were still more astonished when they found, that men like themselves could guide it at pleasure over the trackless ocean. Could their astonishment have been converted into rational reflection on every great purpose, and every little mean, of this floating world of art, how much higher would their admiration of the human mind have arisen? Whither do not the hands of Europeans at present reach, by means of this single implement? Whither may they not reach thereafter?

Beside this art, others innumerable have been invented within the space of a few years by mankind, that extend their sway over air and water, over Earth and Heaven. And when we reflect, that but few nations were engaged in this contest of mental activity, while the greater part of the rest slumbered in the lap of ancient custom; when we reflect, that almost all our inventions were made at very early periods, and scarcely any trace, scarcely any ruin, of an ancient structure, or an ancient institution, exists, that is not connected with our early history; what a prospect does this historically demonstrated activity of the human mind give us for the infinity of future ages! In the few centuries during which Greece flourished, in the few centuries of modern improvement, how much has been conceived, invented, done, reduced to order, and preserved for future ages, in Europe, the least quarter of the Globe, and almost in its smallest parts! How prolific the seeds, that art and science have copiously shed, while one nourishes, one animates and excites the other! As when a string is touched, not only everything that has music resounds to it, but all its harmonious tones reecho the sound, till it becomes imperceptible; so the human mind has invented and created, when an harmonious point of its interiour has been hit. When a new concord was struck, in a creation where every thing is connected, innumerable new concatenations followed of course.

But, it may be asked, how have all these arts and inventions been applied? Have practical reason and justice, and consequently the true improvement and happiness of the human species, been promoted by them? In reply I refer to what has recently been urged respecting the progress of disorder throughout the whole creation: that, according to an intrinsic law of nature, nothing can attain durability, which is the essential aim of all things, without order. A keen knife in the hand of a child may wound it: yet the art that invented and sharpened the knife is one of the most indispensable of arts. All that use such a knife are not children; and even the child will be taught by pain, to use it better. Artificial power in the hand of a despot, foreign luxury in a nation without controlling laws, are such pernicious implements: but the very mischief they do will render men wiser; and, soon or late, the art, that created luxury as well as despotism, will first confine both within due bounds, and then convert them into real benefits. The heavy plough-share wears itself out by long use: the slight teeth of new watchwork gain merely by their revolution the more suitable and artful form of the epicycloid. Thus in human powers abuses carried to excess wear themselves down to good practices: extreme oscillations from side to side necessarily settle in the desirable mean of lasting fitness in a regular movement. Whatever is to take place among mankind will be effected by men: we suffer under our faults, till we learn of ourselves the better use of our faculties, without the assistance of miracles from Heaven.

We have not the least reason, therefore, to doubt, that every good employment of the human understanding necessarily must and will, at some time or other, promote humanity. Since agriculture has prevailed, men and acorns have ceased to be food. Man found, that he could live better, more decently, and more humanely, on the pleasing gifts of Ceres, than on the flesh of his fellows, or the fruits of the oak; and was compelled so to live by the laws of men wiser than himself. After men had learned to build houses and towns, they ceased to dwell in caves: under the laws of a commonweal, the poor stranger was no longer liable to death. Thus trade brought nations together: and the more its advantages were generally understood; the less murders, oppressions, and deceptions, which are always signs of ignorance in commerce, would necessarily be practised. Every addition to the useful arts secures men's property, diminishes their labour, extends their sphere of activity, and necessarily lays therewith the foundations of farther cultivation and humanity. What labour was saved, for example, by the single invention of printing! What an extensive circulation of men's ideas, arts, and sciences, did it promote? Were an European Kang-Ti now to attempt, to eradicate the literature of this quarter of the Globe, he would find it impossible. Had the Phenicians and Carthaginians, the Greeks and Romans, possessed this art; the destruction of their literature would not have been so easy to their spoilers, if it could by any means have been accomplished. Let savage nations burst in upon Europe, they could not withstand our tactics; and no Attila will again extend his march from the shores of the Black Sea and the Caspian to the plains of Catalonia. Let monks, sybarites, fanatics, and tyrants, arise, as they will; it is no longer in their power, to bring back the night of the Middle Ages. Now as no greater benefit can be conceived to arise from any art, divine or human, than not merely to bestow on us light and order, but from its very nature to extend and secure them; let us thank the Creator, that he conferred *understanding* on mankind, and made *art* essential to it. In them we possess the secret and the means of securing order in the World.

Neither need we any way repine, that many excellently conceived theories, morals not excepted, have remained so long without being carried into practice among mankind. The child learns much, which the man alone can apply; but he has not therefore learned in vain. The youth heedlessly forgets, what at some future period he must take pains to recollect, or learn a second time. So no truth that is treasured up, nay no truth that is discovered, among a race continually renovating, is wholly in vain: future circumstances will render necessary what is now despised; and in the infinity of things every case must occur, that can in any way exercise the human species. As in the creation we first conceive the *power,* that formed Chaos, and then disposing *wisdom,* and harmonious *goodness;* so the natural order of mankind first developes rude powers: disorder itself must guide them into the path of understanding; and the farther the understanding pursues its work, the more it perceives, that goodness alone can bestow on it durability, perfection, and beauty.

CHAPTER 5

A wise Goodness disposes the Fate of Mankind; therefore there is no nobler Merit, no purer and more durable Happiness, than to cooperate in its Designs

THE sensual contemplator of history, who in it has lost sight of God, and begun to doubt of Providence, has fallen into this misfortune, from having taken too superficial a view of his subject, or from having had no just conception of Providence. If he have considered Providence as an apparition, that was to meet him at every turn, and continually interrupt the course of human actions, to accomplish this or that particular object of his will and fancy; I confess history is the grave of such a Providence, but certainly to the advantage of truth. For what kind of a Providence must it be, that every one could employ as a hobgoblin in the order of things, as the agent of his narrow designs, as the ally of his pitiful follies; so that the whole would ultimately remain without a master! The God, whom I seek in history, must be the same as in nature: for a man is but a small part of the whole; and his history, like that of the grub, is intimately interwoven with that of the web he inhabits. In it, therefore, natural laws must prevail, that are inherent in the essence of things; and with which the deity is so far from being able to dispense, that he reveals himself in his supreme power, with invariable wisdom, goodness, and beauty, even in those which himself has founded. Every thing, that can take place upon Earth, must take place upon it, provided it happens according to rules, that carry their perfection within themselves. Let us repeat these rules, which we have already developed, as far as they regard the history of mankind: they all bear in themselves the stamp of wise goodness, of exalted beauty, and even of intrinsic necessity.

1. Every thing, that can live on our Earth, lives upon it: for every organization carries in its essence an union of various

powers, which limit each other, and thus limited are capable of attaining in themselves a maximum of durability. Could they not attain this, the powers would separate, and form unions of a different kind.

2. Among these organized bodies man arose, the crown of the terrestrial creation. Innumerable powers united in him, and attained a maximum, the understanding; as their material parts, the human body, did also, in the centre of gravity, according to laws of the most beautiful symmetry and order. Thus in the character of man were given the basis of his duration and happiness, the stamp of his destination, and the whole course of his earthly fate.

3. This character of man is termed intelligence: for it understands the language of God in the creation, that is, it seeks the rule of order, according to which things are founded connectedly on their essences. Thus its intrinsic law is the perception of existence and truth; the connexion of creatures according to their relations and qualities. It is an image of the deity: for it investigates the laws of nature, the ideas in conformity to which the Creator connected them, and which he made essential to them. Reason, therefore, can no more act arbitrarily, than God himself has thought at random.

4. Man began to perceive and to examine the powers of nature from his immediate wants. His aim extended no farther than to his well being, that is, to the due employment of his own powers in exercise and rest. He became connected with other beings; and still his own state of existence was the measure of his connexions. The rule of equity pressed itself upon him; for this is nothing more than practical reason, the measure of the actions and reactions of similar beings for the general security.

5. Human nature is constructed on this principle; so that no individual can suppose himself to exist for the sake of another, or of posterity. If the lowest in the rank of men follow the law of reason and justice, that is within him; he possesses consistency; that is, he enjoys durability and well being; he is rational, just, and happy. These he is not by the will of another creature,

or of the creator, but by the laws of a general order of nature, founded on that order itself. If he deviate from the rule of equity, his avenging faults themselves must show him the disorder, and induce him to return to reason and justice, as the laws of his existence and his happiness.

6. As his nature is composed of very different elements, this he seldom does in the shortest way; he vibrates between two extremes, till he accommodates himself to his state of existence, and reaches the temperate mean in which he imagines his well being to consist. If he err in this, he must be secretly conscious of it, and suffer the consequences of his fault. These, however, he suffers but to a certain degree; for either fate corrects them by means of his own endeavours, or his being no longer finds an internal capacity of subsistence. Supreme wisdom could not impart more beneficial uses to physical pain and moral evil, for nothing superior can be conceived.

7. Had one single man alone trodden the Earth, the object of human existence would have been accomplished in him; as we must consider it to be accomplished, in so many individuals and nations, whom circumstances of time and place separated from the general chain of the species. But as every thing, that can live upon the Earth, endures as long as it can remain in its state of permanency; so the human species, like every other kind of living beings, possesses such intrinsic transmissive powers, as could find, and have found, proportion and order suitable to the whole. Thus reason, the essence of man, and its organ, tradition, have been inherited through a series of successive generations. The Earth was gradually filled, and man became everything, that, in such a period and no other, he could become upon Earth.

8. Thus the propagation of families and traditions, connected human reason: not as if it were in each individual no more than a fragment of the whole, a whole existing no where in one subject, and therefore by no means the end of the Creator; but because the disposition and concatenation of the whole species led to this. As men are propagated, so are animals; yet no general animal reason arises from their generations: but as

reason alone gives permanency to mankind, it must be propagated, as the characteristic of the species; for without it the species would cease to be.

9. In the species, as a whole, reason has experienced the same fate, as in its individual members; for of individual members the whole consists. It has often been disturbed by the wild passions of men, acting with still more violence from conjunction, turned out of its way for centuries, and lain as if dormant beneath its ashes. To all these disorders Providence has applied no other remedy, than what she administers to individuals; namely, that each fault should be followed by its correspondent evil, and every act of indolence, folly, malice, rashness, and injustice, be its own punishment. But as the species appears in collective bodies in such circumstances, children must suffer for the faults of their parents, the people for the folly of their rulers, and posterity for the indolence of their ancestors; and if they will not, or cannot, correct the evil, they may suffer under it for ages.

10. Thus the weal of the whole is the greatest good of each individual: for it is the inherent right and duty of every one, who suffers under its evils, to ward off these evils from himself, and diminish them for his fellows. Nature has not calculated for sovereigns and states, but for the welfare of men. The former suffer not so speedily for their vices and follies as individuals, because they always reckon only with the whole, in which the miseries of the poor are long suppressed; but the state ultimately suffers, and with so much more violent a concussion. In all these things the laws of retaliation display themselves, as do the laws of motion on the shock of the slightest physical substance; and the greatest sovereign of Europe is not less subject to the natural laws of the human species, than the least of his people. This condition merely binds him, to be an economist of these natural laws; and, by that power, which he enjoys only through the means of other men, to be for other men a wise and good terrestrial divinity.

11. In general history, too, as in the lives of careless individuals, all the follies and vices of mankind are exhausted; till at

length they are compelled by necessity, to learn reason and justice. Whatever can happen, happens; and produces, what from its nature it can produce. This law of nature hinders not even the most eccentric power in its operation; but it confines all by the rule, that one opposing effect destroys another, and what is useful alone ultimately remains. The evil, that destroys another, must submit to order, or destroy itself. The rational and virtuous are uniformly happy in the kingdom of God; for virtue requires external reward, no more than reason covets it. If their works are not accompanied by external success, not to them, but to their age will be the loss: yet neither the discord nor folly of man can for ever counteract them; they will succeed, when their time arrives.

12. Still human Reason pursues her course in the species in general: she invents, before she can apply; she discovers, though evil hands may long abuse her discoveries. Abuse will correct itself; and, through the unwearied zeal of ever-growing Reason, disorder will in time become order. By contending against passions, she strengthens and enlightens herself: from being oppressed in this place, she will fly to that, and extend the sphere of her sway over the Earth. There is nothing enthusiastical in the hope, that, wherever men dwell, at some future period will dwell men rational, just, and happy: happy, not through the means of their own reason alone, but of the common reason of their whole fraternal race.

I bend before this lofty sketch of the general wisdom of Nature with regard to the whole of my fellow creatures the more willingly, as I perceive, that it is Nature's universal plan. The law that sustained the mundane system, and formed each crystal, each worm, each flake of snow, formed and sustained also the human species: it made its own nature the basis of its continuance, and progressive action, as long as men shall exist. All the works of God have their stability in themselves, and in their beautiful consistency: for they all repose, within their determinate limits, on the equilibrium of contending powers, by their intrinsic energy, which reduces these to order. Guided by this clew, I wander through the labyrinth of history, and every where perceive divine harmonious order: for what can any where occur, does occur; what can operate, operates. But reason and justice alone endure: madness and folly destroy the Earth and themselves.

Thus when I hear a Brutus at Philippi, with the dagger in his hand, looking up to the starry sky, say, according to the fabled story. "O Virtue, I believed thee something; but now I perceive, that thou art a dream!" I cannot discover the calm philosopher in the latter part of the complaint. Had he possessed true virtue, this, as well as his reason, would ever have found its own reward, and must have rewarded him even at that moment. But if his virtue were mere Roman patriotism, is it to be wondered, that the weaker yielded to the more strong, that the indolent sunk before the more alert? Thus the victory of Antony, with all its consequences, belonged to the order of things, and to the natural fate of Rome.

In like manner when among us the virtuous man so often complains, that his labours miscarry; that brutal force and oppression prevail upon Earth; and that mankind seem to be given merely as a prey to the passions, and to folly: let the genius of his understanding appear to him, and interrogate him friendly, whether his virtue be of the right kind, and connected with that intelligence, that activity, which alone deserve the name of virtue. Every labour, it must be confessed, does not succeed on all occasions; but do thy best, that it may succeed, and promote its time, its place, and that internal stability, in which real good alone subsists. Rude powers can be regulated only by reason: but they require an actual counterpoise, that is prudence, zeal, and the whole force of goodness, to reduce them to order, and maintain them in it with salutary control.

It is a beautiful dream of future life, that we shall there enjoy friendly intercourse with all the wise and good, who have ever acted for the benefit of mankind, and gone to the regions above with the sweet reward of accomplished labours: but history in a certain degree unlocks to us this arbour of pleasing conversation and intimacy with the intelligent and just of all ages. Here Plato stands before me: there I listen to the friendly interrogations of Socrates, and participate in his last fate. When Marcus Antoninus confers in secret with his own heart, he confers also with mine; and the poor Epictetus issues commands more powerful than those of a king. The afflicted Tully, the unfortunate Boethius, confidentially disclose to me the circumstances of their lives, their sorrows, and their consolations. How ample, yet how narrow, is the human heart! How individual, yet how recurrent, are all its passions and desires, its faults and foibles, its hope and its enjoyment! The problem of humanity has been solved a thousand ways around me, yet every where the result of man's endeavours is the same: "the essence, the object, and the fate of our species, rest on understanding and justice." There is no nobler use of history than this: it unfolds to us as it were the counsels of Fate, and teaches us, insignificant as we are, to act according to God's eternal laws. By teaching us the faults and consequences of every species of irrationality, it assigns us our short and tranquil scene on that great theatre, where Reason and Goodness, contending indeed with wild powers, still, from their nature, create order, and hold on in the path of victory.

Hitherto we have been wandering through the obscure field of ancient nations: we now joyfully advance to approaching day, and view the harvest, that the seed of antiquity has produced for succeeding ages. Rome destroyed the balance of nations; and under her a World bled to death: what new state will arise from this balance destroyed? what new creature will spring from the ashes of so many nations?

III

Near Eastern Beginnings

BOOK XII

We now come to the shores of the Tigris and Euphrates: but how has the face of history changed throughout the whole of this region! Babylon and Nineveh, Ecbatana, Persepolis, and Tyre are no more: nation follows nation, empire follows empire, and of most even their very names, and once celebrated monuments are swept from the Earth. The appellations of Babylonian, Assyrian, Chaldean, Mede, and Phenician, are no longer born by any people; and no distinct traces of their ancient political establishments are now to be found. Their empires and towns are destroyed, and the people are dispersed about under different names.

Whence arises this variation from the deeply imprinted character of the eastern empires? Hindostan and China have been more than once overrun by the Mungals, nay have worn their yoke for centuries; yet neither has Pekin nor Benares vanished, neither the lamas nor bramins are extinct. To me the difference of their destiny appears easily explicable, if we consider the different situations and constitutions of the two regions. In the east of Asia, beyond the great ridge of mountains, the southern nations had but one enemy, the Mungals, to dread. These wandered peaceably for ages on their hills, or in their valleys; and when they overran the neighbouring provinces, their objects were dominion and plunder, not destruction. Accordingly several nations have retained their own constitutions for thousands of years under Mungal sovereigns. The throng of people, that swarmed between the Euxine and the Caspian Sea, down to the Mediterranean, was altogether different; and the Tigris and Euphrates were the principal guides of these hordes in their migrations. The whole of hither Asia was filled with nomades at an early period: and the more flourishing cities, the more polished empires, arose in this fine country, the more did they attract savage nations for the purpose of plunder, or they themselves knew not how to employ their increasing power except in destroying others. How often has Babylon, that delightful centre of the commerce of the east and west, been taken and despoiled! Tyre and Sidon, Jerusalem, Ecbatana, and Nineveh, experienced no better fate: so that this whole region may be considered as the garden of desolation, where one empire subverted another, to be itself destroyed in its turn.

There is no cause to wonder, therefore, that many lost even their very names and left scarcely a trace behind them. For in what were their traces to be left? Most of the people of this region had one language, varied only by different dialects: accordingly, on their downfall, their dialects became confounded with one another, uniting at length in the Chaldee-Syriac-Arabic medley, which now prevails in that region, almost without any discriminating mark of the mingled people. Their states arose from hordes, and returned to hordes again, without any permanent political stamp. The celebrated monuments of a Belus, a Semiramis, and the rest, could still less assure them the eternity of a pyramid: for they were constructed merely of bricks, which, baked in the sun or by fire, and cemented with bitumen, were easily destroyed, if they did not perish beneath the silent foot of time. The despotic sovereignties of the founders of Nineveh and Babylon as gradually decayed; so that in this celebrated part of the World we find nothing to contemplate, but the names once born among the nations by people now no more. We wander over the graves of departed monarchies, and see the ghosts of their former importance on the Earth.

In fact this importance was so great, that, if we include Egypt within this region, no part of the World, Greece and

Rome excepted, has invented and laid the rudiments of so many things for Europe, and through the medium of Europe, for all the nations upon Earth. The number of arts and trades, that appear, from the accounts of the Hebrews, to have been common among many little wandering hordes in these regions, in the earliest periods, is astonishing.[1] Husbandry, with various implements; gardening, fishing, hunting, and in particular the breeding of cattle; the grinding of corn; the baking of bread; the dressing of food; wine; oil; the preparation of wool and leather for garments; spinning, weaving, and sewing; painting, tapestry, and needlework; the coining of money; the engraving of seals, and cutting of gems; the fabrication of glass; coral fishing; mining and metallurgy; various works in metal; the arts of drawing, modelling, and founding; statuary and architecture; music and dancing; writing and poetry; trade by weight and measure; on the sea coasts navigation; in the sciences, some of the elements of astronomy, chronology, and geography; physic and the art of war; arithmetic, geometry, and mechanics; in political institutions, laws, tribunals, religion, contracts, punishments, and a number of moral customs; were all found in use so early among the people of hither Asia, that we could not avoid considering the whole cultivation of this region as the remains of an enlightened anteriour world, if we were led to this by no tradition. Only the people wandering at a distance about the centre of Asia became wild and barbarous, so that sooner or later they were to be civilized a second time in various ways.

CHAPTER 1

Babylon, Assyria, Chaldea

In the extensive region of hither Asia, peopled by wandering hordes, the fertile and pleasant banks of the Tigris and Euphrates must soon have attracted a number of pastoral tribes:

[1] See Goguet's *Origine des Loix, etc.* (Origin of laws, arts, and sciences, and their progress among the ancients), and more particularly Gatterer's *Kurzer Begriff der Weltgeschichte* (Brief sketch of universal history), Vol. I, Göttingen, 1785.

and as they resemble a Paradise, between mountains on the one hand, and deserts on the other, there these tribes must have inclined to fix their residence. At present indeed this country has lost much of its beauty; as it remains almost without cultivation, and has been exposed for centuries to the devastations of predatory hordes: yet particular districts still confirm the general testimony of the ancient writers, whose praises of it knew no bounds.[2] Accordingly this was the birthplace of the first monarchies of history, and an early storehouse of useful arts.

In the course of a wandering life nothing could be more natural, than for some ambitious sheik to conceive the design of appropriating to himself the delightful banks of the Euphrates, and of uniting together a few hordes to maintain the possession of them. The Hebrew chronicle gives this sheik the name of Nimrod, who founded his kingdom with the towns of Babylon, Edessa, Nisibin, and Ctesiphon: and in the neighbourhood it places another, the kingdom of Assyria, with the cities of Resen, Nineveh, Adiabene, and Calah. From the situation of these kingdoms, with their nature and origin, arose the whole of their subsequent destiny, till it terminated in their destruction. For being founded by different races, and bordering too closely on each other, what could follow from the quarrelsome spirit common to the hordes of these regions, but that they must look upon each other as enemies, more than once fall under one sovereignty, and be dispersed various ways, by the incursion of more northern mountaineers? This is the brief history of the kingdoms on the Tigris and Euphrates; which, from such remote periods, and through the mutilated accounts of several nations, cannot have been handed down to us free from confusion. In the origin, spirit, and constitutions of these kingdoms, however, both history and fable agree. They sprang from small beginnings, and wandering tribes: and they ever retained the character of predatory hordes. Even the despotism that arose in them, and the various skill in the arts, for which Babylon was

[2] See Buesching's *Geography*, Vol. V, part I.

particularly famed, are perfectly consistent with the spirit of the country, and the national character of its inhabitants.

For what were the first towns built by these fabled monarchs of the World? Great, fortified hordes; the fixed encampments of a tribe, that enjoyed these fertile regions, and made excursions for the purpose of plundering others. Hence the vast circumference of Babylon, so soon after it was founded on either side the river: hence its huge walls and towers. The walls were lofty thick ramparts of baked clay, erected for the protection of an extensive camp of nomades; and the towers were watchtowers. The whole town, interspersed with gardens, was, according to the expression of Aristotle, a peloponnesus. The country furnished in abundance materials for this sort of architecture natural to nomades; clay, namely, out of which they formed bricks, and bitumen, with which they learned to cement them. Thus nature facilitated their labours; and the foundations being once laid in the nomade style, it was easy to enrich and beautify them, when the horde had made excursions, and returned with booty.

And what were the famous conquests of a Ninus, a Semiramis, and the rest, other than predatory expeditions, like those of the present Arabs, Curdes, and Turcomans? The Assyrians were even by descent mountain banditti, whose names have been handed down to posterity with no other renown, than that of having robbed and plundered. From the remotest periods the Arabs are particularly named in the service of these conquerors of the World: and we know the unchangeable way of life of these people, which will continue as long as the deserts of Arabia shall endure. At a later period the Chaldeans appear on the stage: and these, both from their descent, and their first places of abode, were plundering Curdes.[3] In history they have distinguished themselves by nothing but devastation: for the fame they have acquired for science is probably an honorary title, which they gained as part of their booty in the conquest of Babylon. Thus we may consider the fine country bounded by

[3] See Schlötzer on the Chaldees, in the *Repertorium für die morgenländische Litteratur* (Repertory of oriental literature), Vol. VIII, p. 113.

these streams as the theatre of wandering tribes, or predatory hordes, both in ancient and modern times, who here collected their plunder in strong holds, till at length they sank under the voluptuous warmth of the climate, and, debilitated by luxury, became a prey to others.

The celebrated works of art of a Semiramis, or even a Nebuchadnezzar, cannot easily be supposed to say more. The earliest expeditions of the Assyrians were towards Egypt: the arts of this peaceful civilized country, therefore, furnished in all probability the prototypes for the decoration of Babylon. The famed colossal statue of Belus, and the sculptures on the brick walls of the great city, appear to have been completely in the Egyptian style: and that the fabulous queen repaired to the mountain Bagisthan, to imprint her image on its summit, plainly indicates an imitation of Egypt. For as the southern country afforded her no granite rocks for an eternal monument, she was impelled to this.

The productions of Nebuchadnezzar, likewise, were nothing but colossal statues, palaces of brick, and hanging gardens. What was wanting in art and materials was attempted to be made up by magnitude: and at least a Babylonian character was given to the more feeble monument by pleasant gardens. I do not much regret, therefore, the decay of these huge piles of earth; for, it is probable, they were far from ranking high as works of art: what I wish is, that men would seek among their ruins for tables of Chaldee writing, which are certainly to be found there, according to the testimony of several travellers.[4]

Not properly Egyptian arts, but the arts of erratic hordes, and afterwards of commerce, belonged to this region, as indeed the nature of its situation demanded. The Euphrates was subject to inundations, and consequently required canals to draw off its waters, and enable it to impart fertility to a more extensive district. Hence the invention of waterwheels and pumps, if they were not borrowed from the Egyptians. The country at some distance from this river, which was once inhabited and fruitful,

---

[4] See Della Valle on the ruins near Ardesh, Niebuhr on the heaps of ruins near Hella, etc.

is now sterile, because it is a stranger to the active hand of industry. From the care of cattle to husbandry the step here was easy, as the settled inhabitant was invited to it by Nature herself. The fine fruits of the garden and the field, that spontaneously shot forth on the banks of the Euphrates with uncommon luxuriance, and richly rewarded the little care they required, converted the shepherd, almost without his being conscious of it, into a husbandman and gardener. A wood of beautiful palmtrees gave him food in their fruits, and timber for the erection of a dwelling more secure than his tent. The clay baked with facility assisted him in its construction; and thus the tent was imperceptibly changed for a better, though less moveable habitation. The same earth afforded him vessels, and therewith a hundred conveniences for domestic life. He learned to bake bread, and to dress his victuals, till at length he was led by commerce to those voluptuous feasts and entertainments, for which the Babylonians were famed in very remote times. From making little idols of baked clay, he soon learned to fashion and bake colossal statues; from the models of which to moulds for casting metals the progress was easy. As letters or figures imprinted on the soft clay were rendered firm by the aid of fire, he learned imperceptibly to preserve a knowledge of former times in bricks, and improved on the observations of his predecessors. Even astronomy was a fortunate invention of the wandering tribes of these regions. The shepherd, as he sat feeding his flocks on the beautiful and extensive plain, observed in quiet leisure the rising and setting of the bright stars in his vast and clear horizon. He gave them names, as he gave names to his sheep, and noted down their changes in his memory. These observations were continued on the flat roofs of the houses of Babylon, on which men amused themselves with conversation after the heat of the day: till at length a particular building was erected for the purpose of this attractive and indispensable science, which continued without interruption the records of the celestial periods. Thus has Nature incited man to the acquisition of knowledge and science; so that even these her gifts are as much local productions, as any others upon Earth. At the foot of Caucasus her fountains of naphtha put fire into the hand of man; whence we cannot doubt, that the fable of Prometheus originated there: in the pleasant palm-groves on the banks of the Euphrates she gently moulded the wandering shepherd into an industrious inhabitant of towns and cities.

Another class of Babylonish arts arose from the circumstance of this country's having been from ancient times, as it ever will be, a central point of the commerce between the east and west. No celebrated city arose in the heart of Persia, and no river flowed thence to the sea: but what points of animation were the Hindus and the Ganges, the Tigris and Euphrates! The Persian gulf was near, which early enriched Babylon, by the transport of the merchandize of India, and made it the parent of commercial industry.[5] The splendour of the Babylonians in their linen, tapestry, needlework, and other stuffs, is wellknown: wealth introduced luxury: luxury and industry brought the two sexes closer together than in other Asiatic provinces, to which the reigns of some queens probably not a little contributed. In short, the formation of these people proceeded so entirely from their situation and mode of life, that it would have been a subject for much wonder, had nothing extraordinary been produced from such circumstances, in such a part of the World. Nature has her favourite spots on the Earth, which, particularly on the banks of rivers, and select parts of the seacoast, excite and reward the industry of man. As an Egypt arose on the Nile, a Hindostan on the Ganges; here she created a Nineveh and a Babylon, and in more recent times a Seleucia and Palmyra. Had Alexander attained the accomplishment of his wish, to rule the World from Babylon, how different an aspect would this delightful country have preserved for ages!

The Assyrians and Babylonians shared also in alphabetical writing, the possession of which the wandering tribes of hither Asia had reckoned among their advantages from time immemo-

---

[5] Eichhorn's *Geschichte des Ostindischen Handels* (History of the trade of the East Indies), p. 12; Gatterer's *Einleitung zur synchronistischen Universalhistorie* (Introduction to a synchronistical universal history), p. 77.

rial. I shall not here enter into the question, to what people this noble invention is properly due: suffice it, that all the Aramean tribes boasted of this present of the primitive world, and held hieroglyphics in a sort of religious abomination.[6] I cannot persuade myself, therefore, that hieroglyphics were employed by the Babylonians: their magi interpreted the stars, events, accidents, visions, and secret writing; but not hieroglyphics. Thus the writing of Fate, that appeared to the revelling Belshazzar, consisted of letters and syllables, which, after the oriental manner, appeared to him in confused lines, but not in images.[7] Even the paintings, that Semiramis placed on her walls, the Syrian letters, that she directed to be cut on the rock of her image, confirm the use of letters, without hieroglyphics, among these people, in the remotest times. These alone rendered it possible for the Babylonians so early to have written contracts, chronicles of their kingdom, and a continued series of celestial observations: by these alone they have transmitted themselves to posterity as a civilized people. It is true, neither their astronomical catalogues, nor any of their writings, have reached us, though they were extant in the time of Aristotle: yet, that they once had such gives no small fame to this people.

When we talk of the learning of the Chaldeans, however, we must not measure it by our standard. At Babylon the sciences were confined exclusively to a class of men of learning, who, on the decline of the nation, became ultimately odious impostors. They were called Chaldeans probably from the period when the Chaldeans ruled over Babylon: for the class of literati had been a regular order of the state, established by the government, from the time of Belus: and it is very likely, that this class, by way of flattery to their rulers, assumed the name of their nation. They were the philosophers of the court, and accordingly stooped to all the base arts and deceptions of court philosophy. In these times, it may be presumed, they added as little to their ancient stores, as the Chinese tribunal to the improvement of learning in China.

---

[6] Of this elsewhere.
[7] Daniel 5:25.

The proximity of the mountains, from which so many uncivilized nations came thronging down, was in some respects fortunate, in others unfortunate, to this delightful country. The Assyrian and Babylonian empires were subdued by the Chaldeans and Medes, and these were conquered by the Persians, till at length the whole became a subjugated desert, and the seat of empire was transferred to a more northern region. Thus we have not much to learn from these empires; either in war or politics. Their mode of attack was rude, their conquests only plunderings, their polity the miserable mode of governing by satraps, which has almost always prevailed among the orientals in these parts. Hence the permanent form of these monarchies: hence the frequent revolts against them, and their total overthrow by the capture of a single city, or one or two general battles. Indeed, soon after the empire was first overturned, Arbaces endeavoured to establish a sort of connected aristocracy of satraps: but he did not succeed; as all the Median and Aramean tribes in general knew no mode of government except the despotic. Their mode of life had been that of nomades: accordingly their idea of a king was that of a sheik, and father of a family, and this left no room for political liberty, or the joint sway of many. As one Sun enlightens the Heavens, so should there be but one ruler on Earth, and he soon assumed all the splendour of the Sun, all the glory of a terrestrial divinity. Every thing flowed from his favour: every thing attached to his person: in him the state lived, and with him it commonly terminated. A haram was the court of the prince: he was acquainted with nothing but silver and gold, men-servants and maid-servants, lands that he possessed as fields of pasture, and herds of men whom he drove wherever he pleased, if indeed he forbore from slaughtering them. Barbarous government of wandering hordes! yet occasionally, though but seldom, it enjoyed a good prince, the true shepherd and father of his people.

CHAPTER 2

Medes and Persians

THE Medes are known in the history of the World for warlike deeds and luxury; but have never distinguished themselves by new inventions, or improvements in the constitution of the state. They were mountaineers, brave and skilled in horsemanship, the natives of a northern country for the most part uncultivated. With these qualifications, they subverted the ancient Assyrian empire, the sultans of which indolently slumbered in their harams; and soon withdrew themselves from the new empire of Assyria. But they were as quickly subjected by their sagacious Dejoces to a rigorous monarchical government, which at length exceeded the Persian itself in luxury and splendour. At length they were united, under Cyrus the great, with that multitude of nations, which exalted the Persian monarchs into sovereigns of the World.

If there be any prince, with whom history seems to deviate into fiction, it is Cyrus, the founder of the Persian empire; whether we read the accounts of this child of the gods, the conqueror and lawgiver of nations, given by the Hebrews or the Persians, Herodotus or Xenophon. Unquestionably the last-mentioned pleasing historian, who caught the idea of a Cyropedia from his tutor, collected some truths concerning him, during his campaigns in Asia: but as Cyrus had long been dead, he could have heard them only after the Asiatic manner, in that style of exaggerated praise, which these people always employ in their accounts of their kings and heroes. Thus Xenophon was to Cyrus, what Homer was to Ulysses and Achilles, with regard to whom the poet had some truths, on which to build. To us, however, it is of little importance, which of the two deals most in fiction: it is sufficient for our purpose, that Cyrus subdued Asia, and founded an empire, which extended from the Hindus to the Mediterranean Sea. If Xenophon have truly described the manners of the ancient Persians, among whom Cyrus was educated; the German may be proud, that he is probably of a race allied to theirs, and may the Cyropedia be read by every prince in Germany.

But, thou great and good Cyrus, could my voice reach thy grave in Pasagarda, it should interrogate thy dust, for what purpose thou becamest such a conqueror. In the youthful course of thy victories, didst thou ask thyself of what use the innumerable nations, the unbounded regions, subjected to thy name, would be to thyself and thy posterity? Could thy spirit be always present to them? could it continue to live and operate on all succeeding generations? And if not, what a burden didst thou impose on thy successors, in giving them to wear the royal robe made up of such complicated patches? Its parts could not fail to break asunder, or press the wearer down. This was the history of Persia under the successors of Cyrus. His spirit of conquest set before them so vast an object, that they aimed at enlarging the empire, when it could no longer be enlarged: thus they roamed and ravaged on all sides, till the ambition of a provoked enemy brought them to a melancholy end. The Persian empire subsisted scarcely two centuries; and it is wonderful, that its duration was so long; for its root was so small, and its branches so extensive, that it must of necessity fall to the ground.

Whenever the empire of humanity shall be established among mankind, the mad spirit of conquest, which necessarily destroys itself in a few generations, will immediately be renounced at her dictates. You drive men like cattle; and join them together as if they were inanimate substances, without reflecting, that they have minds, and that perhaps the last, the outermost piece of the fabric will break off, and crush the builder. A kingdom consisting of a single nation is a family, a wellregulated household: it reposes on itself, for it is founded by Nature, and stands and falls by time alone. An empire formed by forcing together a hundred nations, and a hundred and fifty provinces, is no body public, but a monster.

Such was the Persian empire from the beginning; though it became more evident after the time of Cyrus. His son, in every thing else different from his father, was desirous of extending his conquests still farther; and so madly attacked Egypt and Ethiopia, that scarcely famine itself could repel him from the deserts. What did he and his empire gain by it? or in what did he benefit the conquered lands? He ravaged Egypt, and destroyed the splendid temples and other monuments of art in Thebes. Senseless destroyer! Slaughtered generations are replaced by other generations succeeding: but such works are never to be restored. Even now they lie in ruins, unexplored, and hardly to be distinguished: every traveller regrets the madness of the sot, who robbed us of these treasures of antiquity for no cause, and to no end.

Scarcely had Cambyses fallen a victim to his own folly, when even the wiser Darius set out from the point, where he had left off. He attacked the Scythians and Hindoos: he plundered Thrace and Macedonia: yet all that he gained was the dispersion of some sparks among the Macedonians, that in time burst out into a flame, by which the last king of his name was consumed. The Greeks he attacked with little success; and his successor Xerxes assailed them with less. Now if we read the catalogue of ships and men employed in the military expeditions of these despots, and furnished to the mad conqueror by the whole Persian empire; if we consider the seas of blood, that flowed in every revolt of unjustly subjugated countries on the Euphrates, the Nile,, the Hindus, the Halys, and the Araxes, for no other reason but that what once was called Persian might retain the name of Persian still; who would shed feminine tears, such as Xerxes wept at the sight of his innocent flock destined for slaughter, and not rather tears of blood, tears of indignation, that such a senseless empire, and so inimical to mankind, should bear the stamp of a Cyrus on its forehead? Did any Persian ravager of the World found such kingdoms, cities, and edifices, as he destroyed, or endeavoured to destroy; Babylon, Thebes, Sidon, Greece, and Athens? Was any one of them capable of founding such?

It is a rigorous yet beneficent law of fate, that all overgrown power, as well as all evil, should destroy itself. The decline of Persia commenced with the death of Cyrus: for though it maintained its external splendour for a century, particularly in consequence of the measures taken by Darius, the worm, that gnaws the vitals of every despotic empire, lurked within. Cyrus divided his dominions into viceroyalties; and these he kept in due subjection by his own superintendence, having established a speedy communication with them all, and watching over the whole himself. Darius divided the empire, or at least his court, still more nicely, and stood on his elevated station as a just and active ruler. But the great kings, born to the throne of despotism, soon became effeminate tyrants. Xerxes, even on his disgraceful flight from Greece, when far other thoughts should have occupied his mind, began a scandalous amour at Sardis. Most of his successors trod in the same steps: and thus corruptions, revolts, conspiracies, assassinations, unsuccessful enterprises, and the like, are almost the only remarkable occurrences, that the latter history of Persia affords. The minds of the nobles were depraved, and those of the commonalty participated in the corruption. At length no sovereign was secure of his life; and the throne tottered even under the best princes: till Alexander burst into Asia, and in a few battles put an end to the internally unsettled empire. Unhappily this fell out under a monarch, who deserved a better fate: he innocently suffered for the sins of his forefathers, and died by the basest treachery. If any history in the World proclaim in conspicuous characters, that licentiousness destroys itself, that an unlimited and almost lawless power is the most fearful weakness, and that every effeminate government conducted by satraps is the most infallible poison, as well for the prince as for the people; it is the history of Persia.

For these reasons, there was not a single nation, on which the empire of Persia had a happy influence: it destroyed, and did not build up: it compelled the provinces to pay disgraceful tributes, one to the queen's girdle, another to her head-dress, a third to her necklace; but it did not bind them together by better laws and institutions. All the splendour, all the superhuman pomp, all the divine homage, of these monarchs, are now no more: their favourites and satraps are dust, like themselves; and the gold they extorted is perhaps equally buried in the earth. Their very history is a fable: a fable which, coming from the mouth of a Greek and of an Asiatic, can scarcely be reconciled. Even the ancient languages of Persia are dead: and the sole monuments of its magnificence, the ruins of Persepolis, remain, with their elegant letters and colossal figures, hitherto inexplicable. Fate has taken vengeance on these sultans: they are swept away from the face of the Earth, as if by the pestilent simoom, and where their memory survives, as among the Greeks, it survives with disgrace, the basis of more famed and more to be admired greatness.

Time has favoured us with no mental production of the Persians, except the books of Zoroaster, if they could be proved to be genuine.[8] As a whole, however, they agree so little with many other accounts of the religion of these people; they bear, too, such evident marks of a mixture with later opinions of the Bramins and Christians; that the groundwork alone can be admitted to be genuine, and this admits of easy explanation. The ancient Persians, for example, were, like all rude nations, and particularly mountaineers, worshippers of the vital elements of the World: but as they quitted their uncivilized state, and raised themselves by their victories almost to the highest pinnacle of luxury; it was necessary, according to the mode of Asia, that they should have a more refined system or ceremonial of religion.

With this they were furnished by Zoroaster, or Zerdusht, under the auspices of Darius Hystaspes. The ceremonial of the Persian government is evidently the basis of this system. As seven princes stood round the throne of the king, seven spirits stand before God, and execute his commands throughout the World. Ormuzd, the good power of light, had incessantly to contend against Ahriman, the prince of darkness, while every good being aided him in the conflict: a political idea, which the personification of the enemies of Persia, who appear throughout the Zend-Avesta as the servants of Ahriman, as evil spirits, evidently elucidates. All the moral ordinances of this religion too are politic: they relate to purity of body and mind, domestic harmony, and reciprocity of kind actions: they recommend agriculture, and the planting of useful trees; the extermination of vermin, which appear as an army of evil spirits in bodily form; attention to decorum; early and prolific marriages; the education of children; honouring the king and his servants; love towards the state: and all these after the Persian manner. In

[8] *Zend-Avesta, Ouvrage de Zoroastre* (Zend-Avesta, a work of Zoroaster), by Anquetil du Perron, Paris, 1771.

short, the basis of this system appears obviously as a political religion, such as at the time of Darius could no where have been invented and introduced, except in the Persian empire. Ancient national ideas and opinions, too, must necessarily lie at the bottom of this superstition. Hence the adoration of fire, which was undoubtedly an ancient religious worship, in the neighbourhood of the springs of naphtha, near the Caspian Sea. Hence so many superstitious practices for the purification of the body; and that extreme fear of demons, which, in almost every sensible object, forms the base of the prayers, vows, and sacred ceremonies of the Parsees. All these show the low degree of mental cultivation attained by the people, for whose benefit this religion was invented: and this is by no means inconsistent with the idea we entertain of the ancient Persians. Lastly, the small part of this system, which refers to general notions of nature, is altogether drawn from the doctrines of the magi, which it merely refines and exalts in its own manner. It subjects the two principles of creation, light and darkness, to an infinitely superiour being, which it styles boundless time; and lets the good every where overcome the evil, and ultimately so swallow it up, that every thing terminates in a holy kingdom of light. Contemplated on this side the political religion of Zoroaster is a kind of philosophical theodicy, such as he could offer to the age in which he lived, and the notions that then prevailed.

In this origin we perceive the cause, why the religion of Zoroaster could not possess the stability of the institutions of the Bramins and lamas. The despotic empire was established long before it; and thus it was or became only a sort of monkish religion, adapted to the political system. Now though Darius suppressed by force the magi, who formed a distinct body of men in the Persian empire; and was eager to introduce this religion, which laid spiritual fetters alone on the monarch; it could never be any thing more than a sect, though it was the ruling sect for a century. Accordingly the worship of fire extended widely: to the left, beyond Media, as far as Cappadocia, where its temples were standing even in the days of Strabo; to the right, as far as the Hindus. But as the Persian empire completely sunk beneath the fortune of Alexander, this, the religion of the state, also found an end. Its seven amshaspands served no more, and the image of Ormuzd no longer sat on the Persian throne. Its season was past, and it became an empty shadow, as is the religion of the Hindoos out of their own country. By the Greeks it was tolerated; at length it was persecuted with unspeakable rigour by the Mohammedans; and in consequence its melancholy remnant took flight to a corner of India; where, like a ruin of antiquity, without end or purpose, it continues its ancient faith and superstition, calculated for the Persian empire alone, and has amplified it with the opinions of the nations among whom it has been thrown by fate, probably without being conscious of the change. Such an augmentation naturally arises out of the course of time and events: for every religion, when forced from its own soil and sphere, must necessarily be influenced by the living world around it. For the rest, the generality of Parsees in India are quiet, peaceable, industrious people, and, considered as a society, surpass many other religious sects. They assist their poor with great zeal, and expel every irreclaimably immoral person from their community.[9]

CHAPTER 3
The Hebrews

THE descendants of Heber make a very diminutive figure, when we consider them immediately after the Persians. Their country was small; and the part they acted on the stage of the World, both in and out of this country, was insignificant, as they seldom appeared in the character of conquerors. Yet through the will of Fate, and a series of events, the causes of which are easy to be traced, they have had more influence on other nations, than any people of Asia: nay in some degree, through the mediums of Christianity and Mohammedanism, they have been the ground work of enlightening the greater part of the World.

That the Hebrews had written annals of their actions, at a time in which most of the now enlightened nations were totally

[9] See Niebuhr's *Travels.*

ignorant of writing, annals which they ventured to carry up to the beginning of the World, distinguishes them in an eminent manner. But they are still more advantageously distinguished by this, that they neither derived their account from hieroglyphics, nor obscured it by them; for it is taken merely from family chronicles, and interwoven with historical tales or poems; and its value as history is evidently increased by this simplicity of form. This account, too, derives singular weight from its having been preserved for some thousands of years, with almost superstitious scrupulosity, as a divine prerogative of their race, and introduced by Christianity into nations, that have examined and questioned, explained and used it, with a spirit of freedom unknown to the Jews. It is indeed remarkable, that the accounts of these people given by other nations, by Manetho the Egyptian in particular, should differ so widely from the history of the Hebrews themselves: yet, if the latter be impartially considered, and the spirit of the narrative understood, it certainly deserves more credit, than the slanders of foreign enemies, by whom the Jews were despised. I scruple not, therefore, to take the history of the Hebrews, as related by themselves, for my groundwork: begging the reader, at the same time, not absolutely to reject the tales of their enemies with contempt, but merely to read them with caution.

Thus, according to the most ancient national stories of the Hebrews, their progenitor passed the Euphrates as sheik of a wandering horde, and at last arrived in Palestine. Here he found room without opposition, to pursue the pastoral life of his ancestors, and worship the god of his fathers after the manner of his tribe. His posterity of the third generation were led into Egypt by the singular good fortune of one of their family, and there continued to follow the pastoral life, without mixing with the inhabitants of the country; till, it is not exactly known in what generation, they were emancipated by their future legislator from the contempt and oppression, which from their character of shepherds they must have experienced among those people, and conducted into Arabia. Here the great man, the greatest these people had ever had, completed his work; and gave them a constitution, founded on the religion and mode of life of their fathers it is true, but so intermingled with Egyptian polity, as on the one hand to raise them from a wandering horde to the state of a cultivated nation, yet on the other to wean them completely from Egypt, so that they were never after desirous of treading the swarthy soil. All the laws of Moses evince wonderful reflection: they extend from the greatest to the smallest things, to sway the spirit of the nation in every circumstance of life, and to be, as Moses frequently repeats, an everlasting law.

This profound system of laws was by no means the production of a moment: the legislator added to it as circumstances required, and before his death bound the whole nation to the observance of its future political constitution. For forty years he exacted a strict obedience to his injunctions: perhaps so long a time was consumed by the people in the deserts of Arabia, that, the first stubborn generation being dead, a people brought up to these customs might settle in the land of its fathers properly qualified for their exercise.

But the wish of this patriotic man was not fulfilled. The aged Moses died on the confines of the land he sought; and when his successor entered it, he enjoyed not sufficient authority and respect, to follow completely the plan of the lawgiver. The Hebrews pursued not their conquests so far as they ought: they were too precipitate in dividing the land, and sitting down in peace. The more potent tribes first took to themselves the largest portions, so that their weaker brethren could scarcely find a settlement, and one of the tribes indeed was under the necessity of being divided.[10] Beside this, many smaller nations remained in the country: so that the Israelites retained their bitterest hereditary enemies among them, and destroyed that external and internal compact rotundity, which alone could secure their prescribed limits.

From this incomplete establishment, that series of insecure times, which scarcely ever permitted the encroaching people to

[10] The tribe of Dan got a corner above and to the left of the land. See the *Geist der Ebraischen Poesie* (Spirit of Hebrew poetry), Vol. II.

be at rest, could not but ensue. The leaders, that necessity raised up, were for the most part to be considered only as successful partisans: and when at length the people came to be governed by kings, these had so much to do with their land divided into tribes, that the third was the last who reigned over the whole of the disjointed realm. Five sixths of the kingdom withdrew from his successor; and how could two such feeble governments subsist in the neighbourhood of powerful enemies, to whose attacks they were incessantly exposed? The kingdom of Israel had properly no regular constitution; and it embraced the worship of foreign gods, in order to preclude any connexion with its rival, who worshipped the legitimate god of its own land. It was natural, that, according to the language of these people, there should be no king in Israel that feared the Lord: for, if there had, his people would have gone up to Jerusalem to worship, and his dominion, returning to the monarchy from which it had been torn, would have continued no longer in his hands. Thus they wallowed in the most wretched imitation of foreign manners and customs, till the king of Assyria came, and plundered the little realm, as a boy would rob a bird's-nest. The other kingdom, which at least had the support of the ancient constitution, established by two potent kings, and a fortified capital, held out some time longer; though only till a more powerful victor thought it worth his attention. The spoiler Nebuchadnezzar came, and made its feeble monarchs first tributaries, and lastly, after they revolted, slaves. The country was ravaged, the capital was rased, and Judah led to Babylon in as disgraceful captivity, as Israel had been to Media. Thus, considered as a state, scarcely any nation exhibits a more contemptible figure in history than this, the reigns of two of its kings excepted.

What was the cause of all this? In my opinion it is clear, from the course of the narrative itself: for it was impossible, that a nation with such a defective constitution, both internally and externally, should prosper in this part of the World. If David overran the desert as far as the banks of the Euphrates, and thereby only stirred up greater enemies against his successor, could he thus give the nation the stability it wanted, particularly as the seat of government was fixed nearly at the southern extremity of the kingdom? His son introduced foreign wives, trade, and luxury into the land: into a country, that, like the united cantons of Switzerland, was capable of supporting husbandmen and shepherds alone, and actually had such in great multitudes to support. Besides, as he carried on his trade for the most part not by means of his own nation, but of the Edomites, whom he had conquered, luxury was pernicious to his kingdom. For the rest, since the time of Moses no second legislator had been found among these people, who was capable of bringing back the state, shattered from its beginning, to a fundamental constitution suitable to the times. The learned class soon declined; they who were zealous for the laws of the land had voices, but not the arm of power; the kings were for the most part either effeminate, or creatures of the priests. Thus two things diametrically opposite, the refined nomocracy, on which Moses had settled the constitution, and a sort of theocratic monarchy, such as prevailed among all the nations of this region of despotism, contended together: and thus the law of Moses became a law of bondage to a people, to whom it was intended to have been a law of political liberty.

In the course of time the case became altered, but not improved. When the Jews, set at liberty by Cyrus, returned from bondage, much diminished in number, they had learned many other things, but no genuine political constitution. How, indeed, was the knowledge of such a constitution to have been acquired in Assyria or Chaldea? Their sentiments fluctuated between monarchical and sacerdotal government: they built a temple, as if this would have revived the times of Moses and Solomon: their religion was pharisaical; their learning, a minute nibbling at syllables, and this confined to a single book; their patriotism, a slavish attachment to ancient laws misunderstood, so as to render them ridiculous or contemptible to all the neighbouring nations. Their only hope and consolation rested on some ancient prophecies, which, equally misconceived, were supposed to promise them the illusory sovereignty of the

World. Thus they lived and suffered for some centuries, under the Greeks of Syria, the Idumeans, and the Romans; till at length, through an animosity, to which history scarce exhibits a parallel, both the metropolis and the rest of the country were destroyed, in a manner that grieved the humane conqueror himself. On this they were dispersed through all the territories of the Roman empire; and with the dispersion such an influence of the Jews upon the human race commenced, as could hardly have been conceived from a land of such small extent; since these people had never distinguished themselves, in the whole course of their history, as skilled in war or politics, and still less as inventors in the arts and sciences.

But, shortly before the downfall of the Jewish state, Christianity arose in the heart of it, and in the beginning not only retained its connexion with Judaism, and consequently admitted the sacred writings of the Jews, but even rested principally on these the divine mission of its Messiah. Thus through Christianity the books of the Jews were introduced to every nation, that embraced the Christian doctrines; and according to the manner in which they have been understood, and the use that has been made of them, they have benefited or injured the whole Christian World. Their effect was good, so far as in them Moses made the doctrine of one god, creator of the World, the basis of all religion and philosophy, and, in many poems and precepts throughout these writings, spoke of this god with a dignity and importance, a gratitude and resignation, of which few examples are to be found in any other human work. We need not compare these books with the Shoo-King of the Chinese, or the Sadder and Zend-Avesta of the Persians, to perceive the superiority of the Hebrew scriptures over all the other religious writings of antiquity: a comparison of them with the much more recent Koran, even though Mohammed availed himself of the doctrines both of the Jews and Christians, will evince their incontestable preeminence. It was gratifying also to the curiosity of the human mind, to find in these books such popular answers to the questions respecting the age and creation of the World, the origin of evil, and the like, as every man could understand and comprehend: to say nothing of the instructive history of the nation, and the pure morality of several books in the collection. Be the Jewish computation of time as it may, it afforded a received and general standard, and a thread with which to connect the events of universal history. Many other advantages of philology, exegesis, and dialectic, may be passed over; as indeed they might have been obtained from other works. In all these ways the writings of the Hebrews unquestionably have had an advantageous effect in the history of mankind.

With all these advantages, however, it is equally incontestable, that the misconception and abuse of these writings have been detrimental to the human mind in various respects; and the more as they have operated upon it under the claim of being divine. How many absurd cosmogonies have been framed from the simple and sublime history of the creation given by Moses! How many rigid doctrines, and unsatisfactory hypotheses, have been spun from his serpent and apple! For ages the forty days of the deluge have formed the peg, on which natural historians have deemed it indispensable to hang all the phenomena of the structure of our Earth: and for no less a time the historians of the human race have chained down all the nations of the Earth to the people of God, and a misunderstood prophetic vision of four monarchies. Thus many histories have been mutilated, that they might be explained by a Hebrew name: the whole system of mankind, of the Earth, and of the Sun, has been narrowed, for the purpose of vindicating the Sun of Joshua, and a few years in the duration of the World, the precise determination of which could never be the object of these writings. How many great men, among whom even a Newton himself is to be reckoned, have the Jewish chronology and the Apocalypse robbed of time, that might have been employed in more useful inquiries! Nay even with regard to morality and political institutions, the writings of the Hebrews, by being misconceived and misapplied, have imposed fetters on the minds of those nations, by which they have been acknowledged. For want of making a distinction between different periods, and different degrees of intellectual cultivation, the intolerant spirit of the Jewish religion has been deemed a pattern for Christians to follow: and passages of the Old Testament have been adduced to justify the inconsistent attempt of making Christianity, which knows no constraint, and is merely a moral system, a Judaical religion of the state. In like manner it is undeniable, that the ceremonies of the Temple, and even the language of the Hebrew worship, have influenced the religious service of all Christian nations, their hymns, their litanies, and the oratory of their pulpits; so that in many instances the oriental idiom pervades all their prayers. The laws of Moses were intended for that climate, and for a nation very differently constituted: their laws and political constitution, therefore, adapt themselves fundamentally to no Christian people. Thus the choicest good, through various misapplication, verges upon numerous evils. Do not the sacred elements of nature effect destruction? may not the most efficacious medicines act as the most virulent poison?

The nation of the Jews itself, since its dispersion, has done service or injury by its presence to the people of the Earth, according as they have used it. In the early ages Christians were considered as Jews, and despised or oppressed in common with them; they rendering themselves liable to many of the reproaches of the Jews, pride, superstition, and antipathy to other nations. Afterwards, when the Christians themselves became oppressors of the Jews, they almost every where gave them an opportunity of engrossing the internal trade of the country, particularly that in money, by their application as individuals, and the manner in which they were spread abroad as a people; so that the less civilized nations of Europe voluntarily became the slaves of their usury. The system of exchange was not invented by them, it is true, but they soon brought it to perfection; their insecurity in Mohammedan and Christian countries rendering it indispensable to them. Thus this widely diffused republic of cunning usurers unquestionably restrained many nations of Europe for a long time from exercising their own industry in trade; for these thought themselves above a

Jewish occupation, and were as little inclined to learn this intelligent and refined species of industry from the servile treasurers of the holy Roman world, as the Spartans to be taught agriculture by their helotes. Should any one collect a history of the Jews from all the countries, into which they have been dispersed, he would exhibit a picture of mankind, equally remarkable in a natural and political view: for no people upon Earth have been spread abroad like these; no people upon Earth have remained so distinguishable and active in all climates.

Let no one, however, from this, superstitiously infer a revolution, at some period or other to be wrought by these people on all the nations of the Earth. All that was intended to be wrought has probably been accomplished; and neither in the people themselves, nor in historical analogy, can we discover the least foundation of any other. The continuance of the Jews is as naturally to be explained, as that of the Bramins, Parsees, or gipsies.

No one, in the mean time, will deny to a people, that has been such an active instrument in the hand of Fate, those great qualities, which are conspicuous in its whole history. Ingenious, adroit, and laborious, the Jews have always borne themselves up under the severest oppression from other nations; as for more than forty years in the deserts of Arabia. They have not wanted warlike courage also; as the times of David and the Maccabees show, and still more the last and most dreadful downfall of their state. In their own country they were once a laborious, industrious people; who, like the Japanese, contrived by means of artificial terraces, to cultivate their naked mountains to the summit, and raised an incredible number of inhabitants on a narrow space, which was never the first in the World for fertility. In the arts, it is true, the Jews were always inexpert, though their country was situate between Egypt and Phenicia; for even Solomon was obliged to employ foreign workmen in the construction of his temple. In like manner, though they possessed for some time the ports of the Red Sea, and dwelt so near the shores of the Mediterranean, they never became a seafaring people, in a situation so favourable for engrossing the commerce of the World, and with a population their country could scarcely support. Like the Egyptians they dreaded the sea, and always chose rather to live among other nations: a feature of the national character, which Moses powerfully exerted himself to eradicate. In short, they were a people spoiled in their education, because they never arrived at a maturity of political cultivation on their own soil, and consequently not to any true sentiment of liberty and honour. In science, their most eminent men have displayed more servile punctuality and order, than productive freedom of mind; and their situation has almost ever denied them the virtues of a patriot. The people of God, whose country was once given them by Heaven itself, have been for thousands of years, nay almost from their beginning, parasitical plants on the trunks of other nations; a race of cunning brokers, almost throughout the whole World; who, in spite of all oppression, have never been inspired with an ardent passion for their own honour, for a habitation, for a country, of their own.

CHAPTER 4

Phenicia and Carthage

THE Phenicians have rendered the World service in a very different manner. They invented glass, one of the noblest implements in the hands of man; and the accidental occasion of its invention at the mouth of the river Belus is recorded in history. Dwelling on the seacoast, they were addicted to navigation from time immemorial; for Semiramis procured her fleet to be built by the Phenicians. From small vessels they gradually rose to ships of considerable burden: they learned to steer their course by the stars, particularly by the Greater Bear: and at length, being attacked, they were obliged to learn the art of naval war. They sailed all over the Mediterranean, as far as the strait of Gibraltar; they visited Britain with their ships; and it is probable, that from the Red Sea they more than once circumnavigated Africa. This they did, not in the character of conquerors, but in that of merchants, and founders of colonies. Lands, which the sea had divided, they connected together by traffic, by language, and by the productions of art; and they ingeniously devised every thing, by which this traffic could be promoted. They learned the art of arithmetic, to stamp metals, and to form them into various utensils and ornaments. They discovered the purple dye, manufactured fine Sidonian linen, procured tin and lead from Britain, silver from Spain, amber from the Baltic, and gold from Africa, for which they bartered Asiatic productions. Thus the whole of the Mediterranean formed a part of their kingdom, their colonies were planted up and down its coasts, and Tartessus in Spain was the celebrated emporium of their commerce between three quarters of the Globe. However extensive or confined the knowledge they may have imparted to Europeans, the gift of letters, which the Greeks acquired from them, was at least equal in value to every thing besides.

But how came this people thus meritoriously to distinguish itself in the arts? Was it perchance a fortunate race of the primeval world, advantageously endowed by Nature in mental and corporal faculties? By no means. According to all the accounts we have of the Phenicians, they were dwellers in caves, despised, and perhaps driven from their homes, the troglodytes or gipsies of this country. We first find them on the shores of the Red Sea, the barren soil of which probably afforded them but meagre nutriment: and when they had migrated to the coast of the Mediterranean, they long retained their barbarous manners, their inhuman religion, and even their habitations among the rocks of Canaan. Every one knows the description given of the ancient inhabitants of Canaan; and that it is not exaggerated, appears as well from the relics of barbarous superstition, which for a long time remained even in Carthage itself, as from the similar picture of the Arabian troglodytes in Job.[11] The manners of the Phenician seamen, too, were not esteemed by foreign nations: they were pilfering, piratical, sensual, and treacherous; so that Punic faith and honesty became a proverbial stigma.[12]

[11] Job 30:3–8.

[12] See the account which Eumæus gives of the Phenicians, *Odyss.* xv, 414, etc.

Necessity, and circumstances, are for the most part the instruments, that make men every thing. In the deserts near the Red Sea, where the Phenicians lived partly it may be presumed on fish, hunger introduced them to an acquaintance with the watery element; so that, when they reached the shores of the Mediterranean, they were already prepared to launch out on a more extensive sea. What has formed the Dutch, what most other seafaring nations? "Necessity, situation, and accident." [13] All the nations of the race of Shem, believing they had an exclusive claim to the whole of Asia, hated and despised the Phenicians. Thus the descendants of Ham, as intruding foreigners, were confined to the sea and its sterile shores. Now that the Phenicians should find the Mediterranean abounding with ports and islands, so that they gradually proceeded from land to land, from coast to coast, and at length beyond the Pillars of Hercules, and were enabled to gather such a rich harvest by their trade with the uncultivated nations of Europe, arose from the circumstances of the case, from the fortunate situation created for them by Nature herself. As in the primeval period the basin of the Mediterranean Sea was scooped out between the Pyrenees, the Alps, the Appennines, and Atlas, and its islands and points of land gradually rose to view, forming harbours and habitable lands, the way to the civilization of Europe was pointed out by eternal destiny. Had the three quarters of our hemisphere been united in one, Europe would now probably have been as little civilized as Tatary, or the interiour of Africa: at least it would have been much more slowly civilized, and in a different way. To the Mediterranean alone our Earth is indebted for a Phenicia and a Greece, an Etruria and a Rome, a Spain and a Carthage; and through the former four of these did Europe attain the degree of civilization it now enjoys.

---

[13] Eichhorn has shown this in the case of Angria's people also: see *Geschichte des Ostindischen Handels* (History of the East Indian Trade), p. 15, 16. Poverty and oppression have been commonly the causes, that produced most commercial nations, as the Venetians, the Malays, and others, testify.

The situation of Phenicia on the land side was equally happy. Behind it lay the whole of the fine country of Asia, with its wares and inventions with an inland trade long before established. Accordingly it enjoyed the advantages not only of foreign industry, but of the riches, with which Nature had endowed this quarter of the Globe, and the long labours of antiquity. The people of Europe gave the name of Phenician to letters, which the Phenicians brought into Europe, but of which it is probable they were not the inventors. So it is to be presumed the Egyptians, Babylonians, and Hindoos pursued the art of weaving before the Sidonians; as it is a wellknown mode of speaking, both in ancient and modern times, to name wares not from the place where they are manufactured, but from the place that trades in them. The skill of the Phenicians in architecture may be known from Solomon's temple; which certainly was not to be compared with any one in Egypt, as in it two wretched columns were looked upon as wonders. Their only architectural remains are those vast caverns in Phenicia and Canaan, which evince both their troglodytic taste and descent. The people, of Egyptian race, undoubtedly rejoiced, to find in this region mountains, in which they could form their habitations and graves, storehouses and temples. The caves still remain; but their contents have vanished. The archives and collections of books, also, which the Phenicians possessed in the times of their splendour, are all destroyed; and the Greeks, by whom their history was written, no longer exist.

Now if we compare these industrious, flourishing commercial towns, with the conquering states on the Euphrates, the Tigris, and Mount Caucasus, no one will hesitate, to which to give the preference, in respect to the history of mankind. The conquerors conquered for themselves: the commercial nations served themselves and others. They rendered the wealth, industry, and science of a certain part of the World common to all; and thus could not avoid promoting humanity, perhaps without the design. No conqueror, therefore, disturbs the course of nature so much, as he who destroys flourishing commercial towns: for the ruin of these generally occasions the decline of the industry and manufactures of whole countries and regions, unless some neighbouring place quickly succeeded them. In this the coast of Phenicia was happy: its situation renders it indispensable to the trade of Asia. When Nebuchadnezzar depressed Sidon, Tyre sprang up: when the Macedonian conqueror destroyed Tyre, Alexandria flourished: but commerce never completely deserted this region. Carthage, too, was benefited by the destruction of the ancient wealthy Tyre, but not with consequences so important to Europe, as those of the more early Phenician commerce; for the time was gone by.

The internal constitution of the Phenicians has been generally considered as the first transition from the monarchies of Asia to a sort of republic, which commerce requires. The despotic power of the kings in their states was weakened, so that they never attempted conquests. Tyre was a long time ruled by suffetes; and this form of government obtained a more firm establishment in Carthage: thus these two states are the first precedents of great commercial republics in history, and their colonies are the first examples of a more useful and refined dominion, than those which a Nebuchadnezzar and a Cambyses established. This was a great step in the civilization of mankind. Thus commerce awakened industry: the sea repressed or set bounds to the conqueror, and gradually changed him, against his will, from a subjugating robber to a peaceful negotiator. Mutual wants, and particularly the more feeble power of a stranger on a distant shore, gave birth to the first more equitable intercourse between nations. How do the ancient Phenicians put to shame the Europeans for their senseless conduct, when, in so much later ages, and with so much more skill in the arts, they discovered the two Indies! These made slaves, preached the cross, and exterminated the natives: those, in the proper sense of the term, conquered nothing: they planted colonies, they built towns, and roused the industry of the nations, which, after all the deceptions of the Phenicians, learned at length to know and profit by their own treasures. Will any part of the Globe be indebted to Europe rich in arts, so much as Greece was indebted to the less cultivated Phenicians?

The influence of Carthage on the nations of Europe was far from being so important as that of Phenicia: owing assuredly to the change of time, situation, and the state of things. As a colony from Tyre, it was not without difficulty, that it established itself on the distant shore of Africa: and being obliged to fight for the extension of its boundary, it gradually imbibed a lust of conquest. Hence it acquired a more brilliant and artfully contrived form than the parent state; but more advantageous in its consequences, neither to the republic, nor to mankind. Carthage was a city, not a nation: so that it was incapable of diffusing civilization and a spirit of patriotism over any extent of country. The territory it acquired in Africa, and in which, at the commencement of the third Punic war, it reckoned, according to Strabo, three hundred towns, contained subjects, over whom the conquerors ruled as lords, but no fellow-citizens of the sovereign state. This indeed the nearly uncivilized Africans never strove to become: for even in their wars against Carthage they appeared either as revolted slaves, or hired soldiers. Thus the interiour parts of Africa derived very little civilization from Carthage, as the object of this city, a few of the families of which had extended their sway beyond its walls, was not to propagate humanity, but to collect treasure. The crude superstition, that prevailed among the Carthaginians to the latest times; the barbarous manner, in which they tyrannically put to death their unsuccessful generals, even when no blame could be imputed to them; and their general conduct in foreign countries; evince the cruelty and avarice of this aristocratic state, which sought nothing but gain, and African servility.

The situation and constitution of Carthage are sufficient to account for this barbarity. Instead of commercial settlements after the Phenician manner, which the Carthaginians deemed too insecure, they erected fortresses; and at a time when the state of the World was so much improved, they attempted to secure the sovereignty of the coasts, as if every place were

Africa. But being obliged to employ for this purpose mercenaries, or enslaved barbarians; and such a proceeding involving them in quarrels with people, who for the most part refused to be treated any longer as savages; these quarrels could produce nothing but bloodshed, and bitter enmity. The fruitful Sicily, Syracuse in particular, was often assaulted by them: and at first very unjustly, as it was merely in consequence of a treaty with Xerxes. They went against a Grecian people as the barbarous auxiliaries of a barbarian, and showed themselves worthy of the part. Selinus, Himera, and Agrigentum, Saguntum in Spain, and many rich provinces in Italy, were plundered or destroyed by them. Nay more blood was shed on the beautiful plains of Sicily alone, than all the trade of Carthage could compensate. Much as Aristotle praises the constitution of this republic in a political view, as little merit has it in the history of the human race: for in it a few families of the city, consisting of barbarous wealthy merchants, employed the arms of mercenaries to contend for the monopoly of their gain, and appropriate to themselves the sovereignty of every country, by which this gain could be promoted. Such a system has in it nothing amiable: and therefore, however unjust most of the wars of the Romans against Carthage were, and much as the names of Asdrubal, Hamilcar, and Hannibal, demand our reverence, we shall hardly become Carthaginians, when we contemplate the internal state of the mercantile republic, which these heroes served. From it they experienced sufficient trouble, and were frequently rewarded with the blackest ingratitude: for his country would even have delivered up Hannibal himself to the Romans, to save a few pounds weight of gold, had he not withdrawn himself by flight from this Punic reward for his services.

Far be it from me, to rob one noble Carthaginian of the least of his merits: for even Carthage, though erected on the lowest ground of avaricious conquest, has produced great minds, and nourished a multitude of arts. Of warriours the family of Barcha in particular will be immortal; the flame of whose ambition mounted the higher, the more the jealousy of Hanno strove to quench it. But for the most part even in the heroic spirit of the

Carthaginians a certain harshness is observable; whence a Gelo, a Timoleon, a Scipio, appear, on comparison, as free men compared to slaves. Thus barbarous was the heroism of those brothers, who suffered themselves to be buried alive, to preserve an unjust boundary to their country: and in more urgent cases, as when Carthage itself was threatened, their valour in general assumed the appearance of savage desperation. Yet it is not to be denied, that Hannibal in particular was the tutor of its hereditary enemies, the Romans, who from him learned to conquer the World, in the more refined parts of the art of war. In like manner all the arts, that were in any way subservient to commerce, naval architecture, maritime war, or the acquisition of wealth, flourished in Carthage: though the Carthaginians themselves were soon conquered at sea by the Romans. In the fertile soil of Africa agriculture was of all arts that, which tended most to promote their trade; and into this, as a rich source of gain, the Carthaginians introduced many improvements. But unfortunately the barbarous state of the Romans occasioned the destruction of all the books of the Carthaginians, as well as of their town: we know nothing of the nation, but from its enemies, and a few ruins, which scarcely enable us to guess at the seat of the anciently famed mistress of the sea. It is to be lamented, that the principal figure Carthage makes in history is on occasion of her contests with Rome: this wolf, that was afterwards to ravage the World, was first to exercise her powers against an African jackal, till he fell beneath her jaws.

CHAPTER 5
The Egyptians

We now come to a country, which, on account of its antiquity, its arts, and its political institutions, stands like an enigma of the primeval World, and has copiously exercised the conjectural skill of the inquirer. This is Egypt. The most authentic information we have respecting it is derived from its antiquities; those vast pyramids, obelisks, and catacombs; those ruins of canals, cities, columns, and temples; which, with their hieroglyphics, are still the astonishment of travellers, as they were the wonder of the ancient World. What an immense population, what arts and government, but more especially what a singular way of thinking, must have been requisite, to excavate these rocks, or pile them upon one another; not only to delineate and carve statues of animals, but to inter them as sacred; to form a wilderness of rocks as an abode for the dead; and to eternize in stone the spirit of an Egyptian priesthood in such multifarious ways! There stand, there lie, all those relics, which, like a sacred sphinx, like a grand problem, demand an explanation.

Part of these works, of obvious utility, or indispensable to the country, explain themselves. Such are the astonishing canals, dikes, and catacombs. The canals served to convey the Nile to the remotest parts of Egypt, which now, from their ruin, are become silent deserts. The dikes enabled cities to establish themselves in the fertile valley, which the Nile overflows, and which, truly the heart of Egypt, feeds the whole land. The catacombs, too, setting aside the religious notions which the Egyptians connected with them, unquestionably contributed to the healthiness of the air, and prevented those diseases, which are the common pests of hot and humid climates. But to what purpose the enormity of these tombs? whence, and why, the labyrinth, the obelisks, the pyramids? whence the marvellous taste, on which the sphinxes and colossuses have so laboriously conferred immortality? Are the Egyptians the primitive nation, sprung from the mud of the Nile, to branch over all the World? or, if they be not indigenous, what circumstances, what motives, have rendered them so totally different from all the people that dwell around?

In my opinion the natural history of the country is sufficient to show, that the Egyptians are no primitive indigenous nation: for not only ancient tradition, but every rational geogony expressly says, that Upper Egypt was the earlier peopled, and that the lower country was in reality gained from the mud of the Nile by the skilful industry of man. Ancient Egypt, therefore, was on the mountains of the Thebaid; where too was the residence of its ancient kings: for had the land been peopled by the way of Suez, it is inconceivable, why the first kings of Egypt should have chosen the barren Thebaid for their abode. If, on the other hand, we follow the population of Egypt, as it lies before our eyes; in it we shall likewise find the cause, why its inhabitants became such a singular and distinguished people, even from their cultivation. They were no amiable Circassians, but, in all probability, a people of the south of Asia, who came westwards across the Red Sea, or perhaps farther off, and gradually spread from Ethiopia over Upper Egypt. The land here being bounded as it were by the inundations and marshes of the Nile, is it to be wondered, that they began to construct their habitations as troglodytes in the rocks, and afterwards gradually gained the whole of Egypt by their industry, improving themselves as they improved the land? The account Diodorus gives of their southern descent, though intermingled with various fables of his Ethiopia, is not only probably in the highest degree, but the sole key to an explanation of this people, and its singular agreement with some distant nations in the east of Asia.

As I could pursue this hypothesis here but very imperfectly, it must be deferred to another place, availing myself only of some of its evident consequences, with regard to the figure made by this people in the history of mankind. The Egyptians were a quiet, industrious, wellmeaning people, as their political constitution, their arts, and their religion, collectively demonstrate. No temple, no column of Egypt, has a gay, airy, Grecian appearance: of this design of art they had no idea, it never was their aim. The mummies show that the figure of the Egyptians was by no means beautiful; and as the human form appeared to them, such would necessarily be their imitations of it. Wrapped up in their own land, as in their own religion and constitution, they had an aversion to foreigners: and as, conformably to their character, fidelity and precision were their principal objects in the imitative arts; as their skill was altogether mechanical, and indeed in its application to religious purposes was confined to a particular tribe, while at the same time it turned chiefly on religious conceptions; no deviations toward ideal beauty, which without a natural prototype is a mere phantom,[14] were in the least to be expected in this country.[15] In recompense they turned their attention so much the more to solidity, durability, and gigantic magnitude; or to finishing with the utmost industry of art. In that rocky land, their ideas of temples were taken from vast caverns: hence in their architecture they were fond of majestic immensity. Their mummies gave the hint of their statues: whence their legs were naturally joined, and their arms closed to the body; a posture of itself tending to durability. To support cavities, and separate tombs, pillars were formed: and as the Egyptians derived their architecture from the vaults of rocks, and understood not our mode of erecting arches, the pillar, frequently gigantic, was indispensable. The deserts, by which they were surrounded, the regions of the dead, which from religious notions floated in their minds, also moulded their statues to mummies, wherein not action, but eternal rest, was the character, on which their art fixed.

The pyramids and obelisks of the Egyptians appear to me less calculated to excite wonder. Pyramids have been erected on graves in all parts of the World, even in Otaheite; not so much as emblems of the immortality of the soul, as tokens of a lasting remembrance after death. Their origin on these graves may be traced to those rude heaps of stone, which were formed as memorials by several nations in very remote antiquity. The rude heap of stones assumed the form of a pyramid, that it might acquire greater stability. When art applied itself to this general custom, as no occasion of a memorial is so dear to the human mind as the interment of the revered dead, the heap of stones, at first perhaps designed to protect the corpse from the fangs of wild beasts, was naturally transformed into a pyramid, or column, erected with more or less skill. Now that the Egyptians should excel other nations in these structures, arose from the same cause as the durable architecture of their temples and catacombs: namely, they possessed stone sufficient for these

[14] Of this in another place.

[15] That African forms may coalesce with Ideal Beauty, is proved by every head of Medusa; but chiefly that of the palace Rondanini at Rome.

monuments, as the greater part of Egypt is properly one rock; and they had hands enough to build them, as, in their fertile and populous country, the Nile manures the soil, and agriculture demands little labour. Besides, the ancient Egyptians lived with great temperance: thousands of men, who laboured for centuries like slaves at these memorials, were so easily maintained, that it depended merely on the will of a king, to erect inconceivable masses of this kind. The lives of individuals were estimated differently then, when their names were reckoned only in tribes and districts, than they are now. The useless labour of numbers was then more easily sacrificed to the will of a monarch, who was desirous of securing to himself immortality by such a heap of stones, and retaining the departed soul in an embalmed corpse, conformably to his religious notions; till this, like many other useless arts, became in time an object of emulation. One king imitated another, or fought to exceed him; while the easy people consumed their days in the structure of these monuments. Thus probably arose the pyramids and obelisks of Egypt: they were built only in the remotest times; for later ages, and nations, employed in more useful works, cease to erect pyramids. Thus, far from being tokens of the happiness and enlightened minds of the ancient Egyptians, the pyramids are incontrovertible testimonies of the superstition and thoughtlessness, both of the poor by whom they were built, and of the ambitious by whom their erection was commanded. Secrets are in vain sought within the pyramids, or concealed wisdom from the obelisks: for if the hieroglyphics of the latter could be deciphered, what is it possible we should read in them, except a chronicle of forgotten events, or a symbolic apotheosis of their builders? And then, what are these masses to a mountain of Nature's erection?

Besides, instead of inferring profound wisdom from the hieroglyphics of the Egyptians, they rather demonstrate the reverse. Hieroglyphics are the first rude infantile essay of the human mind, when seeking characters to denote its thoughts: the rudest savages of America had hieroglyphics sufficient to answer their occasions; for could not the Mexicans convey information of the most unheard of events, of the arrival of the Spaniards for instance, in hieroglyphics? But what poverty of ideas, what a stagnation of the mind, do the Egyptians display, in so long retaining this imperfect mode of writing, and continuing to paint it for centuries with immense trouble on rocks and walls! How confined must have been the knowledge of a nation, and of its numerous learned order, who could content themselves for some thousands of years with these birds and strokes! For their second Hermes, who invented letters, lived very late; and he was no Egyptian. The alphabetical writing on the mummies consists wholly of the foreign Phenician letters, intermingled with hieroglyphical characters, and therefore in all probability learned from the Phenician traders. The Chinese themselves have advanced farther than the Egyptians, and from similar hieroglyphics have invented actual notations of thought, to which these, as it appears, never attained. Is it to be wondered, then, that a nation so poor in writing, and yet not without capacity, should have been eminent in mechanic arts? Their road to science was obstructed by hieroglyphics, and thus their attention was the more turned towards objects of sense. The fertile valley of the Nile rendered their agriculture easy: they learned to measure and calculate those periodical inundations, on which their welfare depended. A people, whose life and comforts were connected with one single natural change, which, annually recurring, formed an eternal national calendar, must ultimately become expert in the measure of the year and the seasons.

Thus all the acquaintance with nature and the heavens, for which this ancient people is famed, was the natural offspring of the country and climate. Enclosed between mountains, seas, and deserts; in a narrow fertile valley, where every thing depended on one natural phenomenon, and every thing recalled that phenomenon to the mind; where the seasons of the year, and the produce of the harvest, winds and diseases, insects and birds, were governed by one and the same revolution, the overflowing of the Nile: could the grave Egyptian, and his numerous order of idle priests, fail ultimately to collect a sort of history of nature and the heavens? From all quarters of the World it is known, that confined sensual nations have the most copious practical knowledge of their country, though not learned from books. The hieroglyphics of the Egyptians were rather injurious than beneficial to science. They converted the lively observation into an obscure and dead image, which assuredly could not advance, but retarded the progress of the understanding. It has been much disputed, whether the hieroglyphics concealed sacerdotal mysteries. To me it appears, that every hieroglyphic from its nature contained a secret; and a series of them, preserved exclusively by a particular body of men, must necessarily have remained a mystery to the many, even supposing they were presented to them at every turn. They could not be initiated into the study of them, for this was not their business; and of themselves they could not discover their meaning. Hence the necessary want of an extensive diffusion of knowledge in every land, in every body of men, possessed of hieroglyphic wisdom, as it is called, whether taught by priests or laymen. Every one was not capable of deciphering its symbols, and what is not easy to be learned without a tutor must, from its very nature, be kept as a mystery. Thus every hieroglyphical science of modern times is a ridiculous obstacle to a free diffusion of knowledge; while in ancient times hieroglyphics were no more than the most imperfect mode of writing. It would be absurd, to expect a man of himself to learn to understand what might be explained in a thousand different ways; and to study arbitrary symbols, as if they were necessarily permanent things, would be endless labour. Hence Egypt has always remained a child in knowledge, because it always expressed its knowledge as a child, and its infantile ideas are probably for ever lost to us.

Thus we can do little more than guess at the rank attained by the Egyptians in religion and politics, while we have been able to mark that, which many other nations of high antiquity have reached, and can still in some measure observe, what the people in the east of Asia have attained. Indeed, could it be rendered probable, that much of the knowledge of the Egyptians was not easy to have been discovered in their country; but that they merely continued to exercise it after received rules and premises, and adapted it to their own land; their infant state in all these sciences would be much more obvious. Hence probably their long register of kings, and of the ages of the World: hence their ambiguous histories of Osiris, Isis, Horus, Typhon, and the rest: hence a great number of their religious fables. Their principal religious notions were common to several people of Upper Asia; only they were here clothed in hieroglyphics, adapted to the natural history of the country, and the character of the people. The leading features of their political constitution were familiar to other nations in a similar stage of cultivation; but here they were more finished, and employed in their own manner, by a people enclosed in the beautiful valley of the Nile.[16] Egypt would not easily have attained the high reputation it enjoys for wisdom, but for its less remote situation, the ruins of its antiquities, and above all the tales of the Greeks.

This very situation likewise shows the rank it occupies among the nations. Few have sprung from it, or been civilized by it: of the former I know only the Phenicians; of the latter, the Jews and Greeks. How far its influence has extended into the interiour of Africa we are ignorant. Poor Egyptians! how are they changed! Once laborious, and endued with patient industry, a thousand years of despair have reduced them to indolence and wretchedness. At the nod of a pharaoh, they spun and wove, dug in the mountains and raised stones, pursued the arts and cultivated the land. Patiently they suffered themselves to be shut up from the rest of the World, and divided into bands for the purpose of labour; they were prolific, and brought up their children with toil; shunned foreigners, and enjoyed their own secluded country. When once their land was laid open, or rather when Cambyses showed the way to it, it was for ages a prey to nation after nation. Persians and Greeks, Romans, Byzantines, Arabs, Fatimites, Curdes, Mamalukes,

[16] The conjectures on this subject must be deferred to another place.

and Turks, annoyed it one after the other; and its fine climate still remains a melancholy theatre of Arabian depredations and Turkish barbarity.[17]

CHAPTER 6

Farther Hints toward a Philosophy of the History of Man

HAVING now gone over a considerable extent of human events and institutions, from the Euphrates to the Nile, from Persepolis to Carthage, let us sit down, and take a retrospective view of our journey.

What is the principal law, that we have observed in all the great occurrences of history? In my opinion it is this: *that every where on our Earth whatever could be has been, according to the situation and wants of the place, the circumstances and occasions of the times, and the native or generated character of the people.* Admit active human powers, in a determinate relation to the age, and to their place on the Earth, and all the vicissitudes in the history of man will ensue. Here kingdoms and states crystallize into shape: there they dissolve, and assume other forms. Here from a wandering horde rises a Babylon: there from the straitened inhabitants of a coast springs up a Tyre: here, in Africa, an Egypt is formed: there, in the deserts of Arabia, a Jewish state: and all these in one part of the World, all in the neighbourhood of each other. Time, place, and national character alone, in short the general cooperation of active powers in their most determinate individuality, govern all the events that happen among mankind, as well as all the occurrences in nature. Let us place this predominant law of the creation in a suitable light.

1. *Active human powers are the springs of human history:* and as man originates from and in one race, his figure, education, and mode of thinking, are thus genetic. Hence that striking national character, which, deeply imprinted on the most ancient people, is unequivocally displayed in all their operations on the Earth. As a mineral water derives its component

[17] The mind of every reader will add a note to this period.

parts, its operative powers, and its taste, from the soil through which it flows; so the ancient character of nations arose from the family features, the climate, the way of life and education, the early actions and employments, that were peculiar to them. The manners of the fathers took deep root, and became the internal prototype of the race. The mode of thinking of the Jews, which is best known to us from their writings and actions, may serve as an example: in the land of their fathers, and in the midst of other nations, they remain as they were; and even when mixed with other people they may be distinguished for some generations downward. It was, and it is the same with all the nations of antiquity, Egyptians, Chinese, Arabs, Hindoos, etc. The more secluded they lived, nay frequently the more they were oppressed, the more their character was confirmed: so that, if every one of these nations had remained in its place, the Earth might have been considered as a garden, where in one spot one human national plant, in another, another, bloomed in its proper figure and nature; where in this spot one species of animal, in that, another, pursued its course, according to its instincts and character.

But as men are not firmly rooted plants, the calamities of famine, earthquakes, war, and the like, must in time remove them from their place to some other more or less different. And though they might adhere to the manners of their forefathers with an obstinacy almost equal to the instinct of the brute, and even apply to their new mountains, rivers, towns, and establishments, the names of their primitive land; it would be impossible for them, to remain eternally the same in every respect, under any considerable alteration of soil and climate. Here the transplanted people would construct a wasp's nest, or anthill, after their own fashion. The style would be a compound arising from the ideas imbibed in their original country, and those inspired by the new: and this may commonly be called the youthful bloom of the nation. Thus did the Phenicians, when they retired from the Red Sea to the shores of the Mediterranean: thus Moses endeavoured to form the Israelites: and so has it been with several Asiatic nations; for almost every people upon

Earth has migrated at least once, sooner or later, to a greater distance, or a less. It may readily be supposed, that in this much depended on the time when the migration took place, the circumstances by which it was occasioned, the length of the way, the previous state of civilization of the people, the reception they met with in their new country, and the like. Thus even in unmixed nations the computations of history are so perplexed, from geographical and political causes, that it requires a mind wholly free from hypothesis to trace the clew. This clew is most easily lost by one, with whom a particular race of the people is a favourite, and who despises every thing, in which this race has no concern. The historian of mankind must see with eyes as impartial as those of the creator of the human race, or the genius of the Earth, and judge altogether uninfluenced by the passions. To the naturalist, who would acquire a just knowledge and arrangement of all his classes, the rose and the thistle, the polecat, the sloth, and the elephant, are equally dear; he examines that most, from which most is to be learned. Now Nature has given the whole Earth to mankind, her children; and allowed every thing, that place, time, and power would permit, to spring up thereon. Every thing that can exist, exists; every thing that is possible to be produced, will be produced; if not today, yet tomorrow. Nature's year is long: the blossoms of her plants are as various as the plants themselves, and the elements by which they are nourished. In Hindostan, Egypt, and China, in Canaan, Greece, Rome, and Carthage, took place, what would have occurred no where else, and at no other period. The law of necessity and convenience, composed of power, time, and place, every where produces different fruits.

2. If the complexion of a kingdom thus depend principally on *the time and place in which it arose, the parts that composed it, and the external circumstances by which it was surrounded,* we perceive the chief part of its fate spring also from these. A monarchy framed by wandering tribes, whose political system is a continuation of their former mode of life, will scarcely be of long duration: it ravages, and subjugates, till at last itself is

destroyed: the capture of the metropolis, or frequently the death of a king alone, is sufficient to drop the curtain on the predatory scene. Thus it was with Babylon and Nineveh, with Ecbatana and Persepolis, and so it is with Persia still. The empire of the great moguls in Hindostan is nearly at an end: and that of the Turks will not be lasting, if they continue Chaldeans, that is foreign conquerors, and do not establish their government on a more moral foundation. Though the tree lift its head to the skies, and overshadow whole quarters of the Globe, if it be not rooted in the earth, a single blast of wind may overturn it. It may fall through the undermining of a treacherous slave, or by the axe of a daring satrap. Both the ancient and modern histories of Asia are filled with these revolutions; and thus the philosophy of states finds little to learn in them. Despots are hurled from the throne, and despots exalted to it again: the kingdom is annexed to the person of the monarch, to his tent, to his crown: he who has these in his power is the new father of the people, that is the leader of an overbearing band of robbers. A Nebuchadnezzar was terrible to the whole of Hither Asia, and under his second successor his unstable throne lay prostrate in the dust. Three victories of an Alexander completely put an end to the vast Persian monarchy.

It is not so with states, which, springing up from a root, rest on themselves: they may be subdued, but the nation remains. Thus it is with China: we well know how much labour it cost its conquerors, to introduce there a simple custom, the Mungal mode of cutting the hair. Thus it is with the Bramins and Jews, whose ceremonial systems will eternally separate them from all the nations upon Earth. Thus Egypt long withstood any intermixture with other nations: and how difficult was it to extirpate the Phenicians, merely because they were a people rooted in this spot! Had Cyrus succeeded in founding an empire like those of Yao, Crishna, and Moses, it would still survive, though mutilated, in all its members.

Hence we may infer the reason, why ancient political constitutions laid so much stress on the formation of manners by education; as their internal strength depended wholly on this spring. Modern kingdoms are built on money, or mechanical politics; the ancient, on the general way of thinking of a nation from its infancy: and as nothing has a more efficacious influence upon children than religion, most of the ancient states, particularly those of Asia, were more or less theocratic. I know the aversion in which this name is held, as to it all the evil, that has at any time oppressed mankind, is in great measure ascribed. Its abuses I will by no means undertake to defend: but at the same time it is true, that this form of government is not only adapted to the infancy of the human race, but necessary to it; otherwise, assuredly, it would neither have extended so far, nor have maintained itself so long. It has prevailed from Egypt to China, nay in almost every country upon Earth; so that Greece was the first, which gradually separated religion from its legislation. And as every religion is more efficacious in a political view, the more its objects, its gods and heroes, and their various actions, are indigenous; we find every firmly rooted ancient nation has appropriated its cosmogony and mythology to the country it inhabited. The Israelites alone distinguish themselves from all their neighbours in this, that they ascribe neither the creation of the World, nor that of man, to their own country. Their lawgiver was an enlightened foreigner, who never reached the land they were afterwards to possess: their ancestors had inhabited another country: and their laws were framed out of their own territories. This afterwards contributed probably to render the Jews more satisfied in a foreign land, than almost any other ancient nation. The Bramin, the Siamese, cannot live out of his own country: and as the Jew of Moses is properly a creature of Palestine, out of Palestine there should be no Jew.

3. Finally, from the whole region over which we have wandered, we perceive *how transitory all human structures are, nay how oppressive the best institutions become in the course of a few generations.* The plant blossoms, and fades: your fathers have died, and mouldered into dust: your temple is fallen: your tabernacle, the tables of your law, are no more: language itself, that bond of mankind, becomes antiquated: and shall a politi-

cal constitution, shall a system of government or religion, that can be erected solely on these, endure for ever? If so, the wings of Time must be enchained, and the revolving Globe hang fixed, an idle ball of ice over the abyss. What should we say now, were we to see King Solomon sacrifice twenty-two thousand oxen, and a hundred and twenty thousand sheep, at a single festival? or hear the queen of Sheba trying him with riddles at an entertainment? What should we think of the wisdom of the Egyptians, when the bull Apis, the sacred cat, and the sacred goat, were shown to us in the most splendid temples? It is the same with the burdensome ceremonies of the Bramins, the superstitions of the Parsees, the empty pretensions of the Jews, the senseless pride of the Chinese, and every thing that rests on antiquated human institutions of three thousand years date. The doctrines of Zoroaster may have been a praiseworthy attempt, to account for the evil in the World, and animate his contemporaries to all the deeds of light: but what is his theodicy now, even in the eyes of a Mohammedan? The metempsychosis of the Bramins may have its merit as a juvenile dream of the imagination, desirous of retaining the immortal soul within the sphere of observation, and uniting moral sentiments with the well-meant notion: yet has it not become an absurd religious law, with its thousand additions of precepts and practices? Tradition in itself is an excellent institution of Nature, indispensable to the human race: but when it fetters the thinking faculty both in politics and education, and prevents all progress of the intellect, and all the improvement, that new times and circumstances demand, it is the true narcotic of the mind, as well to nations and sects, as to individuals. Asia, the mother of all the mental illumination of our habitable Earth, has drunk deep of this pleasant poison, and handed the cup to others. Great states and sects sleep in it, as, according to the fable, Saint John sleeps in his grave: he breathes softly, though he died almost two thousand years ago, and slumbering waits till his awakener shall come.

IV

The Greeks

BOOK XIII

I TAKE leave of Asia with the regret of a traveller, obliged to quit a country, before he has acquired the knowledge of it he wished. How little do we know of it! and for the most part of how recent times, and from what doubtful authority! Of the eastern part of Asia we have but lately acquired any knowledge; and this through the means of men imbued with religious or political prejudices: while much of what we have thus acquired has been so embroiled by literary partisans in Europe, that great districts of it are still to us a fairy-land. In Hither Asia, and the neighbouring land of Egypt, every thing appears to us as a ruin, or a dream that is past: what we know from records, we have only from the mouths of the volatile Greeks, who were partly too young, partly of too different a way of thinking, for the remote antiquity of these states, and noticed only what concerned themselves. The archives of Babylon, Phenicia, and Carthage, are no more: Egypt was in its decline, almost before its interiour was visited by a Greek: so that the whole is shrunk up to a few withered leaves, containing fables of fables, fragments of history, a dream of the ancient World.

With Greece the morning breaks, and we joyfully sail to meet it. The inhabitants of this country acquired the art of writing at an early period compared with others; and in most of their institutions found springs to guide their language from poetry to prose, as in this to history and philosophy. Thus the Philosophy of History looks upon Greece as her birthplace, and in it spent her youth. Even the fabling Homer describes the manners of several nations, as far as his knowledge extended. They who sung the exploits of the argonauts, the echoes of whose songs remain, entered into another memorable region. When proper history subsequently separated itself from poetry, Herodotus travelled over several countries, and collected with commendable infantile curiosity whatever he saw and heard. The later writers of history in Greece, though their own country was their only object, could not avoid saying many things of other countries, with which the Greeks were connected: thus their canvas was gradually extended, particularly by the expeditions of Alexander. With Rome, to whom the Greeks served not only as guides in history, but as historians, it extended still more; so that Diodorus of Sicily, a Greek, and Trogus, a Roman, ventured to form their materials into a sort of universal history. Let us then rejoice, that at length we have reached a people, whose origin indeed is enveloped in obscurity, whose early ages are uncertain, and whose finest works, both in letters and the arts, have been for the most part destroyed by the rage of enemies, or the fashion of the times; yet of whom we have noble monuments: monuments that speak to us with a philosophic spirit, the humanity of which I in vain endeavour to infuse into my essay on them. I might invoke, as a poet, allseeing Apollo, and the daughter of Memory, the omniscient muse: but my inspiring muse shall be impartial truth; and my Apollo, the spirit of inquiry.

CHAPTER 1

The Situation and Peopling of Greece

The triple Greece, of which we speak, is a land of coasts and bays, surrounded by the sea; or rather a cluster of islands. It lies in a region, where it might receive from various parts not only inhabitants, but the seeds of cultivation, and this speedily. Thus its situation, and the character of the people, which formed itself suitably to the country by early expeditions and revolutions, soon set afloat an internal circulation of ideas, and an external activity, denied by Nature to the nations of the extensive continent. Finally, the period in which the cultivation of

Greece occurred, and the degree of improvement, which not only the neighbouring people, but the human mind in general, had attained, contributed to render the Greeks what they once were, what they no longer are, and what they never more will be. Let us more narrowly examine this fine historical problem; for the solution of which we have nearly sufficient data, particularly from the industry of learned Germans.

A secluded nation, enclosed by mountains, far from the sea-coast, and from any intercourse with other people; that derived its knowledge from a single place, and, in proportion as this was more early received, more firmly fixed it by brazen laws; may acquire great peculiarity of character, and retain it long: but this confined peculiarity will be far from giving it that useful versatility, which can be gained only by active competition with other nations. Egypt, and all the countries of Asia, are examples of this. Had the power, which constructed our Earth, given its mountains and seas a different form; had that great destiny, which established the boundaries of nations, caused them to originate elsewhere than from the Asiatic mountains; had the east of Asia possessed an earlier commerce, and a Mediterranean Sea, which its present situation has denied; the whole current of cultivation would have been altered. It flowed westwards; because eastwards it was unable to flow, or to spread.

If we contemplate the history of islands, and countries connected by straits, in whatever part of the World they lie, we find, that, the more fortunate they were in their peopling, the more easy and diversified the stream of activity, that could be set in motion among them, and the more advantageous the time or situation, in which they had to perform their part; by so much more did the inhabitants of such coasts or islands distinguish themselves above those of the main land. On the continent, in spite of all natural endowments, and acquired capacities, the shepherd remained a shepherd; the hunter, a hunter: even the husbandman and artist were confined like plants to a narrow spot. Compare England with Germany: the English are Germans, and even in the latest times the Germans have led the way for the English in the greatest things. But while England, as an island, early acquired a much more active universality of mind, its situation itself accelerated the means of improvement, and gave them without interruption a consistence unattainable by the more embarrassed continent. A similar difference is perceivable on a comparison of the Danish islands, the coasts of Italy, France, and Spain, the Netherlands, and the North of Germany, with the interiour country of the Slavians and Scythians of Europe, with Russia, Poland, and Hungary. Voyagers in all the seas have found, that on islands, peninsulas, or coasts happily situate, an application and freedom of improvement had been generated, which could not have surmounted the pressure of the uniform ancient laws of the main land.[1] Read the descriptions of the Society and Friendly Islands: in spite of their distance from the rest of the habitable World, they have raised themselves into a sort of Greece, even in luxury and ornamental dress. In many solitary islands of the wide ocean the first voyagers experienced a gentleness and courtesy, which would be sought in vain among inland nations. Thus every where we perceive the great law of human nature, that, where activity and quiet, society and distance, voluntary occupation and its advantages, are happily united, such a course of things is promoted, as is favourable both to the people themselves, and to their neighbours. Nothing is more injurious to the health of mankind, than obstructions of their juices: in the despotic states of ancient institution these were inevitable; and hence, if they were not soon extirpated, their bodies, while alive, underwent a lingering death. On the other hand, where, from the nature of the country, states continued small, and the inhabitants in healthy activity, to which a life divided between sea and land is particularly conducive, favourable circumstances alone were required, to form a highly cultivated and celebrated people. Thus, to say nothing of other countries, the islanders of Crete

[1] Compare the Malays, and the inhabitants of the Asiatic islands, with those of the continent; put even Japan in competition with China; the natives of the Kuriles and Fox Islands, with the Mungals; observe Juan Fernandez, Socotora, Easter Island, Byron's Island, the Maldives, etc.

were the first among the Grecians themselves, to produce a system of laws as a model for all the republics on the main land; and of these the most numerous and celebrated were fixed on the coasts. Thus the ancients placed their seats of bliss on islands not without reason; probably because on islands they found the most free and happy people.

When we apply this to Greece, how different must we expect to find its inhabitants from those of the lofty mountains. A narrow strait divided Thrace from Asia Minor; and this fertile country, rich in nations, was connected along its western shore with Greece by a sound thickly interspersed with islands. It seems as if the Hellespont had been broken through, and the Egean Sea with its islands interposed, to facilitate the passage, and produce a constant wandering and circulation throughout Greece. Thus in the remotest times we find the numerous nations of these coasts roaming the seas: Cretans, Lydians, Pelasgians, Thracians, Rhodians, Phrygians, Cyprians, Milesians, Carians, Lesbians, Phoceans, Samians, Spartans, Naxians, Heretrians, and Eginetans, followed each other, even before the time of Xerxes, in the dominion of the sea: and long before these maritime powers, pirates, colonists, and adventurers, were found upon it; so that there is scarcely a nation of Greece, that has not migrated, and many more than once.[2] Every thing here has been in motion from the oldest times, from the coasts of Asia Minor to Italy, Sicily, and France: no people of Europe has colonized a finer, more extensive country, than these Greeks. This is what we mean, when we talk of the fine climate of Greece. Did the expression signify merely the indolent seat of fertility in wellwatered vales, or meadows overflowed by rivers, how many finer climates would be found in the other three quarters of the Globe, no one of which, however, has yet produced Greeks! [3] But a series of coasts, enjoying an air so favourable to the activity of little states in the progress

[2] Heyne's "Commentary on the Epoch of Castor," in the *Nov. Comment. Soc. Gött.* (New Memoirs of the Göttingen Society), Vol. I, II.

[3] See Riedesel's *Bemerkungen auf einer Reise nach der Levante* (Observations on a tour to the Levant), p. 113.

of cultivation, as those of Ionia, Greece, and Grecia Magna, are no where else to be found upon Earth.

We need not long inquire whence Greece derived its first inhabitants. They were called Pelasgians, that is strangers, and at this distance acknowledged the people beyond the sea, that is, of Asia Minor, as brethren. It would be useless labour, to enumerate all the courses they steered, through Thrace, or over the Hellespont and Archipelago, westward and southward; and how, protected by the northern mountains, they gradually spread over Greece. One tribe followed another; one tribe pressed upon another: Hellenes brought new knowledge to the ancient Pelasgians, as in the progress of time Grecian colonies again settled on the Asiatic shores. It was favourable enough for the Greeks, that they were in the vicinity of such a fine peninsula of the great continent, most of the inhabitants of which were not only of one race, but more early civilized.[4] Hence their language acquired that originality and uniformity, which a mixture of many tongues could not have possessed; and the nation itself participated in the moral condition of the neighbouring primitive race, with whom it was soon connected by the various relations of war and peace. Thus Asia Minor was the parent of Greece, both in peopling it, and in imparting the principal features of its earliest cultivation: while Greece in its turn afterward sent out colonies to its mother country, and lived to see in it a second and superior cultivation.

It is to be regretted, however, that we have very little knowledge of the Asiatic peninsula in the earliest times. Of the kingdom of the Trojans we know nothing except from Homer: and however high he endeavours, as a poet, to exalt his countrymen above their antagonists, the flourishing state of Troy in the arts, and even in magnificence, is evident from his account. In like manner the Phrygians were an ancient and early cultivated nation, whose religion and fables had an unquestionable influence on the earliest mythology of the Greeks. So afterwards the Carians, who called themselves brothers of the Mysians and

[4] See Heyne on the origin of the Greeks, *Commentat. Soc. Götting.* (Memoirs of the Göttingen Society), 1764.

Lydians, and were of the same race with the Pelasgians and Leleges, applied early to navigation, which at that time was merely piracy; while the more civilized Lydians share the invention of coin, as a medium of commerce, with the Phenicians. Thus none of these people were wanting in early cultivation, any more than the Mysians and Thracians, and were capable of becoming Greeks by proper transplantation.

The primitive seat of the Grecian muses was in the north east, toward Thrace. Orpheus, who first converted the savage Pelasgians to humanity, and introduced those religious practices, that prevailed so widely and so long, was a Thracian. The first mountains of the muses were the mountains of Thessaly; Olympus, Helicon, Parnassus, Pindus: here, says the acutest of the investigators of Grecian history, was the most ancient seat of the religion, philosophy, music, and poetry, of Greece.[5] Here dwelt the first Grecian bards: here were formed the first civilized societies: here the lyre and the harp were invented, and the first models cast of every thing, that Grecian genius afterwards produced. In Thessaly and Bœotia, which in later times were so little celebrated for the production of genius, there is not a fountain, a river, a hill, or a grove, which poetry has not immortalized. Here flowed the Peneus, here was the delightful Tempe: here Apollo wandered in the garb of a shepherd, and here the giants piled up their mountains. At the foot of Helicon Hesiod yet learned his fables from the mouths of the muses. In short, the first cultivation of the Greeks was indigenous here; and hence the purer Grecian language flowed through the descendants of the Hellenes in its principal dialects.

In the course of time, however, a series of other fables necessarily arose, on such various coasts and islands, and from such repeated wanderings and adventures, which the poets equally consecrated in the temple of the Grecian muse. Almost every little district, every celebrated tribe, introduced into it its ancestors or national divinities: and this variety, which would form an impenetrable wood, if we were to consider the Grecian mythol-

[5] Heyne on the Muses: see *Gött. Anzeigen* (The Göttingen Review), for 1766, p. 275.

ogy as a system, infused life into the national way of thinking from the actions and manners of every tribe. Without such various roots and germes, that fine garden, which in time produced the most diversified fruits, even in legislation, could not have come to perfection. The land being divided into many portions, this tribe defended its valley, that its coasts and islands; and thus from the long youthful activity of scattered tribes and kingdoms arose the great and free genius of the Grecian muse. Its cultivation was under the control of no universal lord: from the voice of the lyre, at religious ceremonies, games, and dances; from arts and sciences of its own invention; and, lastly, still more from the various intercourse of the different tribes of Greece among each other and with strangers; it adopted, of its own free will, now this, now that law, custom, or principle: thus being a free Grecian people, even in the progress of cultivation. That, as Phenician colonies contributed to this in Thebes, so Egyptian colonies did in Attica, cannot be denied: yet, fortunately, neither the principal race of the Greeks, nor their language and way of thinking, sprung from these. Thanks to their descent, mode of life, and native muses, the Greeks were not destined to become a herd of Egyptian Canaanites.

CHAPTER 2
The Language, Mythology, and Poetry of Greece

WE now come to subjects, which have been for some thousands of years the delight of the more polished part of mankind, and I hope will ever continue to be so. The Grecian language is the most refined of any in the World; the Grecian mythology, the richest and most beautiful upon Earth; the Grecian poetry, perhaps the most perfect of its kind, when considered with respect to time and place. But who gave this once rude people such a language, such poetry, and such figurative wisdom? The genius of nature, their country, their way of life, the period in which they lived, and the character of their progenitors.

The Greek language sprang from rude beginnings: but these

very beginnings contained the seeds of what it was afterwards to become. They were no hieroglyphic patchwork, no series of singly ejected syllables, like the languages beyond the Mungal mountains. Readier and more flexible organs produced among the Caucasean nations a more easy modulation, which was susceptible of being soon reduced to form by the social propensity to music. The words were more smoothly connected, the tone modulated into rhythm: the language flowed in a fuller stream; its images, in pleasing harmony: it raised itself to the melody of the dance. And thus the peculiar character of the Greek language, not constrained by mute laws, arose as a living image of nature, from music and the dance, from history and song, and from the talkative free intercourse of many tribes and colonies. The northern nations of Europe were not thus fortunate in their formation. Foreign manners imparted to them by foreign laws, and a religion devoid of song crippled their language. The German, for example, has unquestionably lost much of its intrinsic flexibility, of its more precise expression in the inflection of words, and still more of that energetic tone, which it formerly possessed in a more favourable climate. Once it was a near sister of the Greek; but how far from this is it now degenerated! No language beyond the Ganges possesses the flexibility and smooth flow of the Greek: no Aramean dialect on this side the Euphrates had them in its ancient form. The Grecian language alone appears as if derived from song: for song, and poetry, and an early enjoyment of freedom, fashioned it as the universal language of the muses. Improbable as it is, that all the springs of Grecian cultivation should again combine together; that the infancy of mankind should return, and an Orpheus, a Musæus, and a Linus, or a Homer and Hesiod, revive with every concomitant circumstance: as little is the generation of a Greek language in our times possible, even in the same regions.

The mythology of the Greeks flowed from the fables of various countries: and these consisted either of the popular faith; the traditionary accounts, that the different generations preserved of their ancestors; or the first attempts of reflecting minds, to explain the wonders of the Earth, and give a consistency to society.[6] However spurious and new-modified our hymns of the ancient Orpheus may be; still they are imitations of that lively devotion and reverence of Nature, to which all nations in the first stage of civilization are prone. The rude hunter addresses his dreaded bear;[7] the Negro, his sacred fetish; the Parsee mobed, his spirits of nature and the elements; nearly after the Orphic manner: but how is the Orphic hymn to Nature refined and ennobled, merely by the Grecian words and images! And how much more pleasing and easy did the Greek mythology become, as in time it rejected even from its hymns the fetters of mere epithet, and recited instead, as in the songs of Homer, fables of the deities! In the cosmogonies, too, the harsh primitive legends were in time amalgamated together, and human heroes and patriarchs were sung, and placed by the side of the gods. Happily the ancient relaters of theogonies introduced into the genealogies of their gods and heroes such striking, beautiful allegories, frequently with a single word of their elegant language, that when subsequent philosophers thought fit merely to unfold their signification, and connect with it their more refined ideas, a new delicate tissue was formed. Thus the epic poets in time laid aside their frequently repeated fables of the generation of the gods, the storming of Heaven, the actions of Hercules, and the like, and sang more human themes for the use of man.

Of these Homer, the father of all the Grecian poets and philosophers that succeeded him, is the most celebrated. His scattered songs had the fortunate destiny to be collected at the most favourable juncture, and erected into a double edifice, shining like an indestructible palace of gods and heroes after thousands of years. As men have endeavoured to explain the wonders of nature, so they have taken pains to investigate the

[6] See Heyne, *De fontibus et causis errorum, etc.* (On the sources and causes of error in mythological history: on the physical causes of fables: on the origin and causes of the fables of Homer: on the theogony compiled by Hesiod: etc.).

[7] See Georgi's *Abbildungen der Voelker des Russischen Reichs* (Delineations of the people of the Russian Empire), Vol. I.

existence of Homer, who was in fact a mere child of Nature, a happy bard of the Ionian shore.[8] Many of his order have sunk perhaps into oblivion, who might have been in part his competitors for that fame, which he alone enjoys. Temples have been erected to him, and he has been adored as a human divinity: but his noblest adoration consists in the permanent influence he had on his own nation, and on all who are capable of feeling his merit. The subjects of his song, indeed, are trifles in our eyes: his gods and heroes, with their passions and manners, are such as the fables of his own and preceding times presented: his knowledge of physics and geography, his morals and politics, are equally confined. But the truth and wisdom, with which he has moulded all the objects of his world into a living whole; the steady outline of every feature of every person in his immortal picture; the easy, unlaboured manner, in which, free as a god, he penetrates into every character, and relates their virtues and vices, their fortunes and misfortunes; and lastly, the music, that incessantly flows from his lips throughout poems of such extent and variety, and will animate every image, every tone, as long as his verses shall live; are the circumstances, for which Homer stands unrivalled in the history of mankind, and which render him worthy of immortality, if aught on Earth can be immortal.

On the Greeks Homer necessarily had a different effect from what he can have upon us, from whom he so often obtains a forced and frigid admiration, or indeed cold contempt. Not so with the Greeks. To them he sung in a living language; at that time perfectly unfettered by what was subsequently termed dialects: to them he sung with patriotic feelings the exploits of their ancestors against foreigners, and recited families, tribes, actions, and countries, which were in part present to their eyes as their own, and in part lived in the memory of their national pride. Thus to them Homer was in many respects the divine herald of national fame, a source of the most diversified national wisdom. The succeeding poets followed him: from him the tragic borrowed fables; the didactic, allegories, examples,

[8] Blackwell's *Inquiry into the Life and Writings of Homer,* 1736: Wood's *Essay on the Original Genius of Homer,* 1769.

and maxims: every one, who first attempted a new kind of writing, took from the artificial structure of Homer's work the model of his own: so that Homer was soon the pattern of Grecian taste, and with weaker heads the standard of all human wisdom. The Roman poets, too, felt his influence; and but for him the Eneid would never have existed. Still more has he contributed, to reclaim the modern nations of Europe from barbarism; so many youth have been formed, while they were delighted by him; so many active as well as contemplative men have imbibed from him the principles of taste, and a knowledge of mankind. Yet it cannot be denied, that, as every great man has been the cause of abuses from an inordinate admiration of his talents, so has the good Homer; insomuch that no one would wonder more than himself, could he arise from the dead, and see what has been extracted from him at various times. Among the Greeks fable maintained its ground more firmly, and for a longer period, than it would have done probably without him: rhapsodists sung after him, frigid poetasters imitated him, and the enthusiasm for Homer became at length among the Greeks such a bald, insipid, wiredrawn art as scarcely has been paralleled for any poet by any other people. The innumerable comments of the grammarians upon him are for the most part lost; otherwise we should see in them the miserable toil God imposes upon the succeeding generations of men in every preponderating genius: for are not examples enough extant of the erroneous study and misapplication of Homer in modern times? This much however is certain, that a mind like his, in the period in which he lived, and for the nation by which his works were collected, was such an instrument of improvement, as scarcely any other people can boast. No oriental nation possesses a Homer: no poet like him has appeared at the proper season, in the bloom of youth, to any people of Europe. Even Ossian was not the same to his Scots: and the Fates alone can tell, whether a second Homer will be given to the new Grecian Archipelago, the Friendly Islands, who will lead them to an equal height with that, to which his elder brother led Greece.

As the cultivation of the Greeks thus proceeded from mythology, poetry, and music, we need not wonder, that a taste for them remained a leading feature of their character, as their most serious writings and institutions evince. To our manners it appears incongruous, that the Greeks should speak of music as the finishing point of education, that they should treat it as a grand engine of state, and ascribe the most important consequences to its decline. Still more singular appear to us the animated and almost rapturous praises they bestow on dancing, pantomime, and the dramatic art, as the natural sisters of poetry and wisdom. Many, who read these encomiums, believed, that the music of the Greeks was a miracle of systematic perfection, as we are so totally unacquainted with any thing like its celebrated effects. But that the Greeks did not principally apply to the scientific perfection of music appears from the very use which they made of it: for they did not cultivate it as a distinct art, but employed it subserviently to poetry, the dance, and the drama. Thus the grand effect of its tones lay in this connexion, and in the general bent of Grecian cultivation. The poetry of the Greeks, proceeding from music, readily returned to it again: sublime tragedy itself originated from the chorus; the ancient comedy, public rejoicings, military expeditions, and the domestic hilarity of the feast, were seldom unaccompanied by music and song; and few games were destitute of the dance. In these, indeed, as Greece consisted of many states and nations, one province differed much from another: the times, the various degrees of civilization and luxury, induced still greater variation: yet on the whole it remains perfectly true, that the Greeks esteemed the joint improvement of these arts the summit of human energy, and attached to it the highest value.

It must be confessed, that neither pantomine nor the drama, neither the dance, nor poetry, nor music, is with us, what it was with the Greeks. With them all these were only one work, one blossom of the human mind, the wild seeds of which we perceive in every nation of gay and pleasing character, if placed in a happy climate. Absurd as it would be, to endeavour to transport ourselves back to this period of youthful levity, which is now past, and to skip as a hobbling graybeard among boys; why should the graybeard be offended with youth for being lively, and dancing? The cultivation of the Greeks fell on this period of youthful jollity, from the arts of which they elicited whatever was capable of being educed, and thus necessarily accomplished effects, the possibility of which is scarce conceivable to us, exhausted and diseased. For I doubt, whether a greater power of operation of refined senses upon the mind can be produced, than the studied supreme point of junction of these arts, particularly on minds educated and formed to them, and living in a world animated by similar impressions. If then we cannot be Greeks ourselves, let us at least rejoice, that there once were Greeks, and that, like every other flower of the human mind, this also found a time and place to put forth its loveliest blossoms.

From what has been said may be conjectured, that many species of Grecian composition, which were designed for animated representation, with music, dancing, and pantomime, appear to us merely as shadows, and may perhaps mislead us even with the most careful explanation. The theatres of Æschylus, Sophocles, Aristophanes, and Euripides, were not our theatres: the proper drama of the Greeks is no more to be seen in any nation, however excellent the pieces of this kind, that many have produced. Without song, without the festivals of the Greeks, and without the exalted notions they entertained of their games, the odes of Pindar must appear to us the exclamations of ebriety; as even in the dialogues of Plato, abounding in melody of language, and beautiful composition of images and words, those very passages, which were clothed with the greatest art, have been exposed to the most numerous objections from critics. Youth, therefore, must learn to read the Greeks; since the aged are seldom inclined to look at them, or appropriate to themselves their beauties. Grant, that their imagination often outflies the understanding; that the refined sensuality, in which they place the essence of accomplishment, sometimes oversteps the bounds of reason and virtue; let us not refuse them due esteem, though we refrain from becoming

Greeks ourselves. From their dress, the fine proportion and outline of their thoughts, the natural vivacity of their sentiments, and lastly from the melodious rhythm of their language, which never yet found its equal, we have much to learn.

CHAPTER 3

The Arts of the Greeks

In all the arts of life, a people endued with such sentiments must necessarily ascend from the necessary to the beautiful and pleasing; and the Greeks attained almost the highest point in every thing relating to them. Their religion required statues and temples; their political institutions demanded monuments and public edifices; their climate and way of living, their activity, luxury, vanity, etc., rendered various works of art indispensable. Thus the genius of beauty put these works into their hands, and assisted them alone of all mortals to finish them; for though their greatest wonders of art have long been destroyed, we still admire and cherish their ruins and fragments.

1. That religion greatly promoted the arts of the Greeks, we see from the catalogues of their works in Pausanias, Pliny, or any of the collections, which speak of their remains: and this is conformable to the universal history of men and nations. All men have been desirous of seeing the objects of their worship; and every where they have attempted, to paint or carve representations of them, where this has not been prohibited by religion or the law. Even the Negro renders his god present to him in a fetish: and of the Greeks we know, that the representations of their gods primarily originated from a stone or a rude billet. This poverty could not long satisfy a people so active: the block became a herm,[9] or a statue; and as the nation was divided into many little tribes and states, it was natural, that each should endeavour to embellish the images of its domestic and family deities. Some successful attempts of the ancient Dedaluses, and probably the view of neighbouring works of art, excited emulation; and thus several states and tribes were

[9] Ερμα, per syncopen pro ἐρεισμα.

soon enabled to contemplate their god, the most sacred of all the things they possessed, in a more agreeable form. The first essays of ancient art, in which it learned as it were to go, were principally images of the gods: hence no nation, to which representations of the gods were prohibited, ever made any great advancement in the imitative arts.[10]

But as the gods of the Greeks were introduced by poetry and song, and animated them in majestic forms, what could be more natural, than that the imitative arts should become the nurslings of the muse, who poured into their ear those splendid forms? From the poets the artist learned the history of the gods, and consequently the manner, in which he was to delineate them: hence the first artists rejected not the most terrible representations, while such the poets sung.[11] In time more pleasing delineations succeeded, poetry itself assuming more agreeable features: and thus Homer was the parent of the improvement of the fine arts of the Greeks, as he was of their poetry. From him Phidias derived the exalted idea of his Jupiter, which was followed by the other performances of this sculptor of gods.[12] From the genealogies and affinities of the gods in the relations of the poets, determinate characters, or family features, entered into their representations, till at length the received poetical tradition became a law for the figures of the gods, throughout the realms of art. Thus no people of antiquity could possess the arts of the Greeks, who had not also the Grecian poetry and mythology, and who acquired not their cultivation in a similar manner. But such are not to be found in history; and consequently the Greeks, with their Homeric arts, remain alone.

Hence may be explained the ideal creation of Grecian art, which arose neither from the profound philosophy of the artists, nor the natural conformation of the people, but from the causes, that have been developed. Unquestionably it was a

[10] See Winckelmann's *Gesch. der Kunst* (History of the arts), Vol. I, chap. 1; and Heyne's confirmation of it, and additions to it, in the German papers of the Göttingen Society, Vol. I, p. 211, etc.

[11] See Heyne, *Über den Kasten des Kypselus* (On the coffer of Kypselus), etc.

[12] Diis quam hominibus fingendis aptior. Plin.

fortunate circumstance, that the Greeks, considered in the whole, were beautifully formed; though this form must not be extended to every individual Greek, as a model of ideal beauty. In Greece, as every where else, copious Nature did not submit to be checked in the thousandfold variation of the human figure; and, if Hippocrates may be believed, as among others, so among the Greeks, deforming accidents and maladies were to be found. But admitting all this, and taking into the account many happy opportunities, when the artist could exalt a beautiful youth into an Apollo, and a Phryne or a Lais into a goddess of love; this would not explain the received ideal of the deities, which was established as a rule among the artists. Perhaps it is as little probable, that a head of Jupiter should ever have been found on a human body, as that the Jupiter of Homer actually existed in this World. The great anatomical draughtsman Camper has clearly shown on what deeply meditated rules the ideal form of the Grecian artist was constructed: but to these rules the representations of the poets, and the aim of producing religious veneration, alone could have led.[13] If, therefore, you would produce a new Greece in images of the gods, give a people again this poetic mythological superstition, with every thing belonging to it, in all its natural simplicity. Travel through Greece, and contemplate its temples, grottoes, and sacred groves; you will soon relinquish the thought, even in wish, of exalting to the height of Grecian art a people totally ignorant of such a religion, that is, of such a lively superstition, which filled every town, every spot, every nook, with the presence of an innate divinity.

2. All the heroic fables of the Greeks, particularly when they relate to the progenitors of their race, are in a similar predicament; for they too passed through the minds of the poets, and in part lived in eternal song: accordingly the artist, who made them his subjects, copied their history with a sort of religious regard to the poets, to gratify the pride of his countrymen, and their attachment to their ancestors. The most ancient history of

---

[13] Camper's *Kleinere Schristen* (Smaller Tracts), p. 18 and following.

the arts, and a view of the Grecian performances, confirm this. Graves, shields, altars, holy places, and temples, preserved the remembrance of their forefathers; and on these, in many tribes, the labours of the artist were employed from the most ancient times. All warlike nations throughout the World painted and adorned their shields: the Greeks went farther; they engraved, or cast and carved upon them memorials of their ancestors. Hence the early performances of Vulcan in very ancient poets: hence in Hesiod the shield of Hercules with the achievements of Perseus. With shields came representations of this kind upon the altars of heroes, or other family memorials; as the coffer of Kypselus shows, the figures on which were completely in the style of Hesiod's shield. Noble works of this kind are of earlier date than the age of Dedalus; and as many temples of the gods were originally tombs, in them the memory of their ancestors, their heroes, and their deities, came so near together, that they coalesced almost into one adoration, at least into one spring of the arts.[14] Hence the ancient stories of their heroes represented on the drapery of their gods, and by the side of the altar and the throne: hence the pictures in honour of the deceased frequently in the market place of the city, or the herms and columns on graves. If to these we add the innumerable works of art presented to the temples of the gods by states, families, or individuals, as memorials, or votive offerings of gratitude; and frequently adorned, according to custom, with subjects from the history of their progenitors, or heroes; what other people can boast such an incentive to the most diversified art? Our galleries of ancestors, filled with the portraits of forgotten forefathers, are nothing in comparison with these; as all Greece was full of stories, and poems, and sacred places, of their gods, and heroic progenitors. Every thing was connected with the bold idea, that gods were related to them; that superiour men, and heroes, were but an inferiour order of deities: and this idea their poets had infused.

[14] As, for example, the temple of Pallas at Larissa was the tomb of Acrisius; that of Minerva Polias at Athens, the tomb of Ericthonius; the throne of Amyclus, the tomb of Hyacinthus, etc.

With this regard to national and family fame, by which the arts were promoted, I reckon the Grecian games. These were instituted by their heroes, and festivals to their memory: beside this, they were public acts of worship to the gods, and practices highly advantageous both to poetry and the imitative arts. Not merely that youths, partly naked, exercised themselves in various contests and feats of activity, and thus presented living models to the artists; but rather as by these exercises their bodies were rendered susceptible of a finer form, and these juvenile victories preserved in their minds an active remembrance of the fame of their relations, their progenitors, and their heroes. From Pindar, and from history, we know how highly these victories were held in estimation throughout all Greece, and with what emulation they were sought. The whole town of the conqueror was honoured by them: the family of the victor was raised to a level with the gods and heroes of old. On this turns the economy of Pindar's odes: works of art, which he raised to a value higher than that of statues. On this depended the honour of the tomb, or statue, commonly a work of fancy, which the victor could claim. By this successful emulation of his heroic ancestors he was raised to something more than man, and became a kind of god. Where now could such games be instituted, equally prized, and equal in consequences?

3. The political institutions of the Greeks likewise promoted the arts: not so much because they were republics, as because these republics employed the artists on grand works. Greece was divided into many states; and in these the arts were fostered, whether they were governed by archons, or by kings. For these kings were Greeks; and every demand for the arts, whether springing from religion or family tales, was their demand: frequently, too, they were the high-priests. Thus from remote periods the decoration of their palaces was distinguished by precious relics of their ancestors or heroic friends, as Homer relates. But the republican constitutions, which in time were diffused throughout all Greece, gave a wider scope to the arts. In a commonwealth, edifices for the assembly of the people, for the public treasure, for general exercise and amuse-

ment, were necessary; and thus arose, in Athens, for example, the magnificent gymnasia, theatres, and galleries, the Odeum and Prytaneum, the Pnyx, etc. As in the Grecian republics every thing was conducted in the name of the people, or of the town, nothing, that concerned their tutelary deities, or the grandeur of their name, was too costly; while individuals, and even the principal citizens, satisfied themselves with less sumptuous habitations. This public spirit of doing every thing, in appearance at least, for the community was the soul of the Grecian states; as Winkelmann no doubt considered, when he esteemed the liberty of the Grecian republics the golden age of the arts. In them grandeur and magnificence were not so divided as in modern times, but concentred in whatever pertained to the state. Pericles flattered the people with these notions of fame, and did more for the arts, than ten kings of Athens would have done. Every thing he built was in the grand style, as it was for the gods, and the immortal city: and assuredly few of the Grecian towns and islands would have erected such edifices, or promoted such works of art, had they not been separate republics, emulous of each other's fame. Besides, as in democratic states the leaders of the people must endeavour to please the public, what means could they more advantageously employ, than such kinds of expense, as, while they tended to propitiate the tutelary deities, were calculated to gratify the eyes of the people, and afford subsistence to many?

This expense, no doubt, had consequences, from which Humanity would willingly avert her eyes. The rigour with which the Athenians oppressed those whom they conquered, and even their colonies; the robberies and wars, in which the states of Greece were perpetually involved; the severe services, which the citizens themselves had to perform for the state; and many other things; rendered the Grecian states not the most desirable: but even these grievances were subservient to the public arts. The temples of the gods were for the most part held sacred even by the enemy; and such temples as the enemy destroyed arose more splendid from their ashes on a reverse of fortune. From the spoils of the Persians a more magnificent Athens was built: and, in almost every successful war, part of the booty that belonged to the state was sacrificed to one or other of the arts. Even in later times, Athens maintained the glory of her name, by her edifices and statues, in spite of all the ravages of the Romans: for several emperors, kings, heroes, and wealthy individuals, were emulous to preserve and adorn a city, which was the acknowledged parent of all refined taste. Hence under the Macedonian empire we perceive the arts of the Greeks did not perish; they only changed their seat. Even in remote countries the Grecian kings were still Greeks, and cherished the Grecian arts. Thus Alexander, and several of his successors, built splendid cities in Asia and Africa. Rome, and other nations, too, learned from the Greeks, when their countries were ripe for the arts: for throughout the whole Earth appeared but one Grecian art, and style of architecture.

4. The climate of the Greeks, too, afforded food for the beautiful in the arts; not principally from the human figure, which depends more on descent than on climate; but from its convenient situation for the materials of the arts, and the erection of the performances of the artist. Their country afforded them the fine Parian and other marbles: ivory, brass, and whatever else the arts required, they derived from a trade, of which they lay as in the centre. These even preceded in a certain degree the birth of their arts themselves; as they were in a situation to obtain from Asia Minor, Phenicia, and other countries, valuable materials, which they yet knew not how to employ. Thus the seeds of their future talents in the arts were early sown; particularly as their proximity to Asia Minor, their colonies in Graecia Magna, etc., excited in them a taste for luxury, and the enjoyments of life, which could not fail to promote the arts. The gay disposition of the Greeks was by no means inclined to waste its industry on useless pyramids. Individual towns and states indeed could never deviate into this wilderness of the monstrous. Thus, if we except perhaps the single Colossus of Rhodes, even in their works of greatest magnitude they adhered to that beautiful proportion, in which the pleasing and sublime are united. For this their serene

climate afforded them sufficient opportunity. It allowed them those numerous uncovered statues, altars, and temples; and in particular the beautiful column, that pattern of simplicity, correctness, and proportion, the slender gracefulness of which could there supply the place of the sullen northern wall.

When we combine all these circumstances, it is obvious, how art could operate, in Ionia, Greece, and Sicily, in that correct and airy style, which the Greeks exhibited in all their works of taste. By rules alone it is not to be learned: but it displays itself in the observation of rules; and, though originally the inspiration of a happy genius, must become mechanical by continued practice. Even the meanest Grecian artist was a Greek in his manner; we may excel him; but the whole genetic spirit of Grecian art we shall never attain: the genius of those times is gone by.

CHAPTER 4

The moral and political Wisdom of the Greeks

THE manners of the Greeks were as different, as their descent, their country, and the way in which they lived, according to their degree of civilization, and the series of successes or misfortunes, in which the fates had placed them. The Arcadians and Athenians, the Ionians and Epirots, the Spartans and Sybarites, were so dissimilar to each other in age, situation, and mode of life, that I want skill to sketch out a deceptive picture of them as a whole, the features of which must appear more contradictory, than those of the genius of the Athenians painted by Parrhassius.[15] Nothing remains for us, therefore, but to mark the general course taken by the moral culture of the Greeks, and the manner in which it coalesced with their political institutions.

As the most ancient moral culture of all the nations upon Earth proceeded chiefly from their religion, so did that of the Greeks, and it continued long in this track. The religious cere-

[15] "Pinxit demon atheniensium argumento quoque ingenioso: volebat namque varium, iracundum, injustum, inconstantem, eundem exorabilem, clementem, misericordem, excelsum, gloriosum, humilem, ferocem, fugacemque, et omnia pariter ostendere." Plin. *Hist. Nat.* lib. xxxv. c. 10.

monies, which were propagated through the means of the various mysteries, even when politics had attained a very considerable height; the sacred rights of hospitality, and of the protection of unfortunate fugitives; the inviolability of holy places; the belief in the furies and vengeance, that pursued even unpremeditated murder, and inflicted a curse upon a whole land for blood unexpiated; the practices of atonement, and appeasing the gods; the responses of the oracles; the sanctity of an oath, of the hearth, of the temples, of graves, etc.; were opinions and institutions, the prevalence of which was to unite a rude people, and gradually form demisavages to humanity.[16] That they happily accomplished their object, we perceive, when we compare the Greeks with other nations: for it is incontestable, that through these institutions they were led, not to the gates of philosophy and political cultivation, but deep into their sanctuary. Of what important service to Greece was the oracle at Delphi alone! Its divine voice pointed out so many tyrants and villains, in warning them of their fate; and not less frequently did it succour the unfortunate, counsel those in need of advice, strengthen beneficial institutions with the authority of the gods, make known works of art or the muse that could reach it, and give a sanction to moral principles and maxims of state. Thus the rude verses of the oracle accomplished more than the most polished lines of later poets: and it had the greatest influence, as it took under its protection the amphictyons, the supreme judges and controllers of the states of all Greece, and gave their sentences in a certain degree the weight of religious laws. What has been proposed in modern times as the sole mean of establishing perpetual peace throughout Europe, a tribunal of amphictyons,[17] existed formerly among the Greeks; and indeed near the throne of the god of truth and wisdom, who sanctified it by his authority.

---

[16] See Heyne on the institutions of the first Grecian legislators for the softening of manners, in *Opusc. academic.* (Academical Tracts), Part I, p. 207.

[17] See *Oeuvres par St. Pierre* (St. Pierre's Works), Vol. I, and almost all his writings.

With religion may be reckoned all those practices, which preserved to posterity the remembrance of their ancestors, from whose institutions they sprung for these continued to operate in the formation of their morals. Thus, for instance, the various public games gave a peculiar turn to education in Greece; as they made bodily exercises its principal object, and the excellencies acquired by them the aim of the whole nation. No tree ever produced such beautiful fruits, as the little branches of olive, ivy, and pine, which crowned the Grecian victors. These rendered youth handsome, healthy, and gay; these gave their limbs suppleness, strength, and symmetry; these struck into their minds the first sparks of love of fame, even of posthumous fame, and impressed on them the indelible character of living publicly for their country; and lastly, what is of all most valuable, they rooted in their hearts that taste for manly intercourse, and manly friendship, for which the Greeks were peculiarly distinguished. In Greece woman was not the supreme object of contest, to gain which the youth bent all his powers: the most beautiful Helen could have formed nothing but a Paris, had her possession or enjoyment been the only scope of manly endowment. The female sex, notwithstanding the fine patterns of every virtue it produced in Greece, remained a subordinate object: the thoughts of nobler youth were bent on something higher: the bands of friendship, which they formed with each other, or with more experienced men, trained them for a school, which no Aspasia could easily supply. Hence, in many states, the manly love of the Greeks; with that emulation, that instruction, that constancy, and that sacrifice of self, the feelings and consequences of which we read in Plato almost as a romance from a foreign planet. Manly hearts united in bonds of love and friendship, that held till death: the friends displayed toward each other a sort of jealousy, which hunted out the minutest spots; and each dreaded the other's eye, as a penetrating flame discovering the most secret inclinations of his mind. Youthful friendships are the sweetest; and no sentiment is so desirable as the love of those, with whom we have exercised ourselves in the course of perfection, during the delightful years of our budding faculties: and this course was publicly prescribed to the Greeks in their gymnasia, and in their military and political occupations, of which those sacred bands of lovers were the natural consequences. I am far from defending the depravity of manners, which in time sprung from the abuse of these institutions, particularly where youth exercised naked; but, alas! this abuse flowed from the character of the people, whose warm imagination, and love almost to madness of every thing beautiful, in which they placed the supreme enjoyment of the gods, rendered such disorders inevitable. Had these been privately performed, they would have been still more pernicious, as the history of all nations in warm climates, or of luxurious manners, sufficiently proves. Thus public institutions, and laudable aims, gave vent to the flame, that raged within: and thus it came under the coercive inspection of the laws, which employed it as an active engine for the purposes of the state.

Lastly. As triple Greece, situate in two quarters of the Globe, was divided into many tribes and states; the moral culture, that appeared in various places, must have been genetic to each tribe, and political in such different ways, that this circumstance alone is sufficient, to explain the happy progress of Grecian manners. The states of Greece were connected only by the gentlest bands; a common religion and language, the oracles, the games, the tribunal of amphictyons, etc.; or by descent and colonization; and lastly by the remembrance of ancient common enterprizes, poetry, and national fame: no despot compelled any farther union; and even their common perils for a long time passed over without destructive consequences. Hence each tribe drew from the source of culture what it esteemed proper, and watered itself from what rivulet it thought fit. And this it did according to its wants; though principally under the guidance of some superiour men, whom forming Nature sent. Even among the kings of Greece there were worthy sons of the ancient heroes, who had advanced with the times, and rendered not less service to their people by good laws, than their fathers had done by their celebrated valour. Thus, excepting the first founders of colonies, Minos was particularly eminent among royal legislators, who formed to war his valiant Cretans, the inhabitants of a mountainous island, and was a pattern in aftertimes for Lycurgus. He was the first, that checked the pirates, and gave security to the Egean Sea; the first general founder of morals by sea and land. That several monarchs resembled him in being the authors of good institutions, appears from the histories of Athens, Syracuse, and other kingdoms. But, it must be confessed, the activity of mankind in moral cultivation, as connected with the state, assumed a very different appearance, when most of the Grecian monarchies were converted into republics: a revolution, certainly one of the most memorable in all the history of mankind. It was not possible in any country but Greece, where a number of individual nations had continued to cherish the remembrance of their origin and race, even under their kings. Every people considered itself as a distinct political body, which possessed the same right to form its own institutions as its wandering ancestors: none of the Grecian tribes were sold at the will of an hereditary succession of kings. From this it does not follow, that the new government was better than the old: almost every where the principal and most powerful persons ruled instead of a king, so that in many cities there was less order, and an insupportable oppression of the people: yet thus the die was cast, and mankind, as emerging from a state of pupillage, learned to think for themselves concerning their political constitution. Accordingly the era of the Grecian republics was the first step of the human mind toward manhood, respecting the important question, how men should govern men. All the mistakes and errours of the governments of Greece are to be considered as the essays of youth, which commonly learns to be wise only from misfortune.

Thus in many states and colonies, that had become free, men of wisdom rose up, and acted as the guardians of the people. They saw the evils under which their fellow-citizens suffered, and turned their thoughts to a constitution, erected on the laws and manners of the community. Most of these ancient Grecian sages filled some public office, were governors of the people, counsellors of the king, or leaders of armies: for from such men of rank alone could proceed a political culture, exerting effective influence on the people. Even Lycurgus, Draco, Solon, were of the first families of the state, or members of administration: in their times the evils of aristocracy, and the discontents of the people, had reached the highest pitch; and hence arose the ready reception of the improved institutions they proposed. These men will inherit immortal praise, for that, possessing the confidence of the people, they declined the sovereign power, both for themselves and their posterity; and applied all their industry, all their knowledge of men and of the world; to a commonwealth, that is, to the state as a state. If their first attempts were far from the summit of perfection, far from being eternal masterpieces of human institutions; such they were not to be: their excellence was local, and their authors were frequently compelled against their will, to adapt them to the manners of the community, and its radical evils. Lycurgus had a freer scope than Solon; but he recurred to times too remote, and founded a state on such principles, as if the World were to persevere eternally in the heroic age of uncultivated youth. He gave perpetuity to his laws without waiting for their effects; and to a mind like his it would have been the severest punishment, could he have looked through all the periods of Grecian history, to perceive the consequences they occasioned to his own state, and sometimes to all Greece, partly by their abuse, and partly by too long continuance. The laws of Solon were injurious in another way. He himself outlived their spirit: the evil consequences of popular government he foresaw, and they remained evident to the wisest and best of his city, even to the last gasp of Athens.[18] But this is some time or other the fate of all human institutions, particularly the most difficult, those that concern countries and people. Time and nature alter every thing; and shall not men's way of life be changed? With every new generation a new way of thinking arises, however government and education may adhere to their ancient modes. New wants and dangers, new advantages of conquest, wealth, or increasing

[18] See Xenophon on the Commonwealth of the Athenians; also Plato, Aristotle, etc.

dignity, and even increase of population, augment the tide: and how can yesterday remain today? or the ancient law be an eternal law? The law is retained, but probably in appearance only; and, alas! chiefly in its abuses, the sacrifice of which appears too severe to selfish and indolent men. This was the case with the laws of Lycurgus, Solon, Romulus, and Moses, and all that outlived their day.

Hence it is very affecting to hear the words of these legislators in their later years: they are commonly the voice of complaint; for they lived long, they outlived themselves. Such are the words of Moses and of Solon, in the few fragments we have of them: nay, if we exclude mere moral maxims, almost all the reflections of the Grecian sages have a plaintive tone. They perceived the mutable destiny and happiness of men, which the laws of nature confine to narrow limits, sadly perplexed by their own conduct, and lamented it. They lamented the transitoriness of human life, and blooming youth; and they contemplated old age, often poor and diseased, but always weak and despised. They lamented the success of the impudent, and the sorrows of the well-meaning: but they omitted not to recommend in an affecting tone to the members of their community the most effectual weapons against these, prudence and a sound understanding, moderation of the passions and quiet industry, simplicity and true friendship, stedfastness and inflexibility of mind, reverence for the gods and love of our country. Even in the remains of the later Grecian comedies these plaintive tones of gentle humanity are heard.[19]

Thus in spite of all the evil consequences, and in part horrible, to the helots, Pelasgians, colonies, foreigners, and enemies, that proceeded from many Grecian states; we cannot overlook the noble sublimity of that public spirit, which flourished, in its day, in Lacedemon, Athens, Thebes, and, in a certain degree, in every part of Greece. It is unquestionably true, that, as it flowed not from particular laws of one particular man, it flourished not equally at all times, and in every member of the state:

[19] Of this elsewhere.

yet it flourished among the Greeks, as even their unjust and jealous wars, their severest oppressions, and the most perfidious traitors to their civic virtue, evince. The monumental inscription of the Spartans that fell at Thermopylae, "Traveller, tell at Sparta, that here we lie, slain in obedience to her laws," will for ever remain the fundamental principle of supreme political virtue; which, after the lapse of two thousand years, gives us only to lament, that once indeed it was the maxim of a few Spartans, with regard to some rigid patrician laws of a narrow country, but never became a principle for the pure laws of collective mankind. The principle itself is the highest, that men could invent and practice for their liberty and happiness. The same may be said of the constitution of Athens, though it struck into a very different path. For if enlightening the people with regard to those things, in which they are most concerned, ought to be the object of a political establishment, Athens was unquestionably the most enlightened city throughout the whole World. Neither Paris nor London, neither Rome nor Babylon, and still less Memphis, Jerusalem, Pekin, or Benares, can enter into competition with it. Now as *patriotism*, and an *enlightened mind*, are the two poles, round which all the moral cultivation of mankind revolves, Athens and Sparta will ever be remembered as the two grand stages, on which human politics first exercised themselves in this career with youthful animation. The other Grecian states for the most part only followed these two grand examples; and a few, that refused to copy the constitutions of Athens and Lacedaemon, fell a prey to conquest.

The philosophy of history, however, considers not so much what was actually done by feeble men on these two points of the Earth, during the short period of their operations, as what followed from the principles of their institutions with regard to mankind in general. In spite of all their faults, the names of Lycurgus and Solon, Miltiades and Themistocles, Aristides, Cimon, Phocion, Epaminondas, Pelopidas, Agesilaus, Agis, Cleomenes, Dion, Timoleon, and others, will live with eternal fame; while Alcibiades, Conon, Pausanias, Lysander, men equally great, will be mentioned with reproach, as subverters of the public spirit of Greece, or traitors to their country. Without an Athens, even the modest virtue of Socrates could scarcely have produced such blossoms as it afterwards did in some of his scholars: for Socrates was no more than a citizen of Athens, and all his wisdom was only the wisdom of an Athenian citizen, which he propagated in domestic dialogues. With regard to the wisdom of common life we are indebted to Athens alone for the most and best in all ages.

As little can be said of practical virtues, we must yet bestow a few words on institutions, of which only an Athenian popular government was susceptible, the forum and the stage. Orators before a tribunal, and particularly on affairs of state, where immediate decision follows, are dangerous instruments; and their bad consequences are sufficiently obvious in the history of Athens. Yet as they presume a people, that have knowledge, or at least are capable of having knowledge of every public business, that is brought before them; the Athenian people, notwithstanding all their parties, remain alone in history, being scarcely equalled even by the Romans. For the business itself, to elect or try a general, to decide on peace and war, life and death, and every public affair of state, a turbulent mob was certainly unfit: yet the conduct of this business, and all the arts employed in it, opened even the ears of the unruly mob, and gave them that enlightened mind, that propensity to political conversation, with which all the Asiatic nations were unacquainted. Eloquence, thus exercised before the public, rose to such a height, as it no where attained, except in Greece and Rome, and as it never can or will reach again, till perhaps popular oratory is united with the universal diffusion of true knowledge. The object is unquestionably great; though in Athens the means fell short of the end. It was the same with the Athenian stage. This exhibited plays for the people, popular, sublime, and ingenious: but with Athens its history is no more; as the narrow circle of determinate subjects, passions, and views, to work upon its people, could scarcely revive for the mixed multitude of another race, and a different political constitution. The moral cultivation of the Greeks, therefore, must never be measured, either in their public history, or in their orators and dramatic poets, by the standard of abstract morality; for in neither of them was such a standard followed.[20] History shows, how the Greeks, in every period, were all, that their situation permitted, both of good and of bad. The orator shows, with what eyes he viewed parties in the pursuit of his profession, and with what colours it was necessary to his purpose to portray them. The dramatic poet brought on the stage such characters as preceding times afforded, or as it suited his object to exhibit to his particular audience. Conclusions respecting the morality or immorality of the people at large drawn from these would be groundless: yet no one will dispute, that the Greeks, at certain periods, and in certain cities, were the most ingenious, gay, and enlightened people of their world, according to the circle of objects then before them. The citizens of Athens afforded generals, orators, sophists, judges, statesmen, and artists, as education, propensity, choice, fate, or accident, directed; and in one Greek many of the best and noblest qualities were often united.

CHAPTER 5

Scientific Acquirements of the Greeks

It is doing justice to no people upon Earth, to judge of them by a foreign standard of science: yet this has been done to the Greeks, as well as to many Asiatic nations, and they have often been unjustly loaded both with blame and praise. The Greeks were unacquainted with any speculative system of doctrines respecting God and the human soul: the inquiries concerning them were private opinions, in which every philosopher was free, so long as he observed the religious rites of his country, and rendered himself obnoxious to no political party. In Greece the human mind had on this point, as it generally has, to fight its way; and in this at length it was crowned with success.

The Grecian philosophy proceeded from ancient tales of the

[20] See the introduction to Gillies's *Translation of the Orations of Lysias and Isocrates,* with other similar works, in which Greece is estimated from its orators and poets.

gods and theogonies; and much indeed was spun from them by the fine invention of the Greeks. The fictions of the births of the gods, of the conflicts of the elements, of the love and hatred of beings towards each other, were so improved in various directions by their different schools, that we may almost say, they had advanced as far as ourselves, when we invent cosmogonies without the aid of natural history. Nay in some respects they advanced farther; as their minds were more at liberty, and no preconceived hypothesis biassed them in their course. Even the numbers of Pythagoras, and other philosophers, are bold attempts, to associate the knowledge of things with the simplest idea of the human mind, a clearly conceived magnitude: but as natural philosophy and mathematics were then in their infancy, the attempt was premature. Yet, like the systems of many other Grecian philosophers, it will ever excite in us a degree of veneration; as these in general, each in its particular sphere, were the fruits of profound reflection and extensive comprehension: many of them are founded on truths and observations, of which, perhaps to the advantage of science, we have since lost sight. That none of the ancient philosophers conceived god, for instance, as a being distinct from the World, or a pure metaphysical monad, but all adhered to the idea of a soul of the World, was perfectly consonant to the childhood of human philosophy, and perhaps will for ever remain consonant to it. It is to be lamented, that we are acquainted with the boldest opinions of philosophers only from mutilated accounts, but not systematically from their own works: still more is it to be regretted, however, that we are disinclined to place ourselves in their times, and eager to intrude on them our way of thinking. In general ideas every nation has its particular way of seeing, founded for the most part on the mode of expression, that is to say, on tradition: and as the philosophy of the Greeks arose from poems and allegories, this gave to their abstract ideas a peculiar stamp, to themselves perfectly clear. Even the allegories of Plato are not merely ornamental: their images are like the classical sentences of old times, ingenious developments of ancient poetical traditions.

The inquiries of the Greeks were principally directed to the philosophy of man and morals; as the time in which they lived, and their political constitution, led them particularly this way. Natural history, mathematics, and natural philosophy, were yet in their rudiments; and the implements of modern discovery were not invented. Every thing, on the other hand, attracted them toward the nature and manners of mankind. This was the predominant tone of the poetry, history, and political institutions of the Greeks: every citizen felt the necessity of knowing his fellow-citizens, and was occasionally liable to be chosen to public offices, which he could not refuse to fill: the passions and active powers of men had then freer play, they suffered not even the retired philosopher to pass unnoticed: to govern men, or to perform the part of an effective member of society, was the predominant propensity of every ambitious Grecian soul. It is nothing wonderful, therefore, that the philosophy of the metaphysician should be occupied on the improvement of morals or the state, as we find in Pythagoras, Plato, and even Aristotle. As citizens they had no call to found states: Pythagoras was not as Lycurgus, Solon, and others, a sovereign, or an archon: and the greater part of his philosophy was speculative, bordering even on superstition. Yet in his school were educated men, whose influence on the states of Graecia Magna was very great; and the society of his disciples, if fate had allowed it longer duration, would probably have been the most efficacious, as it certainly was a very pure engine for the improvement of mankind.[21] But even this step of a man far superiour to the age in which he lived was premature: the wealthy, sybaritish cities of Graecia Magna, and their tyrants, desired no such censors of morals, and the Pythagoreans were martyred.

It is an often repeated encomium, though in my opinion exaggerated, of the benevolent Socrates, that he was the first and chief, who called philosophy from Heaven down to Earth, and imparted to man the boon of morality. This encomium at

[21] See the history of this society in Meiners's *Geschichte der Wissenschaften in Griechenland und Rom* (History of the sciences in Greece and Rome), Vol. I.

most is valid only with regard to the person of Socrates, and the narrow circle of his own life. Long before him there were sages, who had actively inculcated morals upon mankind; as this was the distinguishing character of Grecian lore, even from the fabulous Orpheus.[22] Pythagoras, too, laid much more extensive foundations for the improvement of men's morals by his disciples, than Socrates was capable of doing by means of all his friends. That Socrates was not fond of sublime abstract speculations arose from his situation, and the circle of his knowledge, though chiefly from the time and his mode of life. The systems of imagination, without farther natural experiments, were exhausted; and the Grecian wisdom was become the wordy play of sophists; so that it required no great effort, to despise or throw aside, what was incapable of being carried to a higher pitch. His demon, his native integrity, and the domestic course of his life, guarded him against the dazzling spirit of the Sophists; and offered to his philosophy the proper object of man, which had such beneficial effects on almost all with whom he conversed. These effects, however were promoted by the time, the place, and the circle, in which Socrates lived. Elsewhere the philosophic citizen would have been a virtuous and enlightened man, yet probably we should never have heard of his name; for no invention, no new doctrine, peculiar to himself, marks him in the book of Time: his method and manner of life, the moral cultivation, which he gave himself, and endeavoured to impart to others, and more particularly the manner of his death, point him out as a pattern to mankind.

Much is requisite to form a Socrates; above all the valuable talent of being satisfied with little, and that exquisite taste for moral beauty, which in himself he seems to have refined into a sort of instinct: yet let us not exalt this modest worthy man above the sphere, in which Providence fixed him. He educated few scholars completely worthy of himself: because his wisdom belonged as it were to the household stuff of his own life; and his

[22] Meae noctes—de uno maximè illo versu Homeri quaerunt, quem Socrates prae omnibus semper rebus sibi esse cordi dicebat; "Οττι τοι ἐν μεγαροισι κακον τ' αγαθον τι τετυκται." Gellius. xiv. 6.

excellent method was easily susceptible of degenerating, in the mouths of his immediate disciples, into jest and sophistry, if the ironical questioner possessed not the same stamp of heart and mind as Socrates. Even if we impartially compare his two most celebrated disciples, Xenophon and Plato, we shall find, to use his own modest expression, that he was only the midwife of their natural genius; whence they appear so unlike each other. The most distinguished parts of their works evidently flow from their own way of thinking; and the best thanks they could pay the teacher they loved, were to exhibit his moral picture. It was much to be wished, however, that the scholars of Socrates could have infused his spirit into all the laws and political institutions of Greece: but history shows, that this was not done. He lived at the period, when Athens had attained her highest polish; but at the same time the Grecian states were most at variance with each other: this conjunction of circumstances could not fail to be succeeded by unfortunate times, and the declension of manners; and these soon effected the downfall of Grecian liberty. Against these they were not protected by Socratic wisdom, which was too pure and delicate, to sway the fate of a people. Xenophon, the statesman and general, pointed out defects in the constitution, which he possessed not the power to amend. Plato created an ideal republic, which was no where carried into practice, and least of all in the court of Dionysius. In short, the philosophy of Socrates was more beneficial to mankind, than to Greece; and this is unquestionably its noblest praise.

Far different was the spirit of Aristotle, the most acute, firm, and dry, perhaps, that ever guided the style. His philosophy, indeed, is more the philosophy of the schools, than of common life; particularly in those of his writings which we possess, and in the manner in which they are used: but abstract reason and science have gained so much the more in him, so that in this sphere he stands alone as the monarch of the times. That the schoolmen, for the most part, attended to his metaphysics only, was not the fault of Aristotle, but their own; yet these incredibly sharpened human reason. They put into the hands of barbarous nations implements, by which the obscure dreams of fancy and tradition were first converted into sophisms, and thus gradually destroyed themselves. His better works, however, his natural history and physics, ethics, politics, poetics, and rhetoric, still want much happy application. It is to be regretted, that his historical works are lost, and that of his natural history we have only abstracts. Let those, however, who deny the Greeks the spirit of pure science, read Aristotle and Euclid, writers, never excelled in their kind: then, too, it was the merit of Plato and Aristotle, to awaken the spirit of natural knowledge and mathematics, which in greatness soars beyond all moralising, and labours for all ages. Many of their scholars promoted astronomy, botany, anatomy, and other sciences; while Aristotle himself, with his natural history alone, formed the basis of an edifice, in the completion of which ages yet to come will find employment. In Greece were laid the foundations of every thing knowable in science, as of every thing beautiful in form: alas! that fate has allowed us so little of the works of its profoundest philosophers! What remains is excellent: but, perhaps, the most excellent is gone.

It will not be expected of me to go through the separate sciences of mathematics, physic, natural knowledge, and all the fine arts, to give a string of names of those, who, as inventors or improvers, have served as the groundwork of every thing scientific in them to all subsequent ages. It is universally known, that Asia and Egypt have given us, properly speaking, no true form of knowledge in any art or science: for such we have to thank the acute methodical spirit of the Greeks alone. Now as it is a determinate form of knowledge, that effects their augmentation or improvement in future times, we are indebted to the Greeks for the basis of almost all our sciences. Let them have appropriated to themselves as many foreign ideas as they pleased, so much the better for us: it is sufficient that they methodised them, and aimed at clearer knowledge. In this the various schools of the Greeks were what their several republics were in politics, emulous powers contending together for one common object: without this division so much would not have been done for science even in Greece. The Ionian, Italian, and

Athenian schools, though they had one common language, were parted by lands and seas: each therefore could separately take root, and when it was engrafted, or transplanted, bore so much the finer fruit. No one of the early philosophers was paid by the state, or even by his scholars: he thought for himself; he invented from love of science, or from love of fame. Those whom he instructed were not children, but youths, or men; and frequently men who bore the most important offices in the state. Men did not write then for annual fairs of literature; but their thoughts were so much the more perseveringly and profoundly employed: at the same time, in the fine climate of Greece, the temperate philosopher could think undisturbed by care, as little was required for his support.

In the mean time, we must not here refuse monarchy the praise it deserves. No one of the Grecian republics was capable of affording Aristotle that assistance in natural history, which he received from his royal scholar: still less could the sciences that require leisure and expense, as mathematics, astronomy, etc., have made the advancement they did in Alexandria, without the establishments founded by the Ptolemies. To these we are indebted for an Euclid, an Eratosthenes, Apollonius Pergaeus, Ptolemy, and others, who laid the foundations of sciences, on which not only the present system of learning rests, but, in a certain degree, the government of the whole World. That the period of Grecian eloquence and popular philosophy ended with the republics, was not without its advantages: these had born their fruits; but other germes of science, springing from Grecian minds, were necessary to the human understanding. We readily forgive the Egyptian Alexandria for the inferiority of her poets; she made ample compensation in good astronomers and mathematicians.[23] Poets form themselves: diligence and practice alone makes accurate observers.

There are three subjects, in particular, to which the Grecian philosophy opened the path, in a manner that could scarcely have been accomplished in any other part of the World: lan-

---

[23] See Heyne on the genius of the age of the Ptolemies, in *Opusc. acad.* (Academical Tracts), Part I, p. 76 and following.

guage, history, and the arts. The language of the Greeks received such abundant richness and beauty from their poets, orators, and philosophers, that in later times the instrument itself, when incapable of being applied to such brilliant ends in public life, attracted no inconsiderable attention. Hence the art of the grammarians, who were in part actual philosophers. Time indeed has robbed us of the greater part of these writers; though the sense of this loss is deadened by that of many greater: their influence, however, has not been obliterated; for the study of the Greek language emitted sparks, at which that of the Latin, and of the philosophy of language in general, caught fire. Nay hence sprung the study of the oriental dialects of Hither Asia: for it was from the Greek, that men learned to reduce the Hebrew, Arabic, and other languages, to rules.

In like manner a philosophy of the arts was thought of no where but in Greece; where, from a happy impulse of nature, and a sure habitual taste, poets and artists carried into practice a philosophy of the beautiful, before its rules were analyzed. Thus from the astonishing emulation in epic and dramatic poetry, and in public speaking, a criticism was necessarily formed, to which ours can scarcely be compared. A few late fragments of it only, the writings of Aristotle excepted, have come down to us; but these evince the refined penetration of the Grecian critics.

Lastly, the philosophy of history belongs particularly to Greece; for the Greeks alone possessed what might properly be called history. The orientals had their genealogies and fables; the northern nations, their tales; others, their poems: the Greeks, in process of time, formed from tales, poems, fables, and genealogies, the sound body of a narrative, through all the members of which the current of vitality flows. Here, too, its ancient poetry led the way, for it is not easy to relate a fable in a more pleasing manner, than was done in the epic poem: the division of the subject into rhapsodies introduced similar pauses in history, and the long hexameter was well adapted soon to form the melody of historical prose. Thus Herodotus succeeded Homer; and the subsequent historians of the commonwealths introduced their colouring, the spirit of republican oratory, into their narration. Now as with Thucydides and Xenophon the Grecian history proceeded from Athens, and its writers were themselves statesmen and generals, their history naturally became a collection of facts and reasonings upon them, without their seeking to give them this philosophical form. The public orations, the intricacy of Grecian affairs, the animated appearance of events and their motives, prompted such a form; and we may confidently assert, that no philosophical history would have been known to the World, had the Grecian republics never existed. In proportion as the military art and the science of politics developed themselves, the philosophical spirit of history was rendered more elaborate; till at length it became in the hands of Polybius almost the sciences of war and politics themselves. In models of this kind subsequent speculators had ample materials for their remarks; and the Dionysiuses had certainly ampler opportunities to acquire the rudiments of history, than a Chinese, a Jew, or even a Roman could have possessed.

As we thus find the Greeks so rich and successful in every exercise of the mind, in poetical, oratorical, philosophical, scientific, and historical works; why, Fate of the times, hast thou deprived us of so many of them? Where are the Amazonia of Homer, his Thebaid and Iresione, his Iambics, and his Margites? Where are the many lost pieces of Archilochus, Simonides, Alcaeus, and Pindar; the eighty-three tragedies of Aeschylus, the hundred and eighteen of Sophocles; and the innumerable performances of tragic, comic, and lyric poets, the greatest philosophers, the most indispensable historians, the most memorable mathematicians, natural philosophers, and others, that have perished? For one work of Democritus, Aristotle, Theophrastus, Polybius, or Euclid; for one tragedy of Aeschylus, Sophocles, and so many others; for one comedy of Aristophanes, Philemon, or Menander; for one ode of Sappho or Alcaeus; for the lost natural and political history of Aristotle, or for the five and thirty books of Polybius; who would not give a mountain of modern writings, his own the first in the heap, to heat the baths of Alexandria for a twelvemonth? But the iron foot of destiny takes a far different course, regardless of the immortality of individual performances in science, or in art. The grand Propylaeum of Athens, all the temples of the gods, those magnificent palaces, walls, colossuses, columns, seats, aqueducts, streets, altars, which the ancients erected for eternity, have fallen beneath the fury of the conqueror; and should a few feeble leaves of human industry and reflection be spared? Rather it is a subject of wonder, that we have so many; too many, perhaps, for us to have used them all as they ought to have been used. In conclusion, let us now consider the history of Greece as a whole, after having thus gone through its parts: it instructively carries its philosophy with it, step by step.

CHAPTER 6

History of the Revolutions of Greece

HOWEVER abundant the revolutions, that embroil the pages of Grecian history, the threads of them lead to a few principal points, the natural laws of which are clear. For,

1. That in the three tracts of land, with their islands and peninsulas, which constituted Greece, many tribes and colonies, from the higher countries and the sea, should migrate from place to place, settle, and expel one another, is conformable to the universal history of the ancient world in similar tracts of land and sea. But here the migration was more animated, as the populous northern mountains, and the extensive country of Asia, were near; and the spirit of enterprise was kept in great activity by a series of adventures, the tales of which were current. This is the history of Greece for about seven hundred years.

2. That different degrees of cultivation, and from different quarters, must have come to these tribes, follows equally from the nature of the country, and of circumstances. They spread from the north; they passed over from different parts of the neighbouring civilized regions, and settled in different ways in different places. At length the predominating Hellenes gave uniformity to the whole, and stamped the character of the

Grecian language and way of thinking. Now the seeds of cultivation, thus introduced, must have germinated very differently and unequally in Asia Minor, in Graecia Magna, and in Greece properly so called: but this variety aided the Grecian spirit by means of transplantation and rivalry: for it is an acknowledged fact, both in the history of plants and animals, that the same seed does not eternally flourish on the same spot, but produces more perfect and racy fruits, if transplanted at proper seasons.

3. The separate states, from originally small monarchies, in time became aristocracies, and some of them democracies: both were often in danger of falling again under the will of one ruler; the democracies most frequently. This, too, is the natural progress of political establishments in their early youth. The chief people of the tribe thought proper to withdraw themselves from obedience to the will of a monarch; and, as the people were unable to guide themselves, they became their guides. But according as the occupation, the spirit, and the institutions of the people were, they remained under these leaders, or assumed a share in the government. The former was the case in Lacedaemon; the latter, in Athens. The causes of this may be found in the circumstances and constitutions of the two cities. In Sparta the regents strictly watched each other, so that no tyrant could arise: in Athens the people were more than once decoyed into a tyranny, either avowed or concealed. Both towns, with all they effected, were as natural consequences of their situation, epoch, constitution, and circumstances, as any natural production could be.

4. Several republics, pitted as it were more or less against each other, by common occupations, boundaries, or some other interest, but still more by martial spirit and love of fame, would soon find causes of quarrel: the most powerful first; and these, when they could, would draw others to their party, till one obtained a preponderance. This was the case in the long wars between the juvenile states of Greece, particularly between Lacedaemon and Athens, and latterly Thebes. The wars were carried on with animosity, rigour, and often barbarity: as all

wars will be, in which every citizen and soldier takes a common part. They mostly originated from trifles, or points of honour, as battles among youths generally arise: and what appears singular, though it is not so by any means, every vanquishing party, Lacedaemon in particular, fought to impose its laws and constitution on the vanquished, as if these would indelibly impress on it the marks of defeat. For aristocracy is a sworn enemy to tyranny, as well as to popular government.

5. The wars of the Greeks, however, considered as to the manner in which they were conducted, were not the mere incursions of savages: in time they developed the whole spirit of war and politics, which has ever turned the wheel of events.[24] Even the Greeks knew the necessities of a state, and the sources of its wealth and power, which they often endeavoured to create, though in a rude way. They understood the meaning too of the balance of power between the republics, and the different ranks in the state; of secret and open confederacies; of stratagems of war; of preventing, abandoning, etc. Both in military and political affairs, the most expert of the Romans, and of the moderns, have learned from the Greeks: for however military manoeuvres may change, with change of weapons, times, and the circumstances of the World; the spirit of man, which invents, deceives, conceals its purposes, attacks, defends, advances, retreats, discovers the weakness of an enemy, and in this way or that avails itself of advantages, or abuses them, will remain at all times the same.

6. The war with the Persians makes the first grand era in Grecian history. It was occasioned by the Asiatic colonies, which had been unable to resist the spirit of conquest of the vast oriental monarchy, but, accustomed to be free, sought the earliest opportunity, to shake off the yoke. That the Athenians sent twenty ships to their aid, arose from the pride of democracy; for Cleomenes, the Spartan, had refused them assistance: and with their twenty ships they led all Greece into the wildest war. When once it had commenced, however, it was a prodigy

[24] A comparison of several nations, in this respect, will arise from the progress of history.

of valour, that a few inconsiderable states should gain important victories over two great kings of Asia. But it was no miracle: the Persians were drawn altogether out of their focus; the Greeks contended for land, life, and liberty. They fought against slavish barbarians, who had shown them, in the example of the Eretrians, what they had to expect; and therefore neglected nothing, that human wisdom and valour could perform. The Persians under Xerxes attacked as barbarians: in one hand they brought chains to enslave; in the other, fire to lay desolate: but this was not fighting with prudence. Themistocles employed merely the advantage of the wind against them: and it must be confessed, that to an unwieldy fleet a contrary wind is a dangerous opponent. In short, the Persians conducted the war with a great force, and much fury; but without skill: consequently the event could not be successful. Even had the Greeks been defeated, and their whole country laid waste like Athens; the Persians, from the centre of Asia, and with such an internal state of the kingdom, could never have retained them in subjection; for they found it extremely difficult even to hold Egypt. The sea was the friend of Greece, as the Delphian oracle said in another sense.

7. But the defeated Persians left behind them in Athens, with their spoils and disgrace, a spark, which kindled flames, that destroyed all the Grecian institutions. This consisted of the wealth and glory, the splendour and jealousy, in short all the ingredients of that pride, which followed the war. In Athens the age of Pericles soon arose; the most brilliant ever experienced by a state so small: and it was quickly followed, from very natural causes, by the unfortunate Peloponnesian war, and the two Spartan; till at length a single victory enabled Philip of Macedon, to throw his chains over all Greece. Let no one say, that an unpropitious deity controls the fate of mankind, and enviously seeks to cast them down: men are the malignant demons of each other. As Greece was in those days, could it fail of being an easy prey to a conqueror? And whence could this conqueror come, but from the mountains of Macedon? From Persia, Egypt, Phenicia, Rome, Carthage, it was secure: but

near it was an enemy, who griped it in his strong and wily talons. The oracle was here more prudent than the Greeks: it philippized; and the whole of the event confirmed the general position, "that a race of united mountaineers, expert in war, and seated on the neck of a divided, enfeebled, enervated nation, must necessarily conquer it, if it pursue its object with prudence and valour." This Philip did, and seized on Greece, which had long before been vanquished by itself. Here the history of Greece would have terminated, had Philip been a barbarian like Alaric or Sylla: but he was himself a Greek, and his still greater son was the same; and thus, even with the loss of their liberty, the Greeks obtained a name in the annals of the World, which few have equalled.

8. The young Alexander, who was scarcely twenty years old when he ascended the throne, and fired with the unchecked ardour of ambition, proceeded to execute the plan, for which his father had made all the necessary preparations: he went over into Asia, and invaded the dominions of the Persian monarch himself. This too was an event most naturally to be expected. All the expeditions of the Persians against Greece by land had passed through Thrace and Macedon; and in consequence these two nations cherished an ancient grudge against the people of Persia. The weakness of the Persians, too, was sufficiently known to the Greeks, not only from the ancient battles of Marathon, Plataea, etc., but, from the more recent retreat of Xenophon with his ten thousand Greeks. Now whither should the Macedonian, the ruler of Greece and generalissimo of its forces, direct his arms, and lead his phalanx, but against the wealthy monarchy, which had been deeply decaying internally for a century? The young hero fought three battles, and Asia Minor, Syria, Phenicia, Egypt, Lybia, Persia, and India, were his own: nay he might have advanced to the boundaries of the ocean, if his Macedonians, more prudent than himself, had not compelled him to retreat. Little as all this success deserves the name of miraculous, as little was his death at Babylon the work of envious fate. How grand was the conception, from Babylon to rule the World! a world, that

extended from the Hindus to Lybia, and even over all Greece as far as the Icarian Sea. How vast the idea, to make of all this country a Greece in language, manners, arts, trade, and colonization; and to render Bactra, Susa, Alexandria, and many other cities, each a new Athens! And behold, the conqueror was cut off in the bloom of his life; and with him died every hope of a new-created Grecian world! Should a man say thus to Fate, he would receive for answer: "Let Babylon or Pella be the residence of Alexander; let the Bactrians speak the language of Greece or of Parthia; if the son of a mortal would execute his projects, let him be temperate, and not drink himself to death." This Alexander did, and his kingdom was at an end. It is no wonder, that he destroyed himself; it is much rather to be wondered, that he, who had long ceased to be able to support his good fortune, did not sooner finish his career.

9. The empire was now divided: the vast bubble burst. When and where was the event different under similar circumstances? The dominions of Alexander were in no respect united: they were scarcely consolidated into a whole even in the mind of the conqueror himself. The cities he had founded in different places were unable to defend themselves in their infant state without such a protector as he, much less to keep in check the nations, on which they were imposed. Now as Alexander died in a manner without an heir, how could it be otherwise, than that the birds of prey, who had assisted him in his victorious flight, should begin to plunder for themselves? They quarrelled among each other, and contended together for a long time, till each had established his nest on the spoils of victory. This has been the case with every state formed by such extensive and speedy conquest, and supported only by the mind of the conqueror: the nature of various nations and countries soon reclaims its rights; so that it can be ascribed only to the superiority of the polished Greeks over the barbarians, that so many forcibly united regions did not sooner return to their old constitutions. Parthia, Bactra, and the countries beyond the Euphrates did this first: for they lay at too great a distance from the centre of an empire, which had nothing to

protect it against mountaineers of Parthian descent. Had the Seleucidae made Babylon their residence, as Alexander intended to have done, or their own Seleucia, they would probably have retained more power toward the east; but then, it may also be presumed, they would sooner have sunk into enervating luxury. It was the same with the Asiatic provinces of the Thracian empire: they availed themselves of the right to which their conquerors had resorted, and, when the thrones of the companions of Alexander were filled by their feebler successors, became separate kingdoms. In all this the invariably recurring natural laws of political history are conspicuous.

10. The kingdoms that lay nearest to Greece were of longest duration: and they might have endured still longer, had not the disputes between themselves, and more particularly those between the Romans and Carthaginians, involved them in that ruin, which, proceeding from the queen of Italy, gradually overspread the whole shore of the Mediterranean Sea. Feeble, worn out kingdoms staked their fortunes in an unequal contest, against which no great share of prudence was requisite to forewarn them. Still, however, they retained as much of the Grecian arts and polish, as their rulers and the times would admit. The sciences flourished in Egypt under the guise of learning, as thus only they had been there introduced: like mummies they lay buried in the libraries and museums. In the Asiatic courts the arts became licentious pomp. The kings of Pergamus and Egypt rivalled each other in collecting books: an emulation, which was both injurious and beneficial to all future literature. They collected books and falsified them: and afterwards, with the burning of what was collected a whole world of ancient learning was destroyed at once. It is obvious, that in these things fate no otherwise interfered, than it does in all worldly events, which it leaves to the wise, or foolish, yet ever natural, conduct of men. When the man of letters laments over a lost book of antiquity, how many things of more importance have we to lament, which have followed the invariable course of fate! The history of the successors of Alexander particularly

claims our notice; not only because it involves so many causes of the fall or preservation of empires, but as a melancholy pattern of kingdoms founded on foreign acquisitions, as well of territory, as of sciences, arts, and cultivation.

11. That Greece in such a state could never more regain its pristine splendour, needs no demonstration: the period of its bloom had long been over. Many vain rulers, indeed, laboured to raise up Grecian freedom: but it was an empty labour for a freedom without spirit, a body without a soul. Athens never ceased to idolize its benefactors; and the arts, as well as declamations on philosophy and science, maintained themselves in this seat of the general cultivation of Europe, as long as it was possible; but prosperity and devastation continued to alternate with each other. The little states were strangers to harmony, and the principles of mutual support, though they formed the Aetolian confederacy, and renewed the Achaian league. Neither the prudence of Philopoemen, nor the rectitude of Aratus, restored the ancient times of Greece. As the declining Sun, surrounded by the vapours of the horizon, assumes a greater and more romantic appearance; so did the political state of Greece at this period: but the beams of the setting luminary no longer impart meridian warmth, and the politics of dying Greece remained ineffective. The Romans came upon them as cajoling tyrants, the judges of all the differences in the country to their own advantage; and scarcely any barbarians could have acted worse, than Mummius in Corinth, Sylla in Athens, and Aemilius in Macedon. The Romans long continued to rob Greece of every thing, that could be carried away; till at length they respected it just as much as men respect a plundered corpse. They paid flatterers there, and sent thither their sons, to study in the sacred paths of the ancient philosophers the sophisms of wordy pedants. At length succeeded the Goths, the Christians, and the Turks, who put a complete end to the empire of the Grecian divinities, which had been long sunk in decrepitude. They are fallen, the great gods, the Olympian Jupiter and Athenian Pallas, the Apollo of Delphi and the Juno

of Argos: their temples are ruins, their statues heaps of stone, and even their fragments may now be sought in vain.[25] They are vanished from the face of the Earth, so that it is difficult to conceive the sway their faith once held, and the wonders it effected, among the most ingenious of all people. As these most beautiful idols of the human imagination have fallen, will the less beautiful fall like them? and for what will they make way; for other idols?

12. Graecia Magna, though in a different vortex, experienced at last a similar fate. The most flourishing, populous cities, in the finest climate of the Earth, founded under the laws of Zaleucus, Charondas, and Diocles, and taking the lead of most of the Grecian provinces in civilization, science, arts, and commerce, were not, it is true, in the way of the Persians, or of Philip; and in consequence maintained themselves longer than their European and Asiatic sisters: but the period of their destiny arrived. Involved in various wars between Rome and Carthage, they at length fell, and ruined Rome by their manners, as Rome had ruined them by her arms. There lie their beautiful and spacious ruins, lamentably desolated by earthquakes and volcanoes, but still more by the rage of man.[26] The nymph Parthenope mourns; the Ceres of Sicily seeks her temple, and can scarcely find again her golden plains.

CHAPTER 7

General Reflections on the History of Greece

We have considered the history of this celebrated region in several points of view, as it is in some measure a general basis for a philosophy of history in all countries. The Greeks not only remained free from any intermixture with foreign nations, so that their progress has been entirely their own; but they so perfectly filled up their period, and passed through every stage of civilization, from its slightest commencement to its completion, that no other nation can be compared with them. The people of the continent have either stopped at the rudiments of

[25] See the travels of Spon, Stuart, Chandler, Riedesel, and others.
[26] See the travels of Riedesel, Howel, and others.

civilization, and unnaturally perpetuated them by laws and customs; or become a prey to conquest, before they had advanced beyond them: the blossom withered before it was blown. Greece, on the contrary, enjoyed its full time: it formed every thing it was capable of forming, and a happy combination of circumstances aided it in its progress to perfection. On the continent undoubtedly it would soon have fallen a victim to some conqueror, like its Asiatic brethren: had Darius and Xerxes accomplished their designs, the age of Pericles would never have appeared. Or had a despot ruled over the Greeks, he would soon have become himself a conqueror, according to the disposition of all despots, and, as Alexander did, have empurpled distant rivers with Grecian blood. Foreign nations would have been introduced into their country, and their victories would have dispersed them through foreign lands. From all this they were protected by the mediocrity of their power, and even their limited commerce, which never ventured beyond the pillars of Hercules and of Fortune. As the botanist cannot obtain a complete knowledge of a plant, unless he follow it from the seed, through its germination, blossoming, and decay; such is the Grecian history to us: it is only to be regretted, that, according to the usual course, it is yet far from having been studied like that of Rome. At present it is my place, to indicate, from what has been said, some points of view in this important fragment of general history, which most immediately present themselves to the eye of observation: and here I must repeat the first grand principle:

Whatever can take place among mankind, within the sphere of given circumstances of time, place, and nation, actually does take place. Of this Greece affords the amplest and most beautiful proofs.

In natural philosophy we never reckon upon miracles: we observe laws, which we perceive every where equally effectual, undeviating, and regular. And shall man, with his powers, changes, and passions, burst these chains of nature? Had Greece been peopled with Chinese, our Greece would never have existed: had our Greeks been fixed where Darius led the enslaved Eretians, they would have formed no Athens, they would have produced no Sparta. Behold Greece now: the ancient Greeks are no more to be seen; nay frequently their country no longer appears. If a remnant of their language were not still spoken; if marks of their way of thinking, if ruins of their cities and works of art, or at least their ancient rivers and mountains, were not still visible; it might be supposed, that Greece was not less fabulous, than the island of Calypso, or the gardens of Alcinous. But as the modern Greeks have become what they are only by the course of time, through a given series of causes and effects, so did the ancient; and not less every other nation upon Earth. The whole history of mankind is a pure natural history of human powers, actions, and propensities, modified by time and place.

This principle is not more simple, than it is luminous and useful, in treating of the history of nations. Every historian agrees with me, that a barren wonder and recital deserve not the name of history: and if this be just, the examining mind must exert all its acumen on every historical event, as on a natural phenomenon. Thus in the narration of history it will seek the strictest truth; in forming its conceptions and judgment, the most complete connexion: and never attempt to explain a thing which is, or happens, by a thing which is not. With this rigorous principle, every thing ideal, all the phantoms of a magic creation, will vanish: it will endeavour to see simply what is: and as soon as this is seen, the causes why it could not be otherwise will commonly appear. As soon as the mind has acquired this habit in history, it will have found the way to that sound philosophy, which rarely occurs except in natural history and mathematics.

This philosophy will first and most eminently guard us from attributing the facts, that appear in history, to the particular hidden purposes of a scheme of things unknown to us, or the magical influence of invisible powers, which we would not venture to name in connexion with natural phenomena. Fate reveals its purposes through the events that occur, and as they occur: accordingly, the investigator of history developes these purposes merely from what is before him, and what displays itself in its whole extent. Why did the enlightened Greeks appear in the World? Because Greeks existed; and existed under such circumstances, that they could not be otherwise than enlightened. Why did Alexander invade India? Because he was Alexander, the son of Philip; and from the dispositions his father had made, the deeds of his nation, his age and character, his reading of Homer, etc., knew nothing better, that he could undertake. But if we attribute his bold resolution to the secret purposes of some superiour power, and his heroic achievements to his peculiar fortune; we run the hazard, on the one hand, of exalting his most senseless and atrocious actions into designs of the deity; and, on the other, of detracting from his personal courage, and military skill; while we deprive the whole occurrence of its natural form. He who takes with him into natural history the fairy belief, that invisible sylphs tinge the rose, or hang its cup with pearly dew-drops, and that little spirits of light encase themselves in the body of the glow-worm, or wanton in the peacock's tail, may be an ingenious poet, but will never shine as a naturalist or historian. History is the science of what is, not of what possibly may be according to the hidden designs of fate.

Secondly. *What is true of one people, holds equally true with regard to the connexion of several together: they are joined as time and place unites them; they act upon one another, as the combination of active powers directs.*

The Greeks have been acted upon by the Asiatics, and the Asiatics reacted upon by the Greeks. They have been conquered by Romans, Goths, Christians, and Turks: and Romans, Goths, and Christians have derived from them various means of improvement. How are these things consistent? Through place, time, and the natural operation of active powers. The Phenicians imparted to them the use of letters: but they had not invented letters for them; they imparted them by sending a colony into Greece. So it was with the Hellenes and Egyptians; so with the Greeks that migrated to Bactra; so with all the gifts of the muse, which we have received from their hands. Homer sung; but not for us: yet as his works have reached us, and are in our possession, we could not avoid being instructed by him. Had any event in the course of time deprived us of these, as we have been deprived of many other excellent works, who would accuse some secret purpose of fate, when the natural cause of the loss was apparent? Let a man take a view of the writings that are lost, and those that remain, of the works of art that are destroyed, and those that are preserved, with the accounts that are given of their destruction and preservation, and venture to point out the rule, which fate has followed in transmitting to us these, and depriving us of those. Aristotle was preserved in a single copy under ground, other writings as waste parchments in chests and cellars, the humourist Aristophanes under the pillow of St. Chrysostom, who learned from him to compose homilies; and thus the whole of the cultivation of our minds has depended precisely upon the most trivial and precarious circumstances. Now mental cultivation is unquestionably a thing of the greatest importance in the history of the World: it has thrown almost all nations into commotion, and now with Herschel explores the Milky Way. Yet on what trifling events has it hinged; the events to which we are indebted for glass and a few books! insomuch, that, but for these, we should still perhaps be wandering about in waggons, with our wives and families, like our elder brothers, the immortal Scythians. Had the course of things so ordered, that we had received Mungal letters instead of Greek, we should now be writing in the Mungal manner: yet the Earth would still pursue her grand career of years and seasons, nourishing every thing, that lives and acts upon her, according to the divine laws of nature.

Thirdly. *The cultivation of a people is the flower of its existence; its display is pleasing indeed, but transitory.*

As man, when he comes into the World, knows nothing, but has all his knowledge to learn; so an uncultivated people acquires knowledge from its own practice, or from intercourse with others. But every kind of human knowledge has its particular circle, that is its nature, time, place, and periods of life. The cultivation of Greece, for example, grew with time, place, and circumstances, and declined with them. Poetry and certain arts preceded philosophy: where oratory or the fine arts flourished, neither the patriotic virtues, nor martial spirit, could shine with their highest splendour: the orators of Athens displayed the greatest enthusiasm, when the state drew near its end, and its integrity was no more.

But all kinds of human knowledge have this in common, that each aims at a point of perfection, which when attained by a concatenation of fortunate circumstances, it can neither preserve to eternity, nor can it instantly return, but a decreasing series commences. Every perfect work, as far as perfection can be required from man, is the highest of its kind: nothing, therefore, can possibly succeed it, but mere imitations, or unsuccessful attempts to excel. When Homer had sung, no second Homer in the same path could be conceived: he plucked the flower of the epic garland, and all who followed must content themselves with a few leaves. Thus the Greek tragedians chose another track: they ate, as Aeschylus says, at Homer's table, but prepared for their guests a different feast. They too had their day: the subjects of tragedy were exhausted, and their successors could do no more, than remould the greatest poets, that is, give them in an inferiour form; for the best, the supremely beautiful form of the Grecian drama had already been exhibited in those models. In spite of all his morality, Euripides could not rival Sophocles, to say nothing of his being able to excel him in the essence of his art; and therefore the prudent Aristophanes pursued a different course. Thus it was with every species of Grecian art, and thus it will be in all nations: the very circumstance, that the Greeks in their most flourishing periods perceived this law of nature, and fought not to go beyond the highest in something still higher, rendered their taste so sure, and its development so various. When Phidias had created his omnipotent Jove, a superiour Jupiter was not within the reach of possibility: but the conception was capable of being applied to other gods, and to every god was given his peculiar character: thus this province of art was peopled.

Poor and mean would it be, if our attachment to any object

of human culture would prescribe as a law to alldisposing Providence, to confer an unnatural eternity on that moment, in which alone it could take place. Such a wish would be nothing less, than to annihilate the essence of time, and destroy the infinitude of all nature. Our youth returns not again: neither returns the action of our mental faculties as they then were. The very appearance of the flower is a sign, that it must fade: it has drawn to itself the powers of the plant from the very root; and when it dies, the death of the plant must follow. Unfortunate would it have been, could the age, that produced a Pericles and a Socrates, have been prolonged a moment beyond the time, which the chain of events prescribed for its duration: for Athens it would have been a perilous, an insupportable period. Equally confined would be the wish, that the mythology of Homer should have held eternal possession of the human mind, the gods of the Greeks have reigned to infinity, and their Demosthenes have thundered for ever. Every plant in nature must fade; but the fading plant scatters abroad its seeds, and thus renovates the living creation. Shakespeare was no Sophocles, Milton no Homer, Bolingbroke no Pericles: yet they were in their kind, and in their situation, what those were in theirs. Let every one, therefore, strive in his place, to be what he can be in the course of things: this he will be, and to be any thing else is impossible.

Fourthly. *The health and duration of a state rest not on the point of its highest cultivation, but on a wise or fortunate equilibrium of its active living powers. The deeper in this living exertion its centre of gravity lies, the more firm and durable it is.*

On what did those ancient founders of states calculate? Neither on lethargic indolence, nor on extreme activity; but on order, and a just distribution of never slumbering, ever vigilant powers. The principle of these sages was genuine human wisdom, learned from nature. Whenever a state was pushed to its utmost point, though by a man of the greatest eminence, and under the most flattering pretext, it was in danger of ruin, and recovered its former state only by some happy violence. Thus when Greece entered the lists with Persia, it was on a dreadful verge: thus when Athens, Lacedaemon, and Thebes, contended together at outrance, the loss of liberty to all Greece ensued. Thus, too, Alexander, with his brilliant victories, erected the edifice of his state on a bubble: he died, the bubble burst, and the edifice was dashed to pieces. How dangerous Alcibiades and Pericles were to Athens their history shows: though it is not less true that epochs of this kind, particularly if they terminate speedily and happily, display rare effects, and set incredible powers in motion. All the splendour of Greece was created by the active operation of many states and living energies: every thing sound and permanent, on the contrary, in its taste, and in its constitution, was produced by a wise and happy equilibrium of its active powers. The success of its institutions was uniformly more noble and permanent, in proportion as they were founded on humanity, that is, reason and justice. Here the constitution of Greece affords us an ample field for reflection, in what it contributed by its inventions and institutions both to the happiness of its own citizens, and to the welfare of mankind. But for this it is yet too early. We must first take a view of many periods and nations, before we can form conclusions on these subjects with security.

V

The Rise and Decline of Rome

BOOK XIV

We now approach the shore, that brought destruction, often terrible, on most of the nations we have hitherto considered: for the spreading flood of devastation, that overwhelmed the states of Graecia Magna, Greece itself, and all the kingdoms that were formed from the ruins of the throne of Alexander, burst forth from Rome. Rome destroyed Carthage, Corinth, Jerusalem, and many other flourishing cities of Greece and Asia; as it brought to a melancholy end every thing civilized in the south of Europe, that lay within the reach of its sword, particularly its neighbours Etruria, and the brave Numantia. It rested not till it attained the sovereignty over a world of nations, from the Euphrates to the Atlantic Ocean, from Mount Atlas to the Rhine: at length, breaking over the boundary prescribed it by fate, the valiant resistance of the northern people, or inhabitants of the mountains, its internal dissensions and luxury, the barbarous pride of its rulers, the horrible sway of the soldiery, and the fury of uncivilized nations, who rushed upon it like the waves of the sea, brought it to a lamentable end. The fate of nations was never so long and so absolutely dependent on one city, as when Rome possessed the sovereignty of the World: and while on this occasion it displayed, on the one hand, all the force of human courage and resolution, and still more military and political skill; on the other, it exhibited in the mighty context vices and barbarities, at which human nature must shudder, as long as it is capable of feeling the least sentiment of its rights. This Rome has become, in a wonderful manner, the fearful, precipitous passage to all the cultivation of Europe; for not only were the melancholy remains of the plundered treasures of all art and science preserved in its ruins, but through a singular revolution its language became the instrument, by which men learned to make use of all those treasures of antiquity. Even now the Latin tongue is the medium of our learned tuition from our early youth; and we, who possess so little of the Roman mind and spirit, are destined to form an acquaintance with the Roman ravagers of the World, before we are introduced to the milder manners of more gentle nations, or the principles that conduce to the happiness of our own country. The names of Marius and Sylla, of Caesar and Octavius, become familiar to us, before we know any thing of the wisdom of Socrates, or the institutions of our forefathers. The history of Rome, likewise, as the cultivation of Europe has hinged on its language, has received political and literary illustrations, of which scarcely any other can boast: for the greatest minds, that have reflected on history, have reflected on this, and have taken the principles and actions of the Romans as the groundwork, on which to develope their own thoughts. Thus we tread the blood-drenched soil of Roman glory as the sanctuary of classical learning and ancient art, where at every step some new object reminds us of the sunken treasures of an universal empire, never more to return. We consider the fasces of the conqueror, beneath which innocent nations once groaned, as shoots of a lordly cultivation, which was planted among us also through cruel events. But before we seek a knowledge of this conqueror of the World, we must bring an offering to humanity, and cast at least a look of pity on a neighbouring people, that contributed most to the early formation of Rome, but, alas! lay too close in the way of its conquests, and thence experienced a melancholy end.

CHAPTER 1
Etruscans and Latins

THE protruding peninsula of Italy lay exposed from its situation to a number of different settlers and inhabitants. As it is joined at its upper part of the great continent, which extends from

Spain and Gaul over Illyria to the Euxine Sea, while its shore lies immediately opposite to the coasts of Illyria and Greece; that, in the times of ancient migration, different tribes of various nations should pass into it, was inevitable. Above were some of Illyrian, others of Gallic descent: below dwelt Ausonians, whose origin can be traced no higher: and as with most of these Pelasgians, and afterwards Greeks, nay probably Trojans too, intermingled at different times from diverse parts; Italy may be considered, on account of these memorable strangers, as a hothouse, in which sooner or later something worthy of notice must be produced. Many of these people came hither not altogether uncivilized: the Pelasgian tribes had their letters, their religion, and their fables: so, it is probable, had many of the Iberians likewise, from their intercourse with the commercial Phenicians: thus the question was, on what spot, and in what manner, the blossoms of the country would put forth.

These first appeared among the Etruscans, who, from whatever part they came, were one of the most early and original people in taste and cultivation. Their minds were not bent on conquest: but on establishments, institutions, commerce, arts, and navigation, for which their coasts were well adapted. They planted colonies throughout almost all Italy, as far as Campania, introduced arts, and pursued trade, so that a number of the most celebrated towns in this country are indebted to them for their origin.[1] Their civil constitution, in which they served as a pattern to the Romans themselves, was far superiour to the governments of barbarians; and bears so completely the stamp of an European spirit, that it certainly could not have been borrowed from any African or Asiatic people.

Long before the time of its destruction Etruria was a federated republic of twelve tribes, united on principles, which were not introduced into Greece till a much later period, and then from the pressure of extreme necessity. No separate state could engage in a war, or conclude a peace, without the common consent. War itself they had already formed into an art; by the

[1] See Demster's *Etrur. Regal.* (Regal Etruria, with the observations of Buonaroti, and supplement of Passerius), Florence, 1723, 1767.

invention, or use of the trumpet, light javelin, pilum, etc., as signals of attack, of retreat, of marching, or of fighting in close order. With the solemn rights of heralds, which they introduced, they observed a sort of law of war and of nations; as their auguries, and many religious practices, which to us appear mere superstitions, were evidently engines of their political institutions, through which they may justly claim to be considered as the first people of Italy, that attempted to form an artful alliance between religion and the state. In almost all these things, they were the tutors of Rome: and if it be undeniable, that similar institutions contributed to the stability and greatness of the Roman power, the Romans are indebted principally for this to the Etruscans.

These people pursued navigation likewise as an art, at an early period; and maintained, by their colonies or trade, the sovereignty of the Italian coasts. They were acquainted with architecture and fortification: the Tuscan column, more ancient even than the Doric of Greece, derives its name from them, and was borrowed from no foreign nation. They were fond of chariot-races, theatrical performances, music, and even poetry; and had naturalized the Pelasgian fables, as their monuments of art evince. Those remains and fragments of their art, which the protecting realms of the dead have principally transmitted to us, show, that they rose from the rudest beginnings; and afterwards, when acquainted with many nations, even with the Greeks, were capable of remaining true to their own way of thinking. They have actually a particular style of art;[2] and preserved this, as well as the use of their religious fables, even when their liberty was no more.[3] Thus, too, in good civil laws for both sexes, and institutions for the cultivation of corn and

---

[2] See Winkelmann's *Geschichte der Kunst* (History of the arts), Vol. I. chap. 3.

[3] See Heyne, "On the Nature and Causes of the Frequent Employment of the Fables and Religion of the Greeks by Etruscan Artists," "On the Remains of the Religion of the Country in the Monuments of Etruscan Art," "Etruscan Antiquity Freed from Fanciful Interpretations," and "The Monuments of Etruscan Art Restored to Their Proper Age and Rank," in *Nov. Commentariis Soc. Götting.* (The new Memoirs of the Göttingen Society), Vol. III, and following.

the vine, the internal security of commerce, the reception of foreigners, and other things, they appear to have come nearer to the rights of man, than even many of the Grecian republics at a much later period: and as their alphabet was the immediate pattern of all those of Europe, we may consider Etruria as the second nursery of the cultivation of our quarter of the Globe. It is the more to be regretted, that we have so few monuments or accounts of the exertions of this polished and skilful people; for an unfriendly accident has deprived us even of the immediate history of their downfall.

Now to what must we ascribe this flourishing state of Etruria? And why, instead of equalling that of Greece, did it fade before it reached the point of perfection? Little as we know of the Etruscans, still we perceive in them the grand principle pursued by nature in the forming of nations, limiting them by their internal powers, and their external circumstances of time and place. They were an European people, more remote from anciently inhabited Asia, the parent of early civilization. The Pelasgian tribes, too, were half-savage wanderers, when they arrived on the different shores of Italy; while Greece, on the contrary, lay as a central point in the conflux of nations already civilized. In Italy many nations mingled together, so that the Etrurian language seems to have been a compound of several; and thus it enjoyed not the advantage of growing up from an uncontaminated seed.[4] The single circumstance of the Appennines, covered with rude mountaineers, stretching through the middle of Italy was sufficient, to prevent that uniformity of national taste, on which alone the permanence of a general culture can be founded. Even in later times no country occasioned more trouble to the Romans than Italy: and as soon as their sovereignty was at an end, it returned to its natural state of various division. The face of the country with regard to its mountains and coasts, and the different hereditary character of its inhabitants, made this division natural: for even now, when it is the object of politics, to reduce all under one chief, or link

[4] See the supplement of Passerius, in Demster's *Etrur. Regal.*

all in one chain, Italy has remained the most divided country in Europe.

Several nations, likewise, soon pressed upon the Etruscans; and as they were more of a commercial than a warlike people, even their more skilful tactics were compelled to give way to almost every attack of ruder nations. By the Gauls they were deprived of their footing in upper Italy, and confined to what may properly be called Etruria; and their colonial towns in Campania became subsequently a prey to the Samnites. As a commercial people addicted to the arts, they could not long stand against barbarous nations: for arts and commerce introduce luxury, from which their colonies on the most delightful shores of Italy were by no means free. At length they were fallen upon by the Romans, to whom they were unfortunately too near; and whom, in spite of their noble resistance, neither their civilization, nor their federal union, could withstand for ever. By their refinement, indeed, they were already in part enfeebled, while the Romans were yet a warlike hardy people: and from their confederation they derived little advantage, as their adversaries had the art to divide their states, and engage them separately. Thus they were subdued one after another, though not without the labour of many years; while in the mean time the Gauls were making continual incursions upon Etruria. Pressed upon by two powerful enemies, they fell a prey to that, which most systematically pursued their subjugation: and this was Rome. After the reception of the haughty Tarquins in Etruria, and the success of Porsenna, they looked upon this city as their most dangerous neighbour: for the humiliations, which Rome had experienced from Porsenna, were such, as it could never forgive. No wonder, that a rude warlike people should overpower a softened commercial nation; that a city firmly united should subdue a disjointed confederacy. To prevent Rome from destroying it, Rome must have been early destroyed: and as the good Porsenna refrained from this, his country at length became a prey to the enemy he spared.

Thus, that the Etruscans never became wholly Greeks in the

style of their arts, is to be accounted for from the time and situation in which they flourished. Their poetic mythology was merely the old heavy Grecian mythology, into which however they infused astonishing spirit and animation. The subjects, on which their arts were employed, appear to have been confined to a few religious or civil festivities, the key to which we have nearly lost. Besides, we know little of these people except from funerals, graves, and urns. Etruscan liberty survived not to the brightest era of Grecian art, which the conquest of the Persians produced; and the situation of Etruria denied it any similar native impulse, to wing its fame and genius to such a height. Thus it must be considered as an immature fruit, which, placed in the corner of the garden, could not attain the delicious flavour of its fellows, enjoying the more genial warmth of the Sun. Fate allotted a later period to the banks of the Arno, in which they were capable of producing more mature and beautiful fruits.

The marshy shores of the Tiber were already destined for a sphere of action, that should include three quarters of the Globe; and the circumstances of the times prepared this, long before the foundation of Rome. In this region, according to ancient stories, landed Evander; as did Hercules also with his Greeks, and Æneas with his Trojans: here, in the centre of Italy, Pallantium was built, and the kingdom of the Latins, with Alba Longa, was founded: here, too, was a settlement of more early civilization, insomuch, that some, indeed, have admitted a prior Rome, and imagined they have discovered the new city to have been erected on the ruins of one more ancient. But the last opinion is without foundation: for Rome was probably a colony from Alba Longa, under the direction of two successful adventurers; as this undesirable region would scarcely have been chosen in other circumstances. Let us examine, however, what Rome had here before and around her from the beginning, so that, the moment she quitted the breast of the wolf, she betook herself to war and plunder.

She was wholly surrounded by little nations; whence she was soon impelled to contend, not for her support alone, but even for her territory. Her early contests with the Caeninenses, Crustumini, Antemnates, Sabines, Camerini, Fidenates, Veientes, and others, are well known: they rendered Rome, when scarcely risen above the ground, standing thus on the frontiers of so many different nations, from the very beginning a kind of fortified camp; and accustomed the generals, the senate, the knights, and the people, to festivals of triumph over plundered countries. These triumphal processions, which Rome borrowed from the neighbouring Etruscans, were the grand lures, that animated this needy state, of confined domains, but populous and warlike, to hostile enterprises, and foreign incursions. In vain did the peaceful Numa erect the temples of Janus and Public Faith: in vain did he set up terminal gods, and celebrate a boundary feast. These peaceable institutions were obeyed only during his life: for Rome, accustomed to plunder by the thirty years victories of her first ruler, thought she could not pay more acceptable homage to her Jove, than by offering him the spoils of war. A renovated martial spirit arose after this just legislator; and Tullius Hostilius already made war on Alba Longa, the mother of his country. Necessarily nothing of this would have taken place, had Rome been built in a different situation, or speedily crushed by some powerful neighbour. But now, as a Latin city, she soon made her way to the head of the Latin confederacy, and at length brought the Latins under her yoke; she interfered with the Sabines, till at last she subjugated them; she learned from the Etruscans, till she became their mistress: and thus she acquired possession of her triple boundary.

To these early undertakings such kings were requisite as Rome had, particularly her first. It was no fable, that Romulus had been nourished by the milk of a wolf: he was evidently a bold, cunning, hardy adventurer, as his first laws and institutions show. His immediate successor, Numa, rendered some of these milder: a clear proof, that they are not to be ascribed to the times, but to the person by whom they were made. At the same time the rude heroism of the early Romans in general appears from the several stories of Horatius Cocles, Junius

Brutus, Mutius Scaevola, and the behaviour of Tullia, Tarquin, etc. It was fortunate for this predatory state, that, in its series of kings, rude valour combined with policy, and both with patriotic magnanimity: fortunate, that to a Romulus succeeded a Numa, to him a Tullius, an Ancus, after these a Tarquin, and then a Servius, whom personal merit alone could have exalted from the condition of a slave to the rank of a king. Lastly, it was fortunate, that these kings, of such different characters, reigned long, so that each had time to secure the benefits of his talents to Rome; till at length an arrogant Tarquin came, and the firmly fixed state chose another form of government. A select and continually renovating succession of warriors and rude patriots now arose, who fought annually to renew their triumphs, and strengthen and exert their patriotism in a thousand ways.

Would any one invent a political romance, to account for the origin of a Rome, he could not easily devise more suitable circumstances, than history, or fable, here gives us.[5] Rhea Sylvia and the fate of her children, the rape of the Sabines and the apotheosis of Quirinus, every rude adventure in war and conquest, and lastly a Tarquin and a Lucretia, a Junius Brutus, a Poplicola, a Mutius Scaevola, etc., serve to indicate a series of future consequences in the early disposition of Rome itself. There is no history on which it is easier to philosophize than the Roman, as the political spirit of its writers points out the chain of causes and effects in the course of events and actions.

CHAPTER 2

The Dispositions of Rome for a sovereign political and military State

Romulus numbered his people, and divided them into tribes, curiae, and centuriae: he measured the land, and parcelled it out to the people, the state, and the service of religion. The

[5] Montesquieu, in his elegant work on the grandeur and decline of the Romans, has almost exalted it into a political romance. Before him, Machiavel, Paruta, and many other sagacious Italians, had tried their skill in political reflections upon it.

people he distinguished into patricians and plebeians: out of the patricians he formed the senate; and to the same order he confined the principal offices of the state, and the sanctity of the priesthood. He likewise selected a body of knights, which in a later period formed a kind of middle rank between the senate and people; and the two grand divisions were more closely connected by the relationship of patron and client. From the Etruscans Romulus borrowed the lictors, with their fasces; a fearful emblem of authority, which every superiour magistrate afterwards assumed in the functions of his office, though with some variations. He excluded foreign gods, to secure to Rome its own tutelar divinity: he introduced augury, and other kinds of soothsaying, establishing an intimate connexion between the popular religion, and civil and military affairs. He determined the reciprocal duties of husband and wife, father and son, regulated the city, celebrated triumphs, was at length murdered, and afterwards adored as a god.

Behold the simple point, on which the wheel of Roman events afterwards incessantly revolved. For though in time the classes of the people were increased, altered, or opposed to each other; though bitter contests arose, whether the classes or tribes of the people, and which of them, should take the lead; though the increasing debts of the plebeians, and the oppressions of the rich, occasioned commotions, and many attempts were made for alleviating the burdens of the people by means of tribunes, agrarian laws, or the administration of justice by a middle rank, the knights; though disputes respecting the limits of the senate, the patricians, and the plebeians, assumed now one form, then another, till the two ranks were confounded together: in all this we perceive nothing more than the necessary consequences of a rudely composed living machine, such as the Roman state within the walls of one city must have been. Thus superiour offices were augmented, as the number of citizens, victories, conquered lands, and necessities of the state increased: thus triumphs, games, expenses, marital power, and paternal authority, were limited or enlarged, according to the different stages of manners and opinions: all however were shades of that ancient constitution, which Romulus invented not, it is true, but which he so firmly established, that it was capable of remaining the basis of the Roman form of government even under the emperours, nay almost to the present day. Its device was S.P.Q.R.,[6] the senate and people of Rome; magic words, which subjugated and ravaged the World, and at length rendered the Romans the instruments of their own ruin. Let us contemplate a few leading points in the Roman constitution, from which the fate of Rome appears to have branched out, as a tree from its roots.

1. *The Roman senate, as well as the Roman people, was, from the earliest times, a body of warriors: Rome, from its highest, to its lowest member in case of necessity, was a military state.* The senate was a deliberative council; but from its patricians it supplied generals and ambassadors: the independent citizen was obliged to serve in the field from his seventeenth year to his forty-sixth or fiftieth. He who had not made ten campaigns was ineligible to any of the higher offices. Hence the political spirit of the Romans in the field: hence their military spirit in the council. Their deliberations were on affairs, with which they were familiar: their resolves were acts. A Roman ambassador was an object of respect to kings: for he might be at the head of an army, and decide the fate of kingdoms either in the senate or in the field. The people of the higher centuriae were by no means a rude mob: they consisted of men of property, experienced in war, and foreign and domestic affairs. The votes of the poorer centuriae had less weight; and in the better times of Rome their members were not thought qualified for the army.

2. *The education of the Romans, particularly in the nobler families, was calculated for this destination.* They learned to deliberate, speak, vote, and persuade the people: they went early to the field, and prepared the way to triumphs, honours, and offices of state. Hence the uniform character of the history and eloquence of the Romans, and even of their jurispru-

[6] *Senatus populusque romanus.*

dence and religion, philosophy and language: all breathe a political and active spirit, a manly, adventurous courage, united with address and urbanity. A wider difference can scarcely be conceived, than appears on comparison of the history and eloquence of China, or Judea, with those of Rome. From the spirit of the Greeks, too, the Spartans themselves not excepted, that of Rome is distinct; as it is founded on a rougher nature, more ancient habit, and principles more fixed. The Roman senate never died: its resolutions, its maxims, and the Roman character inherited from Romulus, were immortal.

3. *The Roman generals were frequently consuls, whose military and civil offices usually continued but a year:* accordingly they hastened to return triumphant, and their successors were eager to emulate their honours. Hence the incredible progress and multiplication of Roman wars: one sprung from another, and gave rise to another in its turn. Occasions for future campaigns were reserved, till the present was ended; and reserved to accumulate with usury, as a capital of spoil, success, and glory. Hence the interest the Romans so greedily took in foreign nations; on which they forced themselves as allies and protectors, or as judges of differences, certainly not from motives of philanthropy. Their friendly alliances were the relation of a guardian to a ward; their advice was command; their decision, war or sovereignty. More cool haughtiness, and latterly shameless impudence, in the exercise of authority assumed by force, were never displayed, than by these Romans, who thought the World was theirs, and made for them alone.

4. *The Roman soldier too shared the glory and reward of his commander.* In the early ages of Rome's patriotic virtues the soldiers served without pay; and afterwards it was sparingly distributed: but out of its conquests, and the increased power of the people by means of the tribunes, grew pay, reward, and booty. The lands of the conquered were often divided among the soldiery; and it is well known, that the most ancient and numerous quarrels in the Roman republic arose from the distribution of lands. Subsequently, in foreign conquests the soldier shared the booty; and participated in the triumph of his general,

both in glory and valuable donations. Civic, mural, and rostral crowns were conferred: and Lucius Dentatus could boast,

> that, having been in a hundred and twenty battles, eight times victorious in single combat, wounded forty five times before, and not once behind, he had disarmed his enemy five and thirty times, and been rewarded with eighteen *hastæ puræ*, twenty five sets of horse furniture, eighty three chains, a hundred and and sixty bracelets, and twenty six crowns, namely, fourteen civic, eight golden, three mural, and one obsidional, beside money, ten prisoners, and twenty oxen.

As beside this, the point of honour in our standing armies, where no one ever serves in a rank inferiour to what he has once born, and every one is promoted in turn, according to the date of his service, was unknown in the Roman state even to the latest period; but the general chose his own tribunes, and the tribune his subordinate officers, at the commencement of a war: a more free competition for posts of honour and military employments was opened, and a more intimate connection between the general, the officers, and the soldiery, was formed. The whole army was a body selected for the campaign, and the spirit of the general was infused into every member of it, by those who commanded under him. In proportion as the wall, that at the commencement of the republic separated the patricians and plebeians, was broken down in the course of time, valour and success in war became the road to honours, wealth, and power, for all ranks; so that in later times the first possessors of undivided power in Rome, Marius and Sylla, were plebeians, and at length the highest dignities were obtained by the meanest persons.[7] Unquestionably this was the ruin of Rome; as, in the beginning of the republic, patrician pride was its support; and it was only by degrees, that the haughtiness and oppression exercised by men of rank became the causes of all the internal dissensions that ensued. To establish an equilibrium between the senate and the people, the patricians and plebeians, was the perpetual bone of contention in the Roman

[7] Sulla was a patrician.

state; where the balance preponderating now to one side, then to the other, at length overturned the commonwealth.

5. *Roman virtue, so highly celebrated, is for the most part inexplicable, without the narrow, severe constitution of the Roman state:* when this was gone, that was at an end. The consuls succeeded in the place of the kings, and were compelled, as it were, in imitation of ancient example, to display something more than a royal, to display a Roman soul. All the magistrates, the censors especially, participated in this spirit. We are astonished at the strict impartiality, the disinterested magnanimity, the busy lives, of the ancient Romans, from the moment their day broke, nay before the break of day, even from the earliest peep of dawn. No state in the World probably went so far in this earnestness of application, this strict discharge of civic duties, as Rome, where all was in close contact. The nobleness of their families, which was honourably designated by patronymic names; dangers continually renewed from without, and incessant contests for an equilibrium between the patricians and plebeians within; again, the bond of union between both in the relationship of patron and client; the crowded intercourse with each other in the market places, in their houses, and in political temples; the fine yet distinct limits between what belonged to the senate, and what to the people; their simplicity in domestic life; and the education of youth in a familiarity with all these things from their infancy; contributed to form in the Romans the first and proudest nation of the World. Their nobility was not, as among others, an indolent nobility, founded on landed possessions, on wealth, or on a name: it was a proud, family, civic, Roman spirit, in the first races; on which their country depended as its firmest support; and in the continued activity, the permanent stream of the same eternal state, it was transmitted from father to son. I am persuaded, that, in the most perilous times, no Roman could conceive any idea of the destruction of Rome: all acted for their city, as if the gods had destined it to be immortal, and them to be the instruments of the gods for supporting it to eternity. But as the astonishing success of the Romans con-

verted their valour into insolence, Scipio could not help applying to his country, on the destruction of Carthage, those verses of Homer, in which the fate of Troy is predicted.[8]

6. *The manner in which religion was interwoven with the state in Rome unquestionably contributed to its civil and military greatness.* As from the foundation of the city, and in the most valiant ages of the republic, the priesthood was in the hands of the most respectable families, who were at the same time statesmen and warriors, so that even the emperours themselves disdained not to execute its functions; in all their ceremonies they guarded against the true pest of every national religion, contempt, which the senate employed its utmost endeavours to obviate. Accordingly, that able politician Polybius ascribes part of the virtues of the Romans, particularly their incorruptible faith and veracity, to religion, by him termed superstition: and even in the late ages of their decline, the Romans were actually so addicted to this superstition, that some commanders, of the most ferocious disposition, professed themselves to have communication with the gods; and believed, that, by their inspiration and assistance, they had not only power over the minds of the people and the army, but even the control of chance and fortune. Religion was connected with every civil and military transaction, so as to sanctify it; and hence the noble families contended with the people for the possession of religious dignities, as for their most sacred privilege. This is commonly ascribed to their policy alone, as their auspices and haruspices put into their hands the direction of affairs by means of artful religious deceptions: but, though I will not deny, that these were occasionally practised, this certainly was not the whole of the business. The worship of their fathers, and of the gods of Rome, was, according to the general belief, the support of their good fortune, the pledge of their preeminence over other nations, and the revered sanctuary of their unparagoned state. As at the beginning they adopted no strange gods, though they respected the deities of every foreign land, so they retained the ancient worship of their divinities, in

[8] They are pronounced by Hector, in his interview with Andromache. *Iliad.* z. 447. seq.

which they became Romans. To alter any thing in this, was to derange the fundamental pillars of the state: hence in the regulation of religious ceremonies the senate and people maintained their sovereign rights, which precluded all the plots and subtleties of a separate priesthood. The religion of the Romans was a civil and military religion; which did not guard them, indeed, from unjust wars, but, giving them at least an appearance of justice by means of their feciales and auspices, placed them under the eyes of the gods, and claimed their assistance.

At a later period it was equally politic in the Romans, abandoning their ancient principles, to allure to them foreign deities. Their state already began to totter, as, after immense conquests, was inevitable: but this politic toleration preserved it from the spirit of persecuting foreign religions, which first appeared under the emperors, by whom it was exercised only occasionally from political motives, and not from hatred or affection to speculative truth. Upon the whole, the Romans troubled themselves about no religion, unless so far as it attacked the state: in this respect they were not men and philosophers, but citizens, soldiers, and conquerors.

7. What shall I say of the *Roman art of war*, certainly at that time the most perfect of its kind, as it united the soldier and citizen, the statesman and general, and ever vigilant, ever pliable and new, acquired knowledge from every enemy? Its rude foundations were of equal antiquity with the city itself, the citizens that Romulus mustered forming the first legion: but they were not ashamed in time to alter the primitive arrangement of the army, to render the ancient phalanx less unwieldy, and thus, by imparting to it a greater capacity for action, to discomfit the veteran Macedonians, whose order of battle was then reckoned the model of the military art. Instead of their ancient Latin arms, they borrowed such as suited them from the Etruscans and Samnites; and they learned the regulation of marches from Hannibal, whose long residence in Italy gave them the severest lessons of war they had ever received. All their great commanders, among whom are to be reckoned the Scipios, Marius, Sylla, Pompey, and Caesar, studied war as an art during the whole of their lives: and as they had to carry it

on against the most various nations, nations too acting valiantly from strength, courage, and despair, they necessarily made great progress in every branch of the science.

The might of the Romans however consisted not wholly in their weapons, their order of battle, and their encampments; but in the imperturbable martial spirit of their generals, and in the tried strength of the soldier; who could brave hunger, thirst, and peril; who was as ready at the use of his weapons, as if they had been his own limbs; and who, standing firm against the shock of the spear, with his short Roman sword in his hand, sought the heart of his enemy even in the midst of the phalanx. This short Roman sword, wielded with Roman valour, conquered the World. It was the Roman art of war to attack rather than defend, to fight rather than besiege, and to take the shortest, straightest way to victory and fame. To the assistance of this came the inveterate principles of the republic, to which all resistance proved vain: never to desist till the enemy was completely overthrown, and therefore to engage only with one enemy at a time; never to accept peace in misfortune, even if peace would give more than victory could obtain, but to stand firm, and act so much the more bravely against the successful victor; to begin with magnanimity, and the mask of disinterestedness, as if they fought only to succour the oppressed, and gain allies, till in time they were enabled to rule their allies, oppress the succoured, and triumph as victors over friend and foe. These and similar maxims of Roman insolence, or, if you please, of cool, prudent magnanimity, reduced a world of nations to the state of provinces: and so they ever would, if similar times, and a similar people, could arise.

Let us now traverse the bloody field, through which these conquerors of the World waded, and examine what they have left behind them.

CHAPTER 3

Conquests of the Romans

When Rome began its career of heroism, Italy was covered with a number of little nations; each living according to its own laws, and hereditary character; more or less enlightened; but active, industrious, prolific. We are astonished at the number of men, that every little state, even in rude mountainous regions, was able to bring against the Romans; men who had there found, and could still find subsistence. The civilization of Italy was by no means confined to Etruria; it was shared by every little people, the Gauls themselves not excepted: the land was cultivated; rude arts, trade, and war, were pursued after the manner of the times; no state was without good laws, though few in number; and even the natural regulation of the balance of power between different states was not unknown. Impelled by pride or necessity, and favoured by various circumstances, the Romans were engaged with them in arduous, bloody wars, for five centuries; so that all the rest of the World that they subdued cost them less trouble, than this little chain of people, which they gradually brought under the yoke.

And what were the consequences of their exertions? Ravage and destruction. I do not reckon the men slain on both sides; and with the loss of whom whole nations, as the Samnites and Etruscans, were swept away: the obliteration of these communities, and the destruction of their towns, were misfortunes of greater magnitude to this country, because affecting remotest posterity. Whether these nations were transplanted to Rome, or their sad remains reckoned in the number of its allies, or treated as subjects and bridled by colonies, their primitive energy was never restored. Once chained to Rome's brazen yoke, they were compelled, for centuries, as subjects or allies, to spill their blood in her service, and for her profit and glory, not their own. Once chained to this yoke, notwithstanding all the privileges conferred on this people, or on that, every individual was at last reduced to seek fortune, honour, wealth, and justice, in Rome alone; so that in a few centuries the great city became the grave of Italy. Soon or late the laws of Rome universally prevailed; the manners of Rome became the manners of Italy; her mad aim to acquire the sovereignty of the World enticed all these people to throng round her, and at length perish in the gulf of Roman luxury. No denial, no restriction, no prohibition, was capable at last of affording any aid: for the course of nature, once turned out of its direction, cannot be altered afterwards at will by human laws.

Thus by degrees Rome drained, enervated, and depopulated Italy; so that at length rude barbarians were requisite, to give it new people, new laws, new manners, and new courage. But what was no more, returned not again: Alba and Cameria, the wealthy Veii, and most of the Etrurian, Latin, Samnite, and Apulian cities were destroyed: the scanty colonies, planted amid their ashes, had restored to none their ancient dignity, numerous population, industry in arts, laws and manners. It was the same with all the flourishing republics of Graecia Magna: Tarentum and Croton, Sybaris and Cumae, Locri and Thurium, Rhegium and Messana, Syracuse, Catania, Naxus, Megara, were no more; and many of them had experienced the severest fate. Thou, wise and great Archimedes, wast slain in the midst of thy geometrical labours; and it is no wonder, that thy grave remained unknown to thy more modern countrymen, since thy country was buried with thee; for the state perished, though the city was spared. The mischief done to the arts and sciences, to the cultivation of the soil and the improvement of the human mind, by the dominion of Rome in this corner of the World, is incredible. Wars and proconsuls laid waste the delightful isle of Sicily; and Lower Italy was ruined by the various ravages committed in it, though still more by its proximity to Rome; till at length both countries were parcelled out into estates and country seats of the Romans, while they were likewise the nearest objects of their extortion. The once flourishing land of Etruria was already in a similar situation, in the time of the elder Gracchus: a fertile solitude, inhabited only by slaves, and drained by the Romans. And what fine country in the World experienced a better fate, when once within the gripe of Roman talons?

When Rome had subjugated Italy, she began with Carthage; and this in a manner, at which her most determined friends must blush. Her assisting the Mamertines, in order to gain footing in Sicily; her seizing upon Corsica and Sardinia, while

Carthage was embroiled with her mercenaries; and lastly, the deliberating of her grave senators, whether a Carthage were to be suffered to exist upon the Earth, with as little ceremony as if the debate had been on a cabbage of their own planting; with a hundred instances of like nature; render the Roman history, with all the valour and address it displays, a history of demons. Be it Scipio himself, that presents to a Carthage, little capable of doing farther injury to Rome, praying even her aid with the offer of an ample tribute, and trusting to her promises, delivering up her weapons, ships, arsenals, and three hundred of her principal inhabitants as hostages; be it Scipio, or a god, that presents to her, in such a situation, the cold, haughty proposal of her destruction, as a decree of the senate; it is still a black, devilish proposal, of which unquestionably the noble deliverer himself was ashamed. "Carthage is taken," he writes back to Rome; as if with this expression he would veil his infamous act: for never have the Romans given, or been the means of giving to the World, such a Carthage. Even an enemy to Carthage, aware of all its vices and defects, beholds with anger its destruction; and respects the Carthaginians at least when he beholds them as disarmed, betrayed republicans, fighting on their graves, and fighting for a burying place.

Why was it denied thee, thou great, thou matchless Hannibal, to prevent thy country's ruin, and march directly to the wolf's den of thy hereditary foe, immediately after the battle of Cannae? Weak posterity, that never crossed the Alps and Pyrenees, condemns thee for this; not reflecting on the people whom thou hadst under thy command, and on the condition in which, after the terrible winter campaign in Upper and Middle Italy, they must have been. It condemns thee, from the mouth of thy enemies, for want of military discipline: though it is almost incomprehensible, how thou couldst keep together thy mercenaries so long, and after such marches and such actions, rest not till thou hadst reached the plains of Campania. Renown will ever deck the name of this brave enemy of Rome, whom she more than once imperiously demanded, to be delivered up to her as some engine of war. Not fate, but the factious avarice of his countrymen, prevented him from completing that victory, which he, not Carthage, had obtained over Rome: and thus he was incapable of becoming more than an instrument for instructing the Romans in the art of war, as they had learned that of navigation wholly from his countrymen. In both fate has given us a fearful warning, never to stop short of the full completion of our purposes; otherwise we shall certainly promote, what we are endeavouring to prevent. Suffice it, that with Carthage fell a state, which the Romans could never replace. Commerce deserted its coasts; and pirates succeeded, as they ever will, to the shores that commerce had abandoned. Under the Roman colonies Africa ceased to be that horn of plenty, which it had long been under Carthage: it was a granary for the people of Rome alone, a menagerie of wild beasts for their amusement, and a magazine of slaves. Desolate to this moment lie the shores and plains of that fine country, which the Romans first robbed of its internal culture. Even every line of the Punic writings is lost to us: Aemilianus presented them to the grandchildren of Masinissa; one enemy of Carthage, to another.

Whatever way I turn my eyes from Carthage, devastation rises before them; for this ever marked the footsteps of these conquerors of the World. Had the Romans really intended to be the deliverers of Greece, when they announced themselves under this proud name at the Isthmian games to the Greeks now sunk into childhood, how different would have been their conduct! But when Paulus Aemilius permitted seventy cities of Epirus to be despoiled, and a hundred and fifty thousand persons to be sold for slaves, merely to reward his army; when Metellus and Silanus ravaged and plundered Macedon, Mummius Corinth, and Sylla Athens and Delphos, as scarcely any cities in the World had been plundered; when this devastation was spread likewise through the Grecian islands, and Rhodes, Cyprus, Crete, experienced no better fate than Greece, namely that of becoming sources of tribute, and magazines of spoil to deck the triumphs of the Romans; when the last king of Macedon was led in triumph with his sons, languished in the most wretched prison, whilst one son escaped death only to gain his livelihood as a skilful turner and scribe at Rome; when the last glimmering of Grecian liberty, the Aetolian and Achaian league, was extinguished, and the whole country became a Roman province, or a field of carnage, on which the plundering, ravaging armies of the triumvirs at length engaged each other: O Greece, what an end was reserved for thee by thy protectress, thy pupil, Rome, the tutoress of the World! Nothing remains of thee but ruins, which the barbarous spoilers carried away with them in triumph, that, at a subsequent period, whatever the art of man had invented might perish amid the ashes of their own city.

From Greece let us steer our course to the shores of Asia and Africa. Into the kingdoms of Asia Minor, Syria, Pontus, Armenia, and Egypt, the Romans soon intruded; either as heirs, or as guardians, umpires, and pacificators: but hence, as a just reward for their services, they drew the poison, that proved fatal to their own constitution. The great military exploits of Scipio Asiaticus, Manlius, Sylla, Lucullus, and Pompey, are known to every one; to the last of whom was decreed a triumph at one time over fifteen conquered kingdoms, eight hundred cities, and a thousand fortresses. The gold and silver displayed in solemn pomp on the occasion were estimated at twenty thousand talents;[9] he augmented the revenues of the state a third part, to the amount of twelve thousand talents;[10] and his whole army was so enriched, that the meanest soldier received from him as a triumphant gift to the value of more than thirty pounds sterling, beside what he had already acquired as booty. What a robber! Crassus, who plundered Jerusalem alone of ten thousand talents,[11] pursued the same steps; and no one penetrated farther into the east, without returning, if he did return, laden with wealth and luxury. What by way of compensation did the Romans bestow on the Asiatics? Neither laws, nor peace; neither institutions, nor arts, nor people. They ravaged countries, burned libraries, despoiled cities, temples, and altars.

[9] About 3,800,000 £ sterling.
[10] About 2,280,000 £.
[11] About 1,900,000 £.

Part of the Alexandrian library was given to the flames by Julius Caesar; and Mark Antony bestowed the greater portion of that of Pergamus on Cleopatra, that both might afterwards perish together. Thus the Romans, endeavouring to spread day over the World, wrapped it in desolating night: treasures of gold and silver were extorted: nations, and myriads of ancient ideas, were whelmed in the abyss: the characters of countries were obliterated, and the provinces were drained, plundered, and abused, under a succession of execrable emperors.

With almost yet more melancholy do I bend my course westwards to the ravaged countries of Spain, Gaul, and wherever the Romans stretched their arms. The nations they destroyed in the east for the most part had already blossomed, and begun to fade: here, yet unripe, but full of buds, they were so injured in their first youthful growth, that the race and family of many are scarcely to be distinguished. Spain, before the Romans entered it, was a well-cultivated, and in most places fertile, rich, and happy land. Its trade was considerable; and the state of civilization among some of its people by no means to be despised; of which the Turdetani, on the banks of the Baetis, to whom the Phenicians and Carthaginians had been longest known, and even the Celtiberians, in the heart of the country, are sufficient proofs. No place upon Earth more stoutly resisted the Romans than the brave Numantia. For twenty years it supported the war; defeated one Roman army after another; and at last defended itself against all the military skill of a Scipio, with a valour, the melancholy fate of which excites the commiseration of every reader. And what did the despoilers seek here, in an inland country, from nations that had never given them offence, and scarcely heard of their names? Gold and silver mines. Spain was to them, what America is now forced to be to Spain, a place for plunder. Lucullus, Galba, and others, plundered in contempt of the faith they had pledged: the senate itself annulled two treaties of peace, which its defeated generals had been fain to conclude with the Numantines. It inhumanly delivered up to them the generals; but was again overcome by the Numantines in generosity to these unfortunate commanders. And now Scipio appeared with all his force before Numantia; completely blockaded it; cut off the right arms of four hundred young men, the only persons who would come to the assistance of this injured town; listened not to the moving intreaties, with which a people oppressed by famine endeavoured to excite his pity and justice; and completed the destruction of these unhappy beings like a true Roman. Like a true Roman, too, acted Tiberius Gracchus; when in the country of the Celtiberians alone he ravaged three hundred towns, even if we suppose them to have been nothing more than fortresses and villages. Hence the inextinguishable hatred of the Spaniards toward the Romans: hence the valiant exploits of Viriatus and Sertorius, both of whom fell by unworthy means, and undoubtedly excelled many Roman commanders in military skill and courage: hence the scarcely ever subdued mountaineers of the Pyrenees, who, in despite of the Romans, retained their savage state as long as possible. Unfortunate land of gold, Iberia, thou, with thy culture, and thy nations, art sunk almost unknown into the realm of Shades, in which Homer already depicted thee, beneath the rays of the setting Sun, as a subterranean kingdom.

Of Gaul we have little to say, as we know nothing of its conquest, but from the military journal of its conqueror. For ten years it cost Caesar himself incredible pains, and required all the powers of his great mind. Though he excelled every other Roman in generosity, still he was unable to change the fate of his Roman destination, and gained the melancholy praise of having been engaged in fifty pitched battles, not reckoning the civil wars, and having slain in fight eleven hundred and ninety two thousand men. Most of these were Gauls. Where are the numerous, lively, valiant people of this extensive country? where were their spirit and courage, their numbers and strength, when centuries after savage nations fell upon them, and shared them among themselves as Roman slaves? Even the name of this leading stock of people, with its peculiar religion, cultivation, and language, is obliterated throughout the whole of the country, that became a Roman province. You great and noble minds, Scipio and Caesar, what are your thoughts, what your feelings, when now, as departed spirits, you look down from your celestial spheres on Rome, that nest of robbers, and the scenes of your murders? How foul to you must appear your honour, how bloody your laurels, how base and inhuman your exterminating arts! Rome is no more: and when it did exist, the feelings of every worthy man must have whispered to him, that all these monstrous, ambitious victories would call down vengeance and destruction on his country.

CHAPTER 4
The Decline of Rome

THE law of retaliation is an eternal ordinance of nature. As in a balance neither scale can be depressed without the ascent of the other; so no political equilibrium can be destroyed, no sin against the rights of nations and of mankind can be committed, without avenging itself; and the more the measure is heaped, the more tremendous will be its fall. If any history proclaim to us this natural truth, it is the history of Rome: but let the reader extend his views, and not confine them to a single cause of the ruin of that state. Had the Romans never beheld Greece or Asia, and proceeded after the manner in which they did against other poorer countries; undoubtedly their fall would have happened at a different period, and under different circumstances: still it would have been equally inevitable. The seeds of destruction lay in the heart of the plant; the worm gnawed its roots, and its vital juices were corrupted: the gigantic tree, therefore, must ultimately fall to the ground.

1. In the essence of the Roman constitution was a leaven of dissension, which, if not removed, could not fail soon or late to effect its destruction: this was *the disposition of the state itself, the unjust or uncertain limits between the senate, the knights, and the citizens.* It was impossible for Romulus to foresee all the future circumstances of his city, when he established this division: he formed it according to its present state and wants; as these altered, he himself lost his life by the hands of those, to whom his power became burdensome. None of his successors

had courage, or occasion, to do what Romulus had not done: they gave a preponderance to either party by their personal authority, and preserved an union between the different ranks in a rude state surrounded with dangers. Servius mustered the people, and put the balance in the hands of the rich. Under the first consuls dangers were extremely pressing: at the same time men of such merit, strength, and greatness, were conspicuous among the patricians, that they could not fail to lead the people.

But circumstances soon changed; and the oppression of the nobles became insupportable. The citizens were overwhelmed with debt: they had too little share in the legislation; they reaped too little advantages from the victories, for which their blood was spilled: so the people retired to the Sacred Mount, and so disputes arose, which the appointment of tribunes was calculated rather to multiply than remove, and with which the whole subsequent history of Rome was accordingly interwoven. Hence the long and frequently renewed contests respecting the division of lands, and the participation of the plebeians in magisterial, consular, and sacerdotal offices; in which contests each party fought its own ends, and no one attempted an unbiassed and equitable adjustment of the interests of both. This contention survived even to the triumvirates: nay the triumvirates themselves were consequences of it. Now as these put an end to the whole of the Roman constitution, and this contention was nearly as old as the republic itself; it appears, that it arose from no external circumstances, but from an internal cause, which from the beginning corroded the vitals of the state. It is singular, therefore, that the Roman constitution should have been represented as a pattern of perfection: a constitution one of the most imperfect in the World, originating from crude temporary circumstances, and never afterwards reformed from a general comprehensive view of the whole, but partially altered from time to time. Caesar alone was capable of giving it a radical reform: but it was too late, and the dagger, that deprived him of life, destroyed all possibility of an improved constitution.

2. There is an inconsistency in the position: Rome, the queen of nations, Rome, the sovereign of the World: for *Rome was merely a city; and its constitution, the constitution of a city alone.* That Rome's resolves for war, however, were the resolves of an immortal senate, not of a mortal king; while the spirit of its world-destroying maxims was naturally more durable in a college, than in a fluctuating series of rulers; unquestionably contributed to its persevering obstinacy in war, and consequently to its victories. Besides, the patricians and plebeians were almost always at variance; so that the senate found it necessary to create wars, for the purpose of employing the unruly multitude, or some turbulent leader, abroad, that peace might be preserved at home. Thus this permanent variance contributed greatly to the continuance of foreign devaluation. Lastly, as the senate itself was often closely beset with dangers, and frequently found victories, or the fame of victories, necessary for its support; and as every daring patrician, who wished the people to espouse his cause, stood in need of donations, games, celebrity, and triumphs, which war alone, or for the most part, could furnish; this divided, restless government was a cause of disturbing the peace of the World, and keeping it in commotion for centuries: for, out of regard to its own happiness, no orderly state, tranquil in itself, would have been the actor of such a fearful tragedy.

To make conquests, however, is one thing; to retain them, another: one thing, to gain victories; another, to render them of advantage to the state. Rome, from its internal constitution, was never capable of the latter: and the former it was enabled to do only by means altogether inimical to the constitution of a city. Already the first kings, that applied their arms to conquest, were compelled to admit some of the conquered towns and nations within the walls of Rome; that the feeble tree, which was desirous of shooting forth such enormous branches, might acquire roots, and a substantial trunk: thus the inhabitants of Rome increased alarmingly. The city afterwards formed alliances, and its allies joined its armies in the field: so that they took part in its victories and conquests, and were Romans, though they were neither citizens nor inhabitants of Rome. Hence soon arose warm contests on the part of the allies for admission to the rights of citizenship: a demand inevitable from the nature of the case. Hence arose the first social war, which cost Italy three hundred thousand of its youths, and brought Rome, which had been obliged to arm even its freedmen, to the brink of destruction: for it was a war between the head and the members, which terminated only by the consolidation of the members into this misshapen head. All Italy was now become Rome, which continued to spread itself, to the great disturbance of the World. I shall pass over the disorder, which this Romanizing must have introduced into the laws of all the Italian states; and only notice the evils, that thenceforward flowed from all corners, and from every region, into Rome.

If there were previously such a conflux to this city, as rendered it so impossible, to keep the tables of the census uncontaminated, that even a man, who was no Roman citizen, was elected consul; how must it have been, when the head of the World was a mixed mob from all Italy; the most monstrous head, that Earth ever bore? Immediately on the death of Sylla, the lords of the World amounted to four hundred and fifty thousand; the admission of the allies infinitely increased the number; and in Caesar's time there were three hundred and twenty thousand, who shared in the public donations of corn. Think of this turbulent mob of mostly idle persons assembling to vote, in company with its patrons, and those who aspired to posts of honour; and it will not be difficult to conceive how donations, spectacles, parade, and flattery, and still more military force, could excite those tumults, spill those seas of blood, and establish those triumvirates, which at length reduced this haughty sovereign of the World into a state of slavery to herself. Where now was the authority of the senate? or what were five or six hundred persons against the innumerable multitude, that claimed the rights of sovereignty, and, marshalled in powerful armies, were at the beck now of this man, now of that? What a poor figure did the divine senate, as the flattering

Greeks styled it, make before Marius or Sylla, Pompey or Caesar, Antony or Octavius! The father of his country, Cicero, appears shorn of his glories, when attacked only by a Clodius; and his best councils were of little avail, not only against what Pompey, Caesar, Antony, and others, actually did, but what even a Catiline had nearly accomplished. Not from the spices of the east, not from the effeminacy of Lucullus, sprung this disorderly state of things; but from the essence of the constitution of Rome, which, merely as a city, aimed at being the head of the World.[12]

3. *In Rome, however, there were not a senate and people alone, but slaves also; and of these the number increased, in proportion as the Romans extended their sway.* By the hands of slaves they cultivated their extensive, fertile lands in Italy, Sicily, Greece, etc. A number of slaves constituted their domestic wealth; and the traffic in them, nay the tuition of them, was an extensive occupation at Rome, of which even Cato was not ashamed. The days when master and servant lived almost like brothers together, and Romulus could promulgate a law, that a father might sell his son for a slave three times, had long been past: the slaves of the conquerors of the World were collected from every quarter of the Globe, and were treated by good masters mildly, by the pitiless frequently as brutes. It would have been wonderful had no detriment accrued to the Romans from this vast multitude of oppressed beings: for, like every other bad institution, this could not fail to avenge itself. The vengeance taken by the bloody war of the slaves, which Spartacus waged against the Romans for three years, with the valour and skill of a consummate general; his followers increasing from seventy-four persons to an army of seventy thousand, with which he defeated different commanders, among whom were two consuls; during which war many cruelties were perpe-

[12] For all the good that can be said of the simplicity of the ancient Romans, and the improvement of the Roman people, read the first volume of Meierotto's well supported work on the manners and way of life of the Romans; and for the progress of luxury, both among the plebeians and patricians, see the second volume of the same book.

trated; was only a prelude. The grand mischief arose from the favourites of their masters, the freedmen, who at length reduced Rome to the state of a slave of slaves, in the strictest sense of the words. This evil commenced as early as Sylla's time; and under the emperors it increased so dreadfully, that I am incapable of describing the disorders and barbarities, which originated with freedmen and favourite slaves. The histories and satires of Roman authors abound with them: no savage nation upon Earth is acquainted with any thing, that will bear a comparison. Thus Rome was punished by Rome: the oppressor of the World became the abject servant of the most infamous slaves.

4. To this *luxury* likewise greatly contributed: towards which unfortunately Rome was not less forcibly impelled by circumstances, than to the conquest of the World by situation. As from a central point she ruled the Mediterranean Sea, and with it the rich shores of three quarters of the Globe: while by the aid of considerable fleets she acquired through the medium of Alexandria the precious commodities of Ethiopia, and the remotest parts of the east. My words are too feeble to describe the gross dissipation and luxury in feasts and public spectacles, in dainties for the table and garments for the body, in houses and in furniture, which prevailed, not only in Rome, but in every place connected with it, after the conquest of Asia.[13] A man can scarcely believe his own eyes, when he reads the descriptions of these things, the high price of foreign commodities, and the profusion of them, with the immense debts of the great men of Rome, who were latterly freedmen and slaves. This extravagance necessarily induced extreme poverty: nay it was in itself a pressing want. Those rivers of gold, which for centuries flowed into Rome from all the provinces, at last dried up: and as all the commerce of the Romans was in the highest

[13] See, beside Petronius, Pliny, Juvenal, and abundance of passages in the ancients; and among modern compilations the second volume of Meierotto's work on the manners and way of life of the Romans, Meiners's *Geschichte des Verfalls der Römer* (History of the decline of the Romans), etc.

degree prejudicial to them, since they exchanged ready money for mere superfluities, it is not to be wondered, that India alone drained them annually of immense sums.

In the mean time, the land was neglected: agriculture was no longer pursued, as it had formerly been, by the Romans and their contemporaries in Italy: the arts of Rome were employed not on the useful, but on the superfluous; on extravagant splendour and expense in triumphal arches, baths, funeral monuments, theatres, amphitheatres, and the like; wonderful structures, such as it must be confessed these plunderers of the World alone could erect. To no Roman are we indebted for any useful art, for any thing contributing to the support of man; which might have benefited other nations, and from which permanent and deserved advantage might have been derived. Hence the empire soon became poor: the standard of the coin was lowered; and in the third century of our era, if we take the baseness of the coin into consideration, a general received scarcely the pay, that was deemed insufficient for a common soldier in the time of Augustus. Obvious natural consequences of the course of things; which, considered merely in a manufacturing and commercial view, could not turn out otherwise.

From these destructive circumstances the human species, too, degenerated; not only in number, but in stature, growth, and vital energy. Rome and Italy, which had rendered the most populous and flourishing countries in the World, Sicily, Greece, Spain, Asia, Africa, and Egypt, nearly deserts, naturally drew upon themselves, by their laws and wars, and still more by their depraved, indolent manner of living, their inordinate vices, the practice of divorce, severity towards their slaves, and latterly tyranny toward the worthiest men, the most unnatural death. Expiring Rome lay for centuries on her deathbed in the most frightful convulsions: a deathbed extending over a whole World, from which she had sucked her delicious poison, and which could then render her no assistance, but that of accelerating her death. Barbarians came to perform this office: northern giants, to whom the enervated Romans appeared dwarfs: they ravaged Rome, and infused new life into expiring Italy. A tremendous yet wholesome proof, that all irregularities in Nature avenge and consume themselves. We have to thank the luxury of the east for having freed the World earlier from a carcase, which victories in other regions indeed would have destroyed, but it is probable neither so speedily, nor so terribly.

5. I have now to consolidate the whole into one view, and unfold the grand ordinance of nature, that, even without luxury, without plebeians, without a senate, and without slaves, *the military spirit of Rome alone must have ultimately destroyed it; and that sword, which it so often drew against innocent cities and nations, have returned into its own bowels.* But here all history speaks for me. When the legions, unsatiated with spoil, found nothing more to plunder, and on the frontiers of Parthia and Germany saw an end to their fame, what could they do, but turn back, and devour the parent state? The fearful tragedy began with the times of Marius and Sylla: attached to their commanders, or paid by them, the returning armies revenged their generals on their antagonists, even in the midst of their country, and Rome was deluged with blood. This tragedy continued. When Pompey and Caesar led against each other dearly paid armies, in the country where once the Muses sung, and Apollo pastured his flocks as a shepherd; Romans, fighting against Romans, decided the fate of their country at this distance. So it proceeded in the barbarous compact of the triumvirs at Modena, which in a single list condemned to death or banishment three hundred senators, and two thousand knights, and extorted two hundred thousand talents[14] chiefly from Rome, and even from the women: as it did after the battle of Philippi, where Brutus fell; before the war against the younger Pompey, the nobler son of a great father; after the battle of Actium; and on other occasions.

It was in vain that the weak, unfeeling Augustus acted the part of clemency and the love of peace: the empire had been won by the sword; the sword must maintain it, or by the sword it must fall. If the Romans began to slumber; the nations that had been injured, or put into commotion, would not slumber too: they demanded vengeance, and retaliated when opportu-

[14] £38,750,000.

nity arrived. In the Roman empire the caesars ever remained nothing more than commanders in chief of the armies: and many of them, who forgot their stations, were dreadfully reminded of them by their soldiers. These set up, and put down emperors: till at length the commander of the pretorian guards made himself grand vizir, and the senators contemptible puppets. In a short time, too, the senate was composed wholly of soldiers; of soldiers whom time had so enfeebled, that they were fit neither for war nor counsel. The empire fell to pieces: rival emperors persecuted and assailed each other: foreign nations pressed into the empire, and enemies were admitted into the army, who allured other enemies. Thus the provinces were torn and ravaged; and proud, eternal Rome fell, deserted and betrayed by its own commanders. A fearful monument of the end, that every where awaits the thirst of conquest, whether in great or little states; and more particularly the spirit of military despotism, according to the just laws of nature. Never was a martial state more firm and extensive than that of Rome: and never was a corpse conveyed more horribly to the grave; so that after Pompey and Caesar another conqueror could never have been expected, or another regiment of soldiers, to arise in a civilized nation.

Powerful Destiny! has the history of the Romans been preserved, has half the World been a victim to the sword, to teach us this lesson? And yet we learn from it nothing but words; or, misunderstood, it has formed new Romans, incapable however of equalling their prototype. Those ancient Romans have appeared but once upon the stage, and acted, chiefly as private persons, a tremendously grand tragedy, the repetition of which, for humanity's sake, we can never desire. Let us examine, however, what greatness and splendour this tragedy has exhibited in its progress.

CHAPTER 5

Character, Sciences, and Arts of the Romans

After what has been said, justice demands, that we should name with due praise those nobleminded individuals, who, in the unfavourable situation, in which destiny had placed them, bravely sacrificed themselves for what they called the good of their country, and in the short course of their lives performed deeds reaching almost the summit of human powers. Following the course of history, I shall mention as deserving fame in different degrees a Junius Brutus and Poplicola, Mutius Scaevola and Coriolanus, Valeria and Veturia, the three hundred Fabii and Cincinnatus, Camillus and Decius, Fabricius and Regulus, Marcellus and Fabius, the Scipios and Catos, Cornelia and her unfortunate sons; to whom, if military glory alone were to be considered, we shall add Marius and Sylla, Pompey and Caesar; and, if good intentions and endeavours deserve praise, Marcus Brutus, Cicero, Agrippa, Drusus, and Germanicus. Neither must we forget among the emperors Titus, the delight of mankind, the just and good Nerva, the fortunate Trajan, the indefatigable Adrian, the good Antoninus, the vigilant Severus, the manly Aurelian, and other powerful props of a sinking edifice. But as these men are better known to every one, than even the Greeks themselves, I may be excused if I speak generally of the character of the Romans in their best ages, and consider this character as a consequence of the circumstances of the times.

If a name were to be given to impartiality and firm resolve, to indefatigable activity in words and deeds, and a determinate ardent pursuit of victory or honour; if to that cool courage, which peril cannot daunt, misfortune cannot bend, and success cannot intoxicate; it must be that of Roman fortitude. Many persons even of the lowest order in this state have displayed this virtue in so conspicuous a manner, that we, particularly in our youth, when we view the Romans chiefly on the most brilliant side, honour such personages of the old World as great departed spirits. Their generals stride like giants from one quarter of the Globe to another, and bear the fate of nations in their prompt and powerful hands. Thrones are overturned by their foot as they pass, and they determine the life or death of myriads with a word. Perilous height, on which they stand! Ruinous game, where crowns are the stake, and where the wealth of nations, and the lives of millions, are played away!

On this height they walk as simple Romans, disdaining the pomp of barbarian kings; the helmet their crown, the coat of mail their only decoration.

And when on this summit of wealth and power I hear their manly eloquence, and see the unwearied activity of their domestic or patriotic virtues; when in the throng of battle, or in the tumult of the Forum, the countenance of Caesar retains its constant serenity, and his heart beats with magnanimous clemency even toward his enemies; great man, even with all the vices, into which levity led thee, if thou didst not deserve to be monarch of Rome, no man ever did! But Caesar was more than this; he was Caesar. The highest throne on Earth decorated itself with his name: O that it could have adorned itself with his spirit also! that for ages it could have been animated with the benevolent, vigilant, comprehensive mind of Caesar!

But there stands his friend Brutus with drawn dagger. Worthy Brutus! thy evil genius appeared to thee not for the first time at Sardis or Philippi: long before hadst thou seen it in the shape of thy country, to which, though of softer soul than thy rude forefathers, thou madest a sacrifice of the sacred rights of friendship and humanity. Wanting the mind of a Caesar and the vulgar ferociousness of a Sylla, thou couldst not profit by the deed imposed upon thee; and wast compelled to abandon Rome, now Rome no longer, to the wild designs of an Antony and an Octavius: Antony, who laid all the glory of Rome at the feet of an Egyptian strumpet; Octavius, who from the chamber of a Livia ruled with a semblance of divine tranquillity the wearied World. Nothing was left for thee, but thy own sword: a melancholy yet necessary resource for an unfortunate Roman.

Whence arose this great character of the Romans? From their education; often from family pride, and the glory of a name; from their occupations; from the condensation of the senate, the people, and all nations, in the central point of the sovereignty of the World; and lastly from the fortunate, unfortunate necessity, in which the Romans found themselves. Hence every part of Roman greatness was common to the people, as well as the nobler families; to the women, as well as the men. The daughters of Scipio and Cato, the wife of a Brutus, the mother and sister of the Gracchi, could not act unbecoming their families: nay, noble Roman ladies frequently excelled the men in prudence and worth. Thus Terentia possessed more heroic courage than Cicero; Veturia, more noblemindedness than Coriolanus; Paulina, more fortitude than Seneca. No natural advantages could produce in an eastern haram, or a gyneceum of Greece, those female virtues, which blossomed in the public and domestic life of the Romans: but it must be confessed, that, in the times of Roman depravity, female vices appeared, at which humanity shudders. Even so early as the subjugation of the Latins, a hundred and seventy Roman wives agreed to poison their husbands; and, when they were discovered, quaffed off the fatal portion like heroes. The deeds, which the women of Rome were capable of perpetrating under the emperors, want a name. The deepest shade borders on the strongest light: a stepmother Livia, and the faithful Antonia-Drusus, a Plancina and Agrippina-Germanicus, a Messalina and Octavia, appear side by side.

If we would estimate the merits of the Romans in regard to science, we must take their peculiar character into consideration, and require from them no Grecian arts. Their language was the Aeolian dialect, intermingled with almost all the tongues of Italy. From this rude form it was slowly improved; and yet, with all its improvement, it could never completely attain that ease, beauty, and perspicuity, which distinguish the Greek. It is concise, grave, and worthy to be the language of the legislators and sovereigns of the World: in every respect a type of the Roman mind. As the Romans did not become acquainted with the Greeks, till their character and political state had long been formed by the Latins, the Etruscans, and their own efforts; it was late, before their native eloquence began, to receive any polish from Greece. We will pass over, therefore, their first dramatic and poetical attempts, which unquestionably contributed much to the formation of their language, and speak of what with them took deeper root; *legislation, oratory,* and *history;* flowers of the intellect, which their occupations produced, and in which the Roman genius is more particularly displayed.

Here, too, we have to regret, that fate has favoured us with so little: for they, whose thirst of conquest deprived us of so many works of other nations, were obliged, in like manner, to submit the productions of their own genius to destructive time. Not to mention the ancient annals of their priests, the heroic histories of Ennius and Naevius, or the attempt of a Fabius Pictor; where are the histories of a Cincius, Cato, Libo, Posthumius, Piso, Cassius Hemina, Servilian, Fannius, Sempronius, Caelius Antipater, Asellio, Gellius, Lucinius, and others? Where are the lives of Aemilius Scaurus, Rutilius Rufus, Lutatius Catulus, Sylla, Augustus, Agrippa, and Tiberius, of an Agrippina-Germanicus, and even of a Claudius, Trajan, etc., written by themselves? where, too, are the numerous historical works of the most important persons of the state in the most important periods of Rome? of Hortensius, Atticus, Sisenna, Lutatius, Tubero, Lucceius, Balbus, Brutus, and Tiro; of Valerius Messala, Cremutius Cordus, Domitius, Corbulo, and Cluvius Rufus? where, the many lost works of Cornelius Nepos, Sallust, Livy, Trogus, Pliny, and others? I insert these names here, to abash those moderns, who set themselves far above the Romans: for where is the modern nation, that can reckon among its princes, generals, and chief officers of state, so many and so great historians, as these pretendedly barbarous Romans, in so short a time, and during events of so much importance, in which they were actively employed? From the few fragments, yet remaining as specimens of a Cornelius, Caesar, Livy, etc., Roman history, it must be confessed, has not the charms and pleasing beauty of the Greek; but it possesses Roman dignity, and much philosophical and political wisdom in a Sallust, Tacitus, and others. Where great actions are achieved, men think and write with dignity: slavery palsies the tongue, as appears from the later Roman history itself: and, alas! the majority of the Roman historians, during the times of Roman liberty, or while that liberty was but half detroyed, are wholly lost. An irreparable loss: for such men can live but once; but once can write their own history.

Roman History walks by the side of Eloquence, her sister, and the Art of War and of Politics, their common mother. Thus several of the greatest of the Romans were not only skilled in these sciences, but writers also. The Greek and Roman historians are unjustly censured for the political and military speeches, which they have frequently introduced into their narrative: for as public speeches formed the chain, to which every affair of the commonwealth was linked, the historian could not find a more natural instrument to connect events, present them in different points of view, and enter into a philosophical elucidation of them. These speeches afford the writer a far more elegant mode of philosophising, than that subsequently adopted by Tacitus and his brethren, who, compelled by necessity, uniformly intermix their own reflections. Tacitus, however, has been unjustly criticised also, for his philosophising spirit; for both in his delineations, and in the severity of their style, he is in heart and mind a Roman. It was impossible for him to relate events, without unfolding their causes, and painting in black colours what was detestable. His history sighs for liberty; and its obscure concise tone displays deeper regret for its loss, than words could have expressed. History and eloquence enjoy only times of freedom, that is of public activity in politics and war: they perish with these; and, as the state grows indolent, their thoughts and expression are benumbed.

With regard to orators, though not inferiour in fame to the historians, we have less to deplore. Cicero alone is sufficient, to indemnify us for the loss of many. In his writings on oratory he gives us the characters, at least of his great predecessors and contemporaries; and to us his orations may supply the place of those of Cato, Antonius, Hortensius, Caesar, and others. The fate of this man is illustrious: more illustrious after his death, than during his life. He has preserved to us not only the eloquence of Rome, in his precepts and examples, but the greater part of the Grecian philosophy; for of many of its schools we should have known little more than the names, and not their doctrines, but for the enviable garb, in which he has preserved them. His eloquence excels the thunder of Demosthenes, not only in philosophical clearness and perspicuity, but in urbanity and true patriotism. Almost to him alone is Europe indebted for the restoration of the pure Latin language; an instrument, that has unquestionably done much for the human mind, notwithstanding its many abuses. Light lie the turf upon thee, therefore, much occupied and much persecuted man, the *pater patriae* of all the Latin schools in Europe! For thy frailties thou didst sufficient penance in thy lifetime: now thou art dead, may men enjoy the fruits of thy learned, elegant, just, and noble spirit, and learn from thy letters and works, if not to adore, at least to love thee with gratitude and high esteem.[15]

The poetry of the Romans was but a foreign flower, which blossomed beautifully in Latium, it is true, and here and there assumed a more delicate tint, but it was incapable of producing any new fruits of its own. The Etruscans, indeed, had already prepared the ruder warrior for poetry by their Salian and funereal songs, and their Fescennine, Atellanian, and scenic games. With the capture of Tarentum and other cities of Graecia Magna, Grecian poets also were captured, who endeavoured to render the rude dialect of the conquerors of Greece more pleasing to them, by the help of the more refined muses of their mother country. The merits of these most ancient Latin poets are known to us only from a few verses and fragments; but we are astonished at the number of their tragedies and comedies, that we find quoted, not only in ancient times, but in part even in the best ages. Time has destroyed them; but I do not think the loss great, compared with that of the Greeks; for many of them were founded on Grecian stories, and probably imitations of Grecian manners. The Roman people delighted too much in farces and pantomimes, in the Circensian games and combats of gladiators, to possess a Grecian ear, or Grecian taste for the theatre. The dramatic muse was introduced to the Romans as a

[15] For the character of this man, which has often been misunderstood, read Middleton's *Life of Cicero,* an excellent work, not only as far as respects the writings of this Roman, but the general history of his time.

slave; and a slave with them she ever remained: still I much regret the loss of the hundred and thirty pieces of Plautus, and the shipwreck of a hundred and eight plays of Terence; as well as the poems of Ennius, a man of strong mind, particularly his Scipio and his didactic poems: for in Terence alone, to use Caesar's expression, we had at least half Menander. Cicero, too, we have to thank for having preserved to us a Lucretius, a poet of a Roman soul; and to Augustus we are indebted for a Semi-Homer in the Aeneid. Let us thank Cornutus, likewise, for not having deprived us of some of the exercises of his noble pupil Persius: and you, also, ye monks, for having saved, as means of learning Latin, Horace, and Boethius, with something of Terence, but above all your Virgil, as an orthodox poet. The sole unspotted laurel in the crown of Augustus is, that he cherished the muses, and allowed science a free wing.

From the Roman poets to the philosophers I turn with pleasure: many were both at the same time, and indeed philosophers in their hearts as well as heads. In Rome no systems were invented; but philosophy was practiced, and introduced into law, politics, and private life. Never did a didactic poet write with more force and fire than Lucretius; for he believed what he taught: never since the time of Plato has the Academy been renovated with greater charms, than in the elegant dialogues of Cicero. The stoic philosophy, likewise, not only obtained great sway in Roman jurisprudence, and formed a strict rule for the conduct of men, but acquired a practical solidity and beauty in the writings of Seneca, the excellent meditations of Marcus Aurelius, the maxims of Epictetus, etc., to which the doctrines of various schools have evidently contributed. Exercise and necessity in many severe situations of the Roman state steeled the breasts of the Romans and fortified their courage: they examined into what was proper to be followed, and availed themselves of what the Greeks had conceived, not as idle ornament, but as weapons and armour of the mind. The stoic philosophy had great effect on the heads and hearts of the Romans: not indeed in exciting them to the conquest of the World, but in promoting justice, rectitude, and the internal consolation of men unjustly oppressed. For the Romans were men; and as innocent posterity suffered for the sins of their progenitors, they fought to strengthen themselves as they could: they firmly appropriated to themselves what was not of their own invention.

The history of Roman literature is to us a ruin of ruins; for, with the collections of it, we have lost, for the most part, the sources whence those collections were drawn. What labour should we have been spared, what light would have been thrown upon antiquity, if the writings of Varro, or the two thousand books from which Pliny compiled, had come down to us! From what was known of the World to the Romans, Aristotle undoubtedly would have made a collection different from Pliny's: yet is the book of Pliny a treasure, which shows the industry and Roman spirit of the writer, notwithstanding his ignorance in particular points. Thus, too, the history of Roman jurisprudence is the history of great diligence and acuteness, which could have been exercised, and so long pursued, in the Roman state alone: what in the course of time has been made out of it, or foisted into it, must not be charged on the lawyers of ancient Rome. In short, defective as Roman literature appears in almost every branch compared with the Greek, this must not be ascribed to the circumstances of the times alone, but to the very nature of the Romans also, for ages proudly aspiring to be the lawgivers of the World. The sequel of the work will show this, when we see a new Rome arising from the ashes of the old, in a very different form, but yet big with the spirit of conquest.

Lastly I have to speak of the arts of the Romans, in which they displayed themselves to the present World, and to posterity, as the sovereigns of the Earth, at whose nod, were the materials of every country, and the hands of every conquered nation. From the beginning they were inspired with the desire of proclaiming the splendour of their victories by monuments of fame, and the majesty of their city by magnificent and durable structures; so that they very early thought of nothing less than the eternity of their proud existence. The temples that Romulus and Numa erected, and the places they assigned for public assemblies, already had victory in view, and a mighty popular government; till, soon after, Ancus and Tarquin laid the firm foundations of that architecture, which ultimately rose almost to immensity. The Etruscan king built the walls of Rome of hewn stone. To supply his subjects with water, and keep the city clean, he erected those vast reservoirs, the ruins of which even now are among the wonders of the world; for modern Rome is unable even to clean them, and keep them in repair. In the same style were its galleries, its temples, its courts of justice, and that immense circus, which, erected for the amusement of the people merely, excites our veneration even now in its ruins. This path was pursued by the kings, the haughty Tarquin in particular; afterwards by the consuls and ediles; then by the conquerors of the World, and the dictators; but chiefly by Julius Caesar; and the emperors followed. Thus by degrees arose those gates and towers, theatres and amphitheatres, circuses and stadia, triumphal arches and honorary columns, splendid monuments and mausolea, roads and equeducts, palaces and baths, which display the eternal footsteps of these lords of the World, in the provinces as well as in Rome and Italy. To contemplate many of these, even in their ruins, almost fatigues the eye; and the mind sinks under the conception of the vast idea, from which the artist generated these grand designs of solidity and magnificence. Still more little do we feel ourselves, when we reflect on the purposes of these structures, the way of life that was pursued in and among them, the people to whose use they were dedicated, and the persons, not unfrequently private individuals, by whom they were erected. Then the mind feels, that the World never contained but one Rome; and that one genius prevailed, from the wooden amphitheatre of Curio, to the Coliseum of Vespasian; from the temple of Jupiter Stator, to the Pantheon of Agrippa, or the temple of Peace; from the first triumphal gate of a returning victor, to the triumphal arches, and honorary columns of Augustus, Titus, Trajan, Severus, and throughout every monument of public or private life. This genius was not the spirit of general liberty and comprehensive benevolence: for, when we reflect on the enormous toil of the labourers, who, as the slaves of war, were often obliged to procure these mountains of stone and marble from distant lands; when we consider the sums expended on these monsters of art, sums wrung from the blood and sweat of plundered and oppressed provinces; when we think of the barbarously proud and savage taste, which most of these edifices cherished, by their bloody combats of gladiators, their inhuman battles with wild beasts, their barbarous triumphal processions, etc.; not to mention the luxury of their baths and palaces; we are compelled to think that Rome was founded by some demon inimical to mankind, to exhibit to all human beings traces of his supernatural, demoniacal sovereignty. On this subject let the reader turn to the complaints of the elder Pliny, and every noble Roman; let him trace the wars and oppressions that brought to Rome the arts of Etruria, Greece, and Egypt: he will probably admire the mountains of Roman magnificence, as the summit of human greatness and power; but at the same time he will learn to detest them, as the murderous and tyrannical graves of mankind. The rules of art, however, remain what they were: and though the Romans, properly speaking, invented nothing in the arts, nay latterly combined together what had elsewhere been invented, in a manner sufficiently barbarous; yet, in this accumulating, piling taste, they show themselves the great lords of the Earth.

Excudent alii spirantia mollius aera:
Credo equidem; vivos ducent de marmore vultus:
Orabunt causas melius: coelique meatus
Describent radio, et surgentia sidera dicent:
Tu regere imperio populos, Romane, memento;
Hae tibi erunt artes, pacisque imponere morem,
Parcere subjectis & debellare superbos.

Aeneid, lib. VI, l. 867–73

Let others better mould the running mass
Of metals, and inform the breathing brass;
And soften into flesh a marble face:
Plead better at the bar: describe the skies,
And when the stars descend, and when they rise.

But, Rome, 'tis thine alone with awful sway,
To rule mankind, and make the world obey;
Disposing peace, and war, thy own majestic way.
Dryden

We would willingly excuse the Romans for the want of all the Grecian arts they despised, and which notwithstanding they employed for use or ornament; nay for the neglect of improving the noblest sciences, astronomy, chronology, etc.; and undertake a pilgrimage to the places, where these flowers of the intellect bloomed in their native soil; had they but left them there, and exercised with more philanthropy that art of government, which they deemed their supreme excellence. But this was not in their power; as their wisdom was subservient only to their overweening authority, and the pretended pride of nations bent to a still greater pride.

CHAPTER 6

General Reflections on the History and Fate of Rome

It has been of old an exercise of political philosophy, to determine, whether Rome was more indebted for her greatness to fortune, or to valour. Already Plutarch, and many other writers, both Greek and Roman, have given their opinions on this point; and in modern times the question has been handled by almost every reflecting adventurer in the paths of history. Plutarch, after all that he is obliged to allow to Roman valour, gives fortune the preponderance: in this inquiry, however, as in his other writings, he shows himself the flowery, pleasing Greek, not the possessor of a comprehensive mind fully equal to his subject. Most of the Romans, on the contrary, ascribe all to their valour; and the philosophers of later times have discovered a system of policy, on which the Roman power was erected, from the first foundation stone to its greatest amplitude. History clearly shows, that neither of these hypotheses is exclusively true; but that all must be taken in conjunction for a solution of the problem. Valour, fortune, and policy must have combined, to effect what was actually accomplished; and we find these three deities leagued in favour of Rome from the days of Romulus. Whether, after the manner of the ancients, we term the whole assemblage of living causes and effects nature, or fortune, the valour of the Romans, not excluding even their barbarous severity, together with their policy and cunning, must be taken as part of this all-ruling fortune. Our view must ever remain incomplete, if we attach ourselves exclusively to either of these qualities, and, while we contemplate the excellencies of the Romans, forget their failings and vices; while we consider their intimate character, omit concomitant circumstances; and, while we admire their firmness and skill in military affairs, overlook those accidents, by which they were often so happily assisted. The geese, that saved the Capitol, were not less the tutelary deities of Rome, than the courage of Camillus, the temporizing of Fabius, or Jupiter Stator. In the physical world all things that act together, and upon each other, whether generating, supporting, or destroying, must be considered as one whole: the same in the natural world of history.

It is a pleasing exercise of the mind, to inquire, on this occasion or that, what Rome would have been under different circumstances: as, if it had been founded on a different spot; if at an early period it had been transported to Veii; if the Capitol had been taken by Brennus: if Italy had been attacked by Alexander; if the city had been conquered by Hannibal; or if his counsel had been followed by Antiochus. In like manner we may inquire, how Caesar would have reigned in the place of Augustus; how Germanicus, in the place of Tiberius: what would have been the state of the World, without the powerful spread of Christianity: etc. These inquiries would lead us to such an accurate concatenation of circumstances, that at length we should learn to consider Rome, after the manner of the oriental sage, as a living creature, capable under such circumstances alone of rising from the banks of the Tiber, as from the sea; gradually acquiring strength to contend with all nations, by sea and land, subdue, and crush them; and lastly finding within itself the limits of its glory, and the origin of its corruption, as it actually did find them. Thus contemplated, every thing arbitrary and irrational vanishes from history. In it, as in every production of nature, all, or nothing, is fortuitous; all, or nothing, is arbitrary. Every phenomenon in history is a natural production, and for man perhaps of all most worthy contemplation; as in it so much depends on men, and he may find the most useful kernel, though included perhaps in a bitter shell, even in what lies without the sphere of his own powers, in the overbearing weight of times and circumstances; in the oppression of a Greece, a Carthage, or Numantia; in the murder of a Sertorius, a Spartacus, or a Viriatus; in the ruin of the younger Pompey, Drusus, Germanicus, or Britannicus. This is the only philosophical method of contemplating history, and it has been even unconsciously practiced by all thinking minds.

Nothing has tended more to obstruct this impartial view, than the attempt to consider even the bloody history of Rome as subservient to some secret limited design of Providence: as, for instance, that Rome was raised to such a height principally for the production of orators and poets, for extending the Roman law and Latin language to the limits of its empire, and smoothing the way for the introduction of Christianity. No one is ignorant of the prodigious evils, under which Rome, and the World around her, groaned, before such orators and poets could arise; how dear, for instance, Sicily bought Cicero's speech against Verres; and how much his orations against Catiline, and his philippics against Antony, cost his country and himself. Thus a ship must be lost, to save one pearl; and thousands must lose their lives, merely that one flower might spring from their ashes, soon to be dissipated by the winds. To purchase the Aeneid of a Virgil, and the tranquil muse and urbane epistles of a Horace, rivers of Roman blood must previously flow, nations and kingdoms innumerable must be destroyed. Were these fine fruits of a forced golden age worth the expense they cost? The case is the same with the Roman law: for who knows not what vexations were suffered through it, and how many more humane institutions in very different countries it destroyed? Foreign nations were judged conformably to manners, with which they were unacquainted; crimes and punishments were introduced among them, of which they had never heard: nay, has not the general progress of this jurisprudence, adapted to the constitution of Rome alone, after a thousand oppressions so extinguished or vitiated the characters of all its conquered nations, that, instead of their peculiar stamp, the Roman eagle at last every where appears, covering with feeble wings the exenterated, eyeless carcases of murdered provinces? The Latin language, too neither gained any thing from conquered nations, nor conferred any thing upon them. It was corrupted, and at length became a mixed jargon, not only in the provinces, but even in Rome itself. Through its means, also, the chaste beauty of the more elegant Greek was contaminated; and the languages of many nations, which would have been far more useful, both to them and to us, than a corrupt Latin, have vanished without leaving behind them the smallest remains. Lastly, with regard to the Christian religion; highly as I venerate the benefits it has conferred on mankind, so far am I from believing, that a single milestone was erected in Rome by human hands on its account. For it Romulus founded not his city, Pompey and Crassus entered not into Judea: still less were all the Roman establishments in Europe and Asia made, to prepare its way over the World. Rome embraced Christianity, no otherwise than it embraced the worship of Isis, and all the contemptible superstitions of the east: it would be derogatory to divine Providence, to suppose, that, for her noblest work, the propagation of truth and virtue, she could employ no other instrument, than the tyrannical and bloody hands of the Romans. The Christian religion raised itself by its own energy, as the Roman empire grew by its own powers; and if they at length united, it was to the advantage of neither: a Romish Christian bastard sprung from the union, of which there are many who wish, that it had never been born.

Natural history has reaped no advantage from the philosophy of final causes, the sectaries of which have been inclined, to satisfy themselves with probable conjecture, instead of patient inquiry: how much less the history of mankind, with its endlessly complicated machinery of causes mutually acting upon each other!

We must also disapprove the opinion, that, the Romans came on the stage in the succession of ages, to form a more perfect link in the chain of cultivation than the Greeks, as in a picture designed by man. In whatever the Greeks excelled, there the Romans never went beyond them: on the other hand, in what was properly their own, they learned nothing from the Greeks. They endeavoured to profit by all nations, of which they had any knowledge, even to the Indians and troglodytes: but this they did as Romans; and it may be questioned, whether to their advantage or to their detriment. Now as little as all other nations existed for the sake of the Romans, or framed for them their political institutions ages before, not more did the Greeks. Athens and the Italian colonies made laws for themselves, not for the Romans: and if Athens had never existed, Rome might have sent to Scythia for her twelve tables. In many respects, too, the Grecian laws were more perfect than the Roman; and the defects of the latter diffused themselves over a far more extensive region. If perchance they were in any points more humane, they were so after the Roman mode; but it would have been altogether unnatural, if the conquerors of so many civilized people had not learned at least a semblance of humanity, by which nations were often deceived.

Nothing remains, therefore, but to consider the Roman nation, and the Latin language, as bridges placed by Providence, for the conveyance of some of the treasures of antiquity to us. Yet for this purpose the bridges were the worst that could have been contrived, for of most of these treasures we were robbed by their very erection. The Romans were destroyers, and in their turn destroyed: but destroyers are no preservers of the World. They irritated all nations, till at length they became their prey; and Providence performed no miracle in their behalf. Let us, therefore, contemplate this, like any other natural phenomenon, the causes and effects of which we would investigate freely, without any preconceived hypothesis. The Romans were precisely what they were capable of becoming: every thing perishable belonging to them perished, and what was susceptible of permanence remained. Ages roll on; and with them the offspring of ages, multiform man. Every thing that could blossom upon Earth, has blossomed; each in its due season, and its proper sphere: it has withered away, and will blossom again, when its time arrives. The work of Providence pursues its eternal course, according to grand universal laws: and to the consideration of this we proceed with unpresuming steps.

VI

The Spread of Early Christianity

BOOK XVII

Seventy years before the dissolution of the Jewish state, a man was born in it, by whom an unexpected revolution was brought about in the sentiments of men, as well as in their manners and institutions. This man, who was named *Jesus,* born in poverty, though descended from the ancient royal lineage, dwelling in the rudest part of the country, and educated remote from the learning and wisdom of his nation, now deeply declined, lived unnoticed the greater part of his short life, till, consecrated by a celestial appearace at the Jordan, he took to himself twelve men of his own condition as disciples, travelled with them through a part of Judea, and soon after sent them round to announce the approach of a new kingdom. The kingdom, that he announced, he styled the kingdom of God, a heavenly kingdom, in which only chosen men could participate, and for the obtaining of which he proposed not external duties and ceremonies, but pure mental and spiritual virtues. The *most genuine humanity* is contained in the few discourses of his, that are preserved: humanity he displayed in his life, and confirmed by his death: and the favourite name, by which he chose to distinguish himself, was that of *the son of man.* That he should have many followers among his countrymen, particularly of the poor and oppressed; and that he should soon be removed out of the way by those, who under the cloak of sanctity oppressed the people, so that we scarcely know with precision the time of his appearance; were the natural consequences of his situation.

But what was this *kingdom of Heaven,* the approach of which Jesus announced, urged others to desire, and strove himself to establish? That it was no worldly sovereignty, is proved by every thing he said and did, to the last unequivocal confession he made before his judges. As a spiritual deliverer of his race, he sought to form *children of God,* who, under whatever laws they lived, should promote the welfare of others from the purest principles; and, patient under sufferings, reign in spite of them as kings in the realm of truth and goodness. It is selfevident, that such a purpose alone could be consistent with the intention of Providence in regard to mankind; a purpose, in the promotion of which all the wise and good upon Earth must cooperate, in proportion to the purity of their thoughts and endeavours; for what can man propose as the standard of his earthly perfection and happiness, but this universally operating, pure humanity?

With reverence I bend before thy noble form, thou head and founder of a kingdom, so great in its object, so durable in its extent, so simple and animated in its principles, so efficacious in its motives, that the sphere of this terrestrial life appears too narrow for it. No where in history find I a revolution so quietly effected in so short a time, planted in such a singular manner by feeble instruments, propagated over all the Earth with yet indeterminable effect, and cultivated so as to produce good or bad fruit, as that, which has spread among nations under the name, not property of *thy religion,* that is to say, of thy vital scheme for the welfare of mankind, but mostly of *thy worship,* that is, an unreflecting adoration of thy cross and person. Thy penetrating mind foresaw this; and it is dishonouring thy name, to affix it to every turbid stream from thy pure fountain. We will avoid it as much as possible: thy placid form shall stand alone before the whole history, that takes its rise from thee.

CHAPTER 1

Origin of Christianity, with the fundamental Principles it included

SINGULAR as it appears, that a revolution affecting more than one quarter of the Globe should originate from a country so despised as Judea, historical grounds for it may be discovered on a closer inspection. The revolution, of which we speak, was intellectual; and however contemptible the Jews may have been deemed by the Greeks and Romans, they had this to boast, that, before any other nation of Asia or of Europe, they possessed writings of ancient date, on which their constitution was founded, and which, in consequence of this constitution, must promote the cultivation of a particular kind of science and literature. Neither Greeks nor Romans could lay claim to such a code of religious and political institutions, which, interwoven with ancient scriptural family records, was confided to the care of a particular and numerous tribe, and preserved by it with superstitious reverence.

In course of time a kind of refined sense naturally grew out of this antiquated letter, which was promoted by the repeated dispersion of the Jews among other nations. In the canon of their sacred writings were intermixed poems, moral maxims, and sublime orations; that, written at various times, and on very different occasions, grew into a collection, which was soon considered as one continued system, and out of which one leading sense was drawn. The prophets of this nation, who, as the appointed guardians of the law of the land, had exhibited to the people a picture of what they ought to be, and were not, each according to his peculiar way of thinking, at one time teaching and exhorting, at another warning or consoling, but always with patriotic hope, had left posterity, in these fruits of their heads and hearts, many seeds of new ideas, which every man might cultivate after his own manner. From all these was gradually formed a systematic expectation of a king, who should deliver his fallen, obedient people; bring them golden days, such as they had never known under the greatest of their ancient sovereigns; and begin a new order of things. Conformably to the language of the prophets, these views were theocratic: with the collected characters of a messiah they were moulded into a lively image, and considered as the certain prerogative of the nation. In Palestine the increasing misery of the people made them hold fast this idea: in other countries, in Egypt for example, where many Jews had resided since the dissolution of the monarchy of Alexander, these notions acquired more of a Grecian form; apocryphal books, which exhibited these prophecies in a new shape, were circulated; and the time was now arrived, when these dreams, having attained their acme, must come to a conclusion. From the people a man arose, whose mind, exalted above all earthly chimeras, united all the hopes, wishes, and predictions of the prophets in the design of an ideal kingdom, which should be nothing less than an Israelitish kingdom of Heaven. In this lofty plan he foresaw the approaching downfall of his nation; and denounced a speedy and lamentable end to their splendid temple, and to their worship, now completely converted into superstition. The kingdom of God was to be extended to all nations; and the people, who deemed it exclusively their own, were considered by him as a lifeless corpse.

What comprehensive force of mind must have been requisite, to discern and announce any thing of the kind at that time in Judea, is evident from the unfriendly reception given to this doctrine by the chief persons and learned men among the Jews: it was looked upon as a rebellion against Moses, and against God; as treason to the nation, whose common hopes it unpatriotically destroyed. Even to the apostles the exjudaism of Christianity was a doctrine above all others difficult to swallow: and the most learned of them, Paul, found all the subtleties of Jewish logic necessary, to render it comprehensible to the Christian Jews, even out of Judea. It was well, that Providence itself gave the first stroke, and that with the destruction of Jerusalem the ancient walls were thrown down, which with unyielding stubbornness separated God's chosen people, as they called themselves, from all others upon Earth. The time of a peculiar national worship, teeming with pride and superstition, was now over: for necessary as such institutions might have been in former days, when every nation, educated in a narrow family circle, ripened as a bunch of grapes on its own stalk, all human exertions in this part of the World had now tended for some centuries, to unite nations, by means of war, commerce, arts, science, and familiar intercourse, and press from the fruit of all one common liquor. The prejudices of national religion stood chiefly in the way of this union: and as, while the Romans exercised a general spirit of toleration throughout their extensive empire, and the eclectic philosophy, that singular compound of all schools and sects, was universally diffused, a *popular* faith now arose, which made of all nations one people, and proceeded immediately from the most obstinate, which had hitherto esteemed itself preeminently distinguished from all others; this was at any rate a great and perilous step in the history of mankind, in whatever manner it was undertaken. It made all people brethren, in leading them to the knowledge of one God and saviour: but it was capable of rendering them slaves, if this religion were imposed upon them as a yoke. The keys of the kingdom of Heaven, both in this world and the next, might introduce phariseeism as dangerous, when in the hands of other nations, as ever they did in the hands of the Jews.

The speedy and firm establishment of Christianity was principally promoted by a belief, which originated from its founder himself: this was the opinion of *his early return, and the revelation of his kingdom upon Earth.* This belief Jesus avowed before his judge, and frequently repeated in the last days of his life: his followers adhered to it, and expected the appearance of his kingdom. The spiritually minded Christian conceived therein the idea of a spiritual kingdom; the carnally minded, of a temporal sovereignty: and as the overstretched imaginations of those times and countries were not over-rational in their reveries, Jewish Christian apocalypses arose, teeming with various prophecies, signs, and dreams. Antichrist was first to be destroyed; and on the delay of Christ's return, this man of sin was first to be revealed, then to increase, and grow up to the utmost height in his abominations, till the saviour should come again, and resuscitate his people.

It cannot be denied, but that such expectations must have occasioned many persecutions of the early Christians; for Rome, the mistress of the World, could not be indifferent to the propagation of such opinions, announcing its approaching overthrow, and representing it as an antichristian object of horrour or contempt. Thus such prophets were soon considered as unpatriotic despisers of their country and the World, nay, as men notoriously guilty of a general hatred to mankind; and many a one, impatient of his saviour's return, ran to meet martyrdom. It is certain, however, that this hope of a kingdom of Christ nigh at hand, in Heaven, or on Earth, powerfully united the minds of men, and detached them from the World. This they despised as sunk in misery; while they beheld every where around them, what they believed so near. Hence they acquired courage, to rise above the spirit of the times, the power of persecutors, the mockery of the incredulous; which otherwise no one could have surmounted: they sojourned here as passengers, whose residence was where their leader was gone before them, and whence he was soon to be revealed.

Beside the leading points of history, that have been mentioned, it appears not unnecessary, to mark some of inferiour magnitude, that contributed greatly to the structure of Christianity.

1. The *benevolent sentiments of Christ* had made fraternal concord and placability, active assistance to the poor and needy, in short every duty of man, the common tie of his followers, so that, conformably to this, Christianity could not be other than *a genuine bond of friendship and brotherly love.* There can be no doubt, that this instrument of humanity contributed much at all times, and particularly in the beginning, to its reception and extension. The poor and needy, the oppressed, the bondsman and the slave, the publican and the sinner, embraced it; and in consequence the first Christian communities were termed assemblies of beggars by the heathen. Now as the new religion was neither capable nor desirous of removing the distinction of ranks, that then existed in the World, nothing was left for it but minds possessed of Christian meekness, with all the weeds that would spring up at the same time on this good ground. Rich widows soon attracted a number of beggars by their gifts, who occasionally disturbed the peace of whole communities. Alms could not fail to be esteemed on one side as

the true treasures of the kingdom of Heaven, and to be sought on the other: in both cases, not only that noble pride, the offspring of independent merit and useful industry, but often impartiality and truth, yielded to base flattery. The almschests of communities became the common property of martyrs: gifts to the community were exalted to the title of the spirit of Chrisianity, while its morals were corrupted by the exaggerated praise bestowed on such acts. Though the necessity of the times may excuse much of this, it is nevertheless certain, that, if human society be considered as one large hospital, and Christianity its common almsbox, a depraved state of morals and politics must necessarily ensue.

2. *Christianity was to be a community governed by elders and teachers without any worldly authority.* These were to guide the flock as shepherds, decide their differences, correct their faults with zeal and affection, and lead them to Heaven by their counsel, their influence, their precepts, and their example. A noble office, when worthily executed, and not prevented by circumstances from being fulfilled: for it blunts the fangs of the law, extracts the thorns from claims and contests, and unites the divine, the father, and the judge. But how was it, when, in course of time, the shepherds treated their human flocks as actual sheep, or led them as beasts of burden to browze on thistles? how, when wolves, legally called, came among the flocks instead of shepherds? Childish obedience then soon became a Christian virtue: it became a Christian virtue, for a man to renounce the use of his reason, and to follow the authority of another's opinion instead of his own conviction, while the bishop, instead of an apostle, was messenger, witness, teacher, expounder, judge, and arbiter. Nothing now was prized so highly as faith, as quietly following the leader: the man, who ventured to have an opinion of his own, was an obstinate heretic, and excluded from the kingdom of God and the church. Bishops and their subalterns, in defiance of the doctrines of Christ, interfered in family disputes and civil affairs; and soon they quarrelled among each other, which should rule the rest. Hence the contests for the chief episcopal sees, and the gradual

extension of their rights: hence the endless dispute, between the sceptre and the crosier, between the crown and the mitre. Certain as it is, that, in times of tyranny, just and pious judges were indispensable aids to men, who had the misfortune to live without political institutions; scarcely any thing more scandalous can be conceived, than the long dispute between the spiritual arm and the temporal, which kept Europe in perpetual confusion for more than a thousand years. In this place the salt was insipid, in that it was too pungent.

3. *Christianity had a certain formulary, of which those who were initiated into it by baptism made profession:* and simple as this formulary was, more disturbances, persecutions, and bitterness, arose in course of time from the harmless expressions, *Father, Son,* and *Spirit,* than from any other three words in human language. The farther men departed from the principles of Christianity, considered as an active institution, founded for the good of mankind; the more men speculated beyond the limits of human reason. Mysteries were discovered; and at length the whole of the Christian doctrine was converted into mystery. After the books of the New Testament were introduced into the church as a canon, things were demonstrated from them, and indeed from books of the Jewish constitution, books which few could read in the original, and of which the primitive signification had long been lost, that from them are not to be proved. Hence systems and heresies multiplied, to stifle which the worst of all means were chosen, *ecclesiastical assemblies and synods.* How many of these are the disgrace of Christianity, and of common sense! Pride and Intolerance called them together; Discord, Party Spirit, Grossness, and Knavery, swayed them: and at length Force, Arbitrary Power, Insolence, Pimping, Deceit, or Accident, decided, under the name of the Holy Spirit, for the whole church, nay for time and eternity. In a short time, none were found so competent to determine articles of faith as the Christianized emperors, to whom Constantine had bequeathed the innate hereditary right, to enjoin creeds and canons concerning Father,

Son, and Spirit, concerning ὁμοούσιος and ὁμοιούσιος, the single or double nature of Christ, Mary the mother of God, and the created or uncreated glory, that appeared at Christ's baptism. These pretensions, with the consequences that ensued from them, will remain an eternal disgrace to the Byzantine throne, and to every throne, by which it was imitated; for which their ignorant power they supported and perpetuated persecutions, schisms, and disturbances, which improved neither the spirit nor the morality of men, but tended to undermine the church, the state, and the thrones themselves. The history of the first Christian empire, that of Constantinople, is such a melancholy exhibition of base treachery, and horrible cruelty, that, to the moment of its deplorable end, it stands a warning monument to all polemic Christian governments.

4. *Christianity had its sacred writings, which sprung in part from occasional epistles, and in part, with few exceptions, from oral communications;* these in time were made the standard of faith, soon became the banner of every contending party, and were abused in every way, that want of sense could dictate. Each party either proved from them what it wished to prove; or men hesitated not to mutilate them, and to forge with unblushing effrontery false gospels, epistles, and revelations, in the name of the apostles. *Pious fraud,* in such things more detestable than perjury, as it lies to a whole series of ages and generations without end, was soon reckoned no sin, but a meritorious act for the honour of God, and the salvation of souls. Hence the many spurious writings of the apostles and fathers of the church: hence the numerous fictions of miracles, martyrs, donations, constitutions, and decretals, the uncertainty of which steals through all the early and Middle Ages of ecclesiastical history, almost down to the reformation, like a thief in the night. When once the corrupt principle was admitted, that a man might deal treacherously, invent lies, and write fictions, for the good of the church, historical faith was wounded: the tongue, the pen, the memory and imagination of men, had lost their rule and compass; so that *Christian veracity* had a more just claim to become proverbial, than Grecian honesty, or Punic

faith. This is the more to be regretted, as the epoch of Christianity follows the period of the most excellent historians of Greece and Rome; after whom true history almost disappears at once with the Christian era for many centuries. It quickly sinks into a chronicle of bishops, churches, and monks; as the pen was employed, not for what is most worthy of man, not for the World and the state, but for the church, or for orders, cloisters, and sects; and as men were accustomed to homilies, and the people were to believe the bishop in all things, writers considered the whole World as a race of believers, as a Christian flock.

5. *Christianity had only two sacred rites, very simple, and well adapted to their purposes;* for nothing was farther from the intention of its founder, than that it should be a ceremonial religion. But deuterochristianity soon became intermixed with Jewish and heathen practices, according to the difference of places and times, so that the baptism of infants was converted into an exorcism of Satan, and a feast in commemoration of a departed friend became the creation of a God, a bloodless sacrifice, a miracle for the remission of sin, a viaticum to the other World. Unfortunately the period of Christianity coincided with that of ignorance, barbarism, and depraved taste; whence little truly great and noble could enter into its ceremonies, the structure of its churches, the institutions of its festivals, statutes, and pageantry, its hymns, prayers, and rituals. These ceremonies rolled on from land to land, from one quarter of the Globe to another: what originally derived some local meaning from ancient custom lost it in foreign countries, and remote times: thus the spirit of Christian liturgies became a singular jumble of Jewish, Egyptian, Greek, Roman, barbarian, practices, in which what was serious frequently became tiresome, or absurd. A history of Christian taste, in festivals, temples, rituals, consecrations, and literary composition, contemplated with a philosophic eye, would exhibit the most chequered picture the World ever beheld, of a subject that was intended to be free of ceremony. And as this Christian taste in time insinuated itself into juridical and political customs, domestic establishments, plays, romances, dances, songs, tourna-

ments, coats of arms, battles, triumphs, and other festivities; it must be confessed, that the human mind received from it an incredible twist; and that the cross erected over nations stamped a singular impression on their foreheads. The *pisciculi christiani* swam for ages in a turbid element.

6. *Christ lived unmarried, and his mother was a virgin: serene and cheerful as he was, he loved occasional solitude, and prayed in private.* The spirit of the orientals, the Egyptians in particular, who were previously inclined to contemplation, seclusion, and religious indolence, carried the notion of the holiness of celibacy, especially in the priesthood, and of the pleasingness to God of virginity, solitude, and a contemplative life, to such an extravagant pitch, that, as Essenes, Therapeutae, and other solitaries, already abounded, above all in Egypt, the spirit of seclusion, vows, fasting, penitence, prayer, and a monastic life, was set in full fermentation by Christianity. In different countries, indeed, it assumed different forms; and according as it was modified, proved either a benefit, or an injury: upon the whole, however, it is incontrovertible, that the injuriousness of this way of life, the moment it becomes an irrevocable law, a slavish yoke, or a political net, is predominant, for society in general, as well as for its individual members. From China and Thibet, to Ireland, Mexico, and Peru, cloisters of bonzes, lamas, and talapoins, and of all Christian monks and nuns, in their several kinds and classes, are the dungeons of religion and the state, seminaries of barbarity, vice, and oppression, or sewers of the most abominable lusts and knaveries. And though we would deprive no spiritual order of its merits with respect to the culture of the earth, the improvement of man, or the promotion of science; we ought never to shut our ears against the secret sighs and lamentations, that echo through these hollow vaults, secluded from humankind; or will we turn our heads, to view the empty visions of supramundane contemplation, or the continued cabals of furious monkish zeal, in a form certainly adapted to no enlightened age. To Christianity they are unquestionably foreign; for Christ was no monk; Mary, no nun; the most ancient of the apostles was accompanied by his wife;

and neither Christ, nor any of the twelve, knew aught of supramundane contemplation.

7. Finally, *Christianity, in seeking to found a heavenly kingdom upon Earth,* and to convince men of the transitoriness of all earthly things, at all times formed those pure and tranquil minds, which sought not the eyes of the World, and performed their good deeds before God; but, alas! it also cherished, by its gross abuse, that false enthusiasm, which, almost from its commencement, gave birth to frantic martyrs and prophets in abundance. They endeavoured to erect a kingdom of Heaven upon the Earth, without knowing where or how it was to stand. They opposed the government, and loosed the bands of order, without giving the World a better; while vulgar pride, base arrogance, scandalous lust, and mad stupidity, concealed themselves under the overflow of Christian zeal. As the deceived Jews followed their Pseudo-Messiahs, the Christians in one place flocked to the banners of bold impostors, in another fawned on the most despicable and dissolute tyrants, as if they had established the kingdom of God upon the Earth, when they built for them churches, or conferred on them donations. Thus the weak Constantine was flattered; and this mystic language of prophetic fanaticism extended itself, according to times and circumstances, both to men and women. The Paraclete has often appeared; and the Spirit has often spoken to a deeply enamoured enthusiast from female lips. History shows what discord and calamity have been introduced into the Christian World by Chiliasts and Anabaptists, Donatists, Montanists, Priscillianists, Circumcellions, and others: how some of heated imaginations have despised and destroyed works of science, demolished and extirpated monuments of art, institutions, and men: how a palpable imposture, or ridiculous accident, occasionally set whole countries in commotion: how, for example, the fancied approach of the World's end drove all Europe into Asia. Let us not, however, refuse its due praise to pure Christian enthusiasm: this, when it took a right course, performed more in a short time for many ages, than all the coolness and indifference of philosophy could ever accomplish. The leaves of

deceit fall off; but the fruit ripens. The flames of time consume the straw and stubble; but real gold they can only refine.

Whatever melancholy has crossed my mind, while my pen has traced many of these shameful abuses of the best of things, I proceed with cheerfulness to the propagation of Christianity in different countries and regions: for as medicine may be converted into poison, poison may be rendered salutiferous; and what is pure and good in its origin must ultimately prove triumphant.

CHAPTER 2
Propagation of Christianity in the East

In Judea Christianity grew under oppression, and retained the stamp of oppression in its form, as long as the Jewish state endured. The Nazarenes and Ebionites, in all probability the remains of the first body of Christians, were poor and low persons, and have long been extinct; their names alone remaining in the list of heretics, on account of their opinion, that Jesus was a mere man, the son of Joseph and Mary. It is to be regretted, that their Gospel is lost; as in it probably we should have the earliest collection, though not altogether pure, of the nearest local traditions of the life of Christ. Thus, too, the ancient books in possession of the Sabeans, or Saint John's Christians, were probably not unworthy notice: for though a pure illustration of the primitive times could by no means be expected from this fabling sect, a compound of Jews and Christians, even fables often throw light on things of this kind.[1]

The influence of the church at Jerusalem on other communities arose chiefly from *the respect paid to the apostles:* for as James, the brother of Jesus, a sensible and worthy man, presided over it for a number of years, there can be no doubt, but its form would be a model to others. A Jewish model, therefore: and as almost every country, and every city, of primitive Chris-

[1] The newest and most authentic account of this sect is in Norberg's *Comment. de relig. et lingua sabaeorum* (Essay on the religion and language of the Sabeans), 1780. This should be printed with the essays of Walch and others, after the manner of older collections.

tendom, would be converted by an apostle, every where imitations of the church at Jerusalem, apostolical communities, arose. The bishop, who received the unction of the Spirit from an apostle, occupied the apostle's place, and with it enjoyed his authority. The power of the Spirit, which he had received, he again imparted, and soon became a kind of high-priest, a mediator between God and man. As the first council at Jerusalem spoke in the name of the Holy Spirit, other councils did the same in imitation of it; and we are startled at the spiritual power very early acquired by the bishops, in the Asiatic provinces. Thus the authority of the apostles, which visibly descended to the bishops, rendered the most ancient constitution of the church aristocratic; and in this constitution lay the germe of a future hierarchy, and a popedom. What is said of the pure virginity of the church during the first three centuries is either fiction, or exaggeration.

It is well known, that *an oriental philosophy*, as it is called, had spread very considerably in the first ages of Christianity. This, however, more closely investigated, appears to have been nothing but a shoot from the eclectric, or modern platonic philosophy, such as the country and time were adapted to produce. It wound itself round Judaism and Christianity; but neither sprang from them, nor produced them any fruits. The Gnostics were branded with the name of heretics, from the commencement of Christianity, because the Christians would not admit among them any subtilizing philosophasters; and many of them would have remained unknown to us, had they not been entered in the rolls of schism. We could wish, that their writings also had been preserved, as they would not be unwelcome to us, with regard to the canon of the New Testament: at present we perceive from a few particular opinions of this numerous sect, yet remaining, nothing more than a crude attempt, to intermix the fictions of the oriental Platonists, respecting the nature of God, and the creation of the World, with Judaism and Christianity, and thence form a metaphysical theology, principally of allegorical names, with a theodicy and moral philosophy. As the name of heretic is unknown to the history of mankind, every one of these unsuccessful attempts is valuable to it, and worthy its notice; though at the same time it is well for the history of Christianity, that such reveries should never become the prevailing system of the church. After the pains that have been bestowed on this sect ecclesiastically, a pure philosophical inquiry, whence their notions were derived, what was their intention, and what effect they produced, would not be unprofitable to the history of the human understanding.[2]

The doctrines of Manes, whose object was nothing less, than to be the founder of a complete Christianity, made farther progress. He perished; and his numerous followers were so persecuted in all places, and at all times, that the name of Manichean, especially after Austin had taken up the pen against them, became one of the most terrible stigmas of a heretic. We now shudder at this ecclesiastical spirit of persecution, and perceive, that many of these heresiarchs were men of reflecting and enterprizing minds, who boldly attempted, not only to combine religion, metaphysics, morals, and natural philosophy, but to unite them for the purpose of an actual society, a philosophico-political religious order. Some of them were lovers of science, and are to be pitied for being denied more ample knowledge by their situation: the Catholic party, however, would have become a stagnant pool, had not these wild winds set it in motion, and compelled them at least to defend their written tradition. The time of pure reason, and a political improvement of morals by it, was not yet arrived; and for the religious community of Manes there was no place, either in Persia, or Armenia, any more than afterwards among the Bulgarians, or Albigenses.

Christian sects penetrated into India, Thibet, and China, though by ways that remain obscure to us: the shock, however, that was given to the remotest regions of Asia in the first

---

[2] After Beausobre, Mosheim, Brucker, Walch, Jablonski, Semler, and others, we may now take a more clear and free view of the subject.

centuries of the Christian era, is observable in their own histories.[3] The doctrine of Budda, or Fo, which is said to have come from Bactra, acquired fresh animation at this period. It spread to Ceylon, Thibet, and China: Hindoo books on the subject were translated into the Chinese language, and the great sect of the bonzes was brought to perfection. Without ascribing to Christianity all the abominations of the bonzes, or the whole of the monastic system of the lamas and talapoins, it seems to have been the leaven, which set all the ancient reveries of the people from Egypt to China in fermentation anew, and modified them more or less. Many fables of Budda, Chrishnoo, and the rest, appear to include Christian ideas enveloped in an Indian garb; and the great lama on the mountains, who probably arose first in the fifteenth century, is, with his personal sanctity and rigid doctrines, his bells and religious orders, in all appearance a distant cousin of the lama on the Tiber: the difference is, there Manicheism and Nestorianism were grafted on Asiatic ideas and manners; here orthodox Christianity was inserted into a Roman stock. The two cousins, however, would not readily recognize each other, so little intercourse has been kept up between them.

We have a clearer knowledge of the more learned Nestorians, who spread themselves far into Asia, particularly after the fifth century, and did much good.[4] Almost from the commencement of the Christian era the school of Edessa flourished as the seat of Syrian learning. King Abgarus, who has been held forth as an epistolary correspondent of Christ himself, when he removed his residence from Nisibis, transported to Edessa the collections of books, which were in the temples. At this period,

[3] It is to be wished, that the essays by De Guignes, in the writings of the French Academy of Inscriptions, were collected and translated as those of Caylus, St. Palaye, and others, have been. This appears to me the easiest mode of drawing things worthy notice out of the wilderness of a society, and of rendering the discoveries of individuals useful, as well as of uniting them together.

[4] Pfeifer's *Auszug aus Assemanni Orientalischer Bibliothek* (Abstract of Assemanni's Oriental Bibliotheca), Erlang, 1776, is an useful work for this almost unknown region of history: a particular, connected history of Eastern Christendom, and of Nestorianism especially, is still a desideratum.

every one, who was desirous of becoming learned, travelled to Edessa, from all parts of the World; for beside Christian theology, the fine arts were taught there in the Greek and Syrian languages, so that Edessa was probably the first Christian university ever established. It flourished for four centuries, till the professors were expelled on account of the doctrines of Nestorius, to which they adhered, and their school was demolished. But in consequence of this the Syrian literature spread not only into Mesopotamia, Palestine, Syria, and Phenicia, but even into Persia; where it experienced an honourable reception, and where at last a Nestorian pope arose, who ruled over all the Christians in this kingdom, and afterwards over those of Arabia, India, Mungalia, and China.

Whether he were the celebrated Prester John (*pres-tadshani,* the priest of the World), of whom many fabulous reports were spread in the Middle Ages; and whether, from a singular mixture of doctrines, the great lama at last arose from him; we shall leave undecided.[5] Suffice it, that in Persia the favoured Nestorians were employed by its monarchs as physicians to the body, ambassadors, and ministers; the Christian writings were translated into the Persian; and the Syriac became the learned language of the country. When the empire of Mohammed gained the sway, particularly under his successors the Ommiades, Nestorians filled the highest posts of honour, and were made viceroys of the conquered provinces; and when the khalifs resided at Bagdad, as well as after they had removed their residence to Samarraja, the patriarch of the Nestorians shared their authority. Under Al-Mamon, who encouraged learning among his people, and appointed physicians and astronomers, philosophers, naturalists, mathematicians, geographers, and annalists, to teach in the academy of Bagdad, the Syrians were associates and instructors of the Arabs. They rivalled each other in translating into Arabic the works of the Greeks, many of

[5] Fischer, in the introduction to his *Siberischen Geschichte* (History of Siberia), § 38 and following, has rendered this opinion very probable. Others are for the *ung-khan,* the khan of the Keraites. See Koch's *Table des Revolutions* (Table of Revolutions), Vol. I, p. 265.

which had already been translated into that language: and if the light of science afterwards dawned on benighted Europe from the Arabic, the Syriac Christians originally contributed to this. Their language, the first of the oriental dialects in this region into which vowels were admitted, and which can boast the most ancient and elegant translation of the New Testament, was the bridge of Grecian science for Asia, and through the Arabs for Europe. Under such favourable circumstances, Nestorian missions then extended themselves far and wide; though other Christian sects found means to suppress them, or chase them away. Under the family of Gengis-khan, too, they were of considerable importance: their patriarch frequently accompanied the khan on his expeditions, and thus their doctrines were spread among the Mungals, Igurians, and other Tatar nations. Samarcand was the seat of a metropolitan; Cashgar, and other cities, of bishops: and if the celebrated Christian monument in China be genuine, there is to be found on it a complete chronicle of the immigration of the priests from Tatsin. If with this be considered, that the whole of the Mohammedan religion, such as it is, would never have arisen, had it not been preceded by Christianity, we find in this, beyond all dispute, a leaven, which, more or less, sooner or later, set in commotion the way of thinking of all the south and part of the north of Asia.

From this commotion, however, no new and peculiar blossom of the human intellect, as perhaps with the Greeks and Romans, was to be expected. The Nestorians, by whom so much was effected, were not a nation, were not a race growing up of itself in a maternal soil: they were Christians, they were monks. Their language, indeed, they were capable of teaching: but what could they write in it? Liturgies, expositions of Scripture, monastic books of devotion, sermons, polemical works, chronicles, and insipid verses. Hence in the Syriac-Christian literature there is not a spark of that poetic genius, which bursts from the soul, and warms the heart: a miserable knack at versifying catalogues of names, homilies, and chronicles, constituted the whole of their art of poetry. In none of the sciences they cultivated did they display the least spirit of invention, in none did they pursue any method of their own. A melancholy proof how little was done by the ascetico-polemic monachal spirit, with all its politic cunning. In this barren form it displayed itself in every quarter of the Globe, and still lords it on the mountains of Thibet; where not the least trace of free inventive genius is to be discovered, throughout the legally established monkish constitution. Whatever proceeds from the cloister is, for the most part, adapted only to the convent.

History, then, need not expatiate long on the particular provinces of Christian Asia. Christianity reached Armenia at an early period, and bestowed on its ancient memorable language an alphabet, with a double and triple version of the Scriptures, and an Armenian history. But neither Misrob with his alphabet, nor his scholar, Moses of Chorene, with his history, could confer on their people literature, or a national constitution.[6] Armenia always lay in the way of other nations: as it had been formerly under Persians, Greeks, and Romans, it now fell under Arabs, Turks, Tatars, and Curdes. Its inhabitants still pursue their ancient occupation, trade: a scientific or political edifice could never have been established in this place, with or without Christianity.

The state of Christian Georgia is still more wretched. There are churches and convents, patriarchs, bishops, and monks: the women are beautiful; the men, brave: yet the parent will sell his child; the husband, his wife; the prince, his subjects; the devotee, his priest. A singular sort of Christianity, among this gay and faithless nation of robbers.

The Gospel was early translated into Arabic, also; and many Christian sects have taken great pains about the fine country of Arabia. In it Jews and Christians often persecuted each other; but neither party, though each occasionally produced even kings, effected any thing of importance. Every thing fell before Mohammed; and now, indeed, there is not a Christian community in Arabia, though there are whole tribes of Jews. Three

---

[6] Whiston's preface to *Mosis Chorensis Hist. Armen.*, 1736; Schroeder's *Thesaur. Ling. Armen. Diss.*, p. 62.

religions, descendants of one another, guard with mutual hatred the sanctuary of their birthplace, the deserts of Arabia.[7]

If we would now take a view of the general result of the effects, produced by Christianity in its Asiatic provinces; we must first agree on the point of view, in which the advantages, that this, or any religion, could confer on one quarter of the Globe, ought to be placed.

1. Christianity may have secretly operated to the furthering of *a heavenly kingdom upon Earth,* that is, a more perfect order of things, for the good of nations: but the flower of this operation, a perfect state, it has never produced, either in Asia, or in Europe. Arabs and Syrians, Persians and Armenians, Hindoos and Druses, have remained what they were; and no political constitution in that country can boast of its being the offspring of Christianity; even if anchoritism and monastic devotion, or a hierarchy of any kind, with their restless endeavours, be taken as the standard of a Christian state. Patriarchs and bishops send missionaries round to extend their sects, their dioceses, their power: they seek the favour of princes, to obtain influence in affairs, or convents and communities: one party strives against another, and endeavours to obtain the superiority. Thus Jews and Christians, Nestorians and Monophysites, hunt each other round; and no party thinks of acting simply and freely for the good of any place or country. The clergy of the east, who were never without a spice of monkery, would serve God, and not mankind.

2. There are three methods of acting upon men; by *teaching, authority,* and *religious ceremonies.* Teaching is the simplest, and most effectual, if it be of the right kind. Instruction of the young and of the old, when it relates to the essential concerns and duties of man, cannot fail to introduce, or keep in circulation, much useful knowledge: the fame and preeminence of having rendered such more clear even to the lower people pertain exclusively to Christianity in many countries. Cate-

[7] Bruce's *Travels into Abyssinia* give a remarkable history of the Christianity of these regions: whether, on the whole, any new conclusions may be derived from it, time will show.

chisms, sermons, hymns, creeds, and prayers, have diffused a knowledge of God, and of morals, among the people: translations and expositions of the holy Scriptures have imparted to them writing and literature: and where nations were still in such infancy, that they were incapable of comprehending any thing but fables, there at least a sacred fable revived. Herein, it is obvious, every thing depended upon this, whether the man, who was to teach, were capable of teaching, and what he taught. In both these points, however, the answer must vary so much, according to the person, the people, the time, and the country, that at last we must confine ourselves to what was to be taught, to what the prevailing church maintained. Fearing the incapacity and boldness of many of its teachers, it preferred brevity, and confined itself within a narrow circle. It thus, we must allow, incurred the danger of having the substance of its doctrines very soon exhausted, and reduced to repetition; so that in a few generations the hereditary religion would lose all the lustre of novelty, and the dull teacher would slumber over his antiquated creed. Thus, for the most part, the first shock of Christian missions alone was truly vivid; soon one dull wave drove on a duller, till at last all gently subsided in the still surface of an accustomed ancient Christian ceremony. By ceremonies compensation was endeavoured to be made for the decay of the soul of ceremony, doctrine; and thus the ceremonial system was invented, which at length became an inanimate puppet, standing immoveable and unmoved in ancient pomp. The puppet was invented for the convenience both of teacher and hearer; for it afforded them both food for reflection, if they chose to reflect; and if not, still, it was said, the vehicle of religion would not be lost. And as from the beginning the church was very tenacious of unanimity, formularies by which the herd would be least distracted were absolutely the best for preserving dull uniformity. The churches of Asia afford the completest demonstration of all this: they still are, what they were almost two thousand years ago, slumbering bodies, destitute of mind: even heresy is extinct in them, for they possess not sufficient energy for heresies.

Possibly, however, the authority of the priests may supply, what is lost by the torpor of the doctrine, or the cessation of impulse? In some measure it may, but not altogether. A sacred person full of years is surrounded with the mild beams of paternal experience, mature judgment, and tranquillity undisturbed by the passions: hence it is so many travellers speak of the reverence, with which they were inspired in the presence of the aged patriarchs, priests, and bishops of the east. A noble simplicity in their carriage, dress, conduct, and way of life, contributes much to this: and many a worthy anchorite, if he keep not his instructions, warnings, and consolations from the World, may have done more good, than a hundred idle preachers amid the bustle of highways and markets. Instruction, however, is the noblest source of authority, united with example founded on knowledge and experience; if shortsightedness and prejudice step into the seat of truth, the authority of the most respectable person is dangerous and detrimental.

3. As the life of man is altogether calculated for the active purposes of general society; it is evident, that, in Christianity also, every thing must soon or late die away, that counteracts these. Every lifeless member is dead; and as soon as the living body is sensible of its own life, and the useless burden of the dead member, this member is removed. As long as the missions in Asia retained their activity, they imparted and received animation: but when the temporal power of the Arabs, Turks, and Tatars, destroyed this, they spread no farther. Their convents and episcopal sees stand as ruins of ancient times, melancholy and confined: many are tolerated only for the sake of their presents, tributes, and abject services.

4. As Christianity operates chiefly by means of its doctrines, much depends on the *language,* in which they are inculcated, and on the degree of mental cultivation already contained in them, to which it orthodoxly adheres. With a cultivated or universal language it not only propagates itself, but it acquires by means of it improvement and respect: but if, as a sacred dialect of divine origin, it remain behind other living languages, or be restricted to the limits of an obsolete, rude paternal

dialect, as to a decayed palace; it must in time be reduced to drag on a wearisome life in it, as a wretched tyrant, or an ignorant prisoner. As in Asia the Greek language, and afterwards the Syriac, were overpowered by the victorious Arabic, the knowledge they contained was thrown out of circulation: they could only propagate themselves as liturgies, as creeds, as a monkish theology. We are mistaken, therefore, when we attribute to the substance of a religion, what properly pertains only to the instruments, with which it operates. Look at the St. Thomas's Christians in India, the Georgians, the Armenians, the Abyssinians, the Copts: what are they? what has Christianity made of them? The Copts and Abyssinians possess libraries of ancient books, unintelligible to themselves, but which might probably be of use in the hands of Europeans: they use them not; they cannot use them. Their Christianity has sunk into the most wretched superstition.

5. Here, then, it is incumbent upon me, to bestow on the *Greek language* that praise, which it so eminently merits in the history of mankind; for by its aid all the light has been kindled, that has illumined or beamed upon Europe. Had not this language been so widely extended, and so long preserved, by the conquests of Alexander, the kingdoms of his successors, and the Roman possessions, Christianity would scarcely have contributed in the least to enlighten Asia: for both the orthodox and the heretic kindled their true or false lights, mediately or immediately, at the Grecian language. From it, too, the Armenian, Syriac, and Arabic languages derived their illumining spark: and had the first Christian writings been composed not in Greek, but in the Hebrew dialect of that time; could not the Gospel have been preached and propagated in Greek; the stream, that now waters nations, would probably have been choked near its fountain. The Christians would have been, what the Ebionites were, and perhaps the St. John's and St. Thomas's Christians are, a poor despised multitude, destitute of all effect on the spirit of nations. Let us, therefore, quit its oriental birthplace, for that stage on which it acted a greater part.

CHAPTER 3

Progress of Christianity in the Grecian Countries

We observed, that *Hellenism,* or a freer manner of thinking of the Jews intermixed with the ideas of others, prepared the way for the rise of Christianity: accordingly Christianity, when it began its course, proceeded far on this way; and in a short time extensive regions, where any Hellenistic Jews resided, were filled with the new mission. The appellation of Christians was first given in a Grecian city: the first writings of Christianity were most extensively circulated in the Grecian language; for this language was more or less diffused from India to the Atlantic, from Lybia to Thule. It may be considered both as fortunate and unfortunate, that Judea was particularly near to a province, which contributed much to the first form of Christianity, the province of Egypt. If Jerusalem were its cradle, Alexandria was its school.

Since the time of the Ptolemies a number of Jews had resided for the sake of trade in Egypt, where they endeavoured to create a Judea of their own, built a temple, translated their sacred writings one after another into Greek, and augmented their number. There had been very flourishing establishments for the promotion of science also at Alexandria, since the time of Ptolemy Philadelphus; such as were to be found nowhere else, even Athens not excepted. Fourteen thousand scholars had been lodged and maintained there for a considerable time at the public expense: here were the celebrated museum, the immense library, the works that conferred renown on ancient poets and learned men of every kind: thus the great school of nations was here, in the centre of the commerce of the World. From this conflux of nations, and the gradual amalgamation of the sentiments of all in the Greek and Roman empire, arose the *modern Platonic philosophy,* as it was called, and particularly that singular *syncretism,* which sought to unite the principles of all parties, and in a short time assimilated the ideas of Indians, Persians, Jews, Ethiopians, Egyptians, Greeks, Romans, and barbarians. This spirit prevailed wonderfully in the Roman empire, as every where philosophers sprung up, who added the notions of their own native places to the general mass: but Alexandria was the spot where it most eminently flourished. Into this ocean the drop of Christianity was cast, and attracted to itself whatever it supposed itself capable of assimilating. Platonic notions had already been introduced into Christianity in the writings of Paul and John: the most ancient fathers of the church, when they entered upon philosophy, were obliged to employ the generally received modes of expression, and some of them found their *Logos,* for example, long before the existence of Christianity, in the soul of every philosopher. Probably it would not have been to be regretted, had the system of Christianity remained, what, according to the representations of a Justin martyr, Clement of Alexandria, and others, it was intended to be, a liberal philosophy, reprobating virtue and the love of truth at no time, and among no people, and yet unacquainted with exclusive verbal formularies, which afterwards obtained the force of laws. It is certain, the earlier fathers of the church, who were formed in Alexandria, were not the worst: Origen alone did more than ten thousand bishops and patriarchs; since, but for the learned critical industry, which he employed on the records of Christianity, this would have almost sunk, with regard to its origin, among unclassic fables. His spirit was transmitted to some of his scholars also; and many fathers of the Alexandrian school thought and argued at least with more address and refinement, than many other ignorant and fanatic heads.

It must be confessed, however, that Egypt, with the philosophy then in fashion, was also a school of corruption for Christianity: for every thing, that, during a period of near two thousand years, has excited disputes, quarrels, tumults, persecutions, and the disturbance of whole nations, arose from these foreign Platonic notions, on which men refined with Grecian subtilty, and which gave Christianity in general that *sophistical* form, so discrepant from its nature. From the single word *logos* arose heresies and acts of violence, at which the *logos* within us, found reason, yet shudders. Many of these disputes were capable of being carried on in the Grecian language alone; to which they should have been for ever confined, and never have been introduced as doctrinal formularies into others. They include no truth, no information, that has afforded an addition to human knowledge, new power to the understanding, or a noble motive to the will: the whole body of Christian polemics, carried on against Arians, Photinians, Macedonians, Nestorians, Eutychians, Monophysites, Tritheites, Monothelites, and the rest, might have been instantly crushed, without the least detriment to Christianity, or human reason. Men were obliged to overlook and forget them altogether, with their consequences, those gross decrees of so many councils of courtiers and robbers, before they could again contemplate the original records of Christianity in their primitive purity, and arrive at an open, simple exposition of them: nay, they still obstruct and afflict many timorous minds, or such as are persecuted on account of them. The speculative spirit of these sects resembles the lernean hydra, or the polypus, which cut in pieces forms a new animal from every limb. This useless tissue, injurious to mankind, runs through many ages of history: rivers of blood have been shed upon it; and innumerable multitudes, often of the worthiest men, have been deprived of property and honour, of friends, of home, and of rest, of health and life, by the most ignorant villains. Even honest barbarians, Burgundians, Goths, Lombards, Franks, and Saxons, in pious orthodoxy have taken part in these massacres, with ardent sectarian zeal, for or against Arians, Bogomilians, Catharians, Albigenses, Waldenses, etc.; and, a true church militant, have drawn their swords as warriors, not idly, for the genuine baptismal form. There is not, perhaps, a more barren field within the domains of literature, than the history of this Christian exercise of the word and the sword; which so deprived the human mind of its proper faculty of thinking, the records of Christianity of their evident purpose, and civil society of its fundamental principles and rules; that at last we are reduced, to thank other barbarians and Saracens, for having destroyed by their wild irruptions the disgrace of the human intellect. Thanks to all those men, who have exhibited to us in their true forms the movers of such disputes, an Athanasius, a Cyril, a Theophilus, a Constantine, and an Irenaeus: for as long as the names of the fathers of the church and their councils are quoted with slavish respect, we are masters neither of Scripture, nor of our own understanding.[8]

Christian morality, likewise, found not a more favourable soil in Egypt, or other parts of the Greek empire: there wretched abuse created that vast army of cenobites and monks, who, not satisfied with mental extasies in the deserts of the Thebaid, frequently traversed countries as mercenary soldiers, interfered in elections of bishops, disturbed councils, and compelled their holy spirit to pronounce, whatever the unholy spirit of these miscreants thought proper. I honour Solitude, the meditating sister of Society, and often her legislator, who converts the experience of active life into principles, and its passions into nutritious juices. Compassion is due likewise to that consoling solitude, which, weary of the yoke of other men, and tired of their persecutions, finds a balm in the heaven within. Many of the first Christians unquestionably were solitaries of the latter kind, whom the tyranny of a great military empire, or the abominations of towns, drove into the desert, where, having few wants, a temperate climate gave them a friendly reception. The more, however, let us despise that proud, selfish retirement, which, contemning active life, places merit in contemplation and penance, nourishes itself with phantoms, and, instead of annihilating the passions, cherishes within the wildest of all, selfish, immoderate pride.

Unfortunately, for this Christianity became a dazzling pretext, when such of its precepts, as were intended for a particular few, were converted into general laws, or indeed conditions for obtaining the kingdom of Heaven, and Christ was sought in

[8] After the labours of the reformers, with those of a Calixtus, Dallaeus, Du Pin, Le Clerc, Mosheim, and others, the name of Semler will ever remain highly respected for a liberal view of ecclesiastical history. He has been followed by Spittler, with penetrating eye, and luminous style: others will succeed; and every period of ecclesiastical history will be exhibited in its true light.

the desert. There Heaven was to be found by men, who disdained being citizens of the Earth, and relinquished the most estimable gifts of human-kind, reason, morality, talents, friendship, and parental, nuptial, and filial affection. Accursed be the praise, that men, from misconception of Scripture, have often so abundantly and imprudently bestowed on an idle, contemplative life of celibacy: accursed the false impressions, that have been stamped on youth with enthusiastic eloquence, thus crippling and distorting the human intellect for ages. Whence is it, that we find in the writings of the fathers so little pure morality: and often good and bad, gold and dross, jumbled together? [9] Whence is it, that we cannot mention a single book of those times, even of the most excellent men, who had still so many Greek authors at their command, which, putting style and composition entirely out of the question, but merely in respect to morality and its general spirit, deserves to be placed by the side of a single work of the Socratic school? Whence is it, that even the select maxims of the fathers have so much of extravagance and monkery in them, when compared with the morals of the Greeks? Men's minds were deranged by the new philosophy, which taught them to wander in the aerial regions, instead of living upon Earth: and as there can be no disease of greater magnitude than this, it is a misfortune much to be deplored, that it was propagated by doctrines, authority, and institutions, and rendered the fountains of pure morality turbid for ages.

When at length Christianity was exalted, and the imperial standard gave it that name, with which, as the paramount religion of the Roman empire, it still flies above all other names upon Earth; the impurity at once became evident, which so singularly mixed the affairs of the church and the state, that scarcely anything could be viewed in its proper shape. While preaching toleration, they, who had long suffered, became

[9] Barbeyrac, Le Clerc, Thomasius, Semler, and others, have shown this; Rösler's *Bibliothek der Kirchenväter* (Bibliotheca of the Fathers of the Church) exhibits it in a very popular manner.

themselves intolerant: and as duties toward the state were confounded with the pure relations of man to God, while a semi-Jewish monkish religion was unconsciously made the base of a Christian Byzantine empire; how could it be otherwise, than that the true affinity between crimes and punishments, rights and duties, and indeed between the members of the constitution itself, must have been basely destroyed? The sacerdotal order was introduced into the state; not, as among the Romans, to cooperate immediately with its other members; but as a monastic and mendicant order, for the benefit of which a hundred ordinances were made, burdensome to the rest, inconsistent with themselves, and obliged to be repeatedly altered, in order that the form of a state might remain. To the great yet weak Constantine we are indebted, without his knowing it, for that two headed monster, which, under the name of the spiritual and temporal power, cajoled or tyrannised over itself and others, and after twice ten centuries has scarcely come to a peaceable agreement on the purposes, which religion and government have to fulfil among mankind. To him we are indebted for that pious imperial arbitrariness in the laws, and with it that Christian-princelike unkingly pliability, from which the most fearful despotism could not fail in a short time to arise.[10] Hence the vices and barbarities in the horrible Byzantine history: hence the venal incense offered to the vilest Christian emperors: hence the miserable perplexity, in which spiritual and temporal affairs, heretics and orthodox believers, Romans and barbarians, eunuchs and generals, women and priests, emperors and patriarchs, are embroiled. The empire was thrown from its centre: the foundering, dismasted ship lost its steersman; whoever could seize the helm managed it, till another drove him away. Ye ancient Romans, Sextus, Cato, Cicero, Brutus,

[10] *The History of Changes in the Government, Laws, and Minds of Men, during the Period from the Conversion of Constantine to the Downfall of the Western Empire,* by an anonymous French writer, is executed with great industry and acuteness. A German translation appeared at Leipsic in 1794.

Titus, Antonine, what would ye have said of this new Rome, the imperial court at Constantinople, from its commencement to its downfall?

The eloquence, too, which this imperial Christian Rome was capable of producing, could nowise be compared with that of the ancient Greeks and Romans. Divine men, indeed, here exercised their elocution; patriarchs, bishops, and priests; but to whom did they address themselves? on what did they discourse? and what fruits could their highest eloquence produce? They had to explain to a stupid, depraved, ungovernable multitude, the kingdom of God, the refined maxims of a moralist, who stood alone in his day, and who certainly had nothing congenial with this mob. Far more attractive for it was it to hear the spiritual orator declaim on the depravity of the court, or the gross luxury of the theatres, public games, amusements, and female dress, or take part in the cabals of heretics, bishops, priests, and monks. Goldentongued Chrysostom, how do I lament, that thy exuberant eloquence fell not on better times! That solitude, the companion of thy better days, was left for a splendid metropolis, which embittered thy life. Thy pastoral zeal had wandered out of its limits: the storms of courtly and priestly cabals overwhelmed thee: expelled, and again restored, thou wast reduced at last, to end thy days in poverty. Such was the fate of many worthy men in this voluptuous court: and, what was worse, their zeal itself was not without faults. As he, who, surrounded by infectious diseases, inhales the contaminated air, if he escape the pestilence, will at least display its effects in his pallid countenance and languid limbs: so here too many dangers and seductions arose on every side, for common prudence to avoid. The greater fame, however, is due to the small number of those, who, in the character of generals and emperors, or bishops, patriarchs, and courtiers, shine like scattered stars in this obscure sulphureous sky: but even their forms are hidden from us by the clouds.

Lastly, if we contemplate the taste in arts, science, and manners, that spread from this first and greatest Christian empire, we can call it nothing else than wretched, and barbarously pompous. After that Jupiter and Christ contended in the senate, in the time of Theodosius, before the face of the goddess of Victory, for the possession of the Roman empire, and Jupiter lost the day; the great monuments of ancient taste, the temples and images of the gods, were ruined gradually or forcibly throughout the World: and the more Christian a country was, the more zealous was it in destroying all remains of the worship of the ancient demons. The origin and object of Christian churches forbad the erection of such edifices as the former temples of idols: accordingly courts of justice, and places for holding assemblies, basilicae, were their models; and though a noble simplicity may be observed in the most ancient of them, of the time of Constantine, as they were in part composed of heathen fragments, and partly constructed amid the greatest monuments of art, yet even this simplicity is Christian. The stolen columns were jumbled together without taste; and the wonder of Christian art in Constantinople, the magnificent church of St. Sophia, was loaded with barbarian ornament. Abundant as were the treasures of antiquity heaped together in this Babel, it was impossible for Grecian art, or Grecian poetry, to flourish in it. We are astonished at the train, which, even in the tenth century, was obliged to attend the emperor, in war and peace, at home and at public worship, as described by a purpleborn slave of it himself; and wonder, that such a kingdom stood so long.[11]

This cannot be charged to the abuse of Christianity; for Byzantium was formed from the beginning for a splendid, dissolute, beggarly state. From it could spring no Rome, which, rising amid oppressions, contests, and dangers, rendered itself the metropolis of the World; the new city was erected at the expense of Rome and the provinces, and immediately burdened with a mob, who lived in idleness and hypocrisy, by right of title or of flattery, on the beneficence and favour of the emperor; in other words, on the marrow of the empire. The new

[11] Constantine Porphyrogenitus, Book II, *De ceremoniis aulae Byzantinae* (Of the ceremonies of the Byzantine court), Leipsic, 1751.

city lay in the lap of pleasure, in a delightful climate, in the centre of three quarters of the Globe. From Asia, Persia, India, and Egypt, she drew all the commodities of that dissolute pomp, which she cherished in herself, and diffused over the northwestern world. Her harbour was filled with ships of all nations; and even in later times, when the Arabs had deprived the Grecian empire of Egypt and Asia, the commerce of the World took the road of the Caspian and Euxine Seas, to supply the wants of ancient voluptuaries. Alexandria, Smyrna, Antioch; the shores of Greece abounding in harbours, with its establishments, cities, and arts; the Mediterranean with its numerous islands; and still more the volatile character of the Greek nation; all contributed, to render the seat of the Christian emperor a receptacle of vices and follies: and what formerly promoted the welfare of Greece, now operated to its detriment.

We will not on this account, however, detract from the smallest benefit, which this empire, so situate, and so constituted, has conferred on the World. It was long a mound, though a weak one, against the barbarians; many of whom lost their rudeness from its neighbourhood, its trade, or in its service, and acquired a taste for the arts, and refinement of manners. The best king of the Goths, Theodoric, was educated in Constantinople: and we may thank the eastern empire, for all the good he did to Italy. From Constantinople more than one barbarian people received the seeds of civilization, letters, and Christianity: thus bishop Ulphilas modified the Greek alphabet for his Goths on the Black Sea, and translated the New Testament into their language: the Russians, Bulgarians, and other Slavish Nations, acquired letters, Christianity, and morals, from Constantinople, in a far milder way, than their western brethren obtained them from the Franks and Saxons. The collection of Roman laws, made by order of Justinian, defective and mangled as it is, remains an immortal record of the genuine ancient Roman spirit, a logic of the active intellect, and a test for every better code. It was a benefit to the whole civilized World, that the

Grecian language and literature were preserved in this empire, however defective the use that was made of them, till western Europe was capable of receiving them from the hands of Byzantine refugees. That the pilgrims and croisaders of the Middle Ages found on their road to the holy sepulchre a Constantinople, whence they returned to their caves, their castles, and their cloisters, with many new ideas of splendour, civilization, and manners, in compensation for much treacherous conduct, at least remotely prepared other times for the west of Europe. The Venetians and Genoese learned their extensive commerce in Alexandria and Constantinople, as they acquired their wealth chiefly from the ruins of this empire, and thence imported much that was useful into Europe. The silk manufacture came to us from Persia through Constantinople: and for how much is the holy see, for how much Europe, as a counterpoise to that see, indebted to the eastern empire!

At length this proud, this wealthy, this magnificent Babylon fell: with all its treasures, and all its splendour, it fell by storm into the hands of its savage conquerors. It had long been unable to protect its provinces: all Greece had been a prey to Alaric so early as the fifth century. East, west, north, and south, the barbarians pressed on it, from time to time, closer and closer; and bands of still greater barbarians often raged in the city. Temples were stormed; statues and libraries were given to the flames: the empire was every where sold and betrayed, as it had no better rewards for its most faithful servants, than to put out their eyes, cut off their noses and ears, or indeed bury them alive; for barbarity and voluptuousness, flattery and the most insolent arrogance, revolt and perfidy, reigned on this throne, all decorated with Christian orthodoxy. Its history, filled with lingering death, is a terrible monitory example for every government of eunuchs, priests, and women, in spite of all its imperial pride and wealth, in spite of all its pomp in arts and science. There lie its ruins: the most ingenious people upon Earth, the Greeks, are become the most despicable, perfidious, ignorant, superstitious, wretched slaves of priests and monks, scarcely again susceptible of the ancient Grecian spirit. Thus ended the first and most magnificent *state-Christianity:* may never such appear again! [12]

CHAPTER 4

Progress of Christianity in the Latin Provinces

ROME was the metropolis of the World: from Rome issued the command, to tolerate, or to suppress the Christians: of necessity, therefore, it must very early have been one of the principal endeavours of the general body of Christians, to influence this centre of grandeur and of power.

The tolerance of the Romans towards all the religions of the people they conquered is beyond dispute: but for this, and the general state of the Roman government at that period, Christianity would not have spread so quickly, and so widely. It arose in a remote quarter, among a people despised, and become proverbial for superstition: wicked, foolish, and weak emperors sat on the Roman throne, so that the control of one allseeing eye was wanting to the state. The Christians were long comprehended under the name of Jews, of whom there was a great number at Rome, as well as in all the Roman provinces. Probably, therefore, it was the hatred of the Jews themselves, that first made the rejected Christians known to the Romans; who, considering them as seceders from the religion of their forefathers, were led to think them either atheists, or, from their secret assemblies, Egyptians, debasing themselves, like other mystagogues, by superstition and barbarity. They were looked upon as a reprobate mob, on whom Nero first laid the

[12] With heartfelt pleasure we can here cite the third classical British historian, the rival of Hume, and of Robertson, whom sometimes perhaps he excels, Gibbon; whose *History of the Decline and Fall of the Roman Empire* is a finished masterpiece; though it seems to want, probably from the fault of the subject, that powerful charm of interest, with which Hume's historical works hurry us along. The cry that has been raised in England, however, against this learned and truly philosophical work, as if the author were an enemy to the Christian religion, seems to me unjust: for Gibbon has spoken of Christianity, as of other matters in his history, with great mildness.

blame of his incendiary madness: the compassion, that was felt for them on account of this extreme injustice, seems to have been nothing more than the pity bestowed on a slave tortured without cause. No farther notice was taken of their doctrines; and they were permitted to propagate them, as all others might be propagated in the Roman empire.

As the principles of their faith and worship came more to light, it was particularly displeasing to the Romans, who were accustomed only to a political religion, that these wretches should insult the gods of the state as demons of Hell, and dare to call the worship paid to the protectors of the empire a school of the Devil. They were displeased, too, that the Christians refused to the images of the emperor that veneration, which they should have thought an honour to themselves to pay, and at the same time restrained from all the duties and worship of the country. In consequence they were deemed its enemies, and deserving of the hatred and abhorrence of other men. According to the dispositions of the emperors, and as they were softened or irritated by fresh reports, injunctions were issued for or against the Christians: and these injunctions were executed more or less strictly in each province, suitably to the sentiments of the governor, or their own conduct. Such persecutions, however, as were carried on in later times, for instance, against the Saxons, Albigenses, Vaudois, Huguenots, Prussians, and Livonians, they never experienced: religious wars of such a kind were not consistent with the Roman way of thinking. Thus the first three centuries of Christianity, during the persecutions enumerated in them, were the triumphal times of the martyrs of the Christian faith.

Nothing can be more noble, than for a man, remaining true to the sentiments he has embraced from conviction, to hold them fast with innocence of manners and integrity of conduct to his last breath. Accordingly the Christians, where as intelligent and good men they displayed such innocence and firmness, gained thereby more followers, than by tales of miraculous gifts and miraculous events. Many of their persecutors were astonished at their courage, even when they could not comprehend, why they should expose themselves to the danger of persecution. Besides, a man attains only what he heartily wills: and what a number of men stedfastly maintain in life and death, cannot easily be suppressed. Their zeal inflames: their example warms, even if it do not enlighten. Thus the church is unquestionably indebted to the stedfastness of its adherents, for that deep foundation of an edifice, capable of enduring with vast enlargement for thousands of years: feeble manners and yielding principles would have suffered the whole soon to evaporate, as an uncovered liquid is dissipated in the air.

In particular cases, however, much depends on that, for which a man struggles and dies. If it be for an internal conviction, for a pledge of faith and truth, the reward of which extends beyond the grave; if it be for a testimony of an event of indispensable importance, which a man himself has seen, and the belief of which, confided to him, would otherwise perish; the martyr dies like a hero, his conscience strengthens him in pain and torment, and Heaven opens before his eyes. Thus every eyewitness of the first events of Christianity could die, when he found it necessary for him, to seal their truth with his blood. To deny them, would have been to contradict facts, which he himself had seen; and every man of probity would rather sacrifice his life, in a case of necessity, than do this. But such witnesses, and such martyrs, the commencement only of Christianity could have had; of these there could not be many; and of their exit out of the World, as well as of their lives, we know little or nothing.

The case was different with the witnesses, who bore testimony centuries later, or hundreds of miles distant, to whom the history of Christianity came only as a report, as tradition, or as a written account. These could not be admitted as authentic witnesses, since it was the testimony of others, or rather their faith in it, which they sealed with their blood. Now as this was the case with all the Christian converts out of Judea; we cannot avoid wondering, that so very much was built, even in the remotest, the Latin provinces, on the testimony of the blood of these witnesses, consequently on a tradition, which they received from far, and could not easily prove. Even after the writings composed in the east had reached these remote regions at the end of the first century, many did not understand them in the original, and were of course obliged to be satisfied with the testimony of their teacher, and the citing of a translation. And how seldom did the western teachers in general refer to the Scripture, while the orientals, even in their councils, determined more from the collective opinions of preceding fathers of the church, than from the Scriptures themselves! Thus tradition and faith, for which men died, were soon the most eminent and victorious argument of Christianity: the more ignorant, poor, and distant, the community was, the more must such a tradition, as delivered by their teacher and bishop, and the testimony of martyrs, as witnesses of the church, be received as it were on their word.

And yet, if we consider the origin of Christianity, it could not easily be propagated otherwise; for, being founded on a fact, like all other facts it demanded narration, tradition, faith. The fact goes from mouth to mouth, till recorded by writing it becomes a confirmed, fixed tradition, subject to general examination, and comparison with other traditions. The ocular witnesses are dead, happy therefore if the tradition tell us, that they sealed their testimony with their blood; human faith demands no more.

And thus the first Christian altars were confidently erected upon graves. In cemeteries the Christians assembled: in the catacombs themselves were placed the altars, on which they celebrated the Lord's Supper, rehearsed their creed, and vowed to be as faithful to it, as those who were gone before them. The first churches were either built over sepulchres, or the bodies of martyrs were brought and placed under their altars, till at length a single bone was forced to suffice for its consecration. By degrees, what once arose from the circumstances of the case, what had been the origin and seal of a society of Christian converts, degenerated into mere form and ceremony. Baptism also, on occasion of which a confession of faith was made, was celebrated over the graves of believers; till at length baptisteries were erected over them, or believers, as a sign that they died in the faith, into which they had been baptised, were interred under baptisteries. One arose from the other, and almost the whole form of ecclesiastical ceremonies in the west sprung from this *profession of faith and sepulchral worship.*[13]

At any rate there was something very affecting in this covenant of truth and obedience entered into at the grave. When, as Pliny says, the Christians assembled before day, to sing hymns to their Christ as to a god, and to bind themselves with the sacrament, as with an oath, to purity of manners, and the exercise of moral duties; the still graves of their brethren must have been to them an impressive symbol of constancy unto death, and a confirmation of their belief in that resurrection, which their lord and teacher, a martyr also, had first attained. To them this terrestrial life must have appeared transitory; death, as an imitation of his, honourable and pleasant; a future life, almost more certain than the present: and such persuasions form the spirit of the most ancient Christian writings. Still such institutions must inevitably have excited an intemperate love of martyrdom; and men, weary of this transient earthly life, contended for the baptism of blood and fire, as the Christian crown of glory, with useless zeal. It was equally inevitable, that in time almost divine honours should be paid to the bones of the dead, and that they should be superstitiously abused to produce ecstasies, heal the sick, and work other miracles. Least of all was it to be avoided, that this army of Christian heroes should in a short time take possession of the whole Heaven of the church; and as their bodies were brought into the nave of the church with adoration, their souls should dispossess all the other benefactors of mankind of their seats: so that a *new Christian mythology* commenced: the mythology, that we behold over altars; the mythology, of which we read in legends.

2. As in Christianity every thing rested on profession, this

---

[13] See the works of Ciampini, Aringhii, Bingham, and others, on this subject. A history of these things, taken from a view of the most ancient churches and monuments themselves, and connected throughout with ecclesiastical history, would exhibit the whole in the clearest light.

profession on a creed, and this creed on tradition; either miraculous gifts, or a strict *ecclesiastical discipline,* were necessary to maintain order and government. With this institution arose the authority of the bishops; and to preserve unity of faith, in other words, a connexion between many communities, councils and synods were requisite. If these were not unanimous, or found opposition in other countries, appeals were made to the most respected bishops, as *arbitrators;* whence it could not ultimately fail, that one *chief aristocrat* should gradually arise out of this apostolical aristocracy. Who must become this chief? The bishop of Jerusalem was too remote, and too poor: his diocese was too much straitened by other apostolical bishops: he sat on his Golgotha, in a manner out of the circle of the sovereignty of the World. The bishops of Antioch, Alexandria, Rome, and lastly of Constantinople also, stepped forward; and owing to the posture of affairs, the bishop of Rome carried it from them all, even from his most eager rival at Constantinople. The Byzantine patriarch was too near the throne of the emperor, who could exalt or depress him at will, so that he could become nothing more than the state prelate of the court. On the other hand, after the emperor had left Rome, and seated himself on the frontier of Europe, a thousand circumstances combined, to give the primacy of the church to this ancient metropolis of the World. Nations had been accustomed for ages, to venerate the name of Rome; and in Rome it was imagined, that the spirit of universal dominion hovered over its seven hills. Here, according to the chronicles of the church, many martyrs had born their testimony, and the greatest of the apostles, Peter and Paul, received their crowns. At an early period, too, was propagated the tale of Peter's episcopal rule over this ancient apostolical church; and the uninterrupted attestation of his successors was quickly demonstrated. Now as the keys of the kingdom of Heaven were delivered expressly to this apostle, and the indestructible edifice of the church was founded on the rock of his profession; how natural was it, that Rome should take the place of Antioch or Jerusalem, and prepare to be considered as the mother church of sovereign

Christendom! The bishop of Rome early enjoyed honour and precedence, even in councils, before others more learned and powerful: in disputes he was employed as a friendly arbitrator; and what had long been a post of free choice in a council became in time a claim of right; his instructive voice was considered as decisive. The situation of Rome in the centre of the Roman World conferred on its bishops a wide field, west, south, and northwards, for counsels and regulations; particularly as the imperial Greek throne was too remote, and soon became too feeble, to control them with much effect. The fine provinces of the Roman empire, Italy with its islands, Africa, Spain, Gaul, and part of Germany, into which Christianity had been early introduced, lay round it as a garden requiring aid and advice: farther to the north were barbarians, whose rude countries were soon to be converted into fertile lands of Christendom. Here being no powerful competition, much more was to be done, and to be gained, than in the eastern provinces, thickly set with bishops, which were soon ravaged and exhausted by speculations, oppositions, and contests, by the dissolute tyranny of the emperors, and by the irruption of the Mohammedan Arabs, and other nations still more savage. The barbarian frankness of the Europeans was much more favourable to it, than the insincerity of the polished Greeks, or the fanaticism of the Asiatics. Christianity, there in a state of ebullition, and occasionally appearing as a febrile delirium of the understanding, was cooled by its regulations and prescriptions in the more temperate climate of the west; without which it would probably have sunk into that state of debility, which we observe in the east succeeding the mad stretch of its powers.

The bishop of Rome unquestionably did much for Christendom: mindful of the Roman name, he not only conquered a World by conversion, but established in it, by means of laws, manners, and customs, a more durable, powerful, and intimate sway, than that of ancient Rome. The Romish see never contended for the palm of learning: this it relinquished to others, to the Alexandrian, the Milanese, the Hipponian even, or any other that coveted it: but to subject the most learned sees, and to rule the World, not by philosophy, but by policy, tradition, ecclesiastical law, and ceremonies, were its aims: and could not fail to be so, as itself rested solely on ceremonies and tradition. Thus from Rome proceeded the numerous rites of the western church, relating to the celebration of festivals, the classing of priests, the institution of sacraments, prayers, and oblations for the dead; altars, chalices, tapers, fasts, praying to the mother of God, the celibacy of priests and monks, the invocation of saints, the worshiping of images; processions, masses for the soul, bells, canonization, transubstantiation, the adoration of the host, etc.; rites, that arose partly from ancient circumstances, in which the enthusiastic conceptions of the orientals had often great share, partly from accommodation to local usages of the west, and chiefly of Rome, incorporated by degrees in the great ecclesiastical ritual.[14] Such weapons now conquered the World: they were the master-keys of Heaven and Earth. Before them bowed nations, that would not have shrunk from the sword: Roman ceremonies had more weight with them, than the speculations of the East. These ecclesiastical laws, it must be confessed, exhibit a fearful contrast to the ancient Roman policy: still they ultimately served, to convert the massy sceptre into a less weighty pastoral staff, and the barbarous custom of heathen nations by degrees into a milder Christian law. The chief shepherd at Rome, after having laboriously attained the supremacy, must have interfered more in the affairs of the west, even against his will, than any of his colleagues in the east or west could do; and if the propagation of Christianity be in itself a merit, this is his in an eminent degree. England and the greater part of Germany, the northern kingdoms, Poland, and Hungary, became Christian through the means of his measures, and his nuncios: nay, that Europe probably was not for ever to be disturbed by Huns, Saracens, Tatars, Turks, and Mungals, is partly also his work. If all the Christian races of emperors,

---

[14] I doubt whether a true history of these rites and institutions, carrying conviction on the face of it, can be written without an accurate knowledge of Rome, with its local circumstances, and the character of the people. What in Rome is evident to the view, is often looked for under the Earth.

kings, princes, counts, and knights, should vaunt the merits, by which they formerly acquired sovereignty over nations, the triple-crowned great lama at Rome, born on the shoulders of unarmed priests, may bless them all with his sacred crosier, and say, "but for me you would never have become what you are." The preservation of antiquity, likewise, is his work; and Rome deserves to be the peaceful temple of its preserved treasures.

3. *Thus the church formed itself with as much locality in the west, as in the east.* Here, also, was a Latin Egypt, the Christian part of Africa, where, as in the other, many African doctrines arose. The strong expressions used by Tertullian respecting satisfaction, by Cyprian respecting the penance of sinners, by Austin respecting grace and freewill, insinuated themselves into the system of the church: and though the bishop of Rome commonly pursued the middle track, he sometimes wanted learning, at others authority, to steer the vessel of the church on the wide ocean of doctrines. The learned and pious Pelagius, for instance, was much too severely treated by Austin and Jerome: Austin contended against the Manicheans only with a more refined species of Manicheism; and what in this extraordinary man frequently proceeded alone from the fire of his imagination, and the heat of dispute, passed into the system of the church in too violent a flame. Yet peace be to thine ashes, thou great contender for what thou calledst the unity of the faith. Thy laborious task is ended; and probably its effect extended too far, and too powerfully, through the succeeding ages of Christianity.

Still I must not pass over the first order introduced into the west, that of the Benedictines. Every attempt to naturalize in the west the monastic life of the east, happily for Europe, was opposed by the climate, till this moderate order established itself, under the favour of Rome, on Mount Cassino. It adopted better clothing and diet, than the hot and abstemious east required: its rule, originally formed by a layman for the laity, also enjoined labour; and thus it was of particular utility in various wild and barren districts of Europe. How many fine lands in all countries have been possessed by Benedictines, who had partly reduced them into a state of cultivation! In every department of literature, too, they did all, that monastic industry could accomplish: individuals have written whole libraries; and congregations have made it their business, to cultivate and enlighten the deserts of the literary World, by editing and illustrating numberless works, particularly of the Middle Ages. But for the order of St. Benedict, probably the greater part of the writings of antiquity would have been lost to us; and when we come to sainted abbots, bishops, cardinals, and popes, the number of them taken from this order, and their labours, are sufficient of themselves to compose a library. Gregory the Great, alone, a Benedictine, did more than ten spiritual or temporal sovereigns: and to this order we are indebted also for the preservation of the ancient church-music, which has had so much effect on men's minds.

Farther we shall not proceed. Before we speak of the effect produced on the barbarians by Christianity, we must take a view of the barbarians themselves, how they entered in great bodies, one after another, into the Roman empire, founded kingdoms, mostly confirmed by Rome itself, and whatever may be farther deduced from this for the history of man.

VII

The Medieval World

BOOK XIX

NEVER was a nominal allusion attended with consequences more important, than that made to St. Peter, that an indestructible church should be built on the rock of his faith, and that to him the keys of the kingdom of Heaven should be entrusted. The bishop, who was supposed to sit in St. Peter's chair, and near his grave, had the art, to interpret this as alluding to himself: and as various circumstances concurred, to render him the primate of the greatest Christian church, and at the same time to confer on him the power of issuing spiritual ordinances and injunctions, calling councils and deciding upon them, establishing and defining articles of faith, absolving irremissible sins, and imparting indulgences, that no other could bestow; so that, in short, he enjoyed the authority of God upon Earth; he soon passed from this spiritual monarchy, to its natural consequence, temporal. As he had formerly limited the power of bishops, he now restrained that of monarchs. He conferred a western imperial diadem, the authority of which he himself did not acknowledge. His dreaded hand, wielding anathemas and interdictions, erected and gave away kingdoms, chastised and pardoned kings, deprived countries of the exercise of religious worship, absolved subjects and vassals from their duties, deprived the whole body of his clergy of wives and children, and founded a system, which a series of ages have shaken indeed, but not yet destroyed. Such a phenomenon demands attention: and as no regent in the world had such obstacles to surmount for the establishment of his power, as the bishop of Rome, it deserves at least to be examined without rancour and animosity, as well as any other political constitution.[1]

CHAPTER 1
Romish Hierarchy

When a man designs to erect an edifice, he usually makes a sketch of the structure, before he lays its foundations: but this is seldom the case with the work of the political architect, which is left to time to complete. It may be doubted, whether the most unremitting attention could ever have been sufficient, to raise the spiritual greatness of Rome. The bishops, that wore the Roman mitre, differed as much as any other potentates; and there were unpropitious times for the ablest operators. But it was the policy of this see, to turn to account even these unpropitious periods, and the faults both of its enemies, and of its preceding occupiers: and by this policy it attained its grandeur and stability. Out of numerous circumstances of history, let us consider a few, with the principles on which the greatness of Rome was erected.

The very name of Rome itself says a great deal: the ancient queen of the World, the head and the crown of nations, inspired her bishops with the desire of being also the head of nations after their manner. No tales of the episcopacy and martyrdom of Peter would have had such political effects at Antioch, or Jerusalem, as in the flourishing church of ancient, immortal Rome: for how much did the bishop of this revered city find, that could not fail to exalt him almost against his will! The ineradicable pride of the Roman people, to which so many emperors were obliged to yield, lifted him on their shoulders; and inspired him, the pastor of the first people upon Earth, with the thought of studying science and politics, in this their

[1] Though particular parts of the papal history have been handled with considerable ability since Sarpi, Puffendorf, etc.; yet I think a philosophical history of the papacy, treated throughout with perfect impartiality, is still wanting. The author of the *Reformationsgeschichte* (History of the Reformation), after he has completed his design, might thus give his work a singular degree of perfection.

high school, to which even in Christian times men journeyed for instruction in the Roman jurisprudence; that, like the ancient Romans he might rule the World by his laws and ordinances. The pomp of pagan worship glared in his eyes; and as this was connected with the sovereign power in the Roman constitution, the people expected in its Christian bishop, likewise, the ancient *pontifex maximus, aruspex, et augur.* Accustomed to triumphs, festivals, and ceremonials of state, they gladly saw Christianity emerging from graves and catacombs into temples worthy of the Roman greatness; and thus Rome became a second time the head of nations, by means of its festivals, rites, and institutions.

Rome early displayed its legislative policy, by inculcating the *unity of the church, purity of doctrine, orthodoxy, and catholicism,* on which it was necessary the church should be built. Even so early as the second century, Victor had the boldness to refuse acknowledging the Christians of Asia as his brethren, because they would not celebrate Easter at the same time with him: nay the first division between Jewish and heathen Christians was probably terminated by Rome, where Paul and Peter lay peaceably interred.[2] This spirit of an universal doctrine maintained itself in the Romanish see: and though some of the popes themselves are scarcely free from the imputation of heresy, their successors always contrived to take a turn, and reenter the pale of the orthodox church. Rome never bowed to heresy, though often threatened by it: the eastern emperors, the Ostrogoths and Visigoths, the Burgundians and the Lombards, were Arians: some of these governed Rome; yet Rome remained Catholic. At length it separated itself without ceremony from the Greek church, though this was almost half a world. This foundation of an immoveable purity and universality of doctrine, professing to rest on Scripture and tradition, must necessarily acquire and support the superstructure, under favourable circumstances, of the throne of a spiritual judge.

Such favourable circumstances occurred. After the emperors

[2] Of this elsewhere.

had left Italy; when the empire was divided, and overrun by barbarians; and Rome had been repeatedly taken and plundered; its bishop had more than once opportunities of being its deliverer. He was the father of the abandoned metropolis; and the barbarians, who venerated the majesty of Rome, respected its chief priest. Attilla retired; Genseric submitted; enraged Lombard kings fell at his feet, even before he was lord of Rome. Long did he hold the balance between Greeks and Barbarians: he had the art to divide, that he might afterwards govern. And when this policy of division would no longer succeed, he had already prepared his Catholic France to assist him: he crossed the mountains, and obtained from his deliverer more than he had asked, his episcopal city, with all the cities of the exarchate. At length Charlemagne became emperor of Rome; and now the word was, one Rome, one emperor, one pope! three inseparable names, thenceforward to work the weal and woe of nations. Unheard of liberties were taken by the Roman bishop even with the son of his benefactor; and his later successors expected still more. He interfered between the emperors, issued his commands to them, deposed them, and tore from their brows the crown, which he conceived he had given to them. The openhearted Germans, who for three hundred and fifty years visited Rome for the sake of this jewel, and readily sacrificed to it the blood of the nation, were they who raised the arrogance of the pope to its most tremendous height. Without a German emperor, and the wretched constitution of his empire, a Hildebrand would never have arisen: and even now the constitution of Germany renders it the pillow of the Roman tiara.

As heathen Rome was happily situate for its conquests, so was Christian Rome. From the North Sea and the Baltic, from the Euxine and the Wolga, came numerous nations, whom the bishop of Rome must finally sign with his orthodox cross, if they would live in peace in this orthodox region: and those, who came not of their own accord, he took care to seek. He sent prayers and incense to the nations; in return for which they dedicated gold and silver to his use, and endowed his numerous servants with woods and fields. But their most valuable present was their raw, unprejudiced hearts; which sinned the more, as they acquired the knowledge of sin; and received from him catalogues of offences, that his absolutions might become requisite. Thus the keys of St. Peter came into employ; but never did they turn without a fee. What a fine inheritance for the clergy were the lands of the Goths, Allemans, Franks, Angles, Saxons, Danes, Swedes, Slavians, Poles, Prussians, and Hungarians! The later these people entered into the kingdom of Heaven, the dearer were they obliged to pay for admission; and not unfrequently their land and liberty were the price. The farther they lay to the north, or to the east; the more tardy was their conversion, and the more ample their gratitude. The greater the difficulty with which a nation was led to the faith, the more firmly did it learn to believe. At length the fold of the Romish bishop extended to Greenland, and stretched from the Dwina and the Nieper to the extreme promontory of the west.

Winifred, or Boniface, the converter of the Germans, raised the authority of the pope over bishops situate out of his diocese to a much higher pitch, than any emperor could have done. As a bishop in a land of infidels he had taken an oath of fealty to the pope, which persuasion or assumption afterwards extended to other bishops, till at length it became a law in all Catholic kingdoms. The frequent division of countries under the Carlovingian race likewise changed the limits of episcopal dioceses, and afforded the pope abundant opportunities of exercising his authority in them. Lastly, the collection of decretals of the Pseudo-Isidorus, which first appeared publicly in these times of the Carlovingians, probably in the interval between the Frank and Germanic empires, being permitted to pass as valid, from inattention, artifice, and ignorance, at once established all the growing abuses of recent times on the basis of ancient authority. This single book was of more service to the pope than ten imperial diplomas: and indeed ignorance and superstition in general, with which the whole western world was deluged, formed the deep and extensive sea, into which the net of St. Peter was cast with ample success.

The political abilities of the Roman bishops were most eminently displayed, in the art with which they turned the most unpromising circumstances to their advantage. Long were they oppressed by the emperors of the east, and often by those of the west: and yet Constantinople was first obliged to allow them the rank of universal bishops, and Germany at last to cede to them the investiture of the spiritual order of the empire. The Greek church separated itself: and by this, too, the pope profited; for in it he could never have obtained that authority, for which he strove in the west, and which he was thus enabled, to render the more compact. Mohammed appeared: the Arabs subdued a great part of the south of Europe: they even cruised in the neighbourhood of Rome, and attempted to land. These calamities, likewise, were of inestimable value to the pope; who well knew how to avail himself of the feebleness of the Greek emperors, and the danger which threatened Europe; taking the field as the deliverer of Italy, and thenceforward assuming to himself the standard of Christendom against all infidels. A fearful species of war, which he had the power to enforce by bans and interdictions, and in which he was not merely the herald, but often both treasurer and commander in chief. He likewise turned to account the successes of the Normans against the Arabs; investing them with lands, to which he had no right, and by means of them securing his rear, that he might be at full liberty, to carry on his operations in front. So true it is, that he advances farthest, who knows not in the beginning how far he shall advance, but avails himself with steady principle of every circumstance, that time throws in his way.

Let us impartially exhibit some of these principles, pursued by the court of Rome to its no small advantage.

1. *The sovereignty of Rome rested on faith:* on a faith, that was to promote the good of men's souls, both in time and in eternity. To this system pertained every thing, that could lead the human mind; and every thing conducive to this end Rome got into her own hands. From his mother's womb to the grave, nay beyond it in the flames of Purgatory, a man was in the power of the church, from which he could not withdraw him-

self, without being irremediably miserable. The church moulded his head: the church disturbed and calmed his heart. Confession placed in her hands the keys of his secrets, of his conscience, of every thing that he carried in or about him. All his lifetime the believer remained a pupil under her discipline: and in the article of death she bound him with sevenfold bonds, the more liberally to loose the penitent and the liberal. This was equally the case with the king and the beggar, the soldier and the monk, the husband and the wife: master neither of his reason, nor of his conscience, every one was doomed to be led, and guides he could not want. Now as man is an indolent animal, and, when once accustomed to have his mind under spiritual direction, cannot easily dispense with it, but rather commends this soft yoke to his posterity, as the pillow of a sick soul; the dominion of the church was hereby interwoven most intimately into the believer's frame. With his reason and conscience she had every thing in her power: it was a trifle, that, sowing her spiritual seed, she reaped his temporal harvest; she was surely the heir of him, whom resignation had stamped her sole property during life.

2. *To guide this faith, the church employed not the greatest, the most important means, but the least, and most comprehensible;* well knowing how little satisfies men's devotion. A crucifix, a picture of Mary and her child, a mass, a rosary, promoted her object more than many refined reasonings would have done: and even these implements she managed with the most frugal diligence. Where a mass was sufficient, it was not necessary to eat the Lord's Supper: when a low mass would answer the purpose, high mass was not required: if a man ate the transubstantiated bread, he might dispense with the transubstantiated wine. This economy afforded the church opportunity for innumerable indulgences, and unexpensive presents: for even the most frugal economist may be defied, to make more of a little water, bread, or wine, a string of glass or wooden beads, a lock of wool, a little ointment, or a cross, than was made by the church of Rome. It was the same with rituals, prayers, and ceremonies. They were never invented and established in vain:

old ceremonies remain, though new are adapted to more modern times: pious posterity must and will be saved after the manner of their fathers. Still less has the church retracted any of the faults committed by her: when too glaring, indeed, they have been artfully glossed over; otherwise every thing has remained as it was, and, when opportunity offered, not corrected, but enlarged. Before Heaven was peopled with saints in this prudent way, the church was filled with wealth and miracles: and even with regard to the miracles of their saints the inventive powers of the narrators have been at little expense. Every thing was repeated, and built on the grand principles of the popular, the comprehensible, and the familiar: for the frequent and bold repetition of what is least credible challenges belief, and at length obtains it.

3. With this principle of the smallest means the Romish policy contrived so to combine the *most refined* and the *most gross,* that it would be difficult to exceed it in either. No one could be more humble, cajoling, and suppliant, than the popes, in time of need, or towards those who were liberal, and prompt to serve them; at one time it is a tender father, at another St. Peter, that speaks through their mouth: but no one could write or act with more openness and vigour, with more coarseness and severity, when it was requisite. They never disputed, but decreed: an artful boldness, which pursues its own course, in spite of tears, or prayers, or demands, or threats, or defiance, or punishment, distinguishes the language of the Romish bulls, almost without a parallel. Hence the peculiar tone of the laws, mandates, and decretals of the church, in the Middle Ages, singularly different from the dignity of the ancient Roman legislation: the servant of Christ is accustomed to speak to laics, or those under his immediate control, always certain of his object, never retracting his words. This holy despotism, glossed with paternal authority, has done more than the empty courtesy of frivolous state policy, in which no one confides. It knew its object, and how obedience was to be ensured.

4. *The Romish policy attached itself to no particular object of civil society in preference: it existed for itself;* it employed

every thing, that was of use to it; it could annihilate every thing, that was an obstacle to it: for it depended solely on itself. An ecclesiastical state, which lived at the expense of all Christian states, could not fail to be of service now to science, now to morality and order, to agriculture, arts, or commerce, when it suited its purpose: but that papacy was never truly inclined to promote the diffusion of genuine knowledge, the advancement to an improved form of government, and whatever is connected with it, is apparent from all the history of the Middle Ages. The best germe might be crushed, if it were at all dangerous: and the more learned papist must conceal or accommodate his knowledge, the moment it interfered with the eternal interest of the see of Rome. On the other hand, whatever promoted this interest, arts, taxes, municipal mutinies, or donations of lands, were cherished and managed for the greater glory of God. In every movement the church was the fixed centre of the universe.

5. *The Romish political supremacy might employ whatever was conducive to this object:* war and devastation, fire and sword, death and imprisonment, forged writings, perjury on the holy sacrament, inquisitorial tribunals and interdictions, poverty and disgrace, temporal and eternal misery. To stir up a country against its prince, it might be deprived of all the means of salvation, except at the hour of death: the keys of Peter exercised an authority over the laws of God and man, over the rights of individuals and of nations.

6. *And as all the gates of Hell were not to prevail against this edifice;* as this system of canonical institutions, the power of the keys to bind and to loosen, the magic power of holy signs, the gift of the spirit, transmitted from Peter to his successors, and those whom they consecrated, preached nothing but eternity; who can imagine a more deeply rooted empire? The clerical order were its own, body and soul: with shaven heads, and irrevocable vows, they were its servants to eternity. The bond that connected the priest to the church was indissoluble: he was deprived of child, of wife, of father, and of heir: cut off from the fruitful tree of the human species, he was engrafted

into the barren evergreen of the church; and his honour was thenceforward its honour, his profit its profit: no change of mind, no repentance, for him, till his slavery was terminated by death. In recompense the church opened to these its vassals an ample field of reward, a lofty ladder, leading them, though servants, to wealth and extensive command, to dominion over all the free and great ones of the Earth. It held out honours to tempt the ambitious, devotion to stimulate the devout, and for every one his proper bait and reward. This legislation, too, has this peculiarity; that, as long as a fragment of it remains, the whole exists; and, with each individual maxim, all must be followed: for it is the rock of Peter, from which the fisherman casts his indestructible net; it is the garment without seam, that can be the lot only of *one,* though soldiers play for it.

7. And who was this *one,* at the head of the sacred college at Rome? Never a whimpering child, to whom men had taken the oath of fealty perhaps in his very cradle, and thereby vowed submission to all his future freaks; never a playful boy, with whom men fought to creep into favour by indulging him in all his youthful follies, that they might afterwards become the spoiled children of his caprice: a man of ripe years, or silvered with age, was elected, already for the most part practised in the affairs of the church, and acquainted with the field, to which he was to appoint labourers; or one closely allied with the princes of his time, and chosen at a critical period, precisely for the difficulty, which he had to surmount. He had but few years to live, and no posterity for whom he could legitimately make provision: and if he did this, it was but as a drop in the great ocean of the Catholic pontificate. The interest of the see of Rome was progressive: the experienced old man was only set up, that he also might put his name to what had been done. Many popes sunk under the burden: others, versed in law and politics, bold, and steady, performed more in a few years, than a weak government could have accomplished in half a century. Were only the most eminently great and worthy popes to be enumerated, they would present a long catalogue of names, many of which must excite our regret, that they who bore them

could not be employed to some other purpose. Fewer effeminate debauchees by far have worn the Roman tiara than secular crowns; and of many of these the faults are striking only because they were the faults of popes.

CHAPTER 2
Effect of the Hierarchy on Europe

First of all it is proper to consider the benefits, that Christianity, even in this garb, must from its nature confer. Compassionate toward the poor and oppressed, it took them under its protection from the wild devastation of the barbarians: many bishops in Gaul, Spain, Germany, and Italy, have proved this as saints. Their habitations and the temples were asylums for the oppressed: they redeemed slaves, liberated prisoners, and repressed the horrible traffic in human beings, carried on by the barbarians, wherever it was in their power. This merit of clemency and generosity to the oppressed part of the human species cannot be refused to the principles of Christianity: from its infancy it laboured for the deliverance of man, as is evinced even by many impolitic laws of the eastern emperors. But this benefit was still more indispensable in the western church; and many decrees of the bishops in Spain, Gaul, and Germany, inculcate it, even without the assistance of the pope.

It is also incontestable, that, in times of general insecurity, temples and convents were the sanctuaries, in which peaceful industry and trade, agriculture, arts, and manufactures, found refuge. Ecclesiastics established annual fairs, still bearing in honour of them the name of masses, and protected them with the peace of God, when no royal or imperial proclamation could give them security.[3] Artists and mechanics retreated within the walls of the convent, as a safeguard against the nobles, who would have held them in a state of vassalage. Monks pursued neglected husbandry, both with their own

[3] The term *messe* is equally applied, in Germany, to the religious office named a mass, and to the great meeting of traders, called a fair; the most important of which are held about Easter and Michaelmas, when a great deal of business is transacted.

hands, and by means of others: they prepared whatever was necessary for their convents, or at least afforded a place for a monastic application to the arts, and bestowed on them a frugal reward. The remains of ancient authors were saved from destruction in convents; and, being occasionally transcribed, were thus transmitted to posterity. Lastly, by means of divine service a slight clew was preserved, such as it was, in the Latin language, which afterwards led men back to the literature of the ancients, and thus to improvement in knowledge. For such times were convents adapted, which afforded even the pilgrim security and protection, food, lodging, and conveniences. Journeys of this kind first brought nations peaceably together; for the pilgrim's staff was a defence, where the sword would have been of little avail: and through their means was acquired a knowledge of foreign countries; while at the same time tales, narratives, romances, and poetry, were cherished by them though in their rudest infancy.

All this is undeniably true: but as much of it might have taken place without the bishop of Rome, let us inquire what advantages his spiritual sovereignty may properly be said to have brought to Europe?

1. *The conversion of many heathen nations.* But in what manner were they converted? Frequently by fire and sword, by secret tribunals, and wars of extirpation. Let it not be said, that the bishop of Rome ordered none of these: he approved them, enjoyed their fruits, and copied them, when it was in his power. Hence that tribunal of the inquisition, at which psalms were chaunted; hence those croisading missions, the plunder of which was shared by popes and princes, knights, prelates, canons, and priests. They who escaped destruction were reduced to the state of vassalage, in which they for the most part still continue. Thus was Christian Europe rounded: thus were kingdoms erected, and their crowns conferred by popes: and thus was the cross of Christ afterwards carried as the signal of death into every quarter of the Globe. America yet smokes with the blood of her slain; and the enslaved nations of Europe still curse their converters. And you, innumerable victims of the

inquisition, in the south of France, in Spain, and in other quarters of the World! your bones are mouldered into dust, and your ashes are dispersed by the winds: but the story of the barbarities exercised towards you remains, an eternal appellant in behalf of human nature outraged in you.

2. To the hierarchy is ascribed the merit *of having united all the nations of Europe in one Christian republic.* But in what did this consist? That all nations should kneel before one cross, and hear one mass, was something, but not much. That they should all be governed by Rome in spiritual affairs, was not of any inestimable advantage to them: for they groaned under the weight of the tribute they sent thither, and an innumerable army of monks and ecclesiastics, nuncios and legates. Peace between the European powers then there was less than now; owing, among other things, to the system of false policy, which the pope himself cherished in Europe. Christianity stopped the piratical depredations of heathenism: but powerful Christian nations rubbed hard against each other; and all were full of disorder within, animated by a spiritual and temporal thirst of plunder. This double sovereignty, too, a papal state within every state, prevented each kingdom from recurring to its principles; to which men have turned their attention only since they have been free from the supremacy of the pope. Europe, therefore, has shown itself as a Christian republic only toward the infidels; and this not often to its honour: for the croisades can scarcely be deemed deserving of fame, even by the epic poet.

3. It has been reckoned to the honour of the hierarchy, that it served to *balance the despotism of the princes and nobles, and exalt the lower classes of men.* True as this is, as to the matter of fact, it must be admitted with great limitations. The original constitution of the Germanic nations was properly so repugnant to all despotism, that, if this disease of the mind were to be learned, it would be much less difficult to maintain, that the bishops taught it to the kings. For instance, the oriental or monastic notion of blind submission to the will of the ruler was first introduced into the jurisprudence and education of the

people by the bishops, who derived it from abuse of Scripture, from Rome, and from their own order: they converted the office of the sovereign into an idle dignity, and infused into him presumption with the oil of divine right. Those who were employed by kings, to establish their despotic power, were almost always ecclesiastics: if these were but well fed with presents and privileges, they little scrupled the sacrifice of others. Then, too, were not the secular princes in general preceded, or at least zealously emulated by the bishops, in extending their powers and privileges? and did not these sanctify the unjust booty? The pope, lastly, as lord paramount of kings, and despot of despots, decided by right divine. In the time of the Carlovingian, Frank, and Suabian emperors, he indulged himself in pretensions, on which a laic could not have ventured without universal disapprobation; and the single life of the emperor Frederic II, of the house of Suabia, from his minority under the guardianship of a pope, of all others most learned in the law, to his own and the death of his grandson Conradin, may serve as a summary of what may be said of the supremacy of the pope over the princes of Europe. The blood of this house can never be washed out from the apostolical chair. What a tremendous height, to be the sovereign lord over all the kings and countries of Christendom! Of this Gregory VII, certainly no ordinary man, Innocent III, and Boniface VIII, are glaring examples.

4. *The great institutions of the hierarchy in all Catholic countries* are palpable; and probably the sciences would long ago have been reduced to beggary, had they not received a support, though scanty, in the crumbs that fell from these ancient holy tables. Let us not, however, mistake the spirit of the times. Agriculture was not the principal object of any Benedictine monk, but cloistered devotion. He ceased to work, as soon as he could dispense with labour: and how considerable was the portion of the sums he gained that went to Rome, or were consumed for purposes, on which they ought not to have been employed! The useful Benedictines were followed by a series of other orders, advantages to the hierarchy indeed,

but then extremely burdensome to arts and science, to the state and to mankind; the mendicants in particular. All these, with the nuns of every description, the brothers and sisters of mercy perhaps alone excepted, were suited only to those harsh, unenlightened, barbarian times. Who would now found a convent according to the rules of Benedict, to promote the cultivation of the ground? or a cathedral, that an annual fair might be held under its protection? Who would expect from a monk instructions in the theory of commerce; from the bishop of Rome, the best system of political economy; or from the teacher in ordinary of a chapter, the most perfect form of education? Still every thing, that promoted science, morality, order, and gentleness of manners, though but collaterally, was of inestimable value.

In this class, however, the forced vows of chastity, idleness, and monastic poverty, are to be reckoned at no time, and in no religious sect. They were indispensable to the supremacy of the papal chair; which found it necessary to break every tie, by which the servants of the church were connected with society, that they might live for it alone: but to mankind they were never adapted, never beneficial. Let any one lead a life of celibacy, beg, sing psalms, count beads, and scourge himself, who can and will: but to whom can it appear a subject of praise, or of approbation, that confraternities of this sort should be favoured with privileges, benefices, and an eternal salary, under the protection of the public, nay under the seal of sanctity and supererogatory merit, at the expense of active, useful industry, a virtuous domestic life, nay the desires and propensities of our very nature itself? The amorous sighs of pining nuns, the furtive gratifications of monks, the secret and crying sins of ecclesiastics, their infringements of the matrimonial tie, the accumulation of property in mortmain, the pampered ambition of the isolated body of the clergy, and every irregularity, that must necessarily grow out of it, gave Gregory the VIIth no concern; but their consequences stand conspicuous in the page of history.

5. The *pilgrimages* of holy idlers, too, deserve no great com-

mendation. Where they were not immediately subservient to commerce and the arts in a clandestine manner, they contributed but very imperfectly and casually to the knowledge of men and countries. Certainly it was very commodious, under the sacred garb of a pilgrim to find every where security, in beneficent convents food and repose, on every road travelling companions, and at last, in the shade of a temple, or sacred grove, the desired comfort and absolution. But if the pleasing revery be reduced to the standard of truth, we shall frequently detect, beneath the holy palmer's weeds, some malefactor, desirous of atoning for flagrant crimes by an easy pilgrimage, or some insane devotee, who has forsaken house and home, perhaps bestowed all he had on some convent, renounced the first duties of his condition, or of man, to remain for the rest of his life a rotten limb of society, a halfmad, arrogant, or dissolute fool. The life of a pilgrim had seldom any claim to sanctity; and the maintenance, which they still derive from certain states at the chief places of their resort, is an actual robbery of the country. The single circumstances, that this pious rage of performing pilgrimages to Jerusalem produced among other things the croisades, gave birth to many ecclesiastical orders, and miserably depopulated Europe, alone bear sufficient testimony against them; and if missionaries made them their stalking-horse, they had certainly no good purpose in view.

6. Lastly, much may be urged against *the colloquial Latin of the monks,* the *band* by which all Roman Catholic countries were unquestionably united. This not only contributed, to keep the vernacular languages of the nations that inhabited Europe, and with them the people themselves, in an uncultivated state; but it was particularly instrumental in depriving the people of their last share in public affairs, because they were ignorant of Latin. The public business of the nation lost a great part of the national character, with the vernacular tongue; while with the monkish Latin crept in that pious monkish spirit, which could flatter, ensnare, or even falsify, as it saw occasion. The writing of all the public acts of the nations of Europe in general, their laws, decrees, testaments, commercial instruments, titledeeds,

and likewise history, for so many centuries, in Latin, could not be otherwise than advantageous to the clergy, as the body of the learned, and prejudicial to the nation. The cultivation of its mother tongue alone can lift a nation out of a state of barbarism: and this very reason kept Europe so long barbarous; a foreign language fettering for near ten centuries the natural organs of its inhabitants, robbing them even of the remains of their monuments, and rendering a native code of laws, a native constitution, and a national history, utterly unattainable by them for so long a period. The Russian history alone is founded on documents in the language of the country; and this is owing to the state having remained unconnected with the hierarchy of the pope of Rome, whose legates Wladimir would not receive. In all other countries of Europe the monkish language has stifled every thing susceptible of being stifled by it, and is to be commended only as a language of necessity, or the slender plank, on which the literature of antiquity saved itself for better times.

These restrictions of the praise of the Middle Ages I have written with reluctance. I am fully sensible of the value, that many institutions of the hierarchy possess even with respect to us; and of the necessity of the times, in which they were formed; and I delight to wander amid the awful gloom of their venerable piles. As a coarse medium of conveyance to us, capable of withstanding the storms of barbarism, it is estimable, and evinces both the ability and circumspection of those, who committed treasures to its charge; but it would be absurd to ascribe to it an absolute and permanent value for all ages. When the seed is ripe, the integument bursts.

CHAPTER 3

Temporal Protectors of the Church

The kings of Germanic tribes and nations were originally generals appointed by election, the superintendents, the chief judges of the people. As soon as they came to be anointed by bishops, they were kings by divine right, the protectors of the church of their country. When the pope inaugurated the Roman emperor, he appointed himself his coadjutor: he the Sun, the emperor the Moon, the other kings the stars, of the Catholic Church. This system, planned in darkness, was first brought out in the twilight, but soon glared into broad day. Already the son of Charlemagne laid down his sceptre at the command of the bishops, and would not again take it up, without their fresh injunction: under his successors the compact was frequently repeated, that the kings should consider their spiritual and temporal orders as coadjutors in the affairs of the church and of the state. Lastly, the Pseudo-Isidorus made the principle universal, that the power of the keys authorised the pope, to lay princes and kings under his ban, and declare them incapable of ruling their states. Over the Roman imperial crown in particular the pope arrogated to himself many rights, and they were not disputed. Henry of Saxony styled himself only king of Germany, till he was inaugurated emperor by the pope. Otto, and his successors down to Frederic II, received from the pope the imperial sceptre, and imagined they thus acquired precedency, or indeed a sort of sovereignty, over all the kings of Christendom. They, who often found it difficult to govern their German dominions, were offended when any thing, of which they did not confer the investiture, was taken from the Grecian empire: they made war upon the heathen, and placed bishops in those lands. When the pope created a Christian king in Hungary, the first Christian prince in Poland was a vassal of the German empire, and many wars afterward arose on account of this feudal dependency. The emperor Henry II received from the pope the golden imperial ball, as an emblem, that the World belonged to him: and Frederic II was laid under the pope's ban, because he declined the croisade he was enjoined to undertake. A council deposed him: the pope declared the imperial throne vacant; and so low was it degraded, that no foreign prince would accept it. Thus the Christian Sun had proved a bad assistant to his Moon; as the protection of Christendom had at length reduced the German emperor to a state of inability to protect himself. He was to travel about, hold diets and tribunals, and confer fiefs, sceptres, and crowns, according to the directions of the pope; who, from his seat on the Tiber, governed the World by his legates, bulls, and interdictions. There is not a Catholic kingdom in Europe, which has not considered its king as a protector of the church, under the sovereign guidance of the pope: nay for a certain period this was the public law of Europe.[4]

All the internal regulations of kingdoms could not avoid being conformable to this notion: for the church was not in the state, but the state in the church.

1. As the spiritual and temporal orders every where composed the states of the kingdom, the most important political, military, and feudal customs were stamped as it were with the seal of the church. The kings held their grand court-days on the ecclesiastical festivals: the ceremony of crowning them was performed in churches: their coronation oath was taken on the gospels, and on relics: their dress, their crown, and their sword, were consecrated. They themselves were considered, in consequence of their office, as servants of the church; and enjoyed the privileges of the clerical order. All the festivities of the state were more or less connected with masses and religion. The first sword given to the bachelor knight was consecrated upon the altar; and when knighthood in time arrived at the solemnities of an order, one third of these consisted in religious ceremonies. Piety took its place in the order with love and honour: for it was the professed object of all the orders of chivalry, to draw the sword in defence of Christendom, as well as of injured innocence and virtue. Christ and the apostles, the mother of God, and other saints, had long been the patrons of Christendom, of all conditions and offices, of particular companies of mechanics, churches, abbeys, castles, and families: their images soon became the banners of armies, standards, seals: their

[4] Leibnitz has touched upon this notion in many of his writings, and occasionally admitted it in his historical system. Puetter's *Geschichte der Entwicklung der Deutschen Staatsverfassung* (History of the development of the German constitution), gives a fine clew to it, which, in former times, led every statist, after his manner, to the prerogatives or pretensions of the German empire.

names, the watchword, and the shout of onset. Men took up their swords at the reading of the Gospel; and went to battle with a *kyrie eleeson.*[5] Practices of this kind so prepared the way for war against heretics, heathens, and infidels, that a loud cry, well timed, and accompanied with spiritual ensigns and promises, was sufficient to set all Europe on the Saracens, Albigenses, Slavians, Prussians, and Poles. Nay the knight and the monk could coalesce in the singular shape of a spiritual order of chivalry: and in particular cases bishops, abbots, and even popes themselves, exchanged the crosier for the sword.

The above mentioned foundation of the kingdom of Hungary by the hand of the pope affords us a brief example of these manners. The emperor and the empire had long considered, how the savage and often defeated Hungarians might be reduced to a state of tranquillity. Their conversion to Christianity was the sole mean, by which it could be effected: and this being accomplished after considerable labour, a king educated in the Christian religion, St. Stephen, pursuing himself the work of conversion, an apostolical crown, probably an Avarian robbery, was sent him; he received, too, the holy lance, or Hungarian battleaxe, and St. Stephen's sword, to protect and extend the church toward all quarters of the Globe; and, at the same time, the imperial ball, the episcopal glove, and the crosier. He was appointed the pope's legate; and delayed not, to found a canonry at Rome, a convent at Constantinople, and hospitals, hostelries, and religious houses, at Ravenna and Jerusalem; to turn the road of the pilgrims through his country; to invite priests, bishops, and monks, from Greece, Bohemia, Bavaria, Saxony, Austria, and Venice: to erect the archbishopric of Gran, with a number of bishoprics, and convents; and to make of the bishops, who were not exempt from the duties of the field, one of the estates of his kingdom. He promulgated a code, the spiritual part of which was borrowed from capitularies of the west, particularly those of the Franks, and ecclesiasti-

[5] "The Lord have mercy upon us": the form of solemn invocation in the Romish liturgy.

cal decrees of Mentz; and left it to his successors, as the fundamental law of the new Christian kingdom. This was the spirit of the times: the whole constitution of Hungary, the relations and condition of its inhabitants, were built upon it: and it was the same in Poland, in Naples and Sicily, in Denmark, and in Sweden, with some trifling variations, according to the circumstances of time and place. All floated on the ocean of the church; the episcopal power formed the starboard side of the vessel; the feudal system, the larboard; the king, or the emperor, served as a sail; and the pope stood at the helm.

2. In all kingdoms the *administration of justice* was arch-Catholic. The customs and statutes of the people must bend before the decrees of the pope and ecclesiastical councils: nay, before the Roman jurisprudence prevailed, the canon law was introduced. It cannot be denied, that many rude asperities of the people were thus rubbed off: for even when Religion stooped to consecrate the trial by combat, or exchange it for the ordeal, she laid these under some restraint, and at least reduced superstition within less pernicious limits.[6] Abbots and bishops were the arbitrators of peace and ministers of divine justice upon Earth: ecclesiastics, for the most part, were the clerks of courts of justice, the makers of laws, ordinances, and capitularies, and often ambassadors on the most important occasions. The judicial authority, which they enjoyed among the heathen of the north, was retained among the Christians; till, at a late period, they were thrust out of their seats by the doctors of law. Monks and confessors were often the oracles of princes; and in the vile affair of the croisades, St. Bernard was the oracle of Europe.

3. The little *physic* of the Middle Ages, except what was practised by the Arabs and Jews, was in the hands of the clergy; whence, as among the northern pagans, it was a tissue

---

[6] No one, to my knowledge, has shown the good effects of the ecclesiastical domination in tranquillizing the then turbulent World, and promoting the cultivation of the land, in a more instructive and philosophical manner, than John Mueller, in his *Schweizergeschichte* (History of Switzerland). This side is not to be overlooked, though it is but one side.

of superstition. The devil and the cross, relics and set forms of words, acted the most conspicuous parts in it; for the true knowledge of nature, a few traditions excepted, had vanished from Europe. Hence so many diseases, that with infectious rage traversed whole countries, under the appellations of the leprosy, the plague, the black death, St. Vitus's dance: no one resisted their progress, for no one was acquainted with them, or knew their proper remedies. Uncleanliness in dress, the want of linen, confined habitations, and even the imagination clouded by superstition, could not fail to promote them. It would have been a truly guardian office, if all Europe had combined, under the direction of the emperor, the pope, and the church, against the influx of such pests, as real works of the devil, and left neither small-pox, plague, nor leprosy, in their land: but they were permitted to enter, rage, and destroy, till the poison exhausted itself. To the church, however, we are indebted for the few institutions formed to counteract them: that was done as a work of compassion, which men yet wanted skill to perform as a work of art.[7]

4. The *sciences* were not so properly in the state, as in the church. What the church thought fit was written and taught: all issued from the schools of monks: accordingly the monkish manner of thinking prevailed in the few literary productions, that then appeared. Even history was written for the church, not for the state, for very few except monks read; and hence the best authors of the Middle Ages smack of the cloister. Legends and romances, to which the invention was then confined, paced round in a narrow circle: for few writings of the ancients had any circulation, so that few ideas had an opportunity of being compared, and the images Christianity then afforded were soon exhausted. Besides, this allowed no poetical mythology: a few

[7] The histories of the small-pox, plague, leprosy, etc., are known from the writings of many skilful physicians; who have likewise proposed means for eradicating these evils, and in some degree accomplished their purpose. Good accounts of the art of physic, and the medical establishments, of the Middle Ages, with remarks, may be found in Möhsen's *Geschichte der Wissenschaften in der Mark Brandenburg* (History of Sciences in the Marche of Brandenburg).

circumstances from the ancient history, or fables, of Rome and Troy, interspersed with the occurrences of more recent times, formed all the rude scenes of the poetry of the Middle Ages. And as soon as these began to be diffused in the language of the country, spiritual subjects were brought forward, with a singular intermixture of heroic fables, and tales of chivalry. On the whole, neither popes nor emperors gave themselves any concern about literature, considered as a mean of diffusing knowledge; the science of jurisprudence alone excepted, which was indispensable, to support the pretensions of both.[8] A pope like Gerbert, who loved the sciences as a man of learning, was a phenix indeed: the ship of the church was ballasted with the sciences of the convent.

5. In like manner, of the *arts* those only were cherished, without which neither churches, nor castles, nor towers, could exist. Gothic architecture, as it is called, so thoroughly accorded with the spirit of the times, the religion and way of life, the wants and climate, of its contemporaries; that it fashioned itself as individually and seasonably, as monkery or knighthood, or as the hierarchy and feudal system. Among the inferior arts such maintained and improved themselves, as were employed in adorning the arms of the knight, and in the decorations and ceremonies of the church, the castle, or the convent: their productions were sculpture and mosaic, painted windows and illuminated books, representations of saints, tapestry, shrines for relics, pixes, chalices, and goblets. From these, not excluding church music, or the huntsman's horn, the revival of the arts in Europe commenced: how different from what was once in Greece![9]

6. The *trade and commerce* of Europe, too, received their broad and deeply indented outline from the all-grasping eccle-

[8] The particular exceptions to this melancholy truth will be noticed in the following book. Here the subject is merely the spirit of the times.

[9] A history of the arts in the Middle Ages, particularly of Gothic architecture as it is called, in their different periods, would be a work well deserving perusal: a selection of such essays as deserve general notice, from the works of the British Antiquary Society, would serve as a preliminary to it.

siastical and feudal systems. The noblest tutelary offices of emperors and kings were unquestionably their delivering towns from plundering violence, and artists and tradesmen from the yoke of vassalage; their protecting and promoting the free exercise of industry and commerce, by justice, exemption from imposts, peaceable fairs, and secure roads; their endeavouring to annihilate the barbarian right of wreck, and to exonerate the useful inhabitants of the town and country from other oppressive burdens: to all which the church very honourably contributed.[10] The bold idea of Frederic II, however, to abolish all guilds and confraternities in his towns, went far beyond his age, like many others of his active mind. Corporate bodies were still necessary, in which, as in the systems of chivalry and monachism, all should be answerable for each, and, even in the most trifling occupations, the learner should rise by degrees; as the monk or the soldier rose in his order. In both, every higher step was accompanied with similar festivities; and the spirit of guilds and associations was extended even to commerce. Its greatest combination, the hanse itself, arose from fraternities of merchants, who first travelled about like pilgrims: danger and necessity by sea and land extended the union higher and farther, till at length, under the protection of European Christendom, such a widespread *commercial republic* arose, as the World had otherwise never seen. Afterwards the universities were similar guilds: Gothic institutions, such as neither Greeks, Romans, nor Asiatics, ever knew; but, as institutions of monachism and chivalry, indispensable to the times, and beneficial to future ages by the preservation of the sciences. In the Middle Ages, too, a particular *municipal law* arose; very different from that of the Romans, but erected on the basis of liberty and security, according to German principles, and productive of

[10] Fisher's *History of the Trade of Germany* has already been quoted as a collection of important inquiries: from it, and other publications of modern days, might be collected materials for a general history of trade and navigation, very different from that which was published at Breslaw in 1754, or from what was in Anderson's power to give in his valuable *History of Commerce*. A history of the arts, manufactures, guilds, towns, and municipal laws, of the Middle Ages, is likewise a desirable work.

industry, arts, and subsistence, on every favourable soil. It bears marks of its origin amid the pressure of princes, nobles, and ecclesiastics; yet operated powerfully on the civilization of Europe. In short whatever could arise under the compressed arch of the hierarchy, feudal system, and tutelary superintendence, has arisen: the firm edifice of Gothic architecture seems to want but one thing, light. Let us see in what singular ways it acquired this.

CHAPTER 4
Kingdoms of the Arabs

THE Arabian peninsula is one of the most distinguished regions of the Earth, apparently intended by Nature herself, to stamp a peculiar character on its nation. The great desert between Syria and Egypt, extending from Aleppo to the Euphrates, afforded, like a southern Tatary, ample room for the predatory and pastoral life, and has been possessed by tribes of wandering Arabs from the remotest periods. The mode of life of these people, to whom a town appeared a prison; their pride of an ancient indigenous origin, of their god, their rich and poetic language, their noble horses, their sword and bow, with every thing else which they fancied sacred to themselves; seem to have prepared the Arabs for a part, which in due time they performed in three quarters of the Globe, in a manner very different from the Tatars of the north.

Even in the age of ignorance, as they call their ancient history, they extended themselves beyond their peninsula: in Irak and Syria they had founded small kingdoms; some of their tribes dwelt in Egypt; the Abyssinians were descended from them; the whole of the African desert appeared to be their inheritance. Their peninsula was separated from the great body of Asia by the desert, which protected them against the frequent expeditions of its conquerors: they remained free, and proud of their descent, of the nobility of their families, of their unconquered valour, and their uncontaminated language. With this they were the centre of the southern and eastern trade; and consequently in the way of acquiring the knowledge of all the nations, that carried on this trade, in which, from the happy situation of their country, they could not avoid taking part. Thus at an early period an intellectual culture arose here, which the Altai or Ural could never have produced: the Arabian language formed itself to an ingenuity in figurative eloquence and prudential apophthegms, long before they, by whom it was spoken, knew how to commit them to writing. On their Sinai the Hebrews received their law, and among them they almost always dwelt. When Christians arose, and persecuted each other, Christian sects also repaired to them. Could it be otherwise, then, that from the mixture of Jewish, Christian, and native ideas, among such a people, with such a language, a new flower in due time should appear? and when it appeared, could it fail, from this point between three quarters of the Globe, to obtain the most extensive spread from commerce, wars, foreign expeditions, and books? Thus the odoriferous shrub of Arabian fame, springing from such an arid soil, is a very natural phenomenon, the moment a man arose, who knew how to rear it into blossom.

In the beginning of the seventh century this man did arise; a singular compound of whatever the nation, tribe, time, and country, could produce; merchant, prophet, orator, poet, hero, and legislator; all after the Arabian manner. *Mohammed* was born of the noblest tribe in Arabia, the guardian of the purest dialect, and of the Caaba, the ancient sanctuary of the nation; a boy of considerable beauty, not rich, but educated in the family of a man of consequence.[11] Already in his youth he had enjoyed the honour of replacing the sacred black stone in its former situation, in the name of the whole people: circumstances brought him early acquainted, on his commercial journeys, with other nations and religions, and led him to the acquisition of considerable property. The praises bestowed on him as an

---

[11] Not to mention Sale's *Introduction to the Koran,* Gagnier's *Life of Mohammed,* and other writers, who have recurred to Arabian documents, Brequigni, in his *Essay on Mohammed,* which is separately translated into German, has given some excellent observations on his situation and mission.

extraordinary youth, the dignity of his tribe and family, and his early employment in the affair of the Caaba, no doubt operated powerfully on his mind; the impression he had received of the state of Christianity united with these; before him stood Mount Sinai decorated with a hundred tales from ancient history; the belief in divine inspirations and missions was common to all these religions, natural to the national way of thinking, and flattering to his own character: all these probably acted so deeply on his mind, in the fifteen years during which he led a life of contemplation, that he believed *himself*, the koreish, *himself* the distinguished man, chosen to restore the doctrines and duties of the religion of his fathers, and to reveal himself as a servant of God. Not the dream of his celestial journey alone, but his life, and the Koran itself, evince the fervour of his imagination, and that no artfully concerted deception was necessary to the persuasion of his prophetic call. Mohammed came forward on the stage, not in the ebullition of youthful blood, but in the fortieth year of his age; first as the prophet of his house, who revealed himself only to few, and gained scarcely six followers in three years: and when, at the celebrated feast of Ali, he had announced his mission to forty persons of his tribe, he thenceforward exposed himself freely to every thing a prophet has to expect from the opposition of the incredulous. His followers justly compute their time from the year of his flight to *Yatreb* (Medina): in Mecca his undertaking would have miscarried, if his life had not been lost.

Thus, if detestation of the barbarous idolatry, which he saw practiced by his tribe, and imagined he perceived in Christianity; with an ardent zeal for the doctrine of the unity of God, and a mode of serving him by purity, devotion, and beneficence; appear to have been the grounds of his prophetic mission: corrupted traditions of Christians and Jews, the poetical way of thinking of his nation, the dialect of his tribe, and his personal talents, may be considered as the wings, that bore him above and out of himself. His Koran, that wonderful mixture of poetry, eloquence, ignorance, sagacity, and arrogance, is a mirror of his mind; displaying his talents and defects, his faults and propensities, the self-deception and necessary pretext with which he imposed upon himself and others, much more perspicuously, than any other Koran of any prophet. He delivered it in separate fragments, as they were called for by occasional circumstances, or when his mind was rapt by contemplation, without thinking of a written system: it consisted of the ebullitions of his imagination, or prophetic discourses of censure and exhortation, at which at other times he himself was astonished, as something above his powers, as a divine gift entrusted to his charge. Hence, like all men of strong minds under the influence of self-deception, he required faith, which at length he contrived to extort even from his bitterest enemies. Scarcely was he lord of Arabia, when he sent his apostles to all the neighbouring kingdoms, Persia, Ethiopia, Yemen, nay to the Greek emperor himself; considering his doctrines, local as they were, as the religion of all nations. The stern expressions that fell from him, when his ambassadors returned, and brought him the refusals of the kings; together with the celebrated passage of the Koran, in the chapter of the Declaration of Immunity; [12] afforded his successors sufficient grounds, to pursue the conversion of nations, from which the prophet was prevented by his early death. To this, alas, Christianity taught him the way; Christianity, the first of all religions, that imposed its belief upon foreign nations, as the necessary condition of salvation: the Arab, however, converted not by means of women, monks, and underhand practices, but in a manner suited to an inhabitant of the wilderness, with sword in hand, and the authoritative demand, "belief, or tribute!"

After Mohammed's death, war spread itself over Babylon, Syria, Persia, and Egypt, like the burning wind of the desert. The Arabs went to battle, as to the service of God, armed with texts of the Koran, and the hopes of Paradise. At the same time

---

[12] "Fight against them who believe not in God, nor in the last day, who forbid not that which God, and his apostle, have forbidden, and who profess not the true religion, of those unto whom the Scriptures have been delivered, until they pay tribute by right of subjection, and they be reduced low." Koran [Sale's version, chap. IX].

they wanted not personal virtue: for as the first khalifs of the house of Mohammed were just, temperate, and excellent men, their blind zeal excepted; so their armies were led by valiant and able generals, as Khaled, Amru, Abu-Obeidah, and many others. They found the empires of the Persians and Greeks so badly constituted, the Christian sects so inveterate in their hatred to each other, perfidy, voluptuousness, selfishness, treachery, pride, vanity, cruelty, and oppression, so universally prevalent, that in the dreadful history of these wars we seem to read a fable of a troop of lions breaking into the folds of sheep and goats, into farms abounding with fat oxen, gaudy peacocks, and helpless lambs. These degenerate people were for the most part a contemptible race, deserving to ride upon asses, as incapable of managing the generous steed, and unworthy the cross upon their churches, which they were unable to defend. What pomp of patriarchs, priests, and monks, in these rich and extensive regions, was now laid at once in the dust!

With this was sunk in a moment, as by an earthquake, the remains of that ancient Grecian cultivation and Roman grandeur, which Christianity was incapable of demolishing. The most ancient cities of the World, and with them innumerable treasures, fell into the hands of valiant robbers, who at first scarcely knew the worth of gold. Above all we have to lament the fate, that befell the remains of science. John the Grammarian begged the library of Alexandria (what would the fool have done with the present?), on which the conqueror, Amru, had never once thought. The petition was referred to the khalif Omar, who answered it by that celebrated argument, which deserves for ever to bear the name of the khalif's syllogism;[13] and the books were committed to the flames. Above a thousand warm baths were heated with them constantly for six months; and thus the most precious thoughts, the most indispensable records, the most elaborate systems in the World, with every

[13] "What is contained in the books, of which thou speakest, either agrees with what is written in the book of God, the Koran, or it is contradictory to it. If it agree with it, the Koran is sufficient without it; if it be contradictory to it, it is fit that the books should be destroyed."

thing that depended upon them for ages to come, was at once lost through the foolish request of a grammarian, and the pious simplicity of a khalif. Gladly would the Arabs have recovered this treasure, when a century afterwards they were sensible of its value.

Almost immediately after the death of Mohammed dissensions arose, which, on the decease of Osman, the third khalif, might soon have checked the conquests of the Arabs, if the valiant, honest, long oppressed Ali, and his son Hassan, had not established the house of the Ommiades. In the person of Moawiyah this now seated itself in the high priest's chair, of which it maintained the hereditary possession for ninety years. Damascus was made the seat of the khalifs: the Arabs soon became a maritime power: and, under an hereditary government, splendour assumed the place of the former simplicity of the court. In Syria, Mesopotamia, Asia Minor, and Africa, indeed, the work of conquest still went on: Constantinople was more than once besieged, but in vain: under Al Waled, Turkestan was taken, and an inroad made even into India: Tarik and Musa conquered Spain with extraordinary success; and the latter conceived the vast project of forming, by the addition of France, Germany, Hungary, and all the country even beyond Constantinople, a more extensive empire, than the Romans had accumulated in the course of several centuries. But how completely was this project frustrated! All the incursions of the Arabs into France miscarried: in Spain itself they lost province after province by incessant revolts: Constantinople was not yet ripe for conquest: and, even under some of the Ommiades, Turkish tribes, afterwards destined to become the conquerors of the Arabs themselves, began to try their strength in the field. On the whole, the first overwhelming flood of their military success subsided with the thirty years of their early enthusiasm, when the house of Mohammed sat on the throne: under the hereditary Ommiades, their conquests proceeded, amid various internal dissensions, with slower and often interrupted steps.

The house of the Abassides followed, who removed their residence from Damascus, and whose second khalif, Al-Mansur, built Bagdad, as the seat of government, in the centre of his dominions. The court of the khalifs now attained the summit of its splendour; and it was also visited by the arts and sciences, in regard to which the names of Al-Raschid and Al-Mamoun will ever be celebrated. Under this race, however, less was done toward foreign conquest, than for the conservation of the monarchy itself. Already under Al-Mansur, the second of this family, Abderahman, the supplanted heir of the Ommiades, founded a separate, independent khalifate in Spain, which continued almost three hundred years, and was afterwards divided into ten kingdoms, which were for some time shared among different Arabian families, but never reunited to the khalifate of Bagdad. On the Western coast of African Barbary (Mogreb) the Edrisiates, a branch of the family of Ali, tore off a kingdom, where they laid the foundations of the city of Fez. In the reign of Haroun Al-Raschid, his viceroy at Kairwan (Cyrene) in Africa made himself independent. The son of this viceroy conquered Sicily. His successors, the Aglabites, removed their residence to Tunis, where they constructed the great aqueduct; and their kingdom endured above a hundred years. In Egypt the attempts of the viceroys to render themselves independent were at first attended with doubtful success, till the family of the Fatimites swallowed up those of the Edrisiates and Aglabites, and founded a third khalifate, extending from Fez to Asia, and including Tunis, Sicily, and Egypt.

Thus there were now three khalifates, at Bagdad, Cairo, and Cordova. However, the kingdom of the Fatimites also fell to ruin: Curds and Zeirites divided it between them; and the valiant Saladin (Selah-eddin), the grand visir of the khalifs, supplanted his masters, and founded the kingdom of the Curds in Egypt; which afterward fell into the hands of the life-guards (*mamalukes,* or slaves), who were at length dispossessed of it by the Osmans. Thus affairs went on throughout all the provinces. In Africa, Zeirites, Morabethians, Muahedians, acted their respective parts; in Arabia, Persia, and Syria, dynasties of every nation and family; till at length the Turks (Seljuks, Curds, Arabecks, Turcomans, Mamalukes, etc.) got every thing into their hands, and the Mungals took Bagdad itself by storm. The son of the last khalif of Bagdad fled to Egypt, where the Mamalukes left him his empty title; till, on the conquest of this country by the Osmans, the 18th of these dethroned princes was carried to Constantinople, but soon sent back to Egypt, there miserably to close the list of these Arabian emperor-popes. The splendid empire of the Arabs was lost in the Turkish, Persian, and Mungal; parts of it fell under the dominion of the Christians, or became independent; and most of its nations still continue to live amid perpetual revolutions.

The causes both of the speedy decline of this vast monarchy, and of the revolutions by which it was incessantly perturbed and torn, were inherent in its nature, arising from its origin and constitution.

1. *The Arabian power arose from the virtues of enthusiasm, and could be upheld only by these virtues;* by valour and fidelity to the law, by virtues of the desert. While their khalifs, either in Mecca, Cufa, or Medina, adhered to the rigid mode of life of their first four great predecessors, and possessed the magic means of binding all their generals and viceroys to their commands with this strong bond, what power could injure this nation? But when the possession of so many fine countries introduced, with a widely extended commerce, wealth, pomp, and luxury; and the hereditary throne of the khalifs attained such splendour in Damascus, and still more in Bagdad, that the description of it appears like a fable of the Arabian Nights Entertainments; the drama, that has been acted a thousand times on the stage of the World, was repeated: Voluptuousness introduced Effeminacy, and at length enfeebled Refinement sunk beneath the arm of rude Strength. The first of the Abassides created a grand visir; and under his successors the authority of this officer grew up to the tremendous power of an *emir al omrah* (*emir of emirs*), and was despotic over the khalif himself. As most of these visirs were Turks, and the life-guards of the khalif were composed of the same people; the evil, that was soon to overpower the whole body of the monarchy, was seated in its very vitals. The territories of the Arabs lay along

those elevated regions, on which these warlike people, Curds, Turks, Mungals, Berbers, were on the watch like beasts of prey; and as most of them were held unwillingly under the dominion of the Arabs, they could not fail to avenge themselves, when opportunity offered. Accordingly, what happened to the Roman empire happened here; visirs and mercenaries were converted into sovereigns and despots.

2. *That the revolution took place more speedily with the Arabs, than with the Romans, must be ascribed to the constitution of their monarchy.* This was khalific; that is despotic in the highest degree, the characters of emperor and pope being most intimately combined in that of khalif. The belief of inevitable destiny, and the word of the prophet, which enjoins obedience in the Koran, promoted submission to the word of his successors, and of their viceroys; and thus this spiritual despotism pervaded the government of the whole empire. But how easy was the transition from the exercise of despotic power in another's name to that of arbitrary authority in a man's own, particularly in the remote provinces of this extensive empire! Add to this, the viceroys were almost every where absolute lords, the chief art of government of the khalifs consisting in distributing, recalling, or changing them, with skill. Thus, for example, when Mamoun allowed his valiant general Taher too much power in Chorasan, he gave the reins of independence into his hand; the countries beyond the Gihon were detached from the khalifate; and a way into the heart of the kingdom was opened to the Turks. Thus it went on throughout all the viceroyalties, till the great empire resembled an archipelago of detached islands, scarcely connected by religion and language, and in a state of the highest disturbance within and without. This empire of varying islands went on for seven or eight hundred years with frequent change of boundary, till most, though not all of them, fell under the power of the Osmans. The empire of the Arabs had no constitution: a circumstance equally unfortunate to the despot, and to his slaves. The constitution of Mohammedan kingdoms consists in submission to the will of God, and of his vicegerent; *Islamism.*

3. *The government of the Arabian empire was attached to one tribe, and properly only to one family of this tribe, the house of Mohammed:* and as almost from the beginning the rightful heir, Ali, was set aside, kept out of the khalifate for a considerable time, and quickly expelled from it with his family, the great schism between the Ommiades and Alites arose; which even now continues with all the animosity of religious rancour between the Turks and Persians, after the lapse of more than a thousand years. In remote countries impostors arose, who forced themselves upon the people as relations of Mohammed, either with sword in hand, or an appearance of sanctity: nay, Mohammed having founded the empire in the character of a prophet, fanatics occasionally ventured, to speak like him in the name of the Lord. Instances of this occurred even in the prophet's lifetime: but Egypt and Africa were the peculiar theatres of such fanatics and impostors.[14]

The religion of Mohammed might appear to have exhausted the abominations of fanaticism and blind credulity, if, alas! they had not reappeared in other religions also: the despotism of the *old man of the mountain,* however, has no where been exceeded. This monarch of a distinct state of murderers, practised, nay born to the trade, may say to any one of his subjects: "Go, and kill": he will do it, though to the sacrifice of his own life. And this kingdom of assassins has continued for centuries.

CHAPTER 5

Effects of the Arabian Kingdoms

QUICK as the spread and division of the khalifate were, it attained with equal celerity the period of its bloom, for which, on a more frigid soil, ten centuries would scarcely have sufficed. The genial power of nature, which accelerates the blossoming of the eastern plant, displays itself equally in the history of these people.

1. *The vast empire of Arabian commerce* had an effect upon

[14] Schloetzer's *Geschichte von Nordafrica* (History of the North of Africa), Cardonne's *Geschichte der Araber in Afrika und Spanien* (History of the Arabs in Africa and Spain), etc.

the World, which, proceeding from the local situation and national character of the people, out-lived their possessions, and still in part survives. The tribe of Koreish, from which Mohammed sprung, and indeed the prophet himself, were leaders of travelling caravans; and Mecca the holy had long been the central point of an extensive commerce between various nations. The gulf between Arabia and Persia, the Euphrates, and the ports of the Red Sea, were the famed repositories, or roads of conveyance, of the produce of India, in all ages: whence many Indian wares bore the epithet of Arabian, and Arabia itself was called by the name of India. Tribes of these active Arabs had early possession of the eastern shores of Africa, and were instruments of the commerce of India even in the times of the Romans. Accordingly, when all the country between the Nile and the Euphrates, and from the Hindus, Ganges, and Oxus, to the Atlantic Ocean, Pyrenees, and Niger, belonged to these people, whose colonies extended even to the land of Caffraria, they were enabled, to become for a time the greatest commercial nation on the face of the Globe. Hence Constantinople suffered, and Alexandria shrunk to a village; while Omar was enabled to build at the confluence of the Tigris and Euphrates the city of Balsora, which received and distributed all the merchandise of the east. Under the Ommiades Damascus became the seat of government; an ancient great emporium, a natural centre of the caravans in its paradisiacal situation, the zenith of wealth and industry. In Africa the city of Kairwan was built so early as the time of Moawiyah, and afterwards Cairo, through which the trade of the World was carried on across the isthmus of Suez.[15] In the interiour parts of Africa the Arabs had monopolized the gold and gum trade, discovered the gold mines of Sofala, and founded the cities of Tombut, Telmasen, and Darah: on its eastern shores they had planted considerable colonies and commercial towns; and had even extended their settlements to Madagascar. When

[15] See Sprengel's *Geschichte der Entdeckung,* in every section of which much is said in few words, and the *Geschichte des Handels* (History of Commerce) already quoted.

India was conquered under Waled, as far as Turkestan and the Ganges, the western World was connected with the extremities of the east. To China they had early traded, partly in caravans, partly over the sea to Kantu (Canton). From this empire they imported brandy, afterward so inordinately increased by the art of chymistry, which they first cultivated; while, fortunately for Europe, it was some centuries later before it spread over this quarter of the World, with the pernicious use of tea, and of coffee, an Arabian drink. They also brought from China into Europe the knowledge of porcelain, and probably of gunpowder likewise. They were masters of the coast of Malabar; visited the Maldivia islands; formed settlements in Malacca; and taught the Malays to write. More recently they planted colonies and their religion in the Moluccas; so that, before the arrival of the Portuguese in these seas, the East India trade was entirely in their hands, and pursued by them to the east and the south, without any European rival. Even the great discoveries of the Portuguese by sea, which changed the whole face of Europe, were led on by war with the Arabs, and the Christian zeal of subduing them in Africa.

2. The *religion and language* of the Arabs produced another important effect on many nations of three quarters of the Globe. For while every where, throughout their extensive conquests, they preached Islamism or tributary submission, the religion of Mohammed extended eastward to the Gihon and the Hindus; westward, to Fez and Morocco; northward, beyond Caucasus and Imaus; southward, to Senegal, Caffraria, the two peninsulas of India, and the neighbouring archipelago; and acquired a greater number of followers than Christianity itself. Now with regard to the doctrines taught by this religion, it cannot be denied, that it has raised the heathen converted to them above the gross idolatrous worship of the powers of nature, the stars of Heaven, and inhabitants of the Earth; and has rendered them zealous adorers of one God, the creator, ruler, and judge of the World, with daily devotion, with deeds of charity, with cleanliness of person, and with resignation to his will. By the prohibition of wine, it has fought to prevent

drunkenness and quarrelling; and by enjoining abstinence from unclean meats, it has endeavoured to promote temperance, and preserve health. In like manner it has forbidden usury, avaricious gambling, and many superstitious practices: and it has raised several nations out of a savage or depraved state to a middle degree of civilization, so that the Moslem, or Mussulman, profoundly despises the vulgar herd of Christians in their gross excesses, and particularly in the impurity of their lives. The religion of Mohammed imprints on the minds of men a degree of tranquillity, an uniformity of character, which, though they may be as dangerous as useful, are in themselves valuable, and deserving esteem: but on the other hand, the polygamy it allows, the prohibition of all inquiry concerning the Koran, and the despotism it establishes in spiritual and temporal affairs, cannot easily avoid being attended with pernicious consequences.[16]

Be this religion, however, what it may, it was propagated in a language, the purest dialect of Arabia, the pride and delight of the whole nation. No wonder, therefore, that the other dialects were thrown by it into shade, and the language of the Koran became the victorious banner of Arabian sovereignty. Such a common standard of the oral and written language is advantageous to a widely extended, flourishing nation. Had the German conquerors of Europe possessed a classic book of their language, such as the Koran was to the Arabs, their tongue would never have been so overpowered by the Latin, and so many of their tribes would not have been left in oblivion. But neither Ulphilas, nor Kaedmon, nor Ottfried, could produce, what Mohammed gave to all his followers in the Koran; which is to this day a pledge of their ancient genuine dialect, by which they are led to the most authentic documents of their race, and remain one people throughout the whole Earth. The language of the Arabs is their noblest inheritance; and even now it forms in various dialects such a bond of intercourse and

---

[16] Good remarks on the subject may be found in Michaelis's *Orientalischer Bibliotheck* (Oriental Bibliotheca), Vol. VIII, p. 33 and following.

commerce, between so many nations of the eastern and southern World, as no other language ever equalled. Next to the Greek, perhaps, it is most worthy too of this general sway: at least the *lingua franca* of those countries appears on comparison with it but as a wretched beggar's cloak.

3. In this elegant and copious language *sciences* were cultivated, which, when roused by Al-Mansur, Haroun Al-Raschid, and Mamoun, spread from Bagdad, the seat of the Abassides, north-east, and still more westward, and flourished for a considerable period throughout the extensive Arabian empire. A chain of cities, Balsora, Cufa, Samarcand, Rosetta, Cairo, Tunis, Fez, Morocco, Cordova, etc., were celebrated schools, whence science was imparted to Persia, India, some Tatarian countries, nay China itself; and even down to the Malays formed the means, whereby Asia and Africa acquired some new improvement in civilization. Poetry and philosophy, history and geography, philology, mathematics, chymistry, and physic, were cultivated by the Arabs; in most of which the spirit of nations has felt their influence as inventors or disseminators, thus conferring benefits on those they conquered.

Poetry was their ancient inheritance: the offspring of freedom, not of a khalif's favour. It flourished long before Mohammed; for the spirit of the nation was poetical, and a thousand circumstances served to excite this spirit. Their country, their way of life, their pilgrimages to Mecca, the poetical contests at Okhad, the honour in which a rising poet was held by his tribe; the pride the people felt in their language and legends; their propensity to adventure, love, and glory; and even their love of solitude, thirst of vengeance, and wandering life, were all incentives to poetry, and their muse distinguished herself by splendid imagery, pride and grandeur of sentiment, acute apophthegms, and something extravagant in the praise or censure of the subjects of her song. Her ideas stand like detached rocks piercing the clouds: the fire of the Arab's words appals like the lightning of his scimitar; his wit is sharp as the arrow from his bow. His noble steed is his Pegasus: often uncomely, but intelligent, faithful, and indefatigable. The poetry of the Persian, on the other hand, which, like his language, descended from the Arabic, has moulded itself to the character of the nation and country; more voluptuous, soft, and gay, a daughter of the terrestrial Paradise. And though neither was acquainted with the forms of Grecian art, the epopee, the ode, the pastoral, still less the drama; though both, when they had acquired the knowledge of them, rejected them as models; the peculiar poetic talent of the Arab and Persian appeared the more distinctly formed and beautified on this very account. No nation can boast of so many passionate votaries of poetry as the Arabs, during their golden age: in Asia this passion spread even to the Tatarian princes and nobles; in Spain, to the Christian. The *gaya ciencia* of the Limosin or Provençal poets was in a manner forced upon them, or inspired by their Arabian foes: and thus Europe by degrees acquired, though rudely and slowly, an ear for more refined and animated poetry.

The fabulous part of poetry, the *romance*, flourished more particularly under an orient sky. An old national story, orally transmitted, became in time a romance: and when the imagination of the people, by whom these stories are told, has a fixed propensity to the extravagant, incomprehensible, grand, and wonderful, the common is exalted into the rare, the unknown into the extraordinary; to which the oriental eagerly lends an ear, for the instruction or amusement of his leisure hours, in his tent, on his journies, or in the social circle. Even in the time of Mohammed there came among the Arabs a Persian merchant with amusing tales, which filled him with apprehensions, that they would obscure the fables of his Koran: and indeed the most pleasing fictions of eastern genius appear to be of Persian origin. The gay talkativeness of the Persians, and their love of splendour, gave their ancient tales in time a romantic form, which was considerably heightened by creatures of the imagination, chiefly formed from the animals of the neighbouring mountains. Hence arose that Fairyland, the country of the peries and neries, for which the Arabs had scarcely a name, and which was copiously introduced into the European romances of the Middle Ages. These tales were arranged by the Arabs at a much later period, when the brilliant reign of the khalif Haroun Al-Raschid was made the scene of their adventures; and this form afforded Europe a new model, for concealing delicate truths under the fabulous garb of incredible events, and uttering the most refined maxims of policy under the pretext of diverting idle hours.

From the romance of the Arabs let us turn to its sister, their *philosophy;* which, according to the oriental mode, was properly erected upon the Koran, and acquired a scientific form only from the translation of Aristotle. As the simple idea of one God was the basis of the whole religion of Mohammed, so we can scarcely conceive an hypothesis, which the Arabs would not connect with this idea, or deduce from it, while they carried it into their metaphysical speculations, and made it the subject of their lofty encomiums, sentences, and maxims. They almost exhausted the synthesis of metaphysical fiction and united it with an exalted mysticism of morality. Sects arose among them, which, in their disputes, already exercised a refined criticism of abstract reason;[17] and indeed scarcely left the schoolmen of the Middle Ages any thing more to do, than to adapt their notions to the doctrines of European Christians. The Jews were the first scholars of this metaphysical theology: afterwards, it came to the newly erected Christian universities, where Aristotle appeared first wholly in the Arabian mode, not in the Grecian, and greatly polished and whetted the speculations, polemics, and language of the schools. Thus the illiterate Mohammed shares with the most learned of the Grecian philosophers the honour of having given the whole metaphysical science of modern times its direction: and as most of the Arabian philosophers were poets also, so among the Christians in the Middle Ages mysticism was constantly united with scholastic lore, in such a manner, that their boundaries were undistinguishable.

Philology was cultivated by the Arabs as the honour of their

[17] *"Eine kritik der reinen vernunft." Kritik der reinen Vernunft* is the title of Kant's celebrated work.

race; so that, from pride in the beauty and purity of their language, they reckoned up all its words, and their inflexions, and in very early times the man of learning might load three-score camels with dictionaries. In this science, likewise, the first scholars of the Arabs were the Jews. They endeavoured to fabricate for their much simpler language an artificial grammar after the Arabian fashion, which remained in use even among the Christians to the most recent times: on the other hand, in our days men have taken from this very Arabic language a living guide, to lead them back to the natural meaning of Hebrew poetry; to consider as figurative what is figurative, and to sweep away a thousand idols of fallacious Hebrew exegesis from the face of the Earth.

In the delivery of *history* the Arabs have not been so happy as the Greeks and Romans; for they were destitute of republics, and consequently strangers to the practice of philosophically discussing public acts and events. They could write nothing but brief and dry chronicles; or, if they attempted biography, ran the hazard of falling into poetical panegyric of their hero, and unjust censure of his enemies. The impartial historical style never formed itself among them; their histories are poems, or interwoven with poetry: but their chronicles, and geographical accounts of countries, with which they had opportunities of being acquainted, and which still remain unknown to us, such as the interiour of Africa, are of much utility.[18]

The most decided merit of the Arabs, however, appears in mathematics, chymistry, and physic; in which sciences, augmented by themselves, they were the teachers of all Europe. So early as the reign of Al-Mamoun, a degree of the meridian was measured on the plain of Sanjar, near Bagdad. In astronomy, though compelled to subserve the purposes of superstition,

[18] Most of these, however, remain unexplored or neglected by us. There are lettered Germans, who possess both knowledge and industry, but want support, to publish them as they ought to be: in other countries, the learned sleep over wealthy institutions and legacies appointed for this purpose. Our Reiske has fallen a martyr to his Arabic-Grecian zeal: peace be to his ashes! but long will be the time, ere we shall see again such learning, as was neglected in him.

celestial atlasses, astronomical tables, and various instruments, were executed and improved with much art by the Arabs; in which they were greatly assisted by the fine climate; and clear sky of their extensive dominions. Astronomy was applied also to the service of geography: they made maps, and composed statistical sketches of many countries, long before such things were thought of by Europeans. By it likewise they fixed the dates of chronology: they employed their knowledge of the courses of the stars in navigation, many technical terms of which are of Arabic derivation: and in general the name of this people is inscribed among the stars with more permanent characters, than it could have imprinted any where upon the Earth. The books produced by the industry of its mathematicians, astronomers particularly, are innumerable: most of them now lie unknown, or unused; and multitudes have been destroyed by war, by the flames, by inattention, or by ignorance. Through its means the noblest sciences of the human intellect penetrated into Tatary, the Mungal countries, and even the secluded China: in Samarcand astronomical tables were constructed, and epochs ascertained, to which we still refer. The characters employed in our arithmetic we received from the Arabs: and algebra derives from them its names. So does chymistry, of which they are the fathers: a science that has put into the hands of man a new key to the secrets of Nature, not only for the purposes of physic, but of every department of natural philosophy. As from attachment to this science they paid less attention to botany, and the pursuit of anatomy was prohibited by their law; they were more sedulous in the application of chymistry to the materia medica, and in the discrimination of diseases and temperaments by an almost superstitious observation of their external signs and symptoms. What Aristotle was to them in philosophy, what Euclid and Ptolemy were in mathematics, such were Galen and Dioscorides in the art of physic: though it cannot be denied, that, in following the Greeks, the Arabs were not merely the keepers, propagaters, and amplifiers, of the sciences most indispensable to man, but occasionally the falsifiers of them. The oriental taste, in which they cultivated the sciences, long adhered to them in Europe, and could not easily be removed. In some of the arts, too, much of what we call the Gothic style is properly the Arabian: as in architecture, which these rude conquerors formed after their own manner from the edifices they found in the Grecian provinces, and brought with them into Spain, whence it spread farther into Europe.

4. Lastly, we should speak of the dazzling and romantic *spirit of chivalry,* which they unquestionably mingled with the European ardour for adventure; but this will soon appear of itself.

CHAPTER 6
General Reflections

If we cast a retrospective view on the form our quarter of the Globe has acquired through the migrations and conversion of nations, through wars and the hierarchy, we shall discern a powerful but helpless body, a giant wanting nothing but eyes. This western end of the ancient World was sufficiently populous: the territories of the Romans, enfeebled by luxury, were abundantly peopled by men of strong bodies and solid courage.[19] For in the early days of their recent possession of these countries, before the distinction of ranks had acquired the oppressive hereditary form, the conquered dominions of the Romans were a real Paradise to the rude enjoyments of these uncultivated people, in the midst of other nations, who had long planted and built for their own convenience. They regarded not the ravages their expeditions occasioned, which kept back the human race more than ten centuries: for we feel not the loss of unknown good; and for the animal man this western part of the northern World, with the slightest remnants of its cultivation, was in every respect preferable to his ancient

[19] The bodily strength of our forefathers is attested by their graves and armour, as well as by history: and without it the ancient and middle history of Europe is scarcely reconcileable to the understanding. The valiant and noble mass possessed but few ideas; and these few were set in motion slowly, yet forcibly.

Sarmatia, Scythia, or remoter eastern Hunland. By the devastations, that took place after the Christian era; in the wars, that these people carried on among themselves; in the new pests and diseases, that ravaged Europe; it must be confessed the human species suffered: but by nothing so much, as by the despotic feudal system. Europe was full of men, but of men in a state of bodily servitude: and the slavery, under which these groaned, was so much the more severe, as it was a Christian slavery, reduced into rule by political laws and blind custom, confirmed by writings, and attached to the soil. The very air conferred property: he who was not emancipated by contract, or a despot by birth, entered into the pretended natural state of subjection, or vassalage.

From Rome no succour was to be expected. Its servants shared with others the sovereignty of Europe; and Rome itself was supported by a multitude of spiritual slaves. Whomever kings and emperors made free, were to be forced from giants and dragons, as in the books of romance, by letters of enfranchisement: accordingly this way was tedious and difficult. The knowledge the Christianity of the west possessed was expended, and turned to profit. Its popular form was become a wretched verbal liturgy: its vile patrician rhetoric had been converted, in monasteries, churches, and communities, into a magic despotism over the mind, which the vulgar adored under whips and scourges, nay licking the dust in penitence. The arts and sciences were no more: for what muse will dwell amid the bones of martyrs, the din of bells and organs, the smoke of incense, and prayers for deliverance from Purgatory? The hierarchy had launched its thunderbolts against all freedom of thought, and crippled with its yoke every noble spring of action. Reward in another World was preached up to the suffering: the oppressor was secure of absolution in the hour of death, for a legacy: God's kingdom upon Earth was let to farm.

In Europe there was no salvation without the pale of the Romish church. For, not to mention the oppressed nations miserably pent up in the corners of the Earth, nothing was to be expected from the Grecian empire, still less from the only kingdom, which had begun to form itself in the east of Europe, out of the jurisdiction of the Roman emperor and pope.[20] Thus nothing remained for the western part, but itself; or the only southern nation, in which a new shoot of mental cultivation bloomed, the Mohammedans. With these Europe soon came into conflict, in its most sensible parts; and this conflict was of long duration: in Spain it continued till the time when knowledge was diffused over all Europe. What was the prize of the contest? and who were the victors? Unquestionably the newly excited activity of mankind was the most valuable prize of the victory.

[20] This is Russia. From the time of its foundation it took a peculiar course, different from that of the other kingdoms of Europe. With these it entered not the lists till late.

VIII

The Origins of Modern Europe

BOOK XX

If the croisades, carried on by Europe in the east, may justly be considered as the epoch of a great revolution in our quarter of the Globe, yet we must take care not to esteem them its first and only cause. They were nothing more than a mad enterprise, which cost Europe some millions of men; and reconveyed to it in the survivors, for the most part, a loose, daring, debauched, and ignorant rabble. The good which was effected in their time arose chiefly from collateral causes, which obtained freer play at this period, and produced advantages, in many respects attended with considerable danger. Indeed, no occurrence in human affairs stands alone: arising from anteriour causes, the spirit of the times, and the disposition of nations, it is to be considered only as the dial, the hand of which is moved by internal springs. Let us proceed, therefore, to examine the movements of Europe in the whole, and observe how every wheel in them cooperated to one common end.

CHAPTER 1

The Spirit of Commerce in Europe

This small portion of the Earth was not in vain surrounded by Nature with so many coasts and bays, and intersected by so many navigable rivers and lakes: the nations, that dwelt on them, were active from the remotest times. What the Mediterranean had been to the south of Europe, the Baltic was to the north; an early incentive to the pursuit of navigation, and a mean of intercourse between different countries. Beside the Gael and Cimbri, we have seen the Frisons, the Saxons, and more especially the Normans, traversing all the seas of the west and the north, nay even the Mediterranean, and effecting much good, and much evil. From the simple excavated trunk of a tree they rose to ships of burden, to a capacity of keeping the open sea, and availing themselves of every wind; so that even now the points of the compass, and many nautical terms, in all the languages of Europe, are of German derivation. Amber in particular was the costly bauble, that attracted Greeks, Romans, and Arabians, and brought the north and the south acquainted with each other. It was conveyed by ships of Massilia (Marseilles) over the ocean; by land, through Carnuntum (Presburg) to the Adriatic; and on the Dnieper, to the Black Sea; in quantities scarcely credible.

The way of the Black Sea was preeminently the path of intercourse between the nations of the North, South, and East.[1] At the mouths of the Don and the Dnieper were two great commercial towns, Azoph (Tanais, Asgard), and Olbia (Borysthenes, Alsheim); the repositories of the wares of Tatary, India, China, Byzantium, and Egypt, which were dispersed over the north of Europe, chiefly by way of barter: and even when the readier way through the Mediterranean was frequented, down to the times of the croisades and beyond them, this north eastern commerce was pursued. After the Slavians became possessed of a great part of the Baltic shores, they established a range of flourishing commercial towns along them. The Germanic nations on the islands and opposite coasts were their eager rivals; and desisted not, till, for the sake of gain and of Christianity, the commerce of the Slavians was destroyed. They then endeavoured to occupy their place; and long before the proper Hanseatic league, a kind of maritime republic, *a league of mercantile towns*, was gradually established, which afterwards rose to the grand hanse. As in the days

[1] Much on this subject is collected in the first volume of Fischer's *Geschichte des teutschen Handels* (History of German commerce).

of plunder there had been maritime kings in the north; so now a much more extensive commercial state was formed of various members, on the genuine principles of mutual aid and security; a prototype, probably, of the future state of all the mercantile nations of Europe. Industry, and useful manufactures, flourished on more than one of the northern shores; first of all particularly in Flanders, which was peopled with German colonists.

The internal constitution of this part of the World, however, was assuredly not the best adapted to the rising industry of its inhabitants: for, on almost every coast, the most promising establishments were frequently ruined by pirates; and, by land, the love of war, that still raged among the nations, and the feudal system, which sprung from it, threw in its way a thousand obstacles. In the earliest times, after the barbarians had dispersed themselves over Europe, when greater equality prevailed among the members of the nation, and the ancient inhabitants experienced gentler treatment, the general spirit of industry required nothing but encouragement: and this would not have been wanting, had more Theodorics, Charlemagnes, and Alfreds, appeared. But when every thing fell under the yoke of bondage, and an hereditary order arrogated to itself the labour and industry of its vassals, for the support of its luxury and splendour; when no man, possessed of talents for any art, could dare to pursue it, till he had redeemed himself out of the clutches of this demon by tribute, or by patent; every thing was unquestionably manacled with heavy chains. Intelligent sovereigns did what they could: they founded cities, and endowed them with privileges: they took artists and mechanics under their protection; invited merchants, and even Hebrew usurers, into their dominions, exempting the former from tribute, and often conferring on the latter pernicious commercial liberties, because they stood in need of Jewish gold: but all these could not establish a freer employment or circulation of human industry on the continent of Europe, under the circumstances we have mentioned. Every thing was confined, mutilated, oppressed; nothing therefore could be more natural, than that the address of the south, aided by convenience of situation, should for a time prevail over the assiduity of the north. Yet it was only for a time: for all that Venice, Genoa, Pisa, Amalfi, have done, is confined within the limits of the Mediterranean: the ocean belongs to the navigators of the north; and, with the ocean, the World.

Venice arose amidst its marshes like Rome. First the asylum of those, who saved themselves from the incursions of the barbarians on wretched, inaccessible islands, and supported themselves as well as they could: afterwards joining with the ancient haven of Padua, it united its villages and islands, acquired a form of government, and rose from a paltry trade in fish and salt, with which it began, to be in a few centuries the first commercial city of Europe, the repository of merchandize for all the surrounding countries, and the mistress of several kingdoms; even in the present day it boasts the honour of being the most ancient republic existing, and a republic never conquered.[2] Its history confirms, what that of many commercial cities has proved, that men may rise from nothing to every thing, and save themselves from the very jaws of destruction, if they unite indefatigable industry with prudence. It ventured not out of its marshes till late, when, like a timid inhabitant of the mud, it fought a little district on the strand. It then advanced a few steps farther, and, to obtain the favour of the wealthy Grecian empire, assisted its feeble exarchs of Ravenna. In return for this, it obtained what it desired; the most important privileges in this empire, then in possession of the principal trade of the World.

When the Arabs had extended their dominions; and with the sovereignty of Syria, Egypt, and almost all the shores of the Mediterranean, had likewise usurped their commerce; the Venetians boldly and successfully withstood their attacks on the Adriatic. As soon as a proper opportunity offered, however, they entered into a treaty with them, and thus became the venders of all the wealth of the east, to their immense profit.

---

[2] This was true when the original was published.

Thus spices, silk, and all the commodities of oriental luxury, were so abundantly diffused over Europe, that almost the whole of Lombardy was converted into a repository of them, and the Venetians and Lombards were, together with the Jews, the general brokers of the western world. The more useful trade of the northern nations suffered from this for a certain period: and now the wealthy Venice, pressed upon by the Hungarians and Avari, established a firm footing on the main land. Embroiling themselves neither with the Greek emperors, nor with the Arabs, they drew advantages from Constantinople, Aleppo, and Alexandria; and opposed the commercial establishments of the Normans with timorous jealousy, till they had enclosed these also in their grasp.

The commodities subservient to the calls of luxury, which they and their rivals imported from the east; and the wealth they acquired thereby; with the reports the pilgrims gave of the magnificence of the oriental nations; inflamed the minds of the Europeans with greater desire for the possessions of the Mohammedans, than did the sepulchre of Christ: and when the croisades broke out, there were none who derived from them so much advantage, as these commercial cities of Italy. They transported over several armies, carried them provision, and hence acquired not only immense sums of money, but new privileges, factories, and possessions, in the newly conquered lands. Venice was particularly fortunate above all the rest: for as it succeeded in taking Constantinople with an army of croisaders, and establishing in it a Latin empire, it shared the plunder with its allies so advantageously, that they had but little, and that little insecure, and but for a short period, while it obtained every thing conducive to its trade, the coasts and islands of Greece. These possessions it retained for a long time, and considerably augmented: and all the dangers that threatened them, from rivals or enemies, it contrived to surmount by success, or ward off by circumspection; till a new order of things, the voyages of the Portuguese round the Cape of Good Hope, and the irruption of the Turks into Europe, restricted it to its own Adriatic. A great part of the booty of the Grecian empire, the croisades, and the commerce of the east, concentred in its marshes: its fruits, both good and bad, were disseminated over Italy, France, and Germany, particularly its southern part. They were the Hollanders of their time; and, beside their commercial industry, beside various arts and manufactures, they have eminently distinguished themselves in the book of human nature by the durability of their form of government.[3]

Genoa acquired a great trade earlier than Venice, and possessed for a long time the sovereignty of the Mediterranean. It shared the Grecian commerce, and afterward the Arabian: and as it was of importance to it, to preserve the security of the Mediterranean, it not only made itself master of Corsica, but also, with the assistance of some Christian princes of Spain, of several places in Africa, and dictated peace to the pirates. During the croisades it was very active: the Genoese supported the armies with their fleets; and assisted, in the first expedition, at the conquests of Antioch, Tripoli, Caesarea, and Jerusalem; so that, beside an honorary inscription over the altar in the chapel of the holy sepulchre, they were rewarded with distinguished privileges in Syria and Palestine. In the trade of Egypt they rivalled the Venetians: but in the Black Sea they bore supereminent sway, where they possessed the great commercial city of Kaffa, the repository of all the commodities, that took their course from the east over land; and they enjoyed magazines and liberty of trade in Armenia, nay far within Tatary. They long defended Kaffa, and the islands they held in the Aegean Sea, till the Turks had conquered Constantinople, and excluded them first from the Black Sea, afterwards from the Archipelago. With Venice they carried on long and bloody wars, and more than once brought this republic to the brink of destruction: Pisa, indeed, they rased to the ground; but at length the Vene-

[3] In Le Bret's *Geschichte von Venedig* (History of Venice), we have such an abstract of every thing most memorable, that has been written respecting the history of this city, as no other language can exhibit. What this maritime city has done in the history of Europe for the church, letters, and in other points, will hereafter appear.

tians succeeded in checking the power of the Genoese at Chiozza, and completing the fall of their greatness.

Amalfi, Pisa, and some other cities of Italy, had part with Genoa and Venice in the Arabian trade of the east. Florence rendered itself independent, and joined to it Fiesole: Amalfi obtained the privilege of a free trade throughout the states of the Egyptian khalifs: Amalfi, Pisa, and Genoa, however, were the principal maritime powers in the Mediterranean. The coasts of France and Spain, likewise, sought to participate in the trade of the Levant and the pilgrims of both countries repaired thither as much for the sake of gain, as of devotion. Such was the situation of the south of Europe, with respect to the possessions of the Arabs; which to the shores of Italy, in particular, expanded like a garden of spices, as a Fairyland of wealth. The Italians, that accompanied the croisades, sought not the body of the Lord, but the spices and treasures in his grave. The bank of Tyre was their Holy Land; and what they any where undertook was in their usual way of trade, which they had trodden for centuries.

Transient as was the prosperity these foreign riches brought to those, by whom they were acquired, still in all probability they were indispensable to the first blooming of Italian cultivation. By them men were taught a less rude and more commodious manner of living; and, instead of their coarse ostentation, to distinguish themselves by more refined magnificence. The many great cities of Italy, which were held only by feeble ties to their weak and absent sovereigns on the other side of the Alps, while they all panted after independence, acquired more than one superiority over the uncivilized marauder of the castle: for they either drew him within their walls, by the attractions of luxury, and the increased enjoyments of social life, and converted him into a peaceable citizen; or by their increase of population they acquired sufficient strength, to destroy his fortress, and compel him to live as a quiet neighbour. Rising luxury awakened industriousness, not only to the pursuit of arts and manufactures, but even of agriculture: the fields of Lombardy, Florence,

Bologna, and Ferrara, with the coasts of Naples and Sicily, flourished under the hand of the husbandman, in the neighbourhood of great and industrious cities. Lombardy was a garden, when a great part of Europe was covered with woods and downs. For as these populous cities must derive their support from the land; and the proprietor of the soil could gain more by the provision, with which he furnished them, in consequence of the increased price given for the necessaries of life; he could not avoid exerting himself in pursuit of this gain, if he were desirous of participating in the luxury recently introduced. Thus one species of activity roused another, and kept it in play: and, with this new course of things, order, the free enjoyment of private property, and submission to the laws, necessarily prevailed. Men were obliged to learn frugality, that they might have money to spend: human invention was sharpened, while one endeavoured to carry the prize from another: every householder, formerly an unconnected individual, now became in some degree himself a merchant. Thus it arose from the nature of things, that fertile Italy, watered by the wealth of the Arabs, should first put forth the blossoms of a new cultivation.

These blossoms, however, were far from perennial. Trade diffused itself, and took a different course: the republics decayed: voluptuous cities became insolent, and at variance within themselves: the whole country was filled with parties, among which enterprizing men, and a few powerful families, raised themselves to great authority. War and oppression succeeded: and as luxury and the arts had banished not only the military spirit, but also faith and probity, one city, one state, after another, fell a prey to foreign or domestic tyrants. The strictest laws of moderation alone were capable of preserving from ruin the distributor of this pleasing poison, Venice itself. Yet let no spring of human action be denied its rightful claims. Happily for Europe, this luxury was at that time far from general, and the greater part of it promoted the gains of the Lombards alone: a spring still more powerful acted in opposition to it, the spirit of chivalry, despising selfinterest, and daring every thing for the sake of glory. Let us examine from what seeds this flower arose; whence it derived its nutriment; and what virtues it possessed, to check the spirit of commerce.

CHAPTER 2
Spirit of Chivalry in Europe

ALL the Germanic tribes, that spread themselves over Europe, consisted of warriours: and as the most arduous part of military service fell upon the calvary, it was natural, that these should amply recompense themselves for their skill in equestrian accomplishments. Accordingly, a fraternity of horsemen soon arose, who learned their art in due form: and as these were the attendants of the commander, duke, or king, a sort of military school was established where the court resided, in which the bachelor knights served their apprenticeship. When this was accomplished, it is probable, that they were sent in quest of adventures, as the means of rendering them perfect in their trade; and, having well approved themselves on this trial, continued to serve as masters of their craft, to the privileges of which they were admitted, or as teachers to instruct others in those arts, which themselves had learned. It is scarcely possible, that the order of chivalry should have had any other origin. The Germanic nations, who carried the corporation spirit into everything, must have applied it particularly to an art familiar to themselves alone: and as this was their grand and sole art, they naturally conferred upon it all the honour, which they were too ignorant to bestow on any other. All the laws and regulations of chivalry may be deduced from this origin.[4]

This company of horsemen being trained for the service of the prince, the first duty incumbent both on the bachelor and the knight was, to swear fealty to him. Horsemanship and the

---

[4] See Möser's *Osnabrueckische Geschichte* (History of Osnabruck), Vol. I. For what follows, instead of the numbers who have written on chivalry, I shall cite only Curne de St. Palaye, whose work is translated into German by D. Klueber. The chief part of the original relates to the French knights alone; the general history of chivalry in Europe has never yet been written to my knowledge.

use of weapons were the exercises of their school; whence tilts and tournaments, with other knightly sports as they were called, afterwards arose. At court the young cavalier was to be about the person of the prince and his consort, to be ready for courtly services: hence the duty of courtesy toward princes and ladies, which he learned as a trade. And as, beside his horse and his arms, a little religion and favour with the ladies were necessary for him, he acquired the former from a short breviary, and obtained the latter as he could, according to his abilities and the fashion of the times. Thus originated chivalry, consisting of a blind faith in religion, a blind submission to the will of the prince, provided he required nothing inconsistent with the principles of the confraternity, courteousness in service, and gallantry toward the ladies: if a knight possessed these virtues, no matter whether his head contained a single idea, his heart a single sentiment, besides. The lower classes were not his equals: the knowledge of the mechanic, the artist, or the man of learning, he, as a soldier and accomplished knight, could despise.

It is obvious, that this military trade must degenerate into unbridled barbarism, as soon as it became an hereditary right, and the genuine, thorough knight was a noble in his very cradle. Sagacious princes, who supported such an idle train about their courts, paid considerable attention to the improvement of this calling, by instilling into the minds of the noble masters some few ideas, and giving them morals, for the security of their own court, family, and country. Hence the severe laws by which every act of baseness was subjected to penalties among them: hence the noble duties of succouring the oppressed, protecting virgin innocence, treating enemies with magnanimity, and the like: the design of which was to obviate their bursts of violence, to temper the rudeness and barbarity of their manners. These laws of the order were not to be obliterated from the virtuous mind, on which they had been impressed from the earliest infancy; so that the probity and faith almost mechanically displayed in word and deed by every worthy knight astonish us. Pliability of character, facility of placing a question in every point of view, and fertility of ideas, were not their failings: hence the language of the Middle Ages was so ceremonious, stiff, and formal, that it seems to move as it were caparisoned in steel, round two or three thoughts, in all the pomp of knighthood.

Causes from two extremities of the Earth concurred, to give this body of chivalry more life and motion: Spain, France, England, and Italy, but principally France, were the places where it received its chief refinements.

1. The national character and country of the *Arabs* rendered a kind of knight-errantry, mixed with the tenderness of love, somewhat like hereditary property to them, from the earliest times. They went in quest of adventures; fought single combats; and washed out the stain of every disgrace, thrown on themselves, or their tribe, with the blood of their enemy. Accustomed to hard fare and slight clothing, their horse, their sword, and the honour of their race, were dear to them above all things. And as while roaming with their tents they sought love-adventures, and then breathed out complaints of the absence of the object of their passion in their much valued poetical language; their songs very soon fell into the regular train of chaunting their prophet, themselves, the honours of their race, and the praises of their mistress; without much attention to the aptness of transition. On their expeditions of conquest the tents of the women were intermingled with theirs: the most courageous animated them in battle, and in return the spoils of the victory were laid at their feet. And as from the time of Mohammed the influence of the women in the formation of the Arabian empire had been great; and the orientals had no enjoyments in a period of peace, except games of pastime, or amusing themselves among the women; the festivities of chivalry, as throwing the javelin at the ring, and other contests, within lists, in the presence of the ladies, were celebrated with great splendour and magnificence in Spain, during the government of the Arabs. The fair dames encouraged the champions, and rewarded them with jewels, scarves, or garments worked with their own hands: for these festivals were held in honour of

them, and the portrait of the conqueror's mistress was hung up to view, surrounded by the portraits of the knights he had overcome. The competitors were divided into bands, distinguished by their colours, devices, and garments; poems were sung in honour of the feast; and the thanks of love were the victor's noblest reward. Thus the more refined customs of chivalry were evidently brought into Europe by the Arabs: what with the heavy-armed heroes of the north remained only professional manners, or mere fiction, were with these nature, light play, sportive exercise.[5]

Thus this gayer spirit of chivalry was first introduced among the Christians in Spain, where the Arabs and Goths lived together for centuries. Here we not only discover the most ancient Christian orders, established either for the purpose of opposing the Moors, for protecting pilgrims on their journeys to Compostella, or for pleasure and amusement; but the spirit of chivalry was so deeply imprinted in the character of the Spaniards, that even knights errant, and chevaliers of love, perfectly in the Arabian style, were not with them mere creatures of the imagination. The romaunt, or historical poem, particularly as dedicated to the adventurers of love and chivalry; and probably the romance, as the old Amadis, and others; were the offspring of their language and way of thinking, in which Cervantes found in latter days the materials for that incomparable national romance, Don Quixote de la Mancha.

But their influence was more eminently displayed in the *lighter poetry,* both here and in Sicily, the two countries of which the Arabs longest maintained possession.[6] For in the land, extending to the Ebro, which Charlemagne conquered from the Arabs, and peopled with Limosins, or the inhabitants of the south of France, the first poetry among the vernacular languages of Europe, the *Provençal* or *Limosin,* gradually formed itself, on either side the Pyrenees, in the neighbourhood

[5] See Reiske on Thograi, Pocock on Abulfaragius, Sale, Jones, Ockley, Cardonne, etc.

[6] See Velasquez on Spanish poetry, and all who have written on the Provençals, minnesingers, etc.

of the Arabs. Tenzonets, sonnets, idyls, villanescas, sirventes, madrigals, canzonets, and other forms, invented for witty questions, dialogues, and envelopes of amorous subjects, gave occasion, as every thing in Europe must assume the court or corporation form, to a singular tribunal, the court of love (*corte de amor*), in which ladies and knights, princes and kings, were concerned as judges and parties. Before it was formed the *gaya ciencia,* the science of the troubadours; first the pursuit of the higher nobility, but afterwards, being considered after the European mode as an amusement of the court, it fell into the hands of the *contadores, truanes,* and *bufones,* the story-tellers, jesters, and court-buffoons, where it became contemptible.

In its early flourishing days the poetry of the Provençals had a softly harmonious, pathetic, and engaging style, which polished the heart and mind, refined the language and manners, and was the general parent of all modern European poetry. The Limosin language extended itself over Languedoc, Provence, Barcelona, Arragon, Valencia, Murcia, Majorca, and Minorca: in these charming countries, fanned by the sea-breeze, love breathed its first sigh, love poured the first language of delight. The poetry of Spain, France, and Italy, were its daughters: by it Petrarch was tutored, of it he was emulous: our minnesingers were its remote and harsh echoes, though the softest of our language is unquestionably theirs. The universally diffused spirit of chivalry transplanted some of its flowers from France and Italy into Swabia, Austria, and Thuringia: some emperors of the Staufish family, and Hermann landgrave of Thuringia, delighted in it, with more German princes, whose names would have sunk into oblivion, had they not been transmitted to posterity with some of their songs. The art, however, speedily degenerated, sinking into the despicable trade of vagrant *jongleurs* in France, of *meistersingers* in Germany. In languages sprung like the Provençal itself from the Latin, and known by the name of Romansh, it could take deeper root; producing far more pleasing fruits as it spread from Spain through France and Italy to the island of Sicily. In Sicily, as in Spain, arose the first Italian poetry on what was once Arabian ground.

2. What the Arabs began from the south, the *Normans* cultivated still more strenuously from the north, in France, England, and Italy. When their romantic character, their love of adventures, heroic tales, and martial exercises, and their native respect to the women, united with the refined chivalry of the Arabs, it gained a wider spread, and deeper root in Europe. The tales called romances, the ground-work of which existed long before the croisades, now came more into vogue: for all the German nations had ever celebrated the praises of their heroes; and these songs and poems had maintained their ground, even amid the darkest ages, in the courts of the great, nay in the convents themselves; and in proportion as genuine history declined, men's minds were the more turned to spiritual legends, or romantic stories. Accordingly, from the first ages of Christianity we find this exercise of the human imagination more employed than any other, first after the African Greek manner, latterly after the Northern European: monks, bishops, and saints, were not ashamed of it; nay, from their mouths, true history, and the Bible itself, spoke the language of romance. Hence arose the suit of Belial against Christ: hence the allegorical and mystical personification of all the virtues and duties: hence the spiritual dramatic moralities and interludes.

Such being the general taste of the times, the offspring of ignorance, superstition, and an awakened fancy, tales and fables (*contes et fabliaux*) were the only food of the human mind, and heroic tales were most admired by the equestrian order. In France, the centre of this cultivation, the subjects most peculiar to it were naturally chosen, according to the two streams that united here. The expedition of Charlemagne against the Saracens, with all the adventures said to have happened in the Pyrenees, was one of these: what already existed in the country of the Normans, in Britanny, in the ancient stories of King Arthur, was the other. Into this were introduced, from the more recent French constitution, the twelve peers, with all the splendour of Charles and his knights, and all the savage deeds they had to tell of the Saracen heroes. Ogier the Dane, Huon of Bordeaux, the children of Aimon, and various stories of the pilgrims and croisaders, entered likewise into this: but the most interesting persons and events were always borrowed from the country of the Provençals, Guienne, Languedoc, Provence, and that part of Spain, where the Limosin poetry flourished. The second stream, the tales of Arthur and his court, came over the sea from Cornwall, or rather from an utopian land, where men indulged in a peculiar species of the wonderful. The mirrour of knighthood was brightly polished in these romances: the vices and virtues of this court were clearly exhibited in the various characters of the Knights of the Round Table; for which there was ample room in the unbounded domains of the romance of Arthur, and in such ancient times.

At length from these two branches of romance issued a third, which excluded no French or Spanish province. Poitou, Champagne, Normandy, the forest of Ardennes, Flanders, nay Mentz, Castile, and Algarva, furnished knights and scenes to the drama: for the ignorance of the times, and the form in which the histories of antiquity then appeared, permitted, or rather urged this jumble of all ages and countries. Troy and Greece, Jerusalem and Trebisond, what was known of old, and what report just bruited about, united in the garland of chivalry: and above all the claim to a descent from Trojan blood was a family honour, of which all the nations and empires of Europe, with its greatest knights and potentates, were firmly persuaded. With the Normans romance passed into England and Sicily: each country afforded it new heroes, and new materials; but no where did it flourish as in France. From the coalescence of various causes, this taste formed the way of life, language, poetry, and even religion and morals of men.[7]

Then, if we pass from the regions of fable into the land of history, is there a kingdom in Europe, where chivalry has blossomed with more elegance than in France? When, after the decline of the Carlovingian race, almost as many courts of little potentates, dukes, counts, or barons, shone forth in power and

[7] Of these directions and ingredients of the romance of the Middle Ages I shall speak elsewhere.

splendour, as there were provinces, castles, and fortresses; every palace, every knight's seat, was also a school of chivalry and honour. The national vivacity of the people; the contests they had maintained for centuries against the Arabs and Normans; the fame their forefathers had thereby acquired; the flourishing state, to which many families had raised themselves; their intermixture with the Normans themselves; but, especially, that peculiarity in the character of the nation, which displays itself throughout their whole history from the days of the Gauls; introduced into chivalry that felicity of expression, that prompt elasticity, easy complaisance, and sparkling grace, which, in any other nation except the French, is to be found but late, or seldom, if ever. How many French knights may be named, whose sentiments and actions, in peace and war, throughout the whole history of France, even down to the times of royal despotism, display so much valour, nobleness, and gallantry, that their families will be eternally honoured! When Fame sounded the trump of the croisades, the knights of France were the flower of European chivalry: French families wore the diadem of Jerusalem and Constantinople; and the laws of the new state were promulgated in French. The language and manners of France seated themselves on the British throne, likewise, with William the Conqueror: and the two nations emulously rivalled each other in the virtues of chivalry, as the plains both of France and Palestine witnessed, till England relinquished to its neighbour the prize of empty splendour, and chose the more useful career of civil virtues. France first braved the power of the pope; and indeed in the easiest way, with a degree of grace: even St. Lewis himself was far from a slave of the holy father. England, Germany, and other countries, have had more valiant kings than France: but policy first entered France from Italy, and there assumed at least the garb of decorum, however disgraceful her actions. This spirit imparted itself likewise to institutions of learning, magisterial dignities, and tribunals of justice, at first to their advantage, afterwards to their detriment.

No wonder, then, that the French nation is become the

vainest in Europe: almost from the origin of its monarchy it has held the lamp to this quarter of the Globe, and given it the tone in its most important revolutions. When all nations flocked together to Palestine, as to a grand carousal, the German knights were led by their connexion with the French, to lay aside their Teutonic turbulence (*furor teutonicus*). The new dress, likewise, which coats of arms and other marks of distinction spread over all Europe in the time of the croisades, was for the most part of French origin.

We should now speak of the three or four orders of spiritual knights, which, founded in Palestine, attained so much wealth, and so many honours; but the heroic and political drama, in which they acquired these, lies before us, with its five, or rather seven acts; to it therefore we will proceed.

CHAPTER 3

The Croisades and their Consequences

PILGRIMS and popes had long complained of the distresses of Christians at Jerusalem. The end of the World was announced to be at hand and Gregory VII believed he had 50,000 men ready to follow him to the holy sepulchre, if he would place himself at their head. At length a native of Picardy, Peter the Hermit, in concert with Simeon, the patriarch of Jerusalem, succeeded in persuading Pope Urban II to set his hand to the work. Two councils were called; and in the latter of them the pope made a speech, at the conclusion of which the people in a frenzy exclaimed: "it is the will of God! it is the will of God!"

Accordingly multitudes were marked with a red cross on the right shoulder; the croisade was preached throughout all papal Christendom; and various privileges were conferred on the holy warriours. They were allowed to alienate or mortgage lands without the assent of their lords; a permission, which was also conferred on ecclesiastics, with respect to their benefices, for a term of three years: all the croisaders were taken under the protection and jurisdiction of the church, with regard both to person and property, and admitted to the rights of the clergy: during the continuance of the holy war they were exempt from all taxes and contributions, from being sued at law for any debts they had contracted, and from paying any interest for what they owed: and they obtained a complete absolution for all their sins. An incredible number of devout, dissolute, giddy, restless, savage, fanatics and dupes, of all ranks and degrees, and even of both sexes, flocked together. The forces were mustered; and Peter the Hermit set out, barefoot, and clad in a long cowl, at the head of an army of 300,000 men. Spurning at all order, they plundered wherever they came. The Hungarians and Bulgarians united; hunted them into the woods and he arrived at Constantinople with a miserable remnant, of about 30,000, in a wretched condition. Gottschalk, a priest, followed with 15,000; and a count of the name of Emich, with 200,000 more.

These men began their holy war with a massacre of the Jews, of whom they murdered twelve thousand in a few towns on the banks of the Rhine: and in Hungary they themselves were either massacred or drowned. The first undisciplined horde of hermits, strengthened by the addition of some Italians, were transported into Asia, experienced the distresses of famine, and would have been totally extirpated by the Turks, had not Godfrey of Bouillon at length arrived before Constantinople with his regular forces, and the flower of European chivalry. The army was mustered in the plains of Chalcedon, and found to consist of 500,000 foot, and 130,000 horse. Nicaea, Tarsus, Alexandria, Edessa, Antioch, and at length Jerusalem, were taken amid incredible dangers and difficulties; and Godfrey of Bouillon was unanimously chosen king. His brother Baldwin was made count of Edessa; and the prince of Tarentum, Boemund, duke of Antioch: Raymond, count of Tholouse, became count of Tripoli; and all the heroes celebrated in Tasso's immortal poem distinguished themselves in this campaign. Misfortune, however, succeeded misfortune: the little kingdom had to defend itself against innumerable swarms of Turks from the east, and of Arabs from Egypt; and defended itself at first with incredible courage and fortitude. But the ancient heroes died: the kingdom of Jerusalem came under a regency: dissensions arose among the princes and knights: a new power sprung up in Egypt, that of the Mamalukes, with which the noble and valiant Saladin straitened the perfidious, depraved Christians, and at length took Jerusalem; thus putting an end to this little shadow of a kingdom, before it had been enabled to celebrate its centennial jubilee.

All the subsequent croisades, to maintain or reconquer this kingdom, were in vain: and the little principalities preceded or soon followed it in their downfall: Edessa remained in the hands of the Christians no more than fifty years: and the immense croisade, the second in order, undertaken by the emperor Conrad III, and Lewis VII king of France, at the war-whoop of St. Bernard, with 20,000 men, was unable to restore it.

In the third croisade, three valiant potentates, the emperor Frederic I, Philip Augustus king of France, and Richard the Lionhearted of England, took the field against Saladin. The first was drowned in a river, and his son died: the other two, being jealous rivals, and the French king in particular envious of the British, could accomplish nothing more than the reconquest of Acre. Unmindful of his word, Philip Augustus returned; and Richard, unable alone to contend against the power of Saladin, was obliged reluctantly to follow him. Nay he had the misfortune, as he travelled through Germany in a pilgrim's guise, to be stopped by Leopold duke of Austria, in revenge for a pretended insult at the siege of Acre, and basely delivered into the hands of the Emperor Henry VI; who still more basely detained him four years in strict confinement, till, all the world murmuring at this unknightly action, he suffered him to ransom himself for 100,000 marks of silver.

The fourth croisade, undertaken by the French, Dutch, and Venetians, under the count of Mountserrat, never reached Palestine; being led by the selfish, revengeful Venetians. They took Zara, and sailed for Constantinople: the imperial city was twice taken and plundered: the emperor fled: Baldwin, count of Flanders, erected a Latin empire in Byzantium: the empire and the spoil were divided, and the Venetians acquired the richest part of the booty, on the Adriatic, the Euxine, and the

Grecian Sea. The commander in chief of the expedition became king of Candia, which island also he sold to his covetous allies: and instead of the countries beyond the Bosphorus he received the crown of Thessalonica. A principality of Achaia, and a duchy of Athens, were created for French barons: wealthy Venetian nobles were made dukes of Naxos and Negropont: there was a count palatine of Zant and Cephalonia: the Grecian empire was sold like ordinary plunder to the best bidder. On the other hand, different branches of the Grecian imperial race erected an empire at Nicaea; a duchy, which afterwards assumed the title of empire, at Trebisond; and a despotism, afterwards styled an empire likewise, in Epirus. As so little was left to the new Latin emperors of Constantinople, this weak and hated throne with difficulty stood for fifty years: the emperors of Nicaea retook the ancient Grecian imperial city; and at length, all these possessions, acquired by adventurers, fell into the hands of the Turks.

The fifth croisade, undertaken by the Hungarians and Germans, was without effect. The kings of Hungary and Cyprus, a titular king of Jerusalem, and the grand masters of the different orders, surrounded Mount Tabor, blocked up the enemy, and had the victory in their hands: but jealousy and discord robbed them of their advantage; and the croisaders returned home, foiled and dejected.

Urged incessantly by the papal court, the emperor Frederic II dispatched a fleet to the Holy Land. An advantageous truce was on the point of being concluded; but it was frustrated by the pope's legate: and as the emperor, compelled greatly against his inclinations, entered on the campaign, the pope himself hindered all probability of its success, by an absurd ban, and a treacherous attack upon the European dominions of the emperor. A truce was concluded with the sultan of Bagdad; Palestine and Jerusalem were yielded to the emperor; but the holy sepulchre remained in the hands of the Saracens, as a free port for pilgrims from all quarters.

This divided possession of Jerusalem, however, continued scarcely fifteen years; and St. Lewis was unable to regain it by his croisade, the seventh in order, and of all the most unfortunate. He himself, with his whole army, fell into the hands of the enemy in Egypt: he was obliged to purchase his ransom at a dear price: and on a second expedition, equally useless and unfortunate, against the Moors, he ended his life before Tunis. His melancholy example at length stifled the senseless propensity to religious wars in Palestine; and the last of the Christian cities there, Tyre, Acre, Antioch, and Tripoli, fell, one after another, into the hands of the Mamalukes. Thus ended this infatuation, which had cost European Christendom immense sums of money, and multitudes of men: and what were its consequences? [8]

It has been customary, to ascribe so many beneficial effects to the croisades, that, conformably to this opinion, our quarter of the Globe must require a similar fever, to agitate and excite its forces, once in every five or six centuries; but a closer inspection will show, that most of these effects proceeded not from the croisades, at least not from them alone; and that, among the various impulses Europe then received, they were at most accelerating shocks, acting upon the whole in collateral or oblique directions, with which the minds of Europeans might well have dispensed. Indeed it is a mere phantom of the brain, to frame one prime source of events out of seven distinct expeditions, undertaken in a period of two centuries, by different nations, and from various motives, solely because they bore one common name.

1. *Trade,* we have seen, the Europeans had already opened with the Arabian states, before the croisades: and they were at liberty to have profited by it, and extended it, in a far more honourable way, than by predatory campaigns. By these, indeed, carriers, bankers, and purveyors, were gainers: but all their gain accrued from the Christians, against whose property they were in fact the croisaders. What was torn from the Greek empire was a disgraceful trader's booty, serving, by extremely

[8] I have never seen the essays and prize papers, concerning the effects of the croisades, written at the instigation of different learned societies: therefore I deliver my own opinion, without reference to any of them.

enfeebling this empire, to render Constantinople an easier prey at a future period to the Turkish hordes, who were continually pressing more closely upon it. The Venetian lion of St. Mark prepared the way, by the fourth croisade, for the Turks to enter Europe, and spread themselves so widely in it. The Genoese, it is true, assisted one branch of the Greek emperors to reascend the throne: but it was the throne of a weakened, broken empire, which fell an easy prey to the Turks; then both the Venetians and Genoese lost their best possessions, and finally almost all their trade, in the Mediterranean and Euxine Seas.

2. *Chivalry* arose not from the croisades, but the croisades from chivalry: the flower of French and Norman knighthood appeared in Palestine in the first campaign. The croisades, indeed, contributed rather to rob chivalry of its proper honours, and to convert real armed knights into mere armorial ones. For in Palestine many assumed the crested helmet, which in Europe they durst not have born: they brought home with them armorial devices and nobility, which they transmitted to their families, and thus introduced a new class, the nobility of the heralds office, and in time also nobility by letters patent. As the number of the ancient dynasties, the true equestrian nobility, lessened, these new men sought to obtain possessions, and hereditary prerogatives, like them: they carefully enumerated their ancestors, acquired dignities and privileges, and in a few generations assumed the title of ancient nobility; though they had not the slightest pretensions, to rank with those dynasties, which were princes to them. Every man, that bore arms in Palestine, might become a knight: the first croisades were years of general jubilee for Europe. These new nobles in right of military service were soon of great use to growing monarchy, which cunningly knew how to avail itself of them against such of the superiour vassals as still remained. Thus passion balances passion, and one appearance counteracts another: and at length the nobility of the camp and the court totally obliterated the ancient chivalry.

3. It is self-evident, that the orders of *spiritual knights*, founded in Palestine, were of no advantage to Europe. They

still consume the capital, once dedicated to the holy sepulchre, an object wholly dead to us. The hospitallers were to receive pilgrims on their arrival, nurse the sick, and administer to the leper: these are the lofty knights of St. John of our time. When a nobleman of Dauphiny, Raymond du Puy, introduced among them the vow of carrying arms, the order of Lazarus separated from them, and adhered to the primitive institution. The templars were regular canons, lived ten years on alms themselves, and protected the pilgrims to the holy sepulchre; till, their property increasing, their statutes were altered, and the knights had their esquires, the order, its lay brothers. Lastly, the Teutonic order was founded for the assistance of the sick and wounded left on the field: bread, water, and clothing, were its rewards; till it also became rich and powerful, from its useful services against the infidels.

All these orders displayed much valour, and much pride, in the Holy Land; and likewise treachery and disloyalty: but with Palestine their history might well have terminated. When the knights of St. John of Jerusalem were compelled to quit this country; when they had lost Cyprus and Rhodes, and Charles V had bestowed on them the rock of Malta; how singular was the commission, to remain to eternity croisaders out of Palestine, and on that score to enjoy possessions in kingdoms safe from the attacks of the Turks, and which no pilgrim could traverse in his way to the Holy Land! Lewis VII received the order of Lazarus into France, and would have reclaimed it to the original purpose of its institution, the care of the sick: more than one pope was desirous of suppressing it: but it was protected by the kings of France, and Lewis XIV united it with some other trifling orders. In this his sentiments differed from those of his ancestor, Philip the Fair, who barbarously exterminated the Templars from motives of avarice and revenge; and appropriated to himself their estates, to which he had no claim. Finally, the Teutonic knights were called in by a duke of Massovia to assist him against the heathen Prussians, and obtained from a German emperor the gift of all the land they could conquer on the occasion, except what belonged to himself. They subdued Prussia; united with the brothers of the sword in Livonia; obtained Esthonia from a king, who was unable to hold it: and thus at length ruled in knightly luxury and licentiousness from the Vistula to the Dwina and Neva. The ancient Prussian nation was exterminated; Lithuanians and Samoiedes, Courlanders, Lettonians, and Esthonians, were divided as live stock among the German nobles. After long wars with the Poles, they lost half Prussia, and then the whole; and at length Livonia and Courland also. In these regions they left nothing behind them, but the repute, that it was scarcely possible for a conquered country, to be ruled more proudly and oppressively, than they ruled these coasts, which, had they been cultivated by some maritime states, would certainly have assumed a very different appearance. Upon the whole it may be said, that the three orders above mentioned belonged not to Europe, but to Palestine. There they were founded; there they appeared in their place. There they might fight the infidels, attend hospitals, protect the holy sepulchre, administer to the leper, and conduct the pilgrim. Their institutions should have been extinguished with these objects: their estates should have been consigned to Christian works, they were the especial property of the sick and the poor.

4. As the new armorial nobility was indebted solely to the growth of monarchy in Europe for its establishment: so the *freedom of cities,* the origin of communities, and lastly the emancipation of the peasantry, in this quarter of the Globe, are to be ascribed to causes very different from the mad croisades. That in their first febrile paroxysm a respite was granted to all prodigal householders and debtors; that vassals and bondsmen were discharged from their duties, tributaries from their tribute, and those who were liable to imposts from their taxes; assuredly formed not the basis, on which the right of liberty in Europe rests. Cities had long been erected; the rights of more ancient cities had long been confirmed and extended: and if the growing industry and commerce of these cities sooner or later embraced the liberty of the peasant also; if the endeavours of such municipalities after independence were necessarily in-

cluded in the progress of rising monarchy; surely we need not seek in Palestine, what the ever changing scene of events in Europe alone could produce. The durable system of Europe could scarcely have proceeded from a religious folly.

5. The *arts and sciences,* too, were nowise promoted by the proper croisaders. The disorderly troops, that first flocked to Palestine, had not the least notion of them; and were not likely to acquire them in the suburbs of Constantinople, or from the Turks and Mamalukes in Asia. In the succeeding campaigns we need only reflect on the short time the armies passed there; and the wretched circumstances, under which this time was often spent merely on the confines of the country; to dissipate the splendid dream of great discoveries imported thence. The pendulum clock, which the emperor Frederic II received as a present from Meledin, introduced not gnomonics into Europe; the Grecian palaces, which the croisaders admired in Constantinople, improved not the style of European architecture. Some croisaders, particularly Frederic I and II, laboured to promote the progress of knowledge: but Frederic I did this ere he beheld Asia; and the short visit paid that country by Frederic II served only as a fresh stimulus, to urge him forward in that course of government, which he had long before chosen. Not one of the spiritual orders of knighthood introduced any new knowledge into Europe, or contributed to its cultivation.

All that can be said in favour of the croisades, therefore, is confined to a few occasions, on which they cooperated with causes already existing, and involuntarily promoted them.

1. As multitudes of wealthy vassals and knights repaired to the Holy Land in the first campaigns, and many of them never returned, their estates were of course sold, or swallowed up in others. By this they profited who could, the liege lord, the church, the cities already established, each after his own manner: this promoted and accelerated the course of things, tending to confirm the regal power by the erection of a middle class, but was by no means its commencement.

2. Men became acquainted with countries, people, religions, and constitutions, of which they were before ignorant; their

narrow sphere of vision was enlarged; they acquired new ideas, new impulses. Attention was drawn to things, which would otherwise have been neglected; what had long existed in Europe was employed to better purpose; and as the World was found to be wider than had been supposed, curiosity was excited after a knowledge of its remotest parts. The mighty conquests made by Genghis-Khan in the north and east of Asia attracted men's eyes chiefly toward Tatary; whither Marco Polo, the Venetian, Rubruquis, a Frenchman, and John de Plano Carpino, an Italian, travelled with very different views; the first, for the purpose of trade; the second, to satisfy royal curiosity; the third, sent by the pope, to make converts of the people. These travels, of course, have no connexion with the croisades, before and after which they were undertaken. The Levant itself is less known to us from these expeditions, than might have been expected: the accounts the orientals give of it, even in the period when Syria swarmed with Christians, are still indispensable to us.

3. Finally, on this holy theatre Europeans became better acquainted with each other, though not in a manner much to be prized. With this more intimate acquaintance kings and princes for the most part brought home an implacable enmity: in particular the wars between England and France derived from it fresh fuel. The unfortunate experiment, that a Christian republic could and might contend in unison against infidels, formed a precedent for similar wars in Europe, which have since extended to other quarters of the Globe. At the same time it cannot be denied, that, while the neighbouring powers of Europe obtained a closer inspection of their mutual weaknesses and strength, some obscure hints were given for a more comprehensive policy, and a new system of relationship in peace and war. Every one was desirous of wealth, trade, conveniences, and luxuries; as an uncultivated mind is prone, to admire these in strangers, and envy them in the hands of another. Few, who returned from the east, could be satisfied with European manners: even their heroism left much behind, awkwardly imitated Asia in the west, or longed for fresh travels and adventures. For

the actual and permanent good produced by any event is always proportionate to its consonancy with reason.

Unfortunate would it have been for Europe, if, at the time when its military swarms were contending for the holy sepulchre in a corner of Syria, the arms of Genghis-Kahn had been sooner and more powerfully turned toward the west. Then probably our quarter of the Globe would have been the prey of the Mungals, like Poland and Russia; and its nations might have dislodged, with the pilgrim's staff in their hands, to tell their beads round the object of their contention. Let us quit these wild fanatics, therefore, and take a retrospect of Europe; that we may see how the course of events, reciprocally acting on each other, gradually enlightened and formed the moral and political reason of mankind.

CHAPTER 4
Cultivation of Reason in Europe

In the early ages of Christianity we observed numerous sects, that attempted to elucidate, apply, and refine the system of religion, through the means of an *oriental philosophy*, as it was called. These were oppressed and persecuted as heretics. The doctrine of *Manes*, which, after the manner of Zoroaster (Zerdusht), included a moral institution, and the design of operating as an active instructor on the community, seems to have struck the deepest root. This was more severely persecuted than theoretical heresies; and took refuge eastwards in the mountains of Thibet, westwards in those of Armenia, and here and there in European countries, in all of which it experienced the same fate as in Asia.

It was long imagined to be suppressed, till, in the profundity of the Dark Ages, it burst forth, as at a signal given, from a country whence it was least expected, and at once occasioned a prodigious uproar in Italy, Spain, France, the Netherlands, Switzerland, and Germany. This country was *Bulgaria;* a barbarous province, for which the Greek and Latin churches had long contended: there was its invisible head, who, far different from the pope of Rome, professed to resemble Christ in poverty. Secret missions went into all parts, and attracted, not only the common people, especially industrious mechanics and the oppressed peasantry, but also the wealthy and the noble, particularly women, with a power, that braved the severest persecution, and death itself. Their placid doctrines, which enforced pure human virtues; industry, chastity, and orderliness, in particular; and held up a pattern of perfection, to which the community should be led in a very distinguished manner; were a loud war-whoop against the prevailing abominations of the church. They directly attacked the morals of the clergy, their wealth, ambition, and licentiousness; rejected their superstitious doctrines and practices, the immoral magic of which they denied; and instead of all these admitted a simple benediction by the imposition of hands, and an union of the members under their leaders, the perfect. According to them, transubstantiation, crucifixes, masses, purgatory, the intercession of saints, and the inherent preeminence of the Romish priesthood, were human doctrines and inventions. The Scriptures, particularly of the Old Testament, they judged very freely, reducing the whole to poverty, purity of body and mind, quiet industry, gentleness, and benevolence; hence in many sects they received the appellation of *bons hommes, the good people*. Among the most ancient of them the oriental Manicheism is palpable: they set out with the contest between light and darkness, held matter for the origin of sin, and entertained very rigid notions of sensual pleasure. By degrees their system was purified. Out of these Manicheans, who were also called cathars (heretics), patarenes, publicans, *passagieri*, and by various other names in different countries, according to local circumstances, individual teachers, particularly Henry and Peter de Bruis, formed less offensive parties; till at length the Waldenses taught, and maintained with great courage, almost every thing, that Protestantism preached some centuries after. The earlier sects appear to have resembled the Anabaptists, Mennonites, Bohemian Brethren, and other sects of modern times. All these spread themselves in silence so powerfully, and with such persuasive impression, that the consequence of the clergy declined extremely in whole provinces, particularly as these were by no means a match for them in disputation. The countries, in which the *Provençal language* prevailed, were the spots in which they most flourished: they translated the New Testament, an undertaking at that time unheard of, into this language; published their *rules of perfection* in Provençal verse; and were the first, who *instructed and formed the people in their vernacular language, after the introduction of the Romish religion.*[9]

On these accounts, however, they were persecuted, as far as they were known, and according to the power possessed by their enemies. So early as the beginning of the eleventh century, Manicheans were burned at Orleans, in the heart of France, and among them even the confessor of the queen: they refused to recant, and died in the profession of their faith. They experienced equal severity in every country, in which the clergy could exercise their authority, as in Italy, and the south of Germany: but in the south of France, and in the Netherlands, where the magistrates protected them as industrious people, they lived a long time in peace; till, after various disputations had taken place, and several councils been held, when the fury of the clergy was wrought to the highest pitch, the tribunal of the inquisition was let loose upon them; and as their protector, Raymond count of Toulouse, a real martyr in the cause of humankind, would not give them up, that dreadful croisade, with all its superabundance of atrocities, burst forth upon them. The order of friars established to preach against heresy, the Dominicans, founded expressly to oppose them, were their detestable judges: Simon of Montford, the leader of the croisade, was the most inhuman monster the Earth ever bore: and from this corner of France, where the poor *bons hommes* had remained concealed for two centuries, the bloody

[9] Among the writings on these sects, of which ecclesiastical history gives a full account, I shall only mention one book, far less known than it deserves, J. C. Fuessli's *Neue und unpartheiische Ketzer-und Kirchenhistorie der mittleren Zeit* (New and impartial history of heresies, and of the Church in the Middle Age), 3 vols. 8vo. in which very useful documents may be found.

tribunal against heretics extended itself to Spain, Italy, and most Catholic countries.

Hence the confusion in which the most opposite sects of the Middle Ages are involved, as they were all indiscriminate objects of this bloody tribunal, and the persecuting spirit of the clergy: yet hence, likewise, their stedfastness, and silent spread, so that after three or four centuries the Protestant Reformation in all countries found the seeds still existing, to which it only imparted a new vivifying power. Wickliff in England acted upon the Lollards, as Huss did upon his Bohemians; for sects of this pious kind had long abounded among the Bohemians, whose language and that of the Bulgarians were the same. The germe of truth now planted, and the decided hatred to superstition, the adoration of mortals, and the insolent, ungodly clergy, were incapable of being again trodden under foot: the Franciscans, and other orders, which, as examples of poverty and the imitation of Christ, were set up in opposition to these sects, to overturn and suppress them, were so far from accomplishing this end, even among the people, that they rather afforded fresh occasion for scandal. Thus the future downfall of the chief of tyrants, the hierarchy, proceeded from the meanest beginnings, from simplicity and sincerity: these simple *bons hommes*, though not without their prejudices and errours, certainly used more freedom of speech in several respects, than many of the reformers could afterwards venture to employ.

What plain common sense did on the one hand, was promoted not ineffectually, though more slowly and with greater refinement, on the other, by *speculative reason.* In the schools of the convents the pupils were taught to dispute on St. Austin and the logic of Aristotle; and accustomed themselves to this art, as a literary trial of skill. The censures passed on this liberty of disputation, as an useless exercise of the Middle Ages, are therefore unjust: for this liberty, at that period, was inestimable. In these disputations many things could be controverted, and sifted by opposing arguments, for the positive or practical questioning of which the times were not yet ripe. Did not the Reformation itself begin by men's taking shelter under the laws of disputation, and claiming the protection of its licence? As the monastic schools became universities, that is theatres of controversy, protected by the papal and imperial licence, a wide field was opened, for exercising and improving the language, presence of mind, wit, and sagacity, of learned polemics. There is not an article of divinity, or a subject of metaphysics, that has not occasioned the most subtile questions, disputes, and distinctions, and in time been spun out to the finest thread. This finespun texture naturally possessed less stability, than that coarse web of positive traditions, to which an implicit faith was required: and being fabricated by human Reason, it could be unravelled and destroyed by that same Reason, as the work of her own hands. Thanks, therefore, to that subtile spirit of disputation of the Middle Ages; and to every sovereign, who erected palaces for its learned webs! If many of the disputants were persecuted from motives of envy, or from their own want of caution; if, after their death, their bodies were disinterred from consecrated ground; still the art, on the whole, continued its progress, and greatly improved the weapons of reason in Europe.

As the south of France was the first permanent stage of an emerging popular religion, its northern part, especially in the celebrated Parisian school, was the theatre of *speculation and scholastic philosophy.* Here Paschasius and Ratramnus lived: Scotus Erigena found favour and a residence in France: Lanfranc and Berengarius, Anselm, Abelard, Peter Lombard, Thomas Aquinas, Bonaventura, Occam, and Duns Scotus, the morning stars and suns of school philosophy, taught in France, either the whole of their lives, or during their best years: and men of all countries flocked to Paris, to learn this chief wisdom of the times. Whoever had rendered himself famous in this succeeded to posts of honour in church and state: for scholastic philosophy was so far from being excluded from political affairs, that Occam, who had defended Philip the Fair, and Lewis of Bavaria, against the pope, could say to the emperor, "defend me with the sword, I will defend you with my pen." The French language is indebted for its superiour philosophical precision to this circumstance among others, that ready and subtile disputation was so long and so much pursued in its native country; for it was allied to the Latin, and easily adapted itself to the expression of abstract ideas.

That *the translation of the works of Aristotle* contributed more than any thing to the subtile philosophy of the schools is evident, from the authority this Grecian sage retained in all the seminaries of Europe for several centuries: but the causes of the avidity, with which his writings, borrowed chiefly from the Arabs, were studied, are to be sought in the disposition and way of thinking of the age, not in the croisades. The first stimulus Europe received from the sciences of the Arabs arose from their mathematical performances, and the secrets men hoped to find in them for the support and prolongation of life, the attainment of immense riches, and the knowledge of mutable destiny. The philosopher's stone, and the elixir of immortality, were sought after; future events were read in the stars, and even mathematical instruments considered as implements of magic. Thus men pursued the wonderful like children, and were prompted by it to the most arduous journeys; a pursuit, which, disappointed of its object, was destined to be rewarded with the future acquisition of truth. As early as the eleventh century, Constantine the African, had spent 39 years in travelling from Carthage over the east, to collect the secrets of the Arabs in Babylon, India, and Egypt. At length he came to Europe, and as a monk at Mount Casino translated many writings, particularly medical, from the Arabic and the Greek. However defective the translations may have been, they came into many hands, and the first school of physic at Salernum arose to great fame, by the help of Arabian knowledge. Such of the French and English as were eager after the learning repaired to Spain, that they might enjoy the benefit of being instructed by the most celebrated Arabian teachers. On their return they were considered as magicians, and even boasted of various secret arts as the effects of magic. Thus mathematics, chymistry, and physic, were introduced into the most celebrated schools of Europe, partly in writings, partly in discoveries and practical experiments. But for the Arabs, no

Gerbert, no Albertus Magnus, Arnold of Villa Nova, Roger Bacon, Raymund Lully, etc., would have arisen. Even the emperor Frederic II, who contributed with indefatigable zeal, to promote the translation of Arabic works, and the revival of every science, was not perfectly free from superstition in his attachment to learning. The propensity to travel, or the rumour of travels to Spain, Africa, and the east, where the most valuable secrets of nature were to be learned from retired sages, prevailed for centuries: many secret orders, and numerous confraternities of travelling scholars, arose from this; and indeed the whole aspect of the philosophical and mathematical sciences betrayed this Arabian origin even beyond the epoch of the Reformation.

No wonder, that *mysticism* united with such a philosophy, thus moulding itself to one of the most refined systems of contemplative perfection. Even in the first Christian church mysticism had passed from the modern Platonic philosophy into several sects; the translation of the spurious Dionysius the Areopagite introduced it into the monasteries of the west, many sects of the Manicheans were infected with it; and at length, with and without the aid of the scholastic philosophy, it attained a degree of consistency among the monks and nuns, in which it displayed sometimes the most subtile sophistry of human reason, at others the most refined tenderness of the enamoured heart. This, however, was not without its benefits, as it called off the mind from mere ceremonial worship, accustomed it to enter into itself, and animated it with mental food. It afforded the languishing, solitary mind, separated from this World, consolation and exercise, while it refined the sentiments by a sort of spiritual romance. It was the precursor of the metaphysics of the heart, as the school philosophy prepared the way for that of the understanding, and each served as a counterpoise to the other. Happy for us, that the time is almost past, in which the use of this opiate is requisite as a medicine.[10]

[10] After all that has been written by Poiret, Arnold, and others, we still want a history of mysticism, particularly of the Middle Ages, composed in a truly philosophical spirit.

Lastly, *the science of jurisprudence,* this practical philosophy of the sense of justice and sound reason, when it began to shine with fresh light, contributed more than mysticism and speculative philosophy to the welfare of Europe, and the firm establishment of the rights of society. In the ages of honourable simplicity few written laws were requisite; and the rude Germanic nations properly strove against the subtilties of the Roman jurists: more polished and partly corrupted countries found written laws of their own, and soon an abstract of the Roman law, altogether indispensable. And as this at length became insufficient in opposition to a progressive papal jurisprudence, increasing with every century, it was not amiss, that the whole code of Roman law should be brought forward, to exercise the judgment and understanding of enlightened and active men. With good reason did the emperors recommend this study, particularly in the higher seminaries of their Italian dominions: for it was a school of arms against the pope, and all rising free-states were equally interested in availing themselves of it, against the pope, the emperor, and their petty tyrants. Accordingly the number of lawyers increased astonishingly: as knights in the realm of literature, as defenders of the liberty and property of nations, they were highly respected in courts, in cities, and in the chair of learning; and on their account the much frequented city of Bologna was esteemed the seat of learning.

The rise of the law rendered Italy what France was in the philosophy of the schools: the old Roman and the canon law contended against each other: even several popes were men of the greatest eminence in jurisprudence. Pity, that the reanimation of this science happened at a time, when the sources were impure, and the spirit of the old Roman law could be seen only through a mist. Pity, that the subtile philosophy of the schools arrogated to itself this practical science, and perverted the decisions of the intelligent by a captious play upon words. Pity too, that an auxiliary study, an exercise of the judgment on the model of the sages of antiquity, should have been taken as a positive rule, as the gospel of the law, in all cases, even the most novel, and farthest from being determined. Hence arose that spirit of chicane, which in time nearly extinguished the character of almost every national legislation in Europe. Barbarous book-learning assumed the place of a living knowledge of things: legal processes became labyrinths of form and quibble: instead of a noble sentiment of justice, men's minds were turned to artifice and cunning, which rendered the language of the laws and of the courts perplexed and unintelligible, and ultimately, in conjunction with the triumphant power of the magistrate, favoured a spurious paramount right of the sovereign. The consequences of this have long continued to be felt.

Were we to compare the state of the human mind on its reawaking in Europe with some of the more ancient times and nations, it would afford a melancholy prospect. Every thing good rises tremblingly from rude and stupid barbarism, under the pressure of spiritual and temporal tyranny: here, the best seeds are trodden down on the stony soil, or scattered by the plundering birds; there, the young plants rise with difficulty amid the thorns, and are choked or stunted, as they want the favourable soil of ancient goodness and simplicity. The first popular religion appeared amid persecuted and in some degree fanatical heretics; philosophy, in the theatres of disputing logicians; the most useful sciences, as magic and superstition; the guidance of the human passions, as mysticism; an improved political system, as the patched and cast-off mantle of a long superannuated and heterogeneous legislation: and through these Europe was to raise herself from a state of the utmost confusion, and form herself anew. What the soil wanted, however, in depth of fertile mould; the implements and auxiliary means, in utility; the air, in serenity and freedom; was compensated, probably, by the extent of the field to be cultivated, and the value of the plants to be produced. Not an Athens, or a Sparta, but an Europe was here to be formed; and this not to the *kalokagathie* of a Grecian philosopher or artist, but to a reason and humanity, that in time should embrace the World. Let us see what institutions have been framed for this, what discoveries have been scattered in the darkness of ages, to be ripened by futurity.

CHAPTER 5

Institutions and Discoveries in Europe

1. The cities of Europe are become as it were fixed camps of cultivation, workshops of industry, and the commencement of an improved political economy, without which this country would be still a desert. In all the territories of the Roman Empire, these cities retained some portion of the Roman arts; and in countries, which the Romans had never possessed, they were mounds opposing the incursion of fresh barbarians, and the asylums of men, of trade, of arts, and manufactures. Praised for ever be the sovereigns, who founded, endowed, and protected them: for with them were founded constitutions, that first gave public spirit room to breathe; aristocratico-democratical bodies were formed, the members of which watched over each other, were often mutual enemies and opponents, and on this very account unavoidably promoted the common security, emulative industry, and progressive exertion. Within the walls of a city, all that could awaken and give consistency to invention, diligence, civil liberty, economy, policy, and order, according to the times, was condensed together in a narrow space: the laws of many cities are masterpieces of civic wisdom. Through the means of cities, nobles, as well as communities, enjoyed the first title of common liberty, *citizenship*. In Italy republics arose, which went farther through the means of their trade, than Athens and Sparta had ever gone: on this side the Alps, not only did individual cities distinguish themselves by industry and commerce, but alliances were formed between them, and ultimately a commercial state, which extended over the Euxine and the Mediterranean, the Atlantic Ocean, the North Sea, and the Baltic. These cities lay in Germany, the Netherlands, and the northern kingdoms, Poland, Prussia, Russia, and Livonia. Lubec was their head, and the chief trading towns of England, France, Spain, Portugal, and Italy joined their association; forming perhaps the most efficacious alliance, that ever existed. This contributed more to give Europe the form of a common-

wealth, than all the croisades and Romish rites; for it rose superiour to religious or national distinctions, and founded the connexion of states on mutual advantage, emulative industry, probity, and order. Cities accomplished what was beyond the power of princes, priests, and nobles: they formed of Europe *one common* cooperative body.

2. The guilds in cities, troublesome as they often were to the magistracy, and even to the growing arts, were at that time indispensable, as little commonwealths, as associated bodies, in which all were answerable for each, to the support of honest trade, the improvement of the arts, and the honour and esteem of the artists themselves. By their means Europe became the manufacturer of all the productions of the Globe; and thus, though the smallest and poorest quarter of it, obtained an ascendancy over the rest. To its industry Europe is indebted for the production of wonders from wool and flax, hemp and silk, hair and skins, earth and clay, stones, metals, plants, juices, and colours, ashes, salts, rags, and excrement, which again served as means to produce other wonders. If the history of inventions be the greatest praise of the human intellect; guilds and corporations have been their school; as by the separation of the arts, and methodical regularity of instruction, by the mutual emulation of many, and by the stimulus of want, things were produced, which the favor of the sovereign or the state scarcely knew, seldom promoted or rewarded, and rarely if ever excited. Discipline and order produced them under the shade of a peaceful city government: the most ingenious arts arose from mechanical labours and enterprises, the garb of which they long wore, particularly on this side the Alps, not to their disadvantage. Let us not ridicule, therefore, or pity the formalities and introductory steps of every such practical regulation; for with them were connected the essence of art, and the common honour of artists. The monk and the knight had far less need of initiatory degrees than the active artificer, for the perfection of whose work the whole fraternity was in some measure answerable: for to every thing, that bears the name of art, nothing is so

detrimental as underhand dealings, and the want of a sense of honour arising from being master of it; by which the very foundations of the art are sapped.

Let us honour, therefore, the master works of the Middle Ages, which evince how much arts and trades are indebted to cities. Gothic architecture would never have attained its flourishing state, had not republics and wealthy commercial cities so eagerly rivalled each other in townhalls and cathedrals, as once the cities of Greece in temples and statues. In each we can discern whence the models of its taste were derived, and the country to which the stream of its commerce flowed: the most ancient edifices of Venice and Pisa display a different style of architecture from those of Milan or Florence. The transalpine cities followed various models; but, on the whole, the better Gothic architecture is most easily explicable from the constitutions of the cities, and the spirit of the times. For as men live and think, so they build and inhabit: foreign models they can copy only after their own manner, as every bird constructs her nest conformably to her figure, and mode of living. The boldest and most ornamental Gothic architecture would never have taken place in convents, or in the castles of knights: it is the peculiar magnificence of public communities. In like manner, the most valuable works of art of the Middle Ages displayed the coats of arms of families, communities, and cities on metals, ivory, glass, wood, tapestry, or vestments; on which account they have in general a permanent intrinsic worth, and are justly an inalienable property of cities and families. Thus civic industry wrote chronicles, also; in which, it is true, the writer's house, family, trade, and city, are his World: but then his heart and soul are proportionally engaged in his subject; and happy the country, that can frame its history from many such, and not from the chronicles of monks. In the councils of cities, too, the Roman jurisprudence was first wisely and efficaciously restricted; otherwise it would have ultimately stifled the best statutes and rights of nations.

3. *Universities* were literary cities and corporations: they were instituted with similar rights, as commonwealths, and

participate in their merits. Not as schools, but as political bodies they weakened the barbarous pride of the nobility, supported the cause of sovereigns against the pretensions of the popes, and opened the way to political services and rank for a properly learned class, instead of the exclusive clergy. Never, perhaps, did men of learning enjoy more esteem, than at the first dawn of science: men beheld the indispensable value of a good they had long despised; and as one party dreaded the light, the other more eagerly hailed the rising morn. Universities were fortresses and bulwarks of science against the belligerent barbarism of ecclesiastical tyranny: they at least guarded a treasure, of which the value was but half known, for better times. After Theodoric, Charlemagne, and Alfred, we would particularly honour the ashes of the emperor Frederic II; who, among his various merits, possesses that of having given universities an impulse toward improvement, the effects of which were not transient. In these institutions Germany has become as it were the centre of Europe: in it the arsenals and magazines of science have acquired the greatest internal abundance, as well as the most durable form.

4. Lastly, we shall enumerate a few of the discoveries, which, carried into practice, became powerful implements in the hands of posterity. The *magnetic needle*, the guide of navigation, was probably introduced into Europe by the Arabs, and first brought into use by the merchants of Amalfi, in their early commercial intercourse with them. With this the World was put into the hands of Europeans. The Genoese soon ventured into the Atlantic: and afterwards the Portuguese evinced, that they possessed not the western shores of the old World in vain. They sought and found a way round Africa, and thus changed the course of the whole Indian trade: till another Genoese discovered a second hemisphere, and thus gave a new face to all the relations of our part of the Globe. The little implement of these discoveries came into Europe with the dawn of science.

Glass, an early commodity of the Asiatics, which was once estimated at its weight in gold, has become of more value than gold in the hands of Europeans. Whether it were Salvino, or some other, who polished the first lens, he thus formed the beginning of an instrument, destined afterwards to discover millions of celestial worlds, regulate time and navigation, and assist the noblest sciences the human mind can boast. Already Roger Bacon, the Franciscan friar, in his cell discovered wonders, in the properties of light, and in almost all the realms of nature, for which he was rewarded with the hatred of his order, and with imprisonment; but which were more happily pursued by others, in more enlightened times. The first beam of light in the mind of this wonderful man showed him a new world in Heaven and on Earth.

Gunpowder also, a murderous, yet on the whole a beneficial gift, was either brought into use by the Arabs, or at least introduced into Europe by their writings. Here and there it appears from these to have been discovered by more than one, and but slowly applied to practical purposes, when it changed the whole face of the art of war. The modern state of Europe was incredibly influenced by this invention; which better subdued the spirit of chivalry, than all the councils that ever were held; promoted the authority of sovereigns, more than any assemblies of the people; checked the blind fury of personally embittered armies; and even set limits to that art of war, to which it gave birth. This and other chemical inventions, above all destructive spirituous liquors, which the Arabs introduced into Europe as medicines, and which have since spread themselves as poisons throughout the wide World, constitute epochs in the history of the human species.

The same may be said of the preparation of *paper* from rags, and the prototypes of *printing* in cards, and other impressions of immoveable characters. That probably owed its origin to the paper fabricated from cotton, and from silk, which the Arabs brought out of Asia: this proceeded by slow steps from one attempt to another, till, from wooden cuts and types, the printer and copperplate engraver produced the most important effects on our quarter of the globe. The *arithmetical figures* of the Arabs; the *musical notes* invented by Guido of Arezzo; *clocks*, for which we are indebted to Asia; oil-painting, an ancient

German invention; and other useful implements, invented, or adopted and imitated, in various places, before the dawn of science; almost always became, in the hothouse of European industry, seeds of new things and events for future ages.

CHAPTER 6
Conclusion

How, therefore, came Europe by its cultivation, and the rank it obtained by it above other countries? Time, place, necessity, the state of affairs, the stream of events, impelled it to this: but, above all, its *peculiar industry in the arts,* the result of many *common exertions,* procured it this rank.

1. Had Europe been rich as India, unintersected as Tatary, hot as Africa, isolated as America, what has appeared in it would never have been produced. Even in the profoundest barbarism its situation on the Globe helped to restore it to light; but from its rivers and seas it derived most advantage. Take away the Dnieper, the Don, and the Dwina; the Euxine, Mediterranean, Adriatic, Atlantic, Baltic, and North Seas with their coasts, islands, and rivers; the great commercial league, to which Europe is indebted for its best activity, would not have existed. But as it was, the two great and wealthy quarters of the Globe, Asia and Africa, embraced their poorer, smaller sister; they sent her their wares and inventions from the remotest limits of the World, from regions the earliest and longest civilized, and thus whetted her industry and powers of invention. The climate of Europe, the remains of the ancient Greek and Roman worlds, assisted all this: and thus the sovereignty of Europe is founded on *activity* and *invention,* on *science* and *united emulative exertions.*

2. The *pressure of the Romish hierarchy* was perhaps a necessary yoke, an indispensable bridle for the rude nations of the Middle Ages. Without it Europe had probably been the prey of despots, a theatre of eternal discord, or even a Mungal wilderness. Thus as a counterpoise it merits praise: but as the first and permanent spring it would have converted Europe into a Tibetian ecclesiastic state. Action and reaction produced an effect,

which neither party had intended: want, necessity, and danger, brought forward between the two a third state, which must be the life-blood of this great active body, or it will run into corruption. This is the *state of science, of useful activity, of emulative industry in the arts;* which necessarily, yet gradually, puts an end to the periods of chivalry and monasticism.

3. Of what kind the modern cultivation of Europe could be is evident from what has been said: only a cultivation of men as they were, and were desirous of being; a cultivation, through the means of industry, arts, and sciences. He, who needed not, despised, or abused these, remained what he was: an universal, reciprocating formation of all ranks and nations, by means of education, laws, and a political constitution, was not then to be thought of; and when will it be? Reason, however, and the effective joint activity of mankind, keep on their unwearied course; and it may even be deemed a good sign, when the best fruits ripen not prematurely.

Index